Integration and Transition in Europe

With the harmonisation of the EU economies, and issues of EU enlargement and integration with Europe's transition economies topping the political agenda, the economic geography of Europe is being recast. Several major forces are in the process of (re)shaping the European economy and society. The ongoing processes of internationalisation and structural change, integration in the West, and transition in the East, along with the EU policy of eastward expansion and enlargement are among the most important of them. All these processes and policies taken together have released market-driven dynamics with a strong spatial dimension that radically change the geography of development and economic relations in Europe.

This important volume analyses the spatial implications of the ongoing integration–transition process, focusing on the key dynamics of emerging pan-European geography. The book examines issues such as the north–south and east–west divides, patterns of regional development, factor movements, regional trade patterns, co-operation and cross-border dynamics. The contributors examine these issues from one of two viewpoints: the first perspective analyses the integration–transition process from a 'macro-geographical' point of view; the second considers spatial adjustments or policy responses at the national or regional level. *Integration and Transition in Europe* reveals that the European geography of Europe has changed in many ways, requiring equivalent changes in policy-making.

George Petrakos is Associate Professor of Spatial Economic Analysis at the Department of Planning and Regional Development, University of Thessaly, Greece. **Gunther Maier** is Associate Professor of Urban and Regional Economics at Vienna University of Economics and Business Administration. **Grzegorz Gorzelak** is Professor at the University of Warsaw and Director of the European Institute for Regional and Local Development.

Routledge Studies in the European Economy

1 Growth and Crisis in the Spanish Economy, 1940–1993
Sima Lieberman

2 Work and Employment in Europe
A new convergence?
Edited by Peter Cressey and Bryn Jones

3 Trans-European Telecommunication Networks
The challenges for industrial policy
Colin Turner

4 European Union – European Industrial Relations?
Global challenges, national developments and transnational dynamics
Edited by Wolfgang E. Lecher and Hans-Wolfgang Platzer

5 Governance, Industry and Labour Markets in Britain and France
The modernizing state in the mid-twentieth century
Edited by Noel Whiteside and Robert Salais

6 Labour Market Efficiency in the European Union
Employment protection and fixed-term contracts
Klaus Schömann, Ralf Rogowski and Thomas Kruppe

7 The Enlargement of the European Union
Issues and strategies
Edited by Victoria Curzon-Price, Alice Landau and Richard Whitman

8 European Trade Unions
Change and response
Edited by Mike Rigby, Roger Smith and Teresa Lawlor

9 Fiscal Federalism in the European Union
Edited by Amedeo Fossati and Giorgio Panella

10 European Telecommunications Liberalisation
Edited by Kjell A. Eliassen and Marit Sjøvaag

11 Integration and Transition in Europe
The economic geography of interaction
Edited by George Petrakos, Gunther Maier and Grzegorz Gorzelak

C H E C K O U T 27/08/2013
15:46:

Mrs Sharon Laverick

Contemporary capitalism : the embeddedne
Barcode:0489509010
Due date:20/06/2014

Capitalism and development
Barcode:034221701X
Due date:20/06/2014

Integration and transition in Europe : t
Barcode:0443355010
Due date:20/06/2014

User ID was removed before
antitheft devic
was disabled on:
Thank you for using the Self Issue
service

Integration and Transition in Europe

The economic geography of interaction

Edited by
George Petrakos, Gunther Maier and Grzegorz Gorzelak

ROUTLEDGE
Taylor & Francis Group
London and New York

First published 2000
by Routledge
11 New Fetter Lane, London EC4P 4EE

Simultaneously published in the USA and Canada
by Routledge
29 West 35th Street, New York, NY 10001

Typeset in Times by
M Rules
Printed and bound in Great Britain by
St Edmundsbury Press, Bury St Edmunds, Suffolk

British Library Cataloguing in Publication Data
A catalogue record for this book is available from the British Library

Library of Congress Cataloging in Publication Data
Petrakos, George.
Integration and transition in Europe: the economic geography of interaction/George Petrakos, Gunther Maier, and Grzegorz Gorzelak.
p. cm.
Includes bibliographical references and index.
1. Europe–Economic integration. 2. Regionalism–Europe. 3. International economic relations. I. Maier, Gunther. II. Gorzelak, Grzegorz. III. Title.
HC241.P48 2000
337.1′42–dc21 99–086053

ISBN 0–415–21808–X

Contents

Figures

Maps

Tables

Contributors

Wilfried Altzinger, Department of Economics, University of Economics and Business Administration, Vienna, Austria

Paul Cheshire, Department of Geography and Environment, London School of Economics and Political Sciences, London.

Nikos Christodoulakis, Department of International and European Economic Studies, Athens University of Economics and Business, Athens, Greece.

Michael Dunford, School of European Studies, University of Sussex, Falmer, Brighton.

Károly Fazekas, Institute of Economics, Hungarian Academy of Science Budapest, Hungary.

Grzegorz Gorzelak, European Institute for Regional and Local Development, University of Warsaw, Poland.

F. E. Ian Hamilton, Department of Geography and Environment, London School of Economics and Political Sciences, London

Maarten Keune, Department of Social and Political Science, European University Institute, Forenze Ferrovia, Italy.

Dimitris Kyrkilis, Department of International and European Economic and Political Studies, University of Macedonia, Thessaloniki, Greece.

Gunther Maier, Institute of Urban and Regional Studies, University of Economics and Business Administration, Vienna, Austria.

József Nemes-Nagy, Department of Regional Geography, Eotvos Lorand University, Budapest, Hungary.

Evangelos Nikolaidis, Department of Geography, University of the Aegean, Mytilini, Greece.

George Petrakos, Department of Planning and Regional Development, University of Thessaly, Volos, Greece.

Daniel Piazolo, Kiel Institute of World Economics, Kiel, Germany.

Thomas Rosenmayr, Economist, Austria

Preface

Several major forces are in the process of (re)shaping the economy and society of Europe. The ongoing processes of internationalisation and structural change, integration in the West, and transition in the East, along with the EU policy of eastward expansion and enlargement are among the most important of them. All these processes and policies taken together and in interaction have released market-driven dynamics that tend to radically change the geography of development and economic relations in Europe.

Understanding the impact of the interaction of policy and market-driven dynamics is a very complex assignment. Various, often conflicting, developments have taken place in a relatively short period of time, requiring examination at various levels and ways. Unavoidably, many issues are still debated in the literature, while new, often controversial and largely unexplored, issues emerge. In addition, empirical findings, so much needed to settle theoretically uncertain or debated issues, often provide mixed evidence. As a result, it is only natural that different approaches, methodologies and views on particular aspects of the phenomena related to East–West integration may coexist for quite some time.

Given that all these processes are expected to have a strong spatial dimension, our goal in this volume is to analyse and discuss the spatial characteristics and implications of the ongoing integration–transition process in Europe. The chapters presented are generally divided into two broad categories: first, those analysing the integration–transition process from a 'macro-geographical' point of view at the European level in both theoretical or empirical ways, and second, those taking a more focused approach and looking at the spatial adjustments or the policy responses at the national or regional level. As no uniformity has been sought or imposed, the chapters in this volume do not necessarily share the same point of view. The plurality of views and ideas presented is intended to help the reader realise that many issues are still being debated in the literature and that definite answers have not yet been provided in a number of cases. The editors and the contributors had the opportunity to discuss the various aspects of integration and transition in Europe in an EU-sponsored conference in Budapest in 1997. The discussion continued in several other occasions, such as lectures, research meetings, workshops and conferences. The interesting issues and debates that arose led to the unanimous conviction that a collection of papers presenting these arguments would be a useful contribution to the literature and this volume is the result.

Abbreviations

AS	Austrian schilling
BC	Balkan countries
BERI	Business Environmental Risk Intelligence
BOT	balance of trade
CEC	Commission of the European Community
CEE	Central and Eastern Europe
CEEC	Central East European country
CMEA	Council for Mutual Economic Aid
COMECON	Council for Mutual Economic Aid
CSF	Community Support Framework
CV	coefficient of variation
EBRD	European Bank for Reconstruction and Development
ECU	European Currency Unit
EFTA	European Free Trade Area
EMU	European Monetary Union
EU	European Union
FDI	foreign direct investment
FURS	functional urban regions
FYROM	Former Yugoslavia and Republic of Macedonia
GC	Gini coefficient
GDP	gross domestic product
GNP	gross national product
HCSO	Hungarian Central Statistical Office
H-O	Heckscher-Ohlin
IIC	indicator of institutional change
IIT	intra-industry trade
ISTC	International Standard Trade Classification
LFS	Labour Force Survey
MNC	multinational corporation
MNE	multinational enterprise
NAFTA	North American Free Trade Area
NUTS	Nomenclature of Statistical Territorial Units (abbreviation is from the initials in French)

OECD	Organization for Economic Cooperation and Development
PPP	purchasing power parity
PPS	purchasing power standards
RCA	revealed comparative analysis
SEM	Single European Market
SITC	Standard International Trade Classification
SME	small and medium-sized enterprise
TC	Theil coefficient
VOT	volume of trade
WAD	weighted absolute deviation
WMAD	weighted mean absolute deviation
WSD	weighted standard deviation

1 The new economic geography of Europe

An introduction

George Petrakos, Gunther Maier and Grzegorz Gorzelak

Introduction

Europe is changing in directions that could hardly be imagined a few decades ago. In many ways it is very different from the last 10–20 years and it is continuing to change at a rapid pace. Its economic structure is changing, its western part is becoming more integrated and its eastern and central part is choosing the difficult road of transition from plan to market. These forces and dynamics along with the rapid development of East–West market interaction and the European Union (EU) policies of enlargement are major factors influencing present and future economic developments.

The 1990s have been a decade of unprecedented changes in all parts of Europe. The policies of integration in the EU and the policies of transition in Central and Eastern Europe (CEE) have released economic forces that have left a permanent mark on the continent. Time has been 'very active' in this period, changing the systemic parameters of the pre-1989 status quo, as well as long-lasting rules of conduct, embedded ideas and perceptions. Yet the interacting market and policy-driven processes that change Europe are not always free of conflict and friction. Changes imply permanent costs and benefits as well as adjustment costs that are not allocated equally among economic actors, social groups or areas. Unavoidably, they generate fears of exclusion, for people and places not prepared to deal with the new reality.

Although significant progress has been made in many respects, Europe will enter the twenty-first century with many important issues open to discussion, debate and challenge. Some of these issues will relate to the spatial aspects of change and the future geography of economic relations and structures. Greater imbalances at the international (macro) level and the intra-national (micro) level, which have already been detected, may not be sustainable in the long term. This raises several interesting questions for policy-making at all the spatial levels of the new European economy.

This introductory chapter intends to present and discuss the main aspects of the emerging pan-European economy, especially those having a spatial dimension. In the next section we will present the basic features of the new European landscape, focusing on the macro-geographical aspects of growth, development and welfare. In the third section, we will analyse the spatial dimension of the main factors shaping the new European economy and briefly discuss the implications of current trends and challenges for policy.

The new European economic landscape

The post-1989 developments in Central and Eastern Europe have given us an opportunity to view Europe[1] as a continuous economic space and study its main economic characteristics without being constrained by profoundly different economic and political systems. As systemic barriers have been removed, it is important for policy-makers and the students of the European economy to be able to understand the characteristics of the new geography of development and economic structure that has emerged at a pan-European scale. A number of interesting questions need to be addressed: what would the potential future size of the European economy be and how does it compare with the present Union of EU-15? How great are the differences in development and welfare levels between European countries? Do these differences have a geographical dimension, in a sense that some macro-regions in Europe tend to have a systematically better or worse than average performance? Have the post-1989 developments and especially the process of transition led to a more coherent or a more divided Europe with respect to economic indicators?

In an attempt to answer these questions, in this section we analyse information related to the size of the European economies and their level of development and welfare. Table 1.1 presents information concerning area, population, GDP, GNP per capita and economic structure, while Table 1.2 presents some additional, mostly physical, indicators of development and welfare for all European countries. Both tables present information for each individual country and also for groups of countries comprising distinct geographical areas or regions of Europe. The regional group labelled 'Central' includes five Central European transition countries: the Czech Republic, Hungary, Poland, Slovakia, and Slovenia. The regional group labelled 'Baltic' includes three Baltic transition countries: Estonia, Latvia and Lithuania. Finally, the group labelled 'Balkan' includes seven Balkan transition countries: Albania, Bosnia, Bulgaria, Croatia, F.Y.R. of Macedonia, Romania and F.R. of Yugoslavia.[2]

This type of regional information serves two goals. On the one hand, it allows comparisons between the EU-15 and the transition countries in Central Europe, the Balkans and the Baltic countries with respect to a number of interesting indicators. It also allows for comparisons within the transition countries group, which are showing differences with respect to progress made and the prevailing economic conditions. These comparisons, which record the depth and type of the East–West and, intra-East development differences, are necessary for any discussion about policy responses to the forces of integration and transition at the European level. On the other hand, this information is a necessary precondition for discussions related to the enlargement of the EU. It is now clear that almost all transition countries have expressed an interest in participating, now or in the future, in the Western institutions and especially the EU. Given this highly encouraging development, it is important to know in which way the basic aggregate figures and statistics of the Union will be affected by the accession of nearly fifteen new members in the future.[3]

The information in columns 1 and 2 in Table 1.1 indicate that a potential Union comprising all European countries will have an area of 5,068 thousand square km, that is 51 per cent larger than the area of the EU-15 and a population of more than 514 million people, that is about 37 per cent greater than the existing population of the EU-15. As a result, this enlargement scenario, that practically doubles the number of member states, significantly increases the EU in terms of both area and population. As area increases relatively more than population, population density is expected to fall. This is so because transition countries have a lower population density than EU countries. The Baltic and partly the Balkan countries in particular are characterised by population densities that are 31 per cent and 62 per cent of the population density in the EU, respectively. Consequently, a future pan-European Union will have a population density that is about 19 per cent lower than the present EU-15 density. Although in principle this would mean that the enlarged Union would have more space for its citizens, this may not be the case for the West if present trends of East–West migration continue in the future.

In column 4 of Table 1.1 we present GDP for 1997 in billion US dollars for all European countries and all regional groups. We observe that the GDP figures for CEE countries are very small compared to those of Western Europe. The GDP of all Central European countries combined is smaller than that of The Netherlands, while the GDP of all Balkan transition countries is smaller than the GDP of Greece. Overall, the increase of the EU-15 GDP by the expansion of the European economic space to the East is relatively small (about 10 per cent), despite the significant size of transition countries in terms of area and population. Clearly, this low GDP level in transition countries is attributed to the bottlenecks and the inefficiency of the pre-1989 system of central planning as well as to the tremendous difficulties these countries have encountered in their first steps from plan to market.

As can seen in column 5, these difficulties (sometimes called the shock of transition) are related to a recession that all ex-socialist countries experienced during the first post-1989 years. Although in the 1989–97 period EU-15 countries increased their GDP level by an average of 16 per cent, transition countries as a whole experienced a contraction of output equal to –11 per cent in the same period. Not all countries, however, or groups of countries experienced the same decline in GDP. Poland, after a short recession period, experienced significant growth rates that led to a net 12 per cent increase in GDP in the 1989–97 period. Also, the other Central European countries had

Table 1.1 Basic indicators of size, economic activity and welfare in Europe

Countries	*Area*	*Population, 1997*		*GDP, 1997*			*GNP per capita (USD), 1997*		*Share of agriculture in*
	th.km² (1)	*million* (2)	*density* (3)	*billion USD* (4)	*89 = 100* (5)	*density* (6)	*USD* (7)	*EU15 = 100* (8)	*GDP, 1997* (9)
Albania	29	3.3	114	2.5	82	85	760	3	63
Bosnia	51	2.3	45	4.5		87	785	3	
Bulgaria	111	8.3	75	10.1	67	91	1,170	5	23
Croatia	57	4.8	84	19.1	76	335	4,060	18	12
The Czech R.	79	10.3	130	52.0	98	659	5,240	23	5
Estonia	45	1.5	32	4.7	76	104	3,360	15	7
Hungary	93	10.1	109	45.7	91	492	4,510	20	6
FYROM	26	2.1	81	2.2	69	85	1,100	5	12
Latvia	65	2.5	38	5.5	57	85	2,430	11	7
Lithuania	65	3.7	57	9.6	63	147	2,260	10	13
Poland	323	38.7	120	135.7	112	420	3,590	16	6
Romania	238	22.6	95	34.8	82	146	1,410	6	20
Slovakia	49	5.4	110	19.5	96	397	3,680	16	5
Slovenia	20	2.0	100	18.2	97	910	9,840	43	5
Yugoslavia	102	10.6	104	15.1	50	149	1,429	6	
Austria	84	8.1	96	206.2	120	2,455	27,920	122	1
Belgium	33	10.2	309	242.5	115	7,349	26,730	117	1
Denmark	43	5.3	123	170.0	122	3,954	34,890	152	4
Finland	338	5.1	15	119.8	107	355	24,790	108	4
France	552	58.6	106	1,392.5	112	2,523	26,300	115	2
Germany	357	82.1	230	2,092.3	120	5,861	28,280	123	1
Greece	132	10.5	80	122.9	114	931	11,640	51	11

Table 1.1 cont.

Countries	*Area*	*Population, 1997*		*GDP, 1997*			*GNP per capita (USD), 1997*		*Share of agriculture in*
	th.km² (1)	*million* (2)	*density* (3)	*billion USD* (4)	*89 = 100* (5)	*density* (6)	*USD* (7)	*EU15 = 100* (8)	*GDP, 1997* (9)
Iceland	103	0.3	3	6.1	116	59	24,900	109	10
Ireland	70	3.7	53	75.0	167	1,072	17,790	78	6
Italy	301	57.5	191	1,145.6	111	3,806	20,170	88	3
Luxemburg	3	0.4	162	12.5	144	4,809	37,100	162	5
Netherlands	41	15.6	380	360.3	123	8,787	25,830	113	3
Norway	324	4.4	14	153.4	134	473	36,100	157	2
Portugal	92	9.9	108	102.1	122	1,110	11,010	48	4
Spain	506	39.3	78	532.0	117	1,051	14,490	63	3
Sweden	450	8.8	20	227.6	107	506	26,210	114	2
Switzerland	41	7.1	173	255.3	105	6,226	43,060	188	3
UK	245	59.0	241	1286.5	116	5,251	20,870	91	2
EU-15	3,350	374.4	137	8,094.1	116	3,966	22,935	100	2
Transition	1,353	128.2	86	379.1	89	318	2,967	13	12
Central	564	66.5	114	271.1	105	481	4,181	18	6
Baltic	175	7.7	43	19.8	64	119	2,524	11	10
Balkan	614	54	85	88.3	72	146	1,534	7	23
Total	5,068	514.1	111	8,881.9	109	3,058	18,346	80	5

Sources: World Bank (1999a), World Bank (1999b).

Table 1.2 Indicators of development and welfare

Countries	*GNP per capita (PPP), 1997*		*Infant mortality*	*Doctors/ 1000 people*	*Beds/ 1000 people*	*Consumption of electricity (kwh) per capita*	*Road (km)/ 1000km²*	*Phone/ 1000 people*	*TV/ 1000 people*
	PPP (1)	*EU-15 = 100 (2)*	*1997 (3)*	*1994 (4)*	*1994 (5)*	*1996 (6)*	*1996 (7)*	*1997 (8)*	*1997 (9)*
Albania	2,170	11	26	1.3	3.0	904	621	23	161
Bosnia			13	0.6	2.0	772	428	80	41
Bulgaria	3,870	19	18	3.3	10.2	3,577	331	323	366
Croatia	4,930	25	9	2.0	5.9	2,291	478	335	267
The Czech Rep.	10,380	52	6	2.9	7.4	4,875	702	318	447
Estonia	5,090	25	10	3.1	8.4	3,293	340	321	479
Hungary	6,970	35	10	3.6	9.6	2,814	1,706	304	436
FYROM	3,180	16	16	2.3	5.5	2,443	407	204	252
Latvia	3,970	20	15	3.0	11.9	1,783	924	302	592
Lithuania	4,140	21	10	4.0	11.1	1,785	1,002	283	377
Poland	6,510	32	10	2.3	6.3	2,420	1,161	194	413
Romania	4,270	21	22	1.8	7.7		644	167	226
Slovakia	7,860	39	9	2.8	7.1	4,450	747	259	401
Slovenia	11,880	59	5	2.2	5.8	4,766	746	364	353
Yugoslavia			14	2.0	5.4	2,972	486	206	255
Austria	22,010	110	5	2.6	9.4	5,952	1,536	492	496
Belgium	23,090	115	6	3.7	7.6	6,878	4,339	468	510
Denmark	23,450	117	6	2.9	5.0	6,113	1,665	633	568
Finland	19,660	98	4	2.7	10.1	12,979	230	556	534
France	22,210	111	5	2.8	9.0	6,091	1,617	575	606
Germany	21,170	105	5	3.3	9.7	5,596	1,773	550	570
Greece	12,540	62	7	4.0	5.0	3,395	886	516	466
Iceland							120	527	353

Table 1.2 cont.

Countries	*GNP per capita (PPP), 1997*		*Infant mortality*	*Doctors/ 1000 people*	*Beds/ 1000 people*	*Consumption of electricity (kwh) per capita*	*Road (km)/ 1000km²*	*Phone/ 1000 people*	*TV/ 1000 people*
	PPP (1)	*EU-15 = 100 (2)*	*1997 (3)*	*1994 (4)*	*1994 (5)*	*1996 (6)*	*1996 (7)*	*1997 (8)*	*1997 (9)*
Ireland	17,420	87	5	2.0	5.0	4,363	1,321	411	455
Italy	20,100	100	5	1.7	6.5	4,196	1,053	447	483
Luxemburg							1,985	525	238
Netherlands	21,300	106	5	2.5	11.3	5,555	3,098	564	541
Norway	24,260	121	4	3.3	13.5	23,487	282	621	579
Portugal	14,180	71	6	2.9	4.3	3,044	747	402	523
Spain	15,690	78	5	4.1	4.0	3,749	682	403	506
Sweden	19,010	95	4	3.0	6.5	14,239	307	679	531
Switzerland	26,580	132	5	3.1	20.8	6,919	1,735	661	536
UK	20,710	103	6	1.5	4.9	5,198	1,518	540	255
EU-15	20,092	100	5	2.7	7.3	5,412	1,489	517	495
Transition	6,024	30	13	2.4	7.2	2,878	859	228	349
Central	7,450	37	9	2.6	7.0	3,095	1,127	240	419
Baltic	4,265	21	12	3.5	10.8	2,070	851	296	467
Balkan	4,042	20	18	2.0	6.9	2,614	530	203	246
Total	16,980	85	7	2.7	7.5	5,051	1,325	447	459

Sources: World Bank (1999a), World Bank (1999b), World Bank (1998).

GDP levels very close to (but below) the 1989 figures in 1997. As a result – influenced by the size of the Polish economy in this group – the Central European region has recorded a small, but positive, GDP change of 5 per cent in the 1989–97 period. The Baltic and Balkan regions, however, had a different transition experience. As the figures in column 5 show, GDP in the period 1989–97 contracted by –36 per cent in the Baltic countries and –28 per cent in the Balkans. As these are average figures, some countries in these two regions, such as Latvia or Yugoslavia, experienced even larger drops in GDP. National GDP growth figures are depicted in Map 1.1, which clearly shows these significant differences in performance.

In column 6, we report GDP density, a rather unusual measure of performance. This figure is the product of GDP per capita and population density and estimates the intensity of economic activity, that is the GDP produced on average per square kilometre of land. This index can be thought of as a measure of efficient use of the territory of each country, or alternatively as a measure of agglomeration economies. According to our estimates, GDP density in the EU-15 is about ten times higher than that in the transition countries. In the EU-15, the highest GDP density figure is reported in The Netherlands followed by Belgium, while among the transition countries the highest figure is reported in Slovenia and the second highest in the Czech Republic. It is worth noting in this column that wide differences exist among transition countries, as the Central region has a GDP density that is more than three times that of the Balkan region and more than four times the Baltic region.[4]

In columns 7 and 8 we present for each country and each regional group information for GNP per capita in USD and GNP per capita as a share of the average EU-15 figure. There are several striking observations to make here. First, the average GNP per capita of transition countries measured in US dollars is equal to only 13 per cent of the EU-15 figure. Wide variations, however are found within both the EU-15 and the transition countries. In the former, Luxembourg has a GNP per capita figure that is more than three times the figure of Greece and Portugal, while in the latter, Slovenia has a GNP per capita figure more than ten times that of Albania and Bosnia. National and regional differences in GNP per capita are depicted in Map 1.2. Second, as already indicated above, wide disparities exist within the transition countries. The Central region seems to have a GNP per capita which is at least 60 per cent higher than the Baltic figure and 150 per cent higher than the Balkan figure. Third, a potential enlargement of the EU to include all European countries will reduce average GNP per capita of the Union by about 20 per cent.[5]

Finally, column 9 presents information about the share of agriculture in GDP, an indicator related to the stage or level of development of each country. In general, the development literature suggests that a greater dependence on agriculture is associated with earlier stages of development. The national and regional figures in column 9 verify our earlier discussion. EU-15 countries

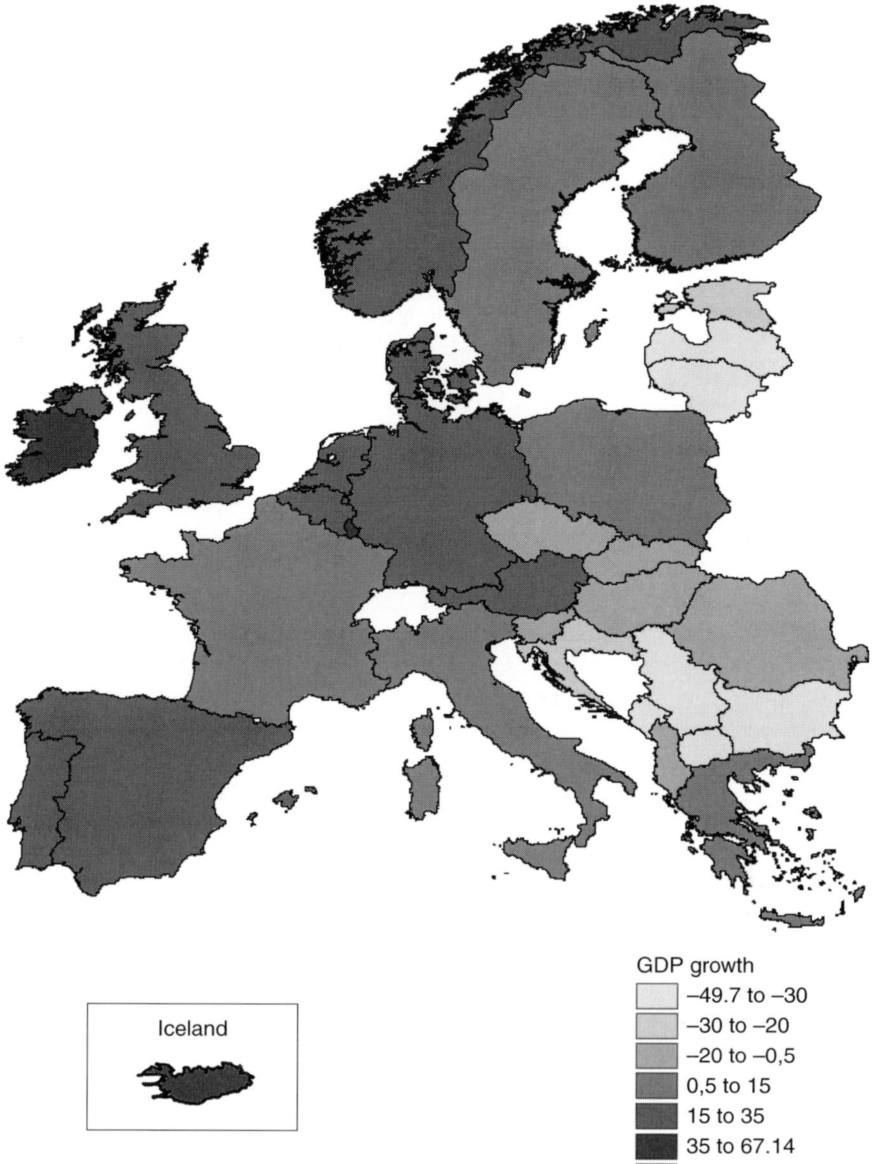

Map 1.1 GDP growth in Europe, 1989–97
Source: Table 1.1.

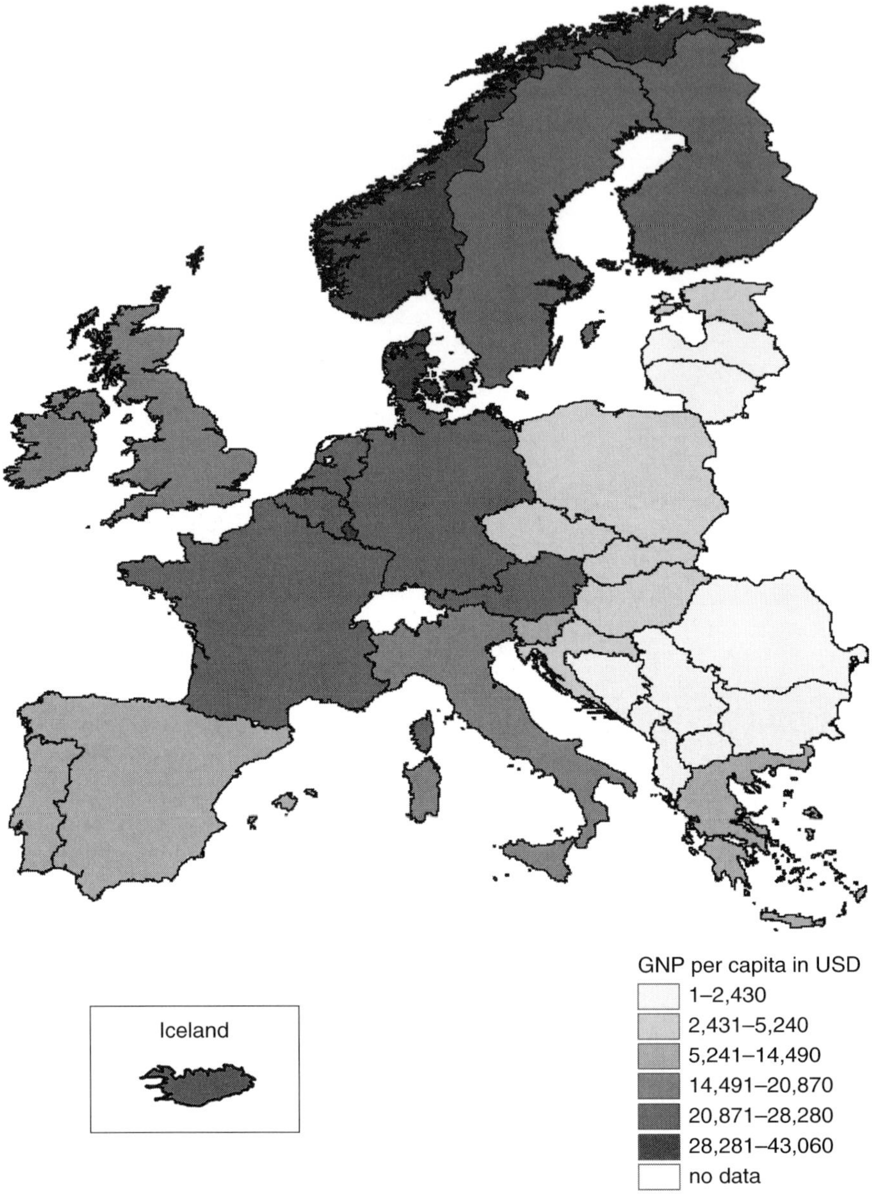

Map 1.2 GNP per capita in Europe, 1997
Source: Table 1.1.

Map 1.3 Share of agriculture in GDP in Europe, 1997

Source: Table 1.1.

have a relatively low dependence on agriculture (2 per cent of GDP), while the transition countries have a much higher dependence (12 per cent of GDP). As Map 1.3 shows, however, within transition countries wide differences exist, with the Central region being much closer to the EU-15 figure than the Baltic or the Balkan region. In particular, the latter is characterised by a productive structure that is not compatible with that of a modern and advanced economy.

Summarising the information of Table 1.1, we could argue that the process of transition may have removed the political and military divide in Europe, but it has not so far removed the economic one. On economic grounds, Europe seems to be still divided between the western and more affluent part and the eastern part that is still faced with a significantly lower development level and a less advanced economic structure. This East–West division is not the only one detectable in Europe. Within the EU-15, the Mediterranean countries or regions have a lower level of development and a less advanced economic structure than the Northwestern countries or regions. Greece, Portugal and Spain have a GNP per capita that is equal to 51 per cent, 48 per cent and 63 per cent respectively of the EU-15 average. On the other hand, Luxembourg, Denmark and Germany have a GNP per capita that is 162 per cent, 152 per cent and 123 per cent of the EU-15 average. Intra-transition divides with respect to development levels and economic structure are even more pronounced. The best performers are found in Central Europe, close to the advanced Western European countries, while the worst performers are found in Southeastern Europe. As a result, it seems that Europe is characterised by a highly unequal geography of development and economic structure. Its most developed part extends from the North of Italy to the Southern part of the UK, including large parts of Austria, Germany, Belgium, Luxembourg, The Netherlands and France. Its least developed part includes the Southeastern European countries in transition, while the Mediterranean zone and the Central European countries take the intermediate positions.

In order to get as precise a picture as possible concerning disparities in Europe, in the remainder of this section we are going to address two further issues. First, we would like to know whether this picture of wide national and macro-regional disparities in Europe is supported by other, mostly physical indicators of development. Second, we are interested in learning whether these disparities will have a tendency to increase or decrease over time. In our view, both issues have important implications for welfare and policy considerations.

In Table 1.2, information is presented about a different measure of GNP per capita and several other measures of welfare and development related to health conditions, infrastructure, and consumption. In column 1 we present GNP per capita in purchasing power parity (PPP) for 1997. This measure differs from that in Table 1.1, as it takes into consideration price level differentials among different countries. It is typical that more developed countries have in general higher price levels than less developed ones, which means that the purchasing power of a given sum of money is greater in the latter than in the former. As a result, compared to US dollars figures based on exchange rate parity, GNP per capita in PPP should be higher in countries and regions lagging behind and lower in advanced ones. Indeed, we observe in column 1 that the purchasing power of the average person in Central Europe is equal to 37 per cent of the EU-15 level, a figure that is twice as high as the one given for GNP per capita in USD in Table 1.1. However, even with this measure of welfare, significant disparities continue to exist. In the EU-15, the highest figure is for Denmark,[6] and is almost twice as high as the figure of Greece, which is the lowest. In the transition countries group, the Baltic and Balkan regions have a higher GNP per capita figure than in Table 1.1, which, however, is still very low and equal to about 20 per cent of the EU-15 figure.

In column 3 we present an index of infant mortality, measured as deaths per 1,000 infants, which intends to capture differences in living and health conditions and the quality of health services. The figures are encouraging for the EU-15, but disappointing for the transition group. The Central European region has a mortality index which is 80 per cent higher than that of the EU-15, while the Baltic and the Balkan region have an index which is 140 per cent and 260 per cent higher than the EU-15 figure, respectively. Some countries like Albania and Romania record alarmingly high infant mortality rates. These figures must be attributed to the low level of living conditions as well as the low quality of health services, as the more quantifiable information on health services provided in columns 4 and 5 do not justify such wide disparities. Indeed, the regional figures for doctors and hospital beds provided in these columns are comparable. In the first indicator the EU-15 figure is 2.7 doctors per 1,000 people and the transition group figure is 2.4 doctors per 1,000 people. In the second indicator the EU-15 and the transition figures are 7.3 and 7.2 hospital beds per 1,000 people respectively. Among all regional groups, the Baltic countries seem to have the best ratio of doctors and beds per resident, which may partly reflect harsh climatic conditions in the region.

Column 6 presents electricity consumption per capita for the year 1996. This index, which includes household and enterprise sector electricity consumption, is often used as a proxy for the level of economic activity in a country or a region. We observe that the differences among regions are relatively limited compared to those recorded in GNP per capita. The average figure for transition countries is equal to 53 per cent of the EU-15 average. Regional differences exist but are not extreme. The Central region has a figure equal to 57 per cent of the EU, while the Baltic and Balkan regions have figures equal to 38 per cent and 48 per cent of the EU, respectively. These figures, recording a lower level of disparities in economic activity and welfare, should be interpreted with caution for two reasons. First, electricity may not be the only or dominant source of energy consumption in all countries. Second, high values may simply reflect harsher climatic conditions, as the figures for Norway, Finland and Sweden clearly show.

The last three columns in Table 1.2 provide information on two indicators related to the conditions of infrastructure and one indicator related to the level of welfare. The index of transportation infrastructure (measured by road density) in column 7 reveals significant East–West and East–East disparities. The EU-15 road network covers 1,489 km of paved road per 1,000 square km, compared to only 859 km in transition countries. Thus, the road density in the East is equal to 57 per cent of the road density in the West. Intra-East regional variations are however significant. The Central region has a figure equal to 75 per cent of the EU-15, while the Baltic and Balkan regions have figures equal to 57 per cent and 35 per cent of the EU-15 figure respectively. Note here that the intra-EU differences are also significant, as the Mediterranean countries have figures that are close to the Baltic ones. The general picture reveals a core–periphery pattern of disparities in terms of the provision of transportation infrastructure, in which the Northwestern countries have a significantly higher road density than the Central, the Mediterranean, the Baltic and Balkan (in this order) regions.

Figures for telephones and TV sets per 1,000 people reveal a similar pattern. On the one hand, the EU-15 has a figure that is significantly higher than the transition countries and on the other some (milder) differences exist among regional groups. The only difference here is that the Baltic countries have a better index than the Central European ones. The Balkans, with a telephone density equal to 39 per cent of the EU-15 and a TV set density equal to the 50 per cent of the EU-15 hold the last place among the transition regions.

Summarising the basic information of Table 1.2, we could say that the evidence tends to verify the pattern of disparities found on the basis of GNP per capita data in Table 1.1. However, the use of GNP per capita figures in PPP, as well as the use of other 'physical' indicators of development and welfare indicate that these disparities are not as profound as the information in Table 1.1 would predict. Figure 1.1 compares 1997 figures of GNP per capita in US dollars and PPP in order to make that point more clear. It shows that differences in terms of the later are smaller, as low level countries tend to have relatively higher figures than the former. The opposite happens for high level countries. Nevertheless, disparities in income and welfare are very serious, with the Central European region (the front runner among transition countries) having figures significantly lower than the EU-15 cohesion countries, while the Baltic and Balkan regions are much further behind.

Given this picture, a question that arises is whether these disparities have shown any tendency to decrease during the 1989–97 period. The driving force of transition from plan to market has been the desire of CEE countries for Western-type institutions and welfare levels. As a result, the very essence of transition policies (liberalisation, openness, and privatisation) has been an effort to catch up with the West. In mainstream economic thinking, this goal is considered highly feasible if the 'correct' mix of transition policies is implemented. Table 1.3 presents some measures of disparity with respect to GDP

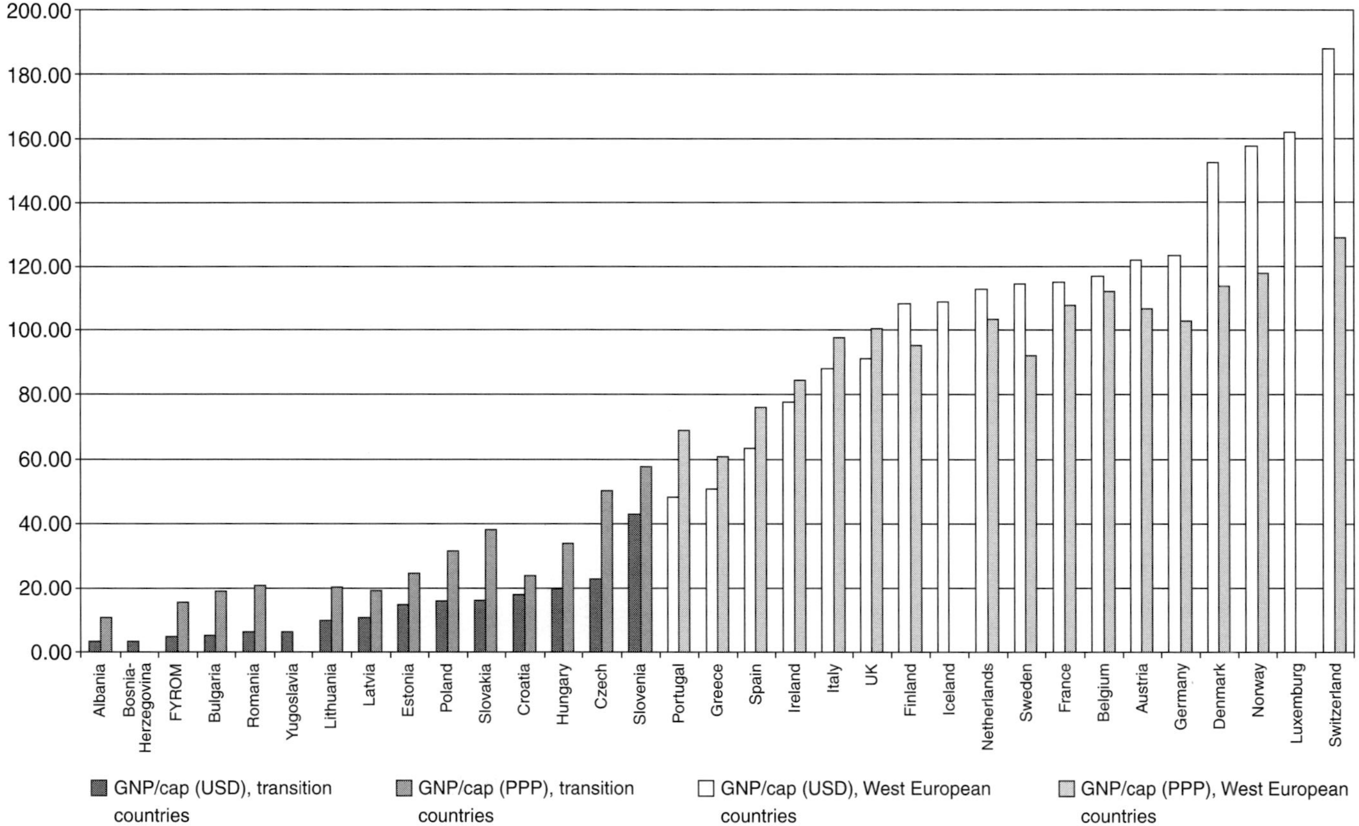

Figure 1.1 GNP per capita in US dollars and PPP in Europe, 1997.

Sources: Tables 1.1, 1.2.

Table 1.3 Indicators of convergence-divergence trends in Europe with the use of GNP per capita, 1989–97

	1989	*1990*	*1991*	*1992*	*1993*	*1994*	*1995*	*1996*	*1997*
c.v. (weighted)	0.65	0.67	0.70	0.72	0.72	0.71	0.70	0.68	0.70
c.v.	0.75	0.77	0.79	0.81	0.81	0.81	0.81	0.81	0.82
max/min	38.03	45.79	60.28	67.99	56.43	53.09	48.6	45.3	48.2
Transition/EU	0.17	0.15	0.13	0.12	0.12	0.12	0.13	0.13	0.14
Mediterranean/EU	0.57	0.57	0.58	0.58	0.57	0.57	0.57	0.59	0.59
CE/EU	0.21	0.19	0.17	0.17	0.17	0.17	0.18	0.18	0.19
Balkans/EU	0.10	0.09	0.07	0.06	0.06	0.06	0.06	0.06	0.07
Baltics/EU	0.20	0.19	0.17	0.13	0.12	0.11	0.11	0.11	0.12

Source: Own calculations from World Bank (1999b).

per capita for the period 1989–97. These measures are the weighted and unweighted coefficient of variation (CV),[7] the max/min ratio[8] and the ratios of the GDP per capita of various regional groups to that of the EU-15. The estimated values of these indicators of disparity, that are presented in Figures 1.2 and 1.3, provide some first evidence of the existing convergence or divergence trends in this period in Europe.

Clearly, the process of transition has increased disparities during the first three or four post-1989 years. This is evident in the increasing values of the coefficient of variation and the max/min ratio, as well as the transition/EU-15 GDP per capita ratio. In the period after 1993 the evidence is less clear. The weighted coefficient of variation starts to decline slowly,[9] while the max/min ratio experiences a more generous decline. On the other hand, the unweighted coefficient of variation continues to increase. In any case, the 1997 values of all these measures are higher than the 1989, indicating that overall disparities in this period have increased.

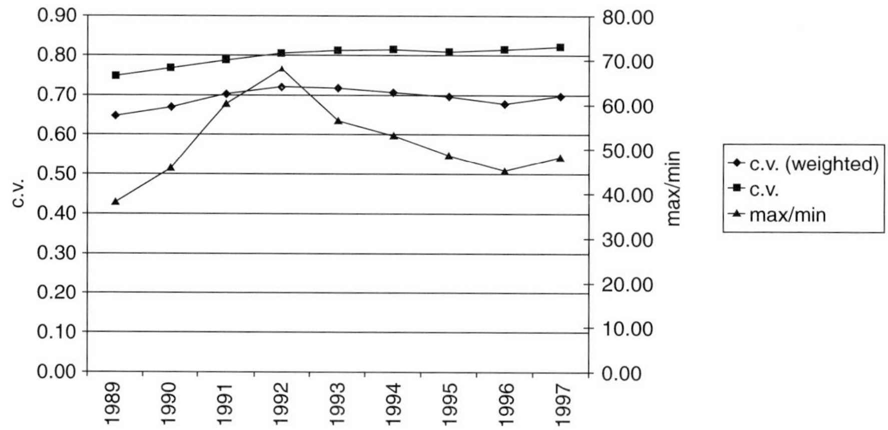

Figure 1.2 Coefficient of variation and max/min ratio based on GNP per capita.

Source: Table 1.3.

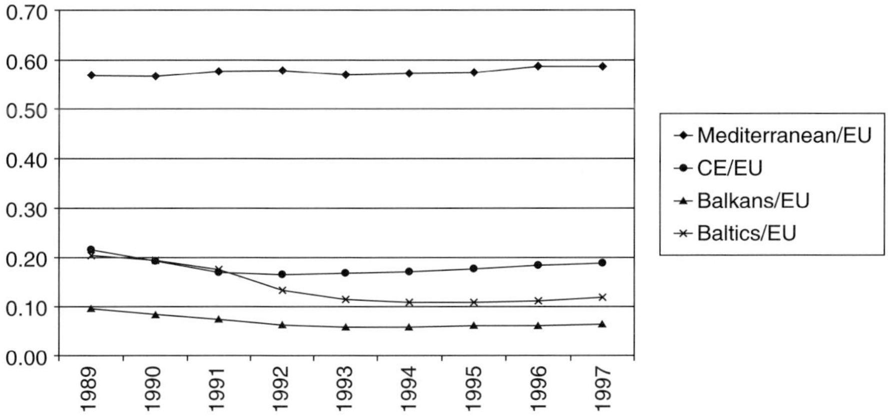

Figure 1.3 Regional GDP per capita compared to EU average.
Source: Table 1.3

Going to the regional ratios, we can make a number of observations. First, at the intra-EU-15 level, disparities have remained constant or decreased slightly, as the Mediterranean countries (Greece, Portugal and Spain) maintain an average GDP per capita equal to 57 or 58 per cent of the EU-15 figure. Second, different regional groups of transition countries have followed different trajectories after 1993. As Figure 1.3 clearly shows, the Central European region shows some weak – but clear – tendency for convergence towards the EU-15. On the other hand, the Baltic and Balkan regions show no clear sign of convergence. Petrakos, in this volume, reaches similar conclusions using a regression model in the tradition of Barro and Sala-i-Martin (1991). Therefore, our findings indicate that there is a visible geographical differentiation in the prospects of transition countries to converge towards the EU-15 development levels. Although the Central European countries have made some steps towards reducing the gap with the West after 1993, the Baltic and Balkan countries have either maintained this gap or increased it further. As a result, in 1997, the European economy is more divided in terms of welfare levels than it was in the beginning of the transition process.

Developments and challenges in the new European economic space

In the previous section we examined on a pan-European scale the basic trends in welfare, structure and performance and found significant differences at the national and macro-regional level. Moreover, several reports indicate that serious disparities also exist at the micro-regional level inside countries in both the West and the East. In this section we would like to examine these issues further, focusing our attention on the factors or processes that are behind these trends and developments and shape, to a large extent, the emerging economic geography of Europe. These are the processes of structural change, integration in the West and transition in the East, as well as the policies of enlargement and the East–West market interaction.

Structural change and its impact on the European space

In Western Europe and in most of the developed world, the last three or so decades have been a period of significant economic restructuring. During this period, important sectors and methods of production have lost, while others have gained ground. The most important features of this restructuring have been (a) the development of service industries and the relative contraction of manufacturing; (b) the gradual shift of output and employment from the traditional labour- and resource-intensive sectors to technology and knowledge-intensive sectors; (c) the contraction and crisis of the Fordist system of industrial organisation and the success and gradual spread of flexible production systems; and (d) the gradual spread of economic networks (Castells 1996; Coffey and Bailly 1996; Piore and Sabel 1984).

These features have been the result of deeper processes related, first of all, to innovation and technological progress that have increased over time the capital and technology intensity of production, imposing labour-saving technologies in manufacturing. Second, they are related to the internationalisation of economic activities through trade and mobile investment that has allowed for a new international division of labour. This has favoured the location of capital-intensive, knowledge-intensive, and technology-intensive activities in the advanced economies and the orientation of labour- and resource-intensive production activities to low-cost developing countries. Finally these features have been affected by the improvements in the standards of living in developed countries, which shifted demand from standardised to personalised and differentiated products.

The changes in the productive structure of the economy are reflected in the spatial structure of the European cities and regions. The decline of manufacturing and the relative contraction of traditional sectors have resulted in the contraction of the economic base and the increase of structural unemployment in traditional industrial areas. Although this development has affected all European countries, its impact was highly differentiated in time and space. Employment losses in manufacturing in the 1970s were much more serious in the traditional industrial cities and regions of the European core, where the higher cost-base imposed structural change earlier and more forcefully than in the less advanced areas of the European periphery, where the lower cost-base postponed this impact for one or two decades.

The crisis in manufacturing was directly associated with the relative decline of the more advanced industrial cities and regions in Europe. In the 1970s these cities and regions lost population and employment positions, not only because of the industrial decline, but also because of the exodus of manufacturing, which gradually left large city centres in order to avoid the high and increasing cost of urban land. These tendencies coincided with the relative improvement of the economic potential of less densely populated cities or regions in the immediate periphery of the European core. Such areas could take advantage of a favourable position with respect to transportation networks, lower land cost, favourable local taxation, local development initiatives and a cleaner and less congested environment.

These developments, that generated prospects for a more balanced development of the urban and regional structure of the European economy, were also favoured by the spread of flexible specialisation. This system is based on differentiated products, external economies of scale and economies of scope, vertical disintegration, flexible and highly differentiated labour markets and the achievement of collective efficiency through a local mix of co-operation and competition and support mechanisms operating at the local level. This system is clearly in contrast with the mass production Fordist system based on economies of scale, vertical integration, large and stable product markets and regulated labour markets (Brusco 1982, 1986; Goodman *et al.* 1989; Petrakos 1996).

These developments were also favoured by the spread of networks, which are intermediate forms of relationship between market transactions on the one hand and full integration within a single firm (Zuscovitch and Justman 1995). According to Castells (1996), networks are a new social morphology that substantially modifies the operation and outcomes in processes of production, experience, power and culture. Firms and increasingly organisations and institutions are organised in networks of variable geometry, whose intertwining supersedes the traditional distinction between corporations and small firms, cutting across sectors and spreading along different geographical clusters of economic units.

As a result it was considered that flexible production systems along with the spread of networks would provide a real opportunity for growth and prosperity, especially for cities and regions outside the traditional development centres of Europe. Indeed, many '*new industrial spaces*' appeared in the 1980s, some more successful than others, attempting to benefit from various mixes of favourable locational and policy characteristics (Komninos 1992; Pyke and Sengenberger 1992).

This optimism in the 1980s about the future of spatial balances in Europe was not bound to last very long. It is now claimed that Europe has entered the fourth phase of its urban cycle. Passing from the phase of *urbanisation and urban concentration* related to the process of industrialisation in the 1950s and the early 1960s to the phase of *suburbanisation,* in the 1960s and *de-concentration* associated with industrial decline in the 1970s, in the mid-1980s it entered the phase of *re-concentration*. At this time, several European countries experienced population changes that were directly related to urban population density, as many large cities and metropolitan areas grew at rates exceeding national averages. Although this trend reversal was not universal, nevertheless it is a significant change of direction in urban balances (Lever and Champion 1996).

As Cheshire and Hamilton show in Chapter 4 of this volume, from 1951 to 1981 there was a very regular pattern of change where European cities moved steadily from stages of centralisation to decentralisation. In the early 1980s, however, the trend reversed towards urban centralisation. Although the balance of forces driving decentralisation has weakened, even often reversed, recentralisation is far from inevitable and it is partly dependent on the functions particular cities perform.

The most important contributor to this trend reversal has been the dramatic development of the tertiary sector of the economy and especially services. The spatial distribution of producer services is very different from that of industry, as these services do not follow the spread of industry but remain concentrated in the metropolitan centre, the large urban regions and the traditional centres of development. Along broad lines, agglomeration economies tend to strengthen in large urban regions complex sets of economic activities, based on the co-operation and spatial clustering of administrative functions of all productive sectors, financial organisations and advanced producer services (Coffey and Bailly 1996).

These trends of re-concentration in the European urban system have both a national and a European dimension. Structural changes in the European economy do not just strengthen the relative position of metropolitan centres in each country, but they also strengthen the position of the metropolitan centres taking the highest places in the European urban hierarchy. Rosenblat and Pumain (1993) have shown that in 1988 London and Paris alone concentrated 50 per cent of the headquarters of the largest 300 European enterprises.

As a result, the structural changes that have taken place in the 1980s and the 1990s have had two distinctive effects. On the one hand, they generated new comparative advantages for the metropolitan regions that this time were not related to industry but to services. On the other hand, new opportunities emerged through the spread of flexible specialisation systems and the operation of economic networks that provided a new potential for a more balanced spatial structure in the future. The moderate number of success stories, however, related to the 'new industrial spaces' and the fact that they had a limited spread and application in the European periphery – where the most disadvantaged areas are found – shows that these opportunities are rarely applicable to the productive structures and realities of the cities and regions lagging behind.

On balance, these trends have generated some concern about the spatial balances at the national and European level and give a new dimension to the discussions about the diverging prospects of many small cities and regions and the discussions for the maintenance of structural and regional policies.

In which way have structural changes affected economic developments in the CEE countries? Although it is difficult to provide solid evidence, it is very likely that the productive structures based on huge industrial plants and mass production, partly dictated by the CMEA division of labour, were responsible for the profound inefficiency of the pre-1989 economic system. Petrakos and Christodoulakis (Chapter 13) in this volume note that it was a historical accident that these structures took momentum at a time when the model of mass production and the Fordist–Taylorist forms of industrial organisation were in serious crisis and openly questioned in the West. As a result, part of the difficulties several CEECs experienced in their transition from plan to market have been attributed to tremendous structural adjustment being overdue. In that respect they are similar to the difficulties that many Western countries faced in the 1970s.

Geography and economic integration

National or regional disparities with respect to development and welfare indicators within the EU have increased in the last thirty years. To a large extent, this is attributed to the accession in the 1980s of members with lower levels of development. These accessions, involving the membership of Greece, Spain and Portugal, transformed the EU gradually from a homogeneous club in the 1960s and 1970s to a heterogeneous union. Several factors, such as economic structure, geography, history and policy can be considered responsible for these inter- and intra-national differences in the level of development.

The relation of EU integration, a process dominated by the operation of the Single European Market (SEM) and the policies for the Economic and Monetary Union (EMU), to disparities at the national or regional level is a topic that has received significant attention in the literature. Petrakos, in this volume, notes that EU integration increases spatial differentiation by exposing to international competition regions with unequal endowments in resources and technology and different economic structures. In general, peripheral regions with weak economic structures and deficient infrastructure and human resources have fared worse. Cheshire and Hamilton in Chapter 4 in this volume make a similar argument about the effects of integration on the European urban system. They claim that these effects favoured advanced urban economies in the core of Europe at the expense of backward urban economies in the periphery through an increased level of territorial competition.

Regional inequality in the EU is analysed by Dunford in Chapter 3 of this volume with the use of figures for GDP per capita. He shows that disparities remain high and of a specific type: poor regions are in the South, while more wealthy regions are urban regions in the North–Central part of the EU. Examining inequality over a period of thirty years he shows that there was a strong convergence until the mid-1970s. Then convergence gave way to divergence until the mid-1980s. From the mid-1980s to 1990 the Member States converged again. At the start of the 1990s there was a further upturn in most measures of inequality. He concludes that over the period from 1974 to 1992 there was no reduction in disparities. A recent European Commission report indicates that in the 1990s most regions of the EU which were lagging behind have made significant progress towards the average EU level of development and this is attributed to the policies introduced after 1988 (EC 1999). Despite this progress, significant disparities remain, as the more advanced regions have also increased their distance from the EU average. Moreover, available data show that within Member States regional inequalities increased and divergence predominated.

The most severely felt and most threatening socio-economic problem in contemporary Europe is beyond doubt unemployment. In 1997 about 18 million people, or 11 per cent of the labour force were unemployed in the European Union. This unemployment rate is slightly lower than that in 1994, but represents a dramatic increase compared to the early 1970s, when in 1973 the respective average figure for the 15 EU Member States was just 2 per cent. The problem of unemployment worsened dramatically despite increasing levels of employment. As it is stated in official documents: 'Over the period 1987 to 1997, employment in the EU increased by 5 million, but this was not enough to keep pace with 7.5 million new entrants into the labour market' (EC 1999).

These aggregate figures, however, obscure substantial regional differences.

> Whereas unemployment in the 25 least-affected regions in the EU averages only 3–4 per cent, only slightly higher than in the early 1970s, in the 25 most affected regions, it now stands at between 20 per cent and 35 per cent, substantially higher than 25 years ago.
>
> (EC 1999)

In many parts of the South, like Spain, Southern Italy and Southern France, we find unemployment rates of 20–30 per cent. Further North, only few regions face comparable problems: East Germany, Northern Finland, and the North-East part of France. Not only are those regions hit by high unemployment, they also show the highest shares of long-term unemployment – a clear indicator of structural problems. The highest shares of unemployed who have been out of work for a year or more can be found in the South of Italy, where typically two-thirds or more of total unemployment is long-term, rising to 80 per cent in Campania (EC 1999).

In these European regions, major parts of the population are practically excluded from society and most likely it is young people and women who are at risk. Women, for example, constitute only about 40 per cent of the European labour force, but 'account for nearly half of the unemployed and slightly over half of the long-term unemployed' (EC 1999). Despite significant improvements in women's position in the EU labour market in recent decades, they still suffer from lower participation rates and higher risk of unemployment – particularly long-term unemployment. This problem, again, has a clear regional dimension. While the respective rates for men and women are quite similar in the ten regions least affected by unemployment, the figures for women are much worse than those for men in the ten most affected regions of the Union.

Underlying the labour market dynamics is the development of the economy and its constant struggle to restructure and to adjust to a turbulent and increasingly competitive environment. The companies in the different regions and sectors of the European economy have to deal with very different challenges. While central regions in the UK were the first to be industrialised, some parts of the Mediterranean are still mainly agricultural. With the EU integration policies of the last decade, all these regions and their economies are becoming more interdependent, and we can see an increasing level of regional specialisation between the different parts of the Union. Not all types of regional specialisation are, however, compatible to long-term development and growth.

Welfare indicators in Tables 1.1, 1.2 and Map 1.2 in the previous section, as well as several European Commission reports reveal a striking pattern: The central part of the European Union that displays average and above average scores, is surrounded by a periphery of poorer countries and regions that consists of all of Greece, Southern Italy, Portugal, almost all of Spain, and stretches around the continent to some Northern and Western regions of the UK to Northern Finland. The New *Länder* of Germany also fall into this group of regions, but are – for obvious reasons – the exception in this pattern.

It is the main objective of the EU regional policy to bring the output levels of those disadvantaged regions closer to the EU average. The effect of this policy is monitored by the European Commission in a series of Cohesion Reports. While the results of earlier such reports were mixed, the latest Cohesion Report can claim that 'the evidence is now unambiguous: the GDP, or output, per head of poorer regions is converging towards the EU average' (EC 1999). In the ten regions where GDP per capita was lowest in 1986, it increased from 41 per cent of the EU average to 50 per cent in 1996, in the twenty-five poorest regions it rose from 52 per cent to 59 per cent. This impressive catch-up process of Europe's poorer regions, however, was accompanied by growing divergence among the regions with above average levels of per capita output. Consequently, the overall level of disparities in output per capita decreased only slightly over this decade. The relative position of the individual regions remained almost the same in a ranking by output per capita during this period.

Moreover, another change in trends has been observed, as increasingly, disparities are not so much between but rather within Member States (EC 1999). The prosperity of a region is clearly related to two interrelated factors: urbanisation and sectoral composition. Urban areas that reach relatively high levels of GDP per capita are concentrated in or around the rich central part of the EU, running from Belgium and The Netherlands through Western Germany to the North of Italy. The larger agglomerations among them typically show the highest employment shares in service, generally a growing sector in the economy. Those larger urban agglomerations therefore tend to be among the most prosperous regions in the EU. The GDP per capita in urban areas lies 22 per cent above the Union average. However, urban areas are at the same time facing major restructuring problems. Loss of the industrial base in some of them has led to poverty and high levels of unemployment. 'The main problems facing the EU – unemployment, poverty, economic restructuring and the destruction of the natural and physical environment – are for the most part concentrated and accentuated in urban areas' (EC 1999).

Evaluating regional trends in the EU and the impact of the integration process, we can make three summary statements. First, intra-EU disparities were and still remain high for a number of reasons, ranging from geography and structure, to history, institutions and policy. Second, the process of EU integration has released strong competitive forces that tend to favour the more advanced cities and regions in the European core, which house the largest and most efficient European enterprises. This is clearly evident in the trends of these regions to grow with rates that are higher than the EU average. Third, although EU and national regional policies seem to have had an impact in alleviating the costs of integration for those regions of Europe lagging behind, regional disparities have been affected rather marginally. This may be an indication that the market forces released by the policies of integration, in interaction with the dynamics of structural change, may be stronger than the policies designed and implemented for the development of those regions lagging behind. This suggests that regional policies need to maintain or even increase their strength, if a reasonable impact in a reasonable time span is to be expected. It may also suggest that as the market forces affecting the location of activities and regional disparities operate increasingly at the European level, spatial development policies should also be designed and implemented at the European – rather than the national – level.

Geography and transition: micro- and macro-spatial perspectives

The process of socio-economic and political transformation in CEE countries is now ten years old. The number and breadth of reforms that were implemented by these countries were unprecedented on this continent in this century and covered all levels of society. In the economic sphere macroeconomic stabilisation had to be achieved simultaneously with microeconomic reforms, privatisation, the creation of central institutions of a market economy, etc. The shock of the transition from a centrally planned to a market economy and the corresponding reorientation of the economy led to contractions of output by 20 to 30 per cent. In some regions and sectors the impact was much more pronounced. Experience shows that particular countries assumed different trajectories of their transition and have achieved differentiated results (De Melo *et al.* 1996; Gorzelak *et al.* 1995; Woo *et al.* 1998; World Bank 1996). On the one hand, there is the success of Poland, Hungary, Estonia and the Czech Republic, on the other, there is the almost permanent recession of several post-Soviet republics and the Balkans.

Several questions arise concerning the process and the policies of transition and several issues are still debated in the literature. What are the factors behind such wide differences in national performance? Are success and failure in transition only a question of policy design and implementation or have other factors mattered more? Is it the circumstances, the endowments of history and geography that shaped the pre-transition conditions or simply reluctant, delayed and poorly implemented policies? To what extent was the post-socialist transformation an unprecedented social, political and economic experiment – and to what extent was it just a repetition of the economic restructuring processes that have been taking place in the more developed part of the world since the 1960s?

Gorzelak (1996, 1998) has recently suggested that the economic decline in Central and Eastern Europe was largely a necessary adaptation to new internal and external conditions in the form of a shift from a Fordist to a post-Fordist organisation of economic, social and political life. This shift was not possible in a closed system, separated by economic and political barriers from global markets and therefore not exposed to economic and political international competition. Once these barriers had been removed, the old patterns of economic production could no longer be maintained and 'imported' patterns of socio-economic and political organisation began to shape the new reality.

According to this interpretation, the post-socialist transformation can be conceived as a 'normal' process of technological and organisational change, performed later than would have been the case if Central Europe (and other socialist countries) had been incorporated earlier into an open global economy. The decline in economic output, which occurred in the post-socialist countries after 1990, is conceived as the price of restructuring similar to that paid by the West for its change in socio-economic structures after 1973, passing from a Fordist to a post-Fordist type of economic organisation.

This line of thinking proceeds one step further based on the concept of the J-curve (which is rooted in the Schumpeterian theory of 'creative destruction') to explain individual country performance in the post-socialist transformation (Bradshaw and Stenning 1999). It is claimed that only those countries willing – and able – to pay the price of the recession (the first, sliding down part of the J-curve), were then able to mount the rising-up part of the curve, since by getting rid of old assets and institutions they had created sound foundations for future growth in the new open market economy. In general, those countries that approached this task most courageously were generally the first to resume economic growth. This policy-based interpretation of performance under transition has received strong support in the literature. Piazolo in Chapter 9 in this volume argues that economic growth in transition countries is positively correlated with reform policies and the advancement of institutional change, an argument shared by several others. For example, Sachs (1996) and de Melo *et. al.* (1996) argue that the transition countries having the highest ranking on various liberalisation scales showed a quicker recovery in total output during the first few years following the date of liberalisation. In general, 'policy failure' explanations attribute poor transition performance to delayed reforms and non-persistent policies of privatisation and market liberalisation.

Although mainstream policy-based explanations of performance under transition have been criticised on several grounds, no coherent alternative has yet been formulated. On the one hand, some reports are concerned with the high social costs of the reform, which led to a sharp decrease in domestic demand and is considered as one of the main causes of the economic decline. Others point to the fact that too wide an opening of the emerging markets to the Western competition created unnecessary difficulties for the post-socialist enterprises, which added to the overall economic decline. They also argue that the shift to Western markets was too fast and that some efforts could have been made to slow down the pace of curtailing sales to the East, i.e. the republics of former Soviet Union and other post-socialist countries (Gatsios 1996). In general, 'market failure' explanations consider the 'shock therapy' of openness, massive privatisation, liberalisation and deregulation in the absence of appropriate institutional arrangements as the primary factor explaining repeated crises in a number of transition countries (Nelis 1999).

On the other hand, some studies point to the importance of 'initial conditions' in shaping national performance under transition, claiming that they had a larger role in determining the output decline than policy choices (Krueger and Ciolko 1998). These differences in initial pre-1989 conditions may concern the structure of the economy and enterprises, the structure of external economic relations (Jackson and Petrakos 1999), the military burden, as well as infrastructure and human capital development.

Along a similar line of argument, others claim that 'geography' also plays an important role in shaping final outcomes. Success and failure in the transition process are considered as being affected by factors such as accessibility, proximity, adjacency and cultural affinity to the Western European core. These geographical features affect the type of trade relations, capital mobility, the attraction of higher functional order activities and the diffusion of technology. This explains why performance has a strong geographical dimension (Mertzanis and Petrakos 1998; Petrakos 1997; Petrakos and Totev 2000; Sachs 1997), with the Visegrad countries in Central Europe having in general a better record than the perimeter Balkan countries in Southeastern Europe.

Other explanations of differential performance under transition are also possible. A non-exclusive list should include significant national differences with respect to prevailing geopolitical conditions or 'border conditions', that inhibit or restrict cross-border economic and social interaction, increasing fragmentation, ethnic rivalry, war and regional instability. Experience has shown that these factors can play an important role, especially in regions and countries with weak institutions and a limited historical experience of the market system.

The evidence provided in the first section of the introduction shows that at the macro-geographical level transition has been more successful in Central Europe and less so in the Baltic and Balkan countries. What has been, however, the spatial impact of transition at the micro-level and how did it affect regional balances in CEE countries? A significant amount of literature has already been published on the regional outcomes of the transformation processes in East-Central Europe (Bachtler *et al.* 1999; EPRC 1996; Gorzelak and Kuklinski 1992; Gorzelak 1996, 1998; Hajdu and Horvath 1994; Jackson and Petrakos 1996; OECD 1995; Petrakos 1999). The regional trajectories of transformation are sharper than the national ones, the amplitudes of recession and growth are greater and failures and successes much more clearly outlined. Almost all countries under transformation have their own regional winners and losers. Petrakos in this volume examines the way in which the processes of internationalisation, marketisation and structural change affect the performance of cities and regions. Gorzelak, also in this volume, presents four different types of regions depending on their reaction to the new economic social and international conditions: (a) the leading regions, which represent a case of positive continuity and are in most cases the metropolitan regions of each country; (b) the losers, which represent a case of negative discontinuity and are in most cases old industrial regions undergoing a deep restructuring process; (c) the backward peripheries, which extending along the eastern borders of most CEECs, represent a case of negative continuity; and (d) the newcomers, that is the western regions of CEECs that have become the new winners of the transformation process and represent a case of positive discontinuity.

The factors that have contributed to different regional performances under transition are varied. Most important are the sectoral shift from industry to services, the change in locational advantage associated with the changing pattern of foreign trade, the locational preferences of foreign capital and the initial conditions of each region related to development levels, the quality of human and productive resources and infrastructure.

Most studies indicate that a decline in output and job losses were mainly experienced in industry, while service sector employment expanded. Consequently, it was mainly regions with a high dependence on industry that suffered in the transition process. Regions that were attractive to services, like most of the capital cities, performed much better. Some of them, like Prague, Budapest, and Bratislava even experienced full employment.

During the period of transition, the foreign trade pattern of Central and East European countries changed fundamentally. While in 1985 less than 20 per cent of their exports went to the countries of the European Union, in 1996 almost 60 per cent of their exports ended up there, and almost the same share of their imports came from the Union. Consequently, locational advantage shifted from Eastern to Western regions, both in Central and Eastern Europe as a whole and within the individual countries. As a result, labour market perfomance tends to be better in the Western parts of the countries. This is clearly visible in countries like Hungary and Slovakia.

A factor that adds to both tendencies is foreign direct investments. Although the regional distribution of foreign direct investment in the Central and East European countries is difficult to assess because of a lack of reliable data, it 'is evident, however, that the major part of inflows went to capital cities, large urban centres and Western regions bordering the EU, with, in most cases, better transport links with EU markets and a more skilled labour force' (EC 1999; Kienast 1999). This, too, helped those regions to reduce unemployment.

Three chapters in this volume, however, argue that there were no dramatic changes in the evolution of regional inequalities. Keune (Chapter 8) observes that the regions and cities that were in better shape in the first years of transition have tended to continue their above average performance. In contrast, regions that were lagging at the beginning have not been able to close the gap. Similarly, Nemes-Nagy in Chapter 7 shows that in Hungary regional inequalities have increased and that the regions which originally had higher incomes are still leading, while the traditionally backward regions have not been able to achieve improvements to a substantial degree. Fazekas, in Chapter 6, in a quantitative and detailed study, shows that there were no changes in the position of Hungarian sub-regions after 1994. The winners of the first years remained winners and the losers remained losers. He challenges the view that high unemployment is concentrated in industrially declining or single-employer regions, arguing that these cases are the exception to the rule. According to his findings in Hungary, unemployment is typically low in urbanised central regions and high in remote agricultural regions with poor infrastructure, low educational levels, no tourism, and poorly developed services, with large Gypsy communities and a long distance away from the affluent centres of the country. He concludes that the long-lasting regional differences in unemployment rates can be traced back to other factors related to historical and cultural traditions, economic development and hard-to-change endowments rather than to events occurring in the first years of transition.

With respect to trends in CEE cities, Cheshire and Hamilton in Chapter 4 in this volume argue that they have become more divergent during the decade of transition and are likely to continue to be so in the foreseeable future. The key to this lies in the differentiated speed and depth of reforms between states, regions and cities and their consequent depth of integration into the spatial structure of the wider Europe. The interrelated processes of integration, however, are stronger in the cities and regions most accessible to the EU core and weaken to the East and the South with increasing distance. Within this broad framework, individual cities range at the one extreme from (a) those, often remote small and medium-size, which are still dominated by state-owned enterprises and are stagnating or facing serious restructuring difficulties to the other extreme; and (b) usually (but not always) larger cities and metropolitan areas where reform and privatisation have fostered entrepreneurship and new firm formation as well as inward foreign investment. Yet it is the expansion of producer services that particularly differentiates the capital cities from the remainder of the urban system, especially in the advanced transition economies.

Given the type and magnitude of regional inequality, it is evident that the question of regional policy under transition is receiving increasing attention. As Gorzelak shows in Chapter 5 in this volume, during the entire transformation period there were no comprehensive regional policies formulated in any CEE country. In addition, local policies and initiatives aimed at employment creation, despite their potential importance (Petrakos 1996), have so far received limited attention. One of the reasons is that in most CEECs self-government is limited to the very local level, composed of thousands of small municipalities. With the exception of Poland, regional government either does not exist or is subordinated to the central government. Several arguments concerning the implementation of regional policy are expressed and supported in this volume. An emerging common point is that one dimension of regional policy should be based on a decentralised bottom-up approach that will take into account the particular problems of local areas and explore their specific advantages and opportunities. Different chapters, however, focus on different aspects of policy. Gorzelak expresses his scepticism about 'traditional' approaches and emphasises that regional policies should serve and not contradict the strategic objectives of a given country, which is promoting high rates of economic growth and deep structural changes. Although he recognises the need for support to depressed and lagging behind regions, he is also concerned with the possibility for a disguised return of socialist-type 'egalitarian' practices through a misunderstood regional policy doctrine. Petrakos expresses doubts about the exclusive reliance on a bottom-up approach to regional policy, as depressed regions rarely have the strength or opportunity to break the vicious cycle in which they are locked in from the inside and require co-ordinated action at both the regional, national (and the EU) level. Along a similar line, Keune notes that because of the significant and increasing level of regional disparities in CEECs, the equity objective should have a prominent place in most countries, with the most problematic regions receiving special assistance. Strengthening employment creation requires that national level policies are complemented by a decentralised approach based on local actors and initiatives that will involve and mobilise local societies. 'Top-down' and 'bottom-up' approaches need to be creatively combined in order to face the challenge of employment creation.

Summing up, it is safe to claim that the ten-years-old process of transition has released several forces that tend to generate serious imbalances in Central and East Europe at both the macro and micro geographical levels. The evidence provided in this volume and elsewhere indicates that Central European countries closer or adjacent to the most developed part of Western Europe have fared better than the more distant Baltic and Balkan countries. Within each country, capital and metropolitan regions as well as western regions near the east–west frontier have a better record than eastern and rural regions with respect to growth performance and unemployment rates.

The spatial aspects of East–West interaction

There is already evidence and an increasing concern that these major changes observed in Europe over the last decade, have resulted in an increasing level of division. As Hudson and Williams (1999) note: 'while Europe seems to be becoming an increasingly homogenized politico-economic space, it is also characterized by enduring and, in some instances, deepening social cleavages'. These divisions in society, economy, and the territory of Europe threaten the process of European integration.

Previous analysis and Petrakos in this volume show that both EU integration and CEE transition processes face problems and difficulties that seem to have a clear geographical dimension. As a result, divergence trends prevail in the new European space at both the macro and micro level. Within the EU international disparities still remain high, although they have a declining tendency due to structural and regional policies in the last period. Intra-national disparities, however, tend to increase as different places adjust in various ways and with different rates of success to the new highly internationalised economic environment. Within CEE both inter-national and intra-national disparities are rising for reasons that have already been discussed. At the European level, Cheshire and Hamilton observe that although East–West integration has shifted the European core to the East, it is doubtful whether there are many regions in the East that will be part of the new extended core – at least in the medium term. As a result, despite euphoria about the (unquestionable) progress of integration and transition, Europe is at the turn of the century perhaps more divided in terms of welfare levels and opportunities than it was ten or twenty years ago.

East–West divides may also be affected by the legacies of the past. Besides economic ones, divides can also be conceptual. Maier and Rosenmayr in Chapter 10 in this volume examine the extent to which the pre-1989 division of Europe has left behind its traces in the minds of the people on either side of the former Iron Curtain. They examine the perception students in Vienna and Bratislava have of the geography of both sides of the former divided Europe and find significant differences between these two groups.

The most significant market force that affects the European economy is the East–West trade relations. Several chapters in this volume and elsewhere examine their structure and impact. According to Petrakos, East–West trade relations have experienced a rapid but unbalanced expansion of a basically inter-industry type. This argument is better documented by Landesmann (1995, 1998), who provides evidence of a strong 'developmental gap' between CEE countries and the EU, in a sense that the former tend to develop patterns of specialisation away from capital-, R&D-, and skill-intensive sectors and towards labour-intensive sectors. This move was found to be much more dramatic in the case of Balkan countries than in the case of the other Central European economies.

Despite the dominance of the inter-industry type of trade, intra-industry trade has also increased in CEE countries (Dobrinsky 1995). However, this increase, which is more evident among the more advanced CEECs, such as the Czech Republic and Hungary, is followed by evidence of a significant 'quality gap' between western and eastern products that is likely to persist for a long time (Landesmann 1998).

Further difficulties and problems for transition countries have also been detected. Kyrkilis and Nikolaidis in Chapter 12 in this volume find that many CEECs to a significant extent have overlapping production structures and common competitive advantages, two factors that lead to similar export structures and affect export success. This similarity in export structures does not imply that CEECs are homogeneous with respect to their trade performance *vis-à-vis* the EU. Early reports (Dobrinsky 1995) indicate that the Czech Republic and Hungary appear more advanced in their trade restructuring, displaying changes that bring their export performance and structure closer to that of the EU countries.

The new pattern of economic interaction in Europe, however, may have positive implications for regional trade, especially for the less advanced EU regions that are on the East–West frontier. Petrakos and Christodoulakis show that Greece has developed its trade relations with the Balkan transition countries in a more diversified manner than its trade relations with the EU. Greek trade relations in the Balkans have a greater sectoral spread and a greater intra-industry component than the Greek–EU (largely inter-industry) trade relations. These positive developments for Greece are attributed to factors such as proximity and cultural affinity and highlight the importance of the new geography of Europe for a lagging EU region that suffered from the pre-1989 division of Europe.

The second most significant factor shaping East–West dynamics is the level and direction of foreign direct investment (FDI). EU foreign direct investment to CEE countries is driven by considerations related to proximity, adjacency, cultural affinity and political stability or institutional reform. It has increased significantly during the first decade of transition and – although it has affected the spatial patterns of growth performance in some transition countries – its real impact on most CEE countries is still limited.

The impact of FDI on the countries of origin has also been a point of concern. Altzinger, in Chapter 11 in this volume, shows that Austria's FDI to Central and Eastern Europe is concentrated in its adjacent countries for reasons related to spatial proximity, history and cultural affinity. He provides evidence that investment was largely undertaken by small and medium-sized enterprises (SMEs) that, in most of the cases were investing abroad for the first time. Moreover, this investment was associated with an expansion and not a dislocation of domestic firms resulting in a net positive effect on Austria's economic performance. Overall evidence from Austria and Greece indicates that FDI from EU countries and especially those adjacent to the new frontier has improved the performance of the domestic industries involved. Sectorally these investments represent mostly non-industrial sectors and involve a large number of small firms.

The spatial impact of the EU enlargement policies

There is no doubt that enlargement will on the whole benefit the European economy and society. A wider Union will promote economic efficiency and greater regional specialisation, improving the position of the European economy versus that of US and Japan in world markets. It will also be associated with significant benefits accruing from cultural and social interaction and political stability. We have seen, however, that enlargement will bring greater economic heterogeneity to the Union and as a result some sectoral and regional adjustment problems will arise. In acceding countries, strains resulting from increased competitive pressure could initially be more widespread and could affect large sectors of industry, services, the financial system and the balance of payments (EC 1997). On the other hand, the EU-15 industry as a whole will benefit from the enlargement, although this may not be the case for some sensitive areas and certain industries, especially the labour-intensive and other traditional sectors.

Concerning the EU policies of enlargement, there is already significant discussion in the literature that attempts to evaluate its implications (Bachtler 1998; EC 1997; Fothergill 1998; Grabbe and Hughes 1998; Hall and Rosenstock 1998). Certainly, the Agenda 2000 proposal (which was approved by the European Council in Berlin) makes an admirable effort to maintain sensitive balances. Both existing and new members receive their regional aid without significantly increasing the EU budget. However, there are important questions related to the size and direction of the Structural and Cohesion Funds that have not received clear answers yet. Given the seriousness of East–West disparities recorded, would the new members receive funding that corresponds to the magnitude of their problems and the current practice of the EU-15? Would present members continue to receive funding for the regions that face serious problems in the future or will funding eventually shift eastwards? Given the magnitude of intra-CEE countries disparities in welfare levels and productive structure, would EU-15 enlargement policies manage to promote coherence and convergence among transition countries? Several papers and Petrakos in this volume have made an effort to analyse the implications of EU enlargement policies.

First, it should be noted that the solution adopted by the EC with respect to the allocation of funding is only feasible because of the timing of accession and cannot be repeated in the next programming period. Fothergill (1998) has estimated that granting Objective One status to all the applicant states without corresponding reductions elsewhere, may increase the Structural Funds budget by about 45 per cent and the overall EU budget by 15–20 per cent. As a result, the crucial issue – increase the budget or shift the funds eastwards – has not been addressed. The question of the spatial focus or spread of EU structural policies will unavoidably come back in the near future.

Second, as Grabbe and Hughes (1998) note, the adopted polices have solved the sensitive questions of Structural Funds reform and allocations at the cost of important principles such as solidarity and cohesion, as they miss the traditional key aim of promoting convergence across Member States. It is interesting that CEE acceding countries receive funds that are on a per capita basis less than half the funds allocated to Greece or Portugal, despite the fact that the former have significantly lower levels of development than the latter. Moreover, under present arrangements, the CEE applicant countries that are scheduled to participate in the first round of EU expansion will end up receiving significantly more funding than those scheduled for the second round. Given that these two groups are characterised by different success in restructuring their economy and different growth prospects, this may be a case where enlargement policies favour greater intra-CEE disparities and sharpen the spatial pattern of inequality among transition countries.

Finally, these policies may affect the relative position of applicant versus non-applicant countries, as the different degrees of integration with the EU – including wide differences in the timing and level of support – will reinforce economic disparities between transition countries. Non-applicant countries – such as Albania, Yugoslavia, Bosnia or FYR of Macedonia – that happen to be in the European South are practically excluded from the funds allocated for enlargement.

Summing up, it has to be acknowledged that the EU policy of enlargement is a very difficult and complex task as it has to bridge several, potentially conflicting objectives. On the one hand, it has to make a clear statement that eastwards expansion is a top priority objective of the EU-15 and take some active steps in that direction. In doing so, it has to be careful enough to reward the forerunners of transition, at the same time keeping the laggards in the race. On the other hand, it strives to maintain sensitive funding balances among existing members – a precondition in order to maintain political support for the enlargement project – and stick with current monetary and fiscal policies, that are considered a precondition for the internal and external performance and success of the Union.

Under these conditions and constraints, it is doubtful whether the policy mix could have been any different. This carefully balanced solution of small budget shifts to the East and even smaller budget increases, seems to keep all those involved with the enlargement project satisfied at present. Most importantly, it seems to provide the European Commission with a policy that steps up the process of eastward expansion without jeopardising the prospects of deeper integration and world competitiveness of existing members. The concerns that have been expressed are mostly related to the spatial aspects of this policy. A question that might arise in the near future is to what extent 'balanced' development policies at the European level can effectively deal with the problems and dynamics of a highly 'unbalanced' economic space.

Conclusion

The processes of integration and transition of the last decade have fundamentally changed the geography of the continent. Despite some obvious successes, like convergence in the EU or successful transition in the Visegrad countries, this introduction has shown that many threads and obstacles remain. These problems of integration and transition, either related to market dynamics or policy choices, often have an important spatial dimension. Perhaps not entirely surprising, political processes also have a spatial dimension. The crises in Bosnia and Kosovo make exactly that point, as ethnic conflict and nationalism – that many had assumed to be extinct from the European continent due to economic prosperity and integration – have obviously survived in its poor backyard. This final point shows that European integration and transition still have a long way to go which is unlikely to be smooth and without backlashes. As the chapters presented in this volume intend to show, the interaction of these two processes may generate a new geography of economic relations and structures that requires a better understanding and perhaps a new round of discussion concerning policy responses for the challenges lying ahead.

Notes

1 The definition we use for Europe here is a practical one and includes all regions that have actively shown an interest to be part of the future European economic and political structures. It includes all Western European countries, whether they are members of the EU or not, as well as all Central European countries, the Balkans and the Baltic countries. The fact that Russia, the Ukraine, Byelorussia or Moldova are not included in the analysis is related to their present orientation and does not imply any judgement about the identity of these countries, which have been part of the European history and culture for many centuries.

2 The figures presented for each group are either the sum of the national values (for variables such as area, population, GDP) or the weighted – by population – average of national values (for variables such as GNP per capita and GDP composition).

3 Besides the ten candidate countries that have formally applied for EU membership (Poland, Hungary, the Czech Republic, Slovenia, Slovakia, Estonia, Latvia, Lithuania, Bulgaria and Romania), nearly all other transition countries in Europe have expressed a desire to do the same as soon as the conditions permit it.

4 We should note, however, that the morphology of national territory (more or less mountainous), the quality of land (more or less fertile) and the climatic conditions affect significantly national or regional differences in GDP density.

5 Strictly speaking, this figure is valid if the growth rate of all European countries from 1997 to the year of enlargement was the same. In all other cases it should be taken as an approximate indication of the magnitude of the decline.
6 The PPP figure for Luxembourg is missing.
7 The coefficient of variation is the ratio of the standard deviation of a variable over its mean. In fact, it measures the dispersion of the values of the variable around its mean. High values of CV indicate a greater dispersion and therefore a higher level of disparities.
8 This is the ratio of the maximum value of a variable over its minimum value and it measures the gap between these two extreme values. High values of the max/min ratio are associated with greater disparities.
9 As this measure is weighted by national population size, it is influenced more by the performance of large, rather than small countries. In this case its declining tendency is affected by the positive performance of Poland.

References

Bachtler, J. (1998) 'Reforming the Structural Funds: challenges for EU regional policy', *European Planning Studies* 6, 6: 645–64.

Bachtler, J., Downs, R. and Gorzelak, G. (eds) (1999) *EU Enlargement, Cohesion and Regional Policy*, Dartmouth (forthcoming).

Barro, R.J. and Sala-i-Martin, X., (1991) 'Convergence across states and regions', *Brookings Papers on Economic Activity I*: 107–82.

Blaszczyk, B. and Woodward, R. (eds) (1996) 'Privatization in post-Communist countries' *CASE*, vol. 1–2, Warsaw.

Bradshaw, M. and Stenning, A. (1999) 'The progress of transition in East Central Europe', in J. Bachtler, R. Downs and G. Gorzelak (eds) *EU Enlargement, Cohesion and Regional Policy*, Dartmouth (forthcoming).

Brusco, S. (1982) 'The Emilian model: productive decentralisation and social integration', *Cambridge Journal of Economics* 6: 167–84.

Brusco, S. (1986) 'Small firms and industrial districts: the experience of Italy', in D. Keeble and F. Wever (eds) *New Firms and Regional Development*, London: Croom Helm.

Castels, M. (1996) *The Rise of the Network Society*. Oxford: Blackwell.

CEC (1996) *Employment in Europe*, Luxembourg: Commission of the European Communities.

Coffey, W. and Bailly, A. (1996) 'Economic restructuring: a conceptual framework', in W. Lever and A. Bailly (eds) *The Spatial Impact of Economic Changes in Europe*, Aldershot: Avebury, pp. 13–37.

De Melo, M., Denizer, C. and Gelb, A. (1996) 'From plan to market: patterns of transition', *Policy Research Working Paper*, No. 1564, Washington, DC: The World Bank.

Dobrinsky, R. (1995) 'Economic transformation and the changing patterns of European East–West trade', in R. Dobrinsky and M. Landesmann (eds) *Transforming Economies and European Integration*, Aldershot: Edward Elgar, pp. 86–115.

EC (1997) *Agenda 2000*, Brussels: European Commission.

EC (1999) *Sixth Periodic Report on the Social and Economic Situation and Development of the Regions in the European Union*, Brussels: European Commission, Directory General for Regional Policy and Cohesion.

EPRC (1996) *Draft Final Report to the European Commission (DGXVI)*, University of Strathclyde, Glasgow: EPRC.

Fothergill, S. (1998) 'The premature death of EU regional policy?', *European Urban and Regional Studies* 5, 2: 183–8.

Gatsios, K. (1996) 'Eastern European lessons on economic restructuring: a synthesis of the literature', in P. Scholtes (eds) *Industrial Economics for Countries in Transition*, Cheltenham: Edward Elgar, pp. 39–53.

Goodman, E., Bamford, E. and Saynor, P. (eds) (1989) *Small Firms and Industrial Districts in Italy*, London: Routledge.

Gorzelak, G. (1996) *Regional Dimension of Transformation in Central Europe*, London: Jessica Kingsley Publishers.

Gorzelak, G. (1998) *The Regional and Local Potential for Transformation in Poland*, Warszawa: EUROREG.

Gorzelak, G., Jaowiecki, B., Kuklinski, A. and Zienkowski, L. (1995) *Eastern and Central Europe 2000*, Final Report, Luxembourg: Commission of the EC.

Gorzelak, G. and Kuklinski, A. (eds) (1992) *Dilemmas of Regional Policies in Eastern and Central Europe*, Warsaw: EUROREG.

Grabbe, H. and Hughes, K. (1998) 'Reform of the Structural Funds: Central and East European perspectives', *European Planning Studies* 6, 6: 665–76.

Hajdu, Z. and Horvath, G. (eds) (1994) *European Challenges and Hungarian Reponses in Regional Policy*, Budapest: Pecs.

Hall, R. and Rosenstock, M. (1998) 'Agenda 2000 – the reform of the Cohesion Policies', *European Planning Studies* 6, 6: 635–44.

Hudson, R. and Williams A. (eds) (1999) *Divided Europe, Society and Territory*, London: Sage Publications.

Jackson, M. and Petrakos, G. (Guest Editors) (1996) 'The regional dimension of transition and the role of the new enterprise', *Eastern European Economics* 34, 2–4, in a Special Edition of three issues.

Jackson, M. and Petrakos, G. (1999) 'Regional differences in the impact of EU integration on the industrial structure and competitiveness of CEFTA countries', paper prepared for the Phare ACE P96-6071–R project: *Competitiveness of CEFTA countries: measurement and trends in the period of preparation to join the EU.*

Kienast, H. (1999) 'Die räumliche Dimension ausländischer Direktinvestitionen in ausgewählten Ländern Osteuropas: eine regionalwirtschaftliche Betrachtung der Direktinvestitionstätigkeit ausländischer Investoren in der Tschechischen Republik, der Slowakei und Ungarn', dissertation, Vienna University of Economics and Business Administration, Vienna.

Komninos, N. (1992) 'Science Parks in Europe: flexible production, productive disintegration and R&D', in M. Dunford and G. Kafkalas (eds) *Spatial Implications of Competition and Regulation in the New Europe*, London: Belhaven.

Krueger, G. and Ciolko, M. (1998) 'A note on initial conditions and liberalization during transition', *Journal of Comparative Economics* 26: 718–34.

Landesmann, M. (1995) 'The patterns of East–West European integration: catching up or falling behind?', in R. Dobrinsky and M. Landesmann (eds) *Transforming Economies and European Integration*, Aldershot: Edward Elgar, pp. 116–40.

Landesmann, M. (1998) 'Features of East–West European integration: cost structures and patterns of specialization', paper presented in the international workshop on: *Competitiveness of the CEFTA countries: measurement and trends in the period of preparation to join the EU*, Bratislava, 17–18 April, 1998.

Lever, W. and Champion, A. (1996) 'The urban development cycle and the economic system', in W. Lever and A. Bailly (eds) *The Spatial Impact of Economic Changes in Europe*, Aldershot: Avebury, pp. 204–27.

Mertzanis, H. and Petrakos, G. (1998) 'Changing landscapes in Europe's economic structure', *Transition* 9, 2: 12–13, The World Bank.

Nelis, J. (1999) 'Time to rethink privatization in transition economies?', *Transition* 10, 1: 4–6, The World Bank.

Nesporova, A. and Kyloh, R. (1994) *Economic and Social Dialogue in the Ostrava-Karviná Region*, Budapest: ILO.

OECD (1995) *The Regional Dimension of Unemployment in Transition Countries*, Paris: OECD.

Petrakos, G. (1996) 'The regional dimension of transition in Eastern and Central European countries: an assessment', *Eastern European Economics* 34, 5: 5–38.

Petrakos, G. (1997) 'Industrial structure and change in the European Union: comparative analysis and implications for transition economies', *Eastern European Economics* 35, 2: 41–63.

Petrakos, G. (1999) 'Patterns of regional inequality and convergence-divergence trends in transition economies', paper presented at international conference on Regional Potential in an Integrating Europe, Regional Studies Association, 18–21 September 1999, Bilbao, Spain.

Petrakos, G. and Totev, S. (2000) 'Economic structure and change in the Balkan region: implications for integration, transition and economic cooperation', *International Journal of Urban and Regional Research* 24, 1: 95–113.

Piore, M. and Sabel, C. (1984) *The Second Industrial Divide: Possibilities for Prosperity*, New York: Basic Books.

Pyke, F. and Sengenberger, W. (1992) *Industrial Districts and Local Economic Regeneration*, Geneva: International Institute of Labour Studies.

Rosenblat, C. and Pumain, D. (1993) 'The location of multinational firms in the European urban system', *Urban Studies*, 30: 1691–709.

Sachs, J. (1996) 'The transition at mid decade', *American Economic Review Papers and Proceedings* 86, 2:128–33.

Sachs, J. (1997) *Geography and economic transition*, Working Paper, Centre for International Development, Cambridge, MA: Harvard University.

Tanzi, V. (1993) *Transition to Market*, Studies in Fiscal Reform, Washington, DC: IMF.

Wodz, K. (eds) (1994) *Transformation of Old Industrial regions as a Sociological Problem*, Katowice: Friedrich Ebert Stiftung.

Woo, T.W., Parker, S. and Sachs, J. (eds) (1998) *Economies in Transition: Comparing Asia and Europe*, London: The MIT Press.

World Bank (1996) *From Plan to Market*, World Development Report, New York: Oxford University Press.

World Bank (1998) *World Development Indicators*, Washington, DC: World Bank.

World Bank (1999a) *Knowledge for Development, World Development Report 1998/99*, New York: Oxford University Press.

World Bank (1999b) *World Development Indicators*. Available HTTP: http://www.worldbank.org/data/wdi/home.html.

Zuscovitch, E. and Justman, M. (1995) 'Networking, sustainable differentiation and economic development', in D. Batten, J. Casti and R. Thord (eds) *Networks in Action*, Springer, pp. 269–85.

2 The spatial impact of East–West integration in Europe

George Petrakos

Introduction

The European economy has changed in many important ways during the last decade, either due to market forces and dynamics or institutional change and policy-making. In addition, Europe itself has changed, as the old divides – both actual and perceptual – are in the process of being altered and replaced by new ones. The driving forces of change are two fundamental, parallel and interacting processes: the first is related to the operation of the Single European Market (SEM) and the European Union (EU) policies towards the Economic and Monetary Union (EMU), and the other is related to the economic transformation and the westward orientation of the Central and Eastern European (CEE) countries. Both processes have been associated with strong expectations for growth and prosperity, both currently face difficulties of varying types and degrees and both have a strong spatial dimension.

Our goal here is to analyse the spatial implications of the ongoing interaction of integration and transition processes and focus on the key characteristics and spatial dynamics of the emerging pan-European geography of the twenty-first century. A number of important features of the emerging European geography with long-term implications for policy-making in the next century have to be analysed and understood in depth. Issues such as the north–south and east–west divides, patterns of convergence or divergence, the spatial allocation of costs and benefits of the integration–transition process, factor movements, regional trade patterns, regional co-operation and cross-border dynamics of the new Europe need to be discussed in connection with the new realities imposed by the removal of the artificial barriers to interaction in the post-1989 European economic space.

The forces at work

The policies and the social dynamics

Several forces have been shaping the new European economic space, including the policies of integration and transition, the social dynamics and the market forces. The policies of EU integration are basically the policies of the Single European Market and the policies towards the Economic and Monetary Union. They are mostly market-oriented policies aiming to increase the efficiency and competitiveness of the fragmented European economy in the face of increasing internationalisation of economic interaction. These policies raise an 'efficiency versus equity' conflict at various social and geographical levels, as the process of integration is associated with winners and losers. For this reason they are supported by structural operations (Structural and Cohesion Funds), aiming to offset the negative impact of the forces released and assist less developed and structurally weak regions

On the other hand, the unsustainable pre-1989 economic and political structures and a profound case of government failure in the former planned economies have imposed the policies of transition. They are also market-oriented policies (privatisation, liberalisation, internationalisation) and policies of institutional change. Up to this point and several years after implementation, great variations in results have been recorded, as destructive adjustment processes have persisted in several sectors and a number of countries.

Finally, the policies of EU enlargement depict the political will of the West to integrate with the East and have been expressed through the assistance provided by the Phare Program, the Association agreements and the Structural Funds allocated to the new members in the 2000–6 period (EC 1997; European Council 1999).

Significant social dynamics have also been behind the East–West interaction affecting its type, direction and pace. On the one hand, there is a strong drive in the East for Western-type political organisation, institutions and lifestyle but also resistance to change due to enormous adjustment costs and increasing social fragmentation. On the other hand, there is a strong drive in the West backed by multinational corporations and large business for an eastwards market expansion, but also an uneasiness in labour, related to migration and the mounting problem of unemployment.

The market forces

Market forces are also playing a very significant role in determining the characteristics of the new European economic space. First, Chapter 1 in this volume has shown that the process of transition has expanded the European market by 37 per cent in terms of population, but only about 10 per cent in terms of GDP. The first figure indicates the long-term potential of the new market, while the second indicates the medium-term difficulties and the present limits of East–West interaction. It should be noticed however, that with expansion, first to the South and now to the East, the EU is being transformed from a homogeneous club to a heterogeneous Union, as these expansions involve States with lower than average development levels.

The most significant market force that affects the European economy is East–West trade relations. East–West trade relations have experienced a rapid but unbalanced expansion of a basically inter-industry type. In the 1992–7 period, EU exports to CEE countries increased by 210 per cent, EU imports from CEE countries increased by 121 per cent and EU trade surplus with the CEE countries increased by 904 per cent (see Table 2.1). Italy, Germany and Austria have enjoyed the greatest trade surpluses, indicating that proximity to the East–West frontier is an important factor determining performance in the new markets. Despite rapid growth, however, East–West trade is still a small fraction of EU trade, as only a small share of EU exports (4.4 per cent) go to CEE countries and only a small share of EU imports (3.3 per cent) comes from them. The greatest part of EU trade (67 per cent of exports and imports) is still intra-Community trade. These figures indicate that East–West trade is presently restricted by the capacity of CEE markets.

Several studies (Jackson and Petrakos 1999; Landesmann 1995, 1998; Petrakos 1997a; Petrakos and Totev 2000) also indicate that East–West trade relations, just like North–South relations, have a predominantly inter-industry character. Western Europe tends to specialise in R&D-intensive, capital-intensive and knowledge-intensive products, while Central and Eastern Europe tends to specialise in labour-intensive and resource-intensive products.

In addition, the new economic environment in Europe is obviously characterised by more intensive factor movements with a clear spatial dimension. Flows of labour and capital, despite various sorts of barriers, cross the East–West borders following the predictions of a simple neo-classical two-sector model where price and opportunities differentials result in eastward capital flows and westward labour movements.

Table 2.1 EU trade with the CEE countries (million ECU)

	Exports		*Imports*		*Balance of trade*	
EU Countries	*1992*	*1997*	*1992*	*1997*	*1992*	*1997*
Belgium and Luxembourg	1,105	3,475	884	1,995	221	1,480
Denmark	732	1,513	609	1,127	123	386
Germany	14,476	39,016	14,041	31,024	435	7,992
Greece	450	751	504	1,018	–54	–267
Spain	358	2,055	502	1,376	–144	679
France	2,722	7,108	2,098	4,491	624	2,617
Ireland	65	521	99	279	–34	242
Italy	4,302	14,704	4,180	9,396	122	5,308
Netherlands	1,768	4,401	1,511	2,935	257	1,466
Austria	2,996	9,434	2,203	6,088	793	3,346
Portugal	37	171	70	145	–33	26
Finland	646	1,326	464	639	182	687
Sweden	866	2,513	914	1,257	–48	1,256
United Kingdom	1,642	5,429	1,384	3,506	258	1,923
Total EU	32,165	92,417	29,463	65,276	2,702	27,141

Source: Eurostat (1992), IMF (1998).

Table 2.2 Foreign direct investment in transition countries, 1997

Countries	*Inward stock* *mil. USD*	*%*	*Inward stock* *per capita (USD)*
Central European countries	42,750	83.85	639.97
Czech	6,763	13.26	656.60
Hungary	15,882	31.15	1557.06
Poland	16,463	32.29	422.13
Slovakia	1,293	2.54	243.96
Slovenia	2,349	4.61	1174.50
Balkan countries	5,145	10.09	92.54
Albania	339	0.66	105.94
Bosnia[a]	–	–	–
Bulgaria	943	1.85	112.26
Croatia	1,336	2.62	278.33
FYROM	60	0.12	28.57
Romania	2,467	4.84	109.64
Yugoslavia[a]	–	–	–
Baltic countries	3,090	6.06	400.78
Estonia	1,148	2.25	765.33
Latvia	901	1.77	360.40
Lithuania	1,041	2.04	280.59
Total CEE	50,985	100.00	391.86

Source: UN (1998).

Note: [a]missing data.

Inward foreign direct investment (FDI) in transition economies has increased significantly, but still remains at levels that in several cases are below initial expectations, for reasons related to the existence of many factors remaining from the old system (Richet 1996). By 1997 the stock of FDI in Central and East Europe accounted for only 1.51 per cent of global FDI, which is below the share of Africa (accounting for 1.89 per cent of the stock) or the share of Latin America and the Caribbean (10.86 per cent). Over time, however, significant progress was made as FDI inflows in the region increased from 1.1 per cent of global inflows in 1990 to 3.0 per cent in 1997 (UN 1998).

How is this FDI stock distributed among Central and East European countries and why? Table 2.2 shows that in 1997 the bulk of FDI has been concentrated in the Central European countries (83 per cent), while the Balkans and the Baltic countries have received a relatively insignificant share (10 per cent and 6 per cent, respectively) of the total. When we adjust for country size and examine figures per capita, we observe that the Central European countries have an FDI stock per capita equal to 640 US dollars, which is 50 per cent higher than the Baltic and more than 6 times higher than the Balkan figure. Although the Balkan countries in transition comprise about 42 per cent of the population of the CEE countries, they have managed to attract in a relatively long period of time only 10 per cent of FDI. On the other hand, the Visegrad countries with 52 per cent of the population have managed to attract 84 per cent of the FDI directed in the CEE region.

Three Central European countries (Poland, Hungary and the Czech Republic) have managed to attract the main bulk of the FDI stock invested. On the other hand, most FDI originates from EU countries, with Germany (by far the first), The Netherlands, France and Italy being the most significant investors. This geographical pattern is expected to continue in the future, driven by cultural and geographical proximity, access to large markets, economic recovery and political stability (Collis *et al.* 1997; UNCTAD 1996). Should this be the case, the Balkan transition countries will only marginally benefit from the west–east flows of capital in the post-transition period.

Turning to migration flows, we observe that despite an enormous stock of potential migrants in CEE countries, East–West migration is limited due to EU policies and is to a large extent illegal. The countries that receive the greatest numbers of migrants are Germany, where 8 per cent of the population is already foreign (Faist and Haubermann 1996) and Greece, where illegal immigration from Albania and Eastern Europe is estimated at 500,000 people (Petrakos and Christodoulakis 1997). Migration to the West has in several cases shifted mood in the receiving areas and countries against immigrants. Even a relatively small number of immigrants from Albania to Italy (40,000) has been enough to reverse attitudes (Zinn 1996). In general, newcomers are conceived as a threat to labour markets, social benefits and cultural homogeneity. Xenophobia seems to be a long-term threat that can affect ideology in the 'democratic west'. Whether or not this threat will materialise, xenophobia has certainly affected the East. Liberalisation in CEE product and capital markets combined with protection in EU labour markets generates unequally distributed costs and benefits as market adjustments under this mix of liberalisation and protection clearly work in favour of the West.

The spatial characteristics of EU integration

The process of EU integration is perhaps the most ambitious European project in this century. It aims to generate a larger obstacle-free market for goods and services, that will stimulate efficiency through the operation of economies of scale and the elimination of cross-border and cross-currency transaction costs. Although a positive sum game, EU integration leaves winners and losers (Amin *et al.* 1992; Camagni 1992; CEC 1991; CEC 1992a; CEC 1993a; Peschel 1992) by exposing regions with unequal endowments in resources and technology and different economic structures to international competition. In general, peripheral regions with weak economic structures and deficient infrastructure and human resources have fared worse in the integration process.

One of the reasons is that sectoral specialisation and North–South or core–periphery trade in the EU still maintain an inter-industry character. The core regions specialise and export to the periphery high-tech manufacturing and producer services, while the periphery exports to the core regions low-tech manufacturing or extracting activity products. As a result, the trickle-down effects assumed to stem from the core regions to the peripheral ones will be limited (Mack and Jacobson 1996).

On the other hand, the SEM has resulted in an increase in the market penetration of regions lagging behind increasing trade deficits and increasing the erosion of their productive base. Greece and Portugal, the two weakest members of the EU, have the greatest trade deficits as a share of GDP in the EU (–12.9 per cent and –10.4 per cent, respectively in 1995). In addition, the trade deficit of Greece with the rest of the EU increased in the period 1989–95 by 218 per cent, while the share of manufacturing output shrank to 16 per cent in 1995 (the average EU figure is 23 per cent). As a result, redistribution at the expense of the less favoured regions takes place at the EU level, through the mechanisms of the Single Market.

Under the pressure of market forces EU regional policy (Structural and Cohesion Funds) has been designed to compensate for the effects of increasing competition, by providing less favoured regions with the means to improve social and technical infrastructure, education and the competitiveness of industry. Two points deserve attention here. First, although available funds increased significantly between the 1st (1989–93) and the 2nd (1994–9) Community Support Framework (CSF), they are presumed to stagnate in the 2000–6 period. For the first time in the history of EU structural policy, significant developments such as the launch of the euro and the enlargement of the Union with new – less advanced members – have not been followed by a significant expansion of the resources devoted to economic and social cohesion and have been conducted in a climate of financial austerity (Bachtler 1998). Given the strong North–South type of regional disparities in infrastructure that still exist in the EU (Martin and Steinen 1997), the proposed funds are clearly below the levels required to have a substantial impact in a reasonable time horizon.

Second, despite recent reform, the funds do not have the necessary spatial focus, as a large share of EU population is eligible for EU *and* national regional support. In several cases, advanced EU countries provide state aid per capita in the form of incentives to enterprises that is higher than in poor countries, partly due to the severe budgetary constraints faced by the latter. As a result, national programmes seem to largely offset the impact of EU regional policies at the enterprise level, intensifying the locational disadvantages of the peripheral states and regions (Martin and Steinen 1997). Moreover, first reports show that those funds had the least impact in the regions that needed them the most, raising a question about the implementation of the programmes, but also a question of low regional multiplier impact.

The spatial characteristics of transition

The systemic changes that have taken place in the former socialist countries pose a major challenge for regional economic analysis and regional development policy. This unique situation, where central control mechanisms have been abandoned in favour of market mechanisms and at the same time domestic productive bases have been opened and exposed to international economic forces, raises a number of important questions about the regional characteristics of the transition process and the future organisation of economic activity over space. A number of studies have already appeared discussing the distribution of the costs and benefits of restructuring over space and the impact of the operation of economic forces across regional productive bases (Gorzelak 1996; Jackson and Petrakos 1996; Petrakos 1996a).

The impact of internationalisation

For CEE countries, the openness and westward orientation that followed the 1989 reforms have led, in most cases, to a rapid internationalisation of the economy, its main characteristics being the influx of foreign direct investment and the fast, although unbalanced, increasing volume of trade. Despite a number of temporary constraints associated with political and legal uncertainty and institutional weaknesses that discouraged large immediate expansion (CEC 1993b; Peschel 1992), foreign investment is expected to be an important determinant of gross capital formation in these countries with significant spatial implications.

It becomes increasingly evident that the behaviour of foreign capital with respect to location is highly selective (CEC 1993a), contributing, at least in the early stages of the transformation process, to a polarised pattern of development. In a more integrated economic environment where barriers to international transactions and factor movements are reduced, global pressures require international investors and multinational corporations (MNCs) to select new business locations with a strategic character. As a result the economic, geographical, functional and demographic characteristics of regions at the national and international European level become very important. Central places with respect to the European economic space will attract a larger number of activities with a higher functional order, while non-central places will receive a smaller number of lower order activities (CEC 1992b, 1993a; Cohen 1981; Rosenblat and Pumain 1993).

It seems therefore that a first spatial impact of the openness and westward orientation of the ECE countries will be a disproportionate concentration of foreign capital in the metropolitan area and a polarising pattern of economic growth. The lower the level of development of the host country, the higher the rate of foreign capital concentration (due to inadequate infrastructure and market conditions in smaller cities) and the greater the polarisation effect is expected to be. Because of the adaptive nature of the foreign capital expansion path, where imperfect information and economies of clustering require that new investment is located near to existing ones, this process of concentration will continue until land availability in the metropolis becomes an inescapable problem. As a result, the process of internationalisation has favoured a polarised economic structure.

Openness, however, and economic integration with the Western European economy have an additional spatial implication that depends on the adjacent position and the proximity of an ECE country to Western Europe. For CEE countries having common borders with West Europe there are significant opportunities for trans-frontier co-operation in the form of joint ventures, subcontracting, free trade areas, scientific and technological co-operation, local or regional policy co-ordination as well as expansion of cross-border transportation and communication infrastructure. Therefore, common borders are expected to generate local economic activity and create an alternative route for foreign capital penetration. This may imply a diversion effect for foreign capital originating from neighbouring countries, as a part of it may prefer the benefits of proximity to the benefits of the metropolitan market. It seems therefore that internationalisation and openness have two distinct spatial effects that operate in favour of the metropolitan areas and the western regions, intensifying polarisation and a geographically divided pattern of development.

Besides capital flows, the resumption of international trade with Western European countries and the collapse of the CMEA relations with the other Eastern European countries and the former Soviet Union will be an important factor with serious regional implications. Reduction or elimination of existing trade barriers with the West increases imports and exposes previously protected regional production bases to international competition. As a result, regions that were heavily dependent on CMEA relations or military contracts, monostructure regions or regions with a weakly integrated production structure, are expected to be more sensitive and suffer directly from the openness of the economy. On the other hand, regions with a diversified production base and regions that have implemented a successful land reform and reorganisation of agricultural production may have greater success in adapting to the new international environment.

Finally, openness and integration into the European economy have an additional macro-geographical impact that is related to the proximity of each country to the Western European development centres. Distant countries will be integrated more slowly and selectively while adjacent ones will experience sooner the benefits of an eastward-directed dispersion of development. Because of the gradual elimination of barriers and the creation of a large European market, geographical factors such as distance, accessibility and centrality emerge as important elements in the spatial organisation of activities and the slowly shaped new spatial European economic order (Peschel 1992; Rosenblat and Pumain 1993). In general, it can be argued that the closer to the European gravity centre an CEE country is, the greater the possibility of attracting higher order economic functions and developing multiple strategic location cities or regions that will be placed in the upper part of the European hierarchy is. In other words, as distance from the European centre of gravity increases, so does the number of cities and regions that do not qualify as European-level strategic locations.

Overall, the impact of internationalisation and integration on the spatial regularities of the ECE countries is exerted through a complex set of interacting processes and cannot be attributed to a single overriding factor. The influence, however, of international forces operating through the selective behaviour of foreign capital and the unbalanced pattern of international trade along with the emerging importance of geographical features are expected to have a strong spatially dividing character. Metropolitan areas, western regions, regions with a diversified production base and those located a short distance from the European development centre are expected to experience a positive net effect from internationalisation. On the other hand, declining monostructure, eastern and perimetric regions are more likely to experience an unfavourable net impact from openness that will further intensify their problems and make the task of restructuring even harder. These regions will tend to replace Southern Europe in forming the new European periphery of the next century.

The impact of restructuring

The process of transformation is also expected to have a spatial dimension that is attributed to the operation of more 'endogenous' factors such as the pace and success of the restructuring policies, the existing condition and quality of the labour force and infrastructure and the changes in the sectoral composition of output.

In the first place, it is expected that there will be an inverse relation between restructuring and growth, on the one hand, and regional disparities, on the other. The faster the pace of restructuring and growth, the more likely it is that regional disparities will be diminished. This will occur because of anticipated spread effects and because growth provides the state with the financial resources to intervene and implement an active regional policy. In contrast, a prolonged recession and crisis will have devastating effects on the regions with the weaker and more vulnerable production structures. The experience of the EU, that went from a period of high growth and declining regional disparities that ended in the mid-1970s, to a period of low growth and increasing regional disparities afterwards (CEC 1991; Dunford and Perrons 1993) is very indicative of this inverse relationship. Recent evidence (Petrakos 1999) indicates that countries with a better record in terms of transforming their economy, a larger size and a short distance from the European development centre tend to experience less often and less intensively increasing disparities than countries with a less successful record, a smaller size and more distant from the EU core.

In addition to this, another relationship well established in the literature indicates that beyond some level of development and with stable and favourable socio-political conditions, higher levels of development are associated with lower levels of regional disparities (Petrakos and Brada 1989; Williamson 1965). This inverse relationship is believed to occur either because agglomeration economies tend to be exhausted beyond some concentration level of economic activities, or because of the political awareness of the peripheral regions and the implementation of serious regional policies. In general, and in the case of the CEE countries it can be claimed that high rates of growth and high levels of development are more likely to lead to regional convergence, while low rates of growth and low levels of development are more likely to lead to regional divergence.

Metropolitan areas and industrial regions will also benefit from a sectoral shift in the composition of output that has taken place in the modern post-industrial world and is slowly being transmitted into the CEE economies. This shift is related to the growing importance of the tertiary sector and the benefits of agglomeration and scale that derive from its operation in metropolitan areas and large urban concentrations. Activities with an increasing importance in today's economies, such as high-level producer services, banking, financial services, entertainment and commerce, have a strong urban character and can be important sources of employment creation and growth in large urban concentrations (CEC 1992b; Coffey and Polese 1987; Fournier and Axelsson 1993; Lever 1993). As a result, central and peripheral regions will not share equally in the benefits of the sectoral shift that is expected to follow the process of restructuring.

Empirical evidence

There is now mounting evidence that transition has increased disparities, as western regions and metropolitan areas in general fare better (Downes 1996). Petrakos (1999) has found clear evidence of this pattern of disparities in transition countries adjacent to the east–west frontier. Core–periphery differences have also increased in Estonia, with Talin benefiting the most from the new orientation of the country. Western coastal regions are faced with new opportunities in trade, tourism and joint ventures, while Eastern regions face mounting problems in their primarily agricultural economy as traditional ties with large Russian markets in St Petersburg and Pskov have been interrupted. Talin has the greatest concentration of foreign capital and joint ventures, the greatest number of new enterprises and the highest income per capita in recent estimates (Raagmaa 1996). Evidence from East Germany already indicates that development is highly selective and depends on the behaviour of foreign capital. Berlin emerges as a development pole with strong links with the West German and international economy but weak local linkages and low spread effects (Haussermann 1993).

Similar trends are detected in the Slovak Republic, where Bratislava with

9 per cent of national population, generates 30 per cent of the country's GDP (Balaz 1996), while in Hungary, where disparities have increased during transition (Fazekas 1996; Nemes-Nagy in this volume), FDI and domestic capital prefer metropolitan and western regions), turning the relatively balanced pre-1989 situation of the regions into an east–west disparity.

Similar evidence also comes from Poland, where FDI goes to metropolitan regions and business services and financial activities develop faster in metropolitan areas and western regions (Kratke 1996). In 1994 the metropolitan region of Warsaw, Krakov, Poznan and Katowice had the lowest unemployment rate. Also, the regional pattern of unemployment in Poland shows some considerable stability in the 1990–4 period, indicating that initial best performing regions are the same as final best performing regions and initial losers are final losers also (Ingham *et al.* 1996). The picture is completed with reports from Albania (Petrakos 1996b), Bulgaria (Minassian and Totev 1996) and Romania (Constantin 1997, Ramboll 1996) that indicate that economic activities are polarised and that disparities have increased during transition.

Although regional policies have already been formulated in some cases, especially in the Visegrad group, regional funds as a share of GDP are far behind the figures of the peripheral EU states (Downes 1996). Given the magnitude and the trends in regional disparities, we would add that they are also well behind the level required for a real impact. In addition, it should be clear that the bottom-up approach to regional policy is more rewarding in the prosperous west, where development largely depends on private initiatives (Lorentzen 1996). The vicious circle, however, that in several instances is in motion in the east and the magnitude of forces operating at a regional scale, require co-ordinated action on a local, national and the EU level, if a real impact on regional disparities is to be recorded in a reasonable time period.

The macro-geographical impact of East–West interaction

Towards a new spatial European order

Another influence that is exerted on the performance of the regions in CEE countries comes from the relative position of each country within the slowly shaping new European economic space. Given that in the EU a large part of regional disparities is attributed to inter-country rather than to intra-country disparities, it becomes clear that the relative standing of each country, on the macro-geographical level, affects the internal micro-geographical allocation of activities. Regions can undertake a strategic or central function that is not derived only from their relative position within their country, but also from the position of the country within the emerging hierarchy of the European economic space. In other words, peripheral regions in countries placed high in the European hierarchy will not experience the same difficulties and will not move along the same trajectories as peripheral regions in perimetric countries.

Regardless of the impact of the macro-geographical regularities on the performance of regions, the study of the new European economic space, its hierarchy and structure, has an interest of its own because of the expected impact of the transformation and openness of the CEE countries.

Petrakos (1996a) has outlined the shape of the new European economic hierarchy as well as the expected dynamic benefits that will accrue to CEE countries from their geographical position and their relative size within the new European economic space, by constructing a simple European level population potential index (Z_i), estimated in three different time horizons:

$$Z_i = \Sigma \, (P_i \, P_j \,/\, d_{ij}^{\,k}) \qquad (1)$$

where Z_i is the population potential of a country i, P_i is the population of this country, P_j is the population of any other European country, d_{ij} is the aeroplane flight distance between the Capitals of the i and j countries and k is an exponent that takes the values k = 1 or k = 1.2, differentiating distance from accessibility where barriers other than geographical ones are present. Depending on the time horizon, N takes the value N = 18 (Western European countries only) or N = 33 (Western Europe plus CEE countries). The usefulness of this index relies on the fact that it consists of a composite measure of the market size of a country (approximated by population) and the relative accessibility of the centre of this market to the other European markets. As such, the index depicts the relative importance and strategic advantage that a country offers, as a location site, to its economic activities and especially those operating in international markets.

Therefore, this economic and geographical index can be taken to indicate the level of economic interaction as well as the relative attraction that a country exerts on high order economic activities. This attraction is generated by (a) its own market size, and (b) its strategic position with respect to the entire European market. As a result, a spatial order of the European economy is shaped because of the importance of national market sizes and costs related to distance. High values of Z_i imply that a country maintains a size or locational advantage highly valued by European-level economic activities.

This index, we believe, is also useful for any effort that intends to trace the spatial dynamics generated by the process of integration in Europe. Table 2.3 and Maps 2.1, 2.2 and 2.3 show the spatial order of population or economic potential (Z_i) in three historic phases. Map 2.1 depicts the spatial order of economic potential in the pre-1989 Western Europe (k = 1, N = 18). Map 2.2 takes a short-to-medium term perspective of the openness and integration of the CEE countries into the European economy and accounts for the difficulties of the transition period by setting k = 1.2 when either i or j is a CEE country (k = 1 or k = 1.2 and N = 33). Here, although transformation

Table 2.3 The spatial order of economic potential in the pre-1989 and the new Europe (short-term and long-term scenarios)

Country	*Pre-1989*	*Country*	*Short term*	*Country*	*Long term*
Iceland	1.32	Iceland	1.46	Iceland	1.43
Luxembourg	6.54	Estonia	5.46	Luxembourg	5.73
Finland	49.28	Luxembourg	6.73	Estonia	11.55
Ireland	49.42	FYROM	6.92	FYROM	14.82
Norway	52.55	Slovenia	7.76	Slovenia	16.87
Denmark	79.79	Latvia	12.33	Latvia	25.72
Greece	89.30	Bosnia	12.56	Albania	28.69
Sweden	94.23	Albania	13.65	Bosnia	28.96
Portugal	105.50	Lithuania	18.15	Ireland	36.35
Austria	115.84	Croatia	20.35	Lithuania	37.34
Switzerland	125.05	Slovakia	21.59	Croatia	43.39
Belgium	279.67	Ireland	41.69	Slovakia	45.68
Holland	340.97	Finland	49.34	Norway	46.08
Spain	433.61	Norway	52.44	Finland	47.47
Italy	590.31	Bulgaria	52.65	Denmark	79.16
Britain	855.04	Yugoslavia	53.08	Portugal	86.31
France	940.75	Hungary	84.40	Greece	94.12
Germany	1000.00	Denmark	85.68	Sweden	98.07
		Greece	96.68	Bulgaria	106.24
		Portugal	98.99	Yugoslavia	109.53
		Romania	100.88	Switzerland	112.85
		Sweden	104.49	Austria	133.23
		Czech	118.83	Hungary	162.75
		Switzerland	124.39	Belgium	193.00
		Austria	136.79	Czech	212.04
		Belgium	223.32	Romania	213.50
		Poland	255.53	Holland	245.30
		Holland	277.65	Spain	369.81
		Spain	411.50	Poland	500.93
		Italy	569.38	Italy	552.63
		Britain	821.54	Britain	738.17
		France	901.01	France	814.37
		Germany	1000.00	Germany	1000.00
min= 307936925847		min= 386978554216		min= 477937881266	
max=231741298518588		max=26360089770360		max=333925816980254	
Coefficient of variation =1.15		Coefficient of variation =1.52		Coefficient of variation =1.34	

Source: own estimations from equation (1).

is understood as a distance (in the broad sense of the word) reducing process, well-known existing difficulties do not allow us for the time being to treat distance from Paris, for example, to Warsaw in the same way as distance from Paris to Rome, since accessibility is not, in the short term, the same. Finally Map 2.3 takes a long-term perspective and depicts the spatial order of economic potential of countries in a unified and obstacle-free European economic space (k = 1 for every i, j and N = 33).

From observation and comparison of the maps a number of important

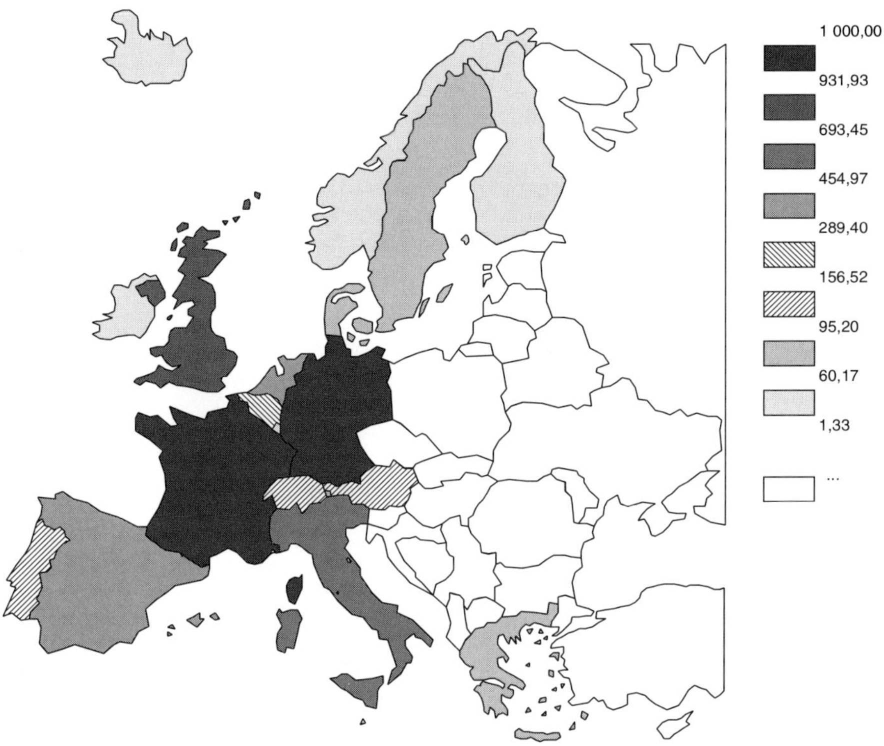

Map 2.1 Spatial order of economic potential in pre-1989 Western Europe (population potential index).

observations about the spatial character of integration can be made. First, it is important to observe that in the pre-1989 European spatial order the gravity centre coincides with the economic development centre. In Table 2.3 we see that Germany takes the highest value of the population potential index (given in relative terms), followed by France and the United Kingdom. Correlation coefficients between the population potential index (Z_i) on the one hand and GDP, industrial product and total exports on the other, give values of 96, 93 and 95 per cent, respectively, indicating that this simple geographical index of distance and size explains a very considerable part of the level of development and the degree of integration between European countries. We also see that the index has a hierarchical structure. Its figure, for example, for Denmark is less than 8 per cent of the German figure and this difference is mainly attributed to the impact of different country (or market) sizes. Serious differences, however exist even for countries of similar size. The figure for Greece for example is less than one-third of the Belgian figure although both countries have the same population. Clearly this difference arises from the more favourable geographical site of Belgium with respect to the other

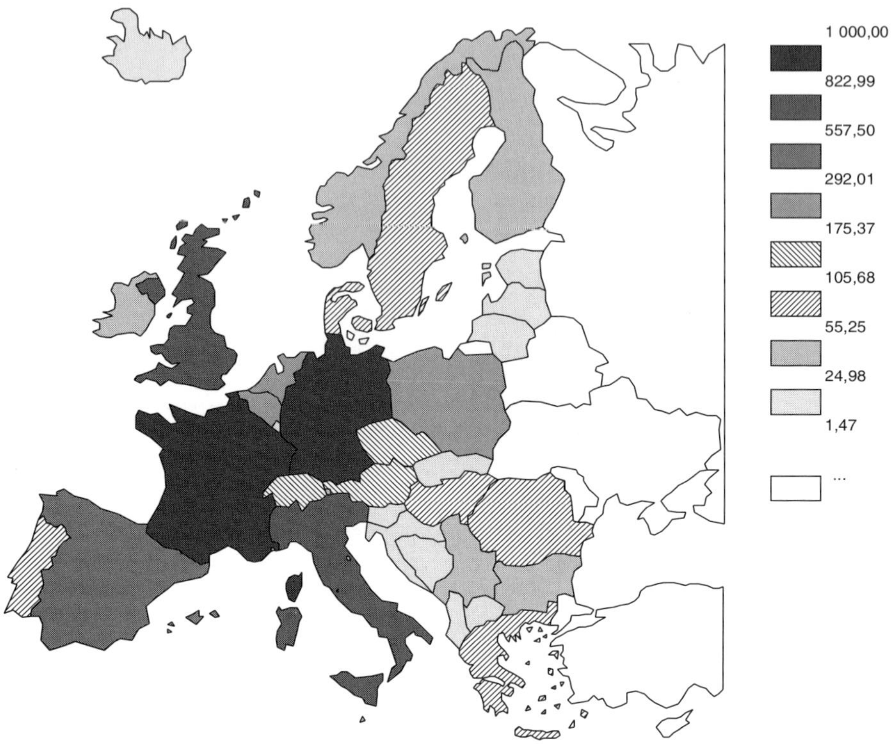

Map 2.2 Spatial order of economic potential in the new Europe (population potential index: the short-to-medium-term perspective).

European countries, which implies better accessibility to the European market and a more strategic location (Petrakos 1996a).

Second, by comparing the Z_i values in Maps 2.1, 2.2 and 2.3 and Figure 2.1, we see that the greater relative improvements in economic potential are expected to be for Germany (explained by the increase in its size due to unification and by its central location), and for the countries with the closest proximity to the new economic space, that is Austria, Greece, Sweden and to a lesser extent Denmark. Most other countries will see their position more or less deteriorating in relative terms (although improving in absolute terms). This suggests a relative shift of the gravity centre to the east giving advantages first of all to Germany which is becoming the centre of the European space instead of being its eastern border. Besides that, the shift also gives advantages to Austria, Greece and Sweden, that in relative terms outweigh the increase in Germany's size. The largest reductions in the relative value of the Z_i index are recorded in the UK, France and Spain that are located away from the expansion of the economic space, and have distance-related constraints that do not allow them to take full advantage of it.

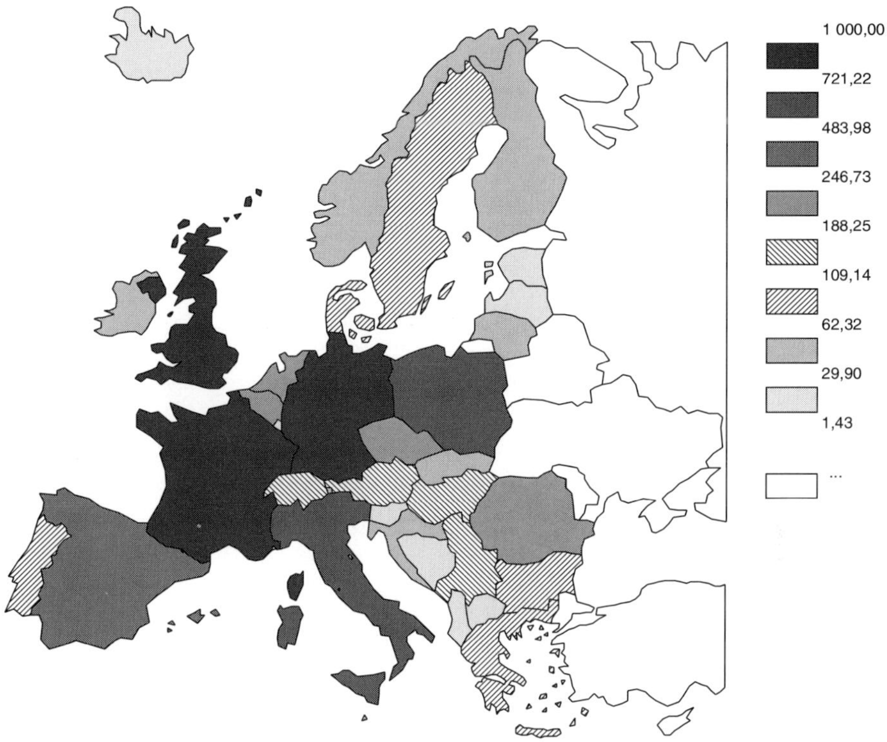

Map 2.3 Spatial order of economic potential in the new Europe (population potential index: the long-term perspective).

Third, in the long run but also to a lesser degree in the short term, the integration of the ECE countries will displace many small and perimeter countries in the spatial European economic order. Portugal, for example, from 10th place in the pre-1989 spatial order moves down to 18th place displaced in the long term by six CEE countries. The same can be said for Ireland which moves from 15th to 25th place surpassed by nine CEE countries. On the other hand, the large European countries (Germany, France, the UK, Italy) maintain in all phases their top-four positions, although Spain is displaced in the long-term from 5th to 6th place by Poland, and Austria and Switzerland are displaced from their pre-1989 top-10 position by Romania and the Czech Republic. It is interesting here to see that, for some Western European countries, the order in which they are placed with respect to each other in the long-term index, has been inverted. Austria is placed ahead of Switzerland, Greece and Sweden ahead of Portugal, and Norway and Finland ahead of Ireland in the long term although the opposite was the case in the pre-1989 hierarchy. This of course indicates the relative improvement of the position of the countries that are closer to the new economic space in the East (Petrakos 1996a).

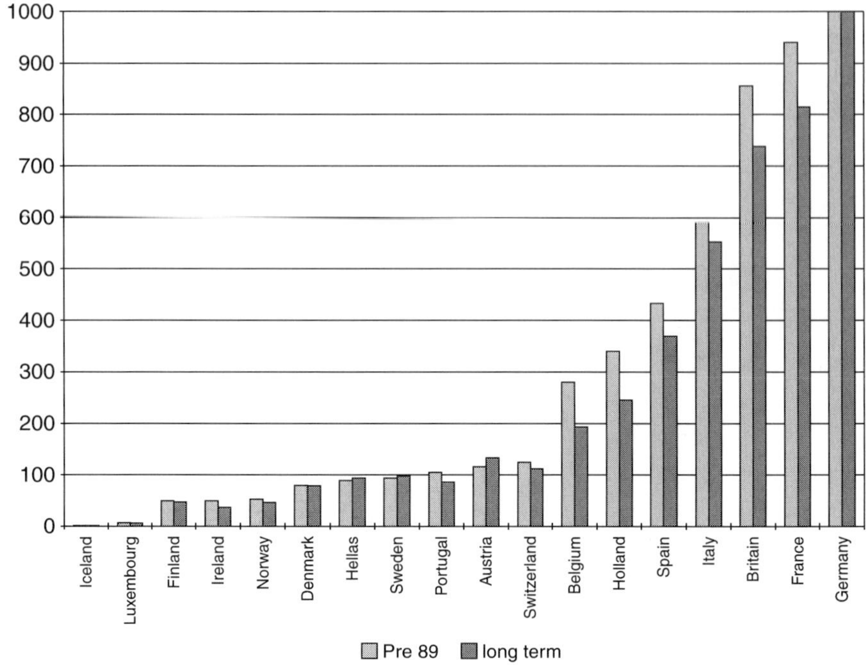

Figure 2.1 Population potential levels in Western Europe in the pre-1989 and the long-term scenario.

Fourth, wide variations are also found in the long-term potential of CEE countries (see Figure 2.2). The one that has benefited most from the process of integration is Poland which has a population potential index half of the German figure and is placed 5th in the pan-European hierarchy. A very good ranking is also attained by Romania and the Czech Republic (8th and 9th place) followed by Hungary (11th place), while the New Yugoslavia and Bulgaria have an economic potential that places them in the upper half of the long-term hierarchy. The rest of the CEE countries have a very small population potential index, being placed at the lower part of the hierarchy. The long-term standing of these countries in the pan-European spatial order may also be interpreted as an indicator of the success of their economic integration with Western Europe. High values of the population potential index imply a strategic location or size that in the long term will result in serious interaction and strong economic links with the western centres of development. On the other hand, a low value on the gravity index implies either a small market size or a really peripheral location.

Fifth, the process of integration has a potentially diverging character as it intensifies disparities with respect to the attractiveness of national central places in a pan-European economic space. We observe in Table 2.3 that the

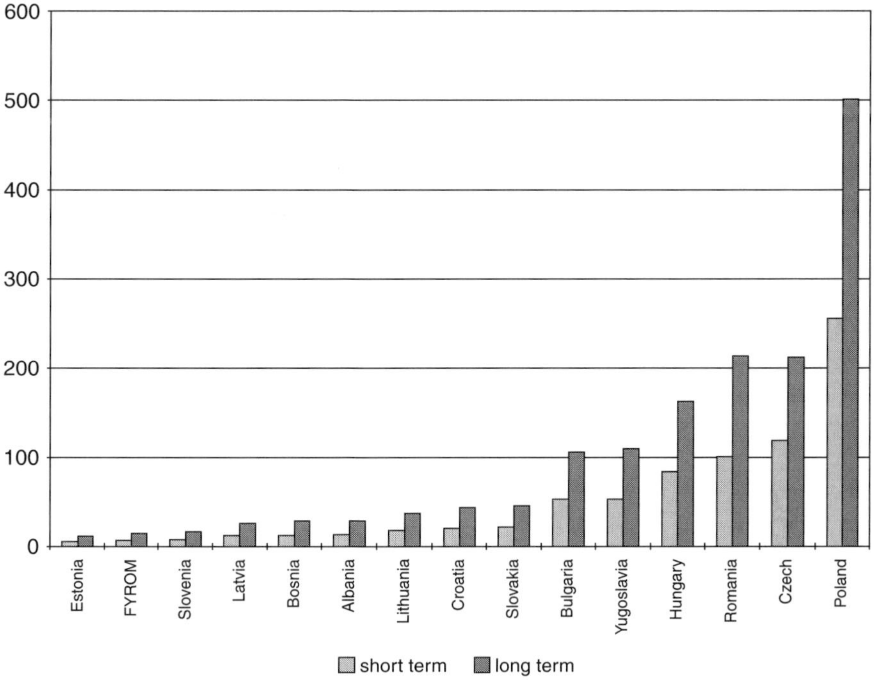

Figure 2.2 Population potential levels in Central and Eastern Europe in the short-term and the long-term scenario.

coefficient of variation ($\sigma/\bar{x}$) of the Z_i index increases from 1.15 in the pre-1989 period to 1.52 in the short to medium-term scenario to drop only in the long-term scenario to 1.34, which, however, is still higher than the initial value of the coefficient. Therefore disparities attributed to geographical conditions such as centrality or accessibility and national market size, will experience a substantial increase during the transition period. This indicates that peripheral CEE countries will, in principle, be in a more unfavourable situation in the new European space than peripheral Western European countries were in the pre-1989 Europe. Although in the long-term scenario the situation improves considerably, the degree of disparities still remains higher. It is worth noting here that, although these trends are expected to influence the prospects of CEE countries for future growth and development, they materialise independently from current economic conditions and existing difficulties in these countries. This, of course, indicates that the tasks of economic convergence and social cohesion will be much harder to achieve in the new Europe than it was in the pre-1989 period (Petrakos 1996a).

This analysis is in line with recent work on transition and development that also emphasises the role of geography in economic processes (Gallup *et al.*

1999; Sachs 1997). Sachs observes that geography is one of the often neglected factors in the literature of integration and transition, despite the fact that it affects directly economic productivity through transport and communication costs. He notices that some of the forerunners of the transition process, such as Poland, Hungary and the Czech Republic lie at the very heart of Europe and have easily accessible markets, while some others, such as Bulgaria or Romania, are more than 1,000 km away from the economic centre of Europe. Using regression analysis, Sachs (1997) finds that physical distance from major economic centres has a significant influence on growth performance and success in liberalising transition economies.

These findings raise some important policy questions that will be discussed latter on. Concluding this section, however, we would like to explore the relation of geography to performance indicators in Europe a little further. For this purpose, we construct a new index (V_i), which is derived from the population potential index (Z_i) as follows:

$$V_i = \Sigma\,(P_j / d_{ij}^{\,k}) + P_i$$

or

$$V_i = (Z_i / P_i) + P_i \tag{2}$$

V_i is in fact the gravity index of each country and should be understood as a measure of accessibility, which is largely independent of country size.[1] Although the relation of geography to economic performance and policy success may be more complicated than this analysis suggests, we would like to explore this issue further with the use of the following simple linear regressions:

$$\Delta Y_i = c_1 + g_1 V_i + e_i \tag{3}$$

$$Y_i = c_2 + g_2 V_i + e \tag{4}$$

$$L_i = c_3 + g_3 V_i + e \tag{5}$$

Y_i is the GDP per capita in 1997, ΔY_i is the GDP per capita growth rate in the period 1989–97 and L_i is an index of success in liberalizing transition economies, used by Piazolo in this volume. Subscript i refers to all European countries in equations (3) and (4), but only to transition countries in equation (5). These regression equations intend to test the hypotheses that more central or more accessible countries in Europe have had a better growth performance (equation 3), a higher level of welfare (equation 4) and a better reform record (equation 5) than less accessible and perimetric ones. The results are presented in Table 2.4.

We observe that all three equations have positive and highly significant slope coefficients (indicated by t-statistics) and a satisfactory for cross-section analysis explanatory power (indicated by R^2). This finding, which is in line

Table 2.4 Regression results for equations 3–5

Coefficient	*Estimated values (t-statistics in parenthesis)* *Equation (2)*	*Equation (3)*	*Equation (4)*
Constant	–29.800 (–4.40)	–3024.350 (–1.22)	23.876 (11.74)
g_1	$1.060(10^{-7})$ (4.91)		
g_2		$6.326(10^{-6})$ (7.90)	
g_3			$3.116(10^{-8})$ (2.48)
N	32	32	13
R^2	44.6%	66.8%	36.0%

with Sachs (1997), indicates that the geographical coordinates of each country play a significant role in determining final outcomes in terms of economic performance and policy success. Countries that are better placed in the new European economic space are *ceteris paribus* more likely to be faster growing and at the top of the development rank than perimetric ones. As far as transition countries are concerned, the message is equally – if not more – important. Success and failure in reforming these economies may not be simply a question of decisiveness, duration or adequate implementation of policies. Geography seems to play an important role here by affecting the size of the markets, the reach of products and services, the type of relations and the level of productivity. Our results support the view that geography matters for growth and development and also matters for transition policies. Of course this relation is far from being a deterministic one, as other factors – including carefully implemented policies – are also found to have an impact on economic outcomes. However, as Gallup *et al.* (1999) have noted, by ignoring geography in assessing economic performance, we tend to overstate the role of policy in economic growth and neglect some deeper – and often very serious – obstacles.

Integration and disintegration in Europe

Recent evidence indicates that EU integration and CEE countries transition processes face serious problems and difficulties that seem to have a clear geographical dimension. On the one hand, integration generates severe pressure for adjustment to the less advanced Southern European countries that have recently internationalised their economies with unsolved, in most cases, problems of efficient organisation of their productive bases. On the other hand, the experience of transition shows that all countries did not adjust or perform in the same way. The introductory chapter of this volume and recent research provide sufficient evidence that in terms of economic structure and performance, a North–South divide is present in both EU and CEE countries (Jackson and Petrakos 1999; Mertzanis and Petrakos 1998; Petrakos 1997a; Petrakos and Totev 2000).

Within the EU, North and Western European countries have a better performance and a more sustainable economic structure than Southern European ones. Within CEE countries, the Visegrad countries have a better performance and a better economic structure than the Baltic countries and the Balkans. Although not explicitly stated, it is beyond any doubt that in this cosmogony of changes that is shaping the new Europe, the worst performing place in all accounts is the Balkan region. With existing trends, the new economic divide in Europe may take a Northwest–Southeast character, where the Southwest, the Central and the Northeast will take the intermediate positions.

With respect to convergence and divergence trends in the new European space, Petrakos, Maier and Gorzelak in this volume provide some initial evidence that transition has increased disparities with respect to development levels. They show that disparities in GDP per capita measured by the coefficient of variation and the max/min ratio were greater in 1997 than in 1989. In this section we conduct a test in order to examine whether the divergence hypothesis is also supported by statistical evidence. Following Barro and Sala-i-Martin (1991, 1992), we estimate the regression:

$$\Delta Y_i = a + b\, Y_i + e_i \tag{5}$$

where Y_i is the 1989 GDP per capita and ΔY_i is the growth of GDP per capita in the 1989-97 period. A positive relation ($b > 0$) of this dependent variable with the initial value Y_{89} would imply that countries with a higher initial value of Y would tend to have a higher growth performance. On the contrary, a negative relation ($b < 0$) of the dependent variable with the initial value would indicate that the best performing countries tend to be those with the lower initial values. This indicates that positive values of the estimated coefficient b are associated with tendencies of divergence, while negative values with tendencies of regional convergence.

The results of the estimation are presented in Table 2.5 and Figure 2.3 and verify the divergence hypothesis. The coefficient of the regression is positive and statistically significant at the 1 per cent confidence interval, indicating that relatively more developed countries had a higher growth rate than relatively less developed ones in the 1989–97 period. If present trends continue, real convergence with respect to development levels will not take place in Europe, at least in the foreseeable future.

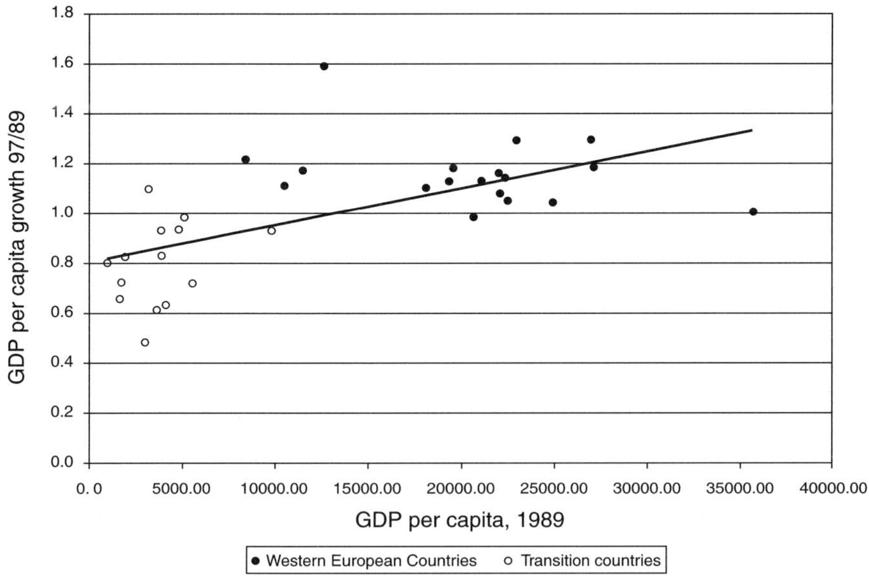

Figure 2.3 Divergence trends with respect to GDP per capita in Europe, 1989–97.

Table 2.5 Regression results of equation (5)

Coefficients	*Estimated values (t-statistics in parenthesis)*
a	0.805 (14.15)
b	$1.443(10^{-5})$ (4.16)
N	32
R^2	36.6%

Policy considerations

Recent evidence and this chapter indicate that a number of important factors can affect the policy response of the EU to present and upcoming challenges. The process of integration in Europe is associated with increasing spatial disparities at all levels, suggesting that, under existing policy trends, our common European future will be a multiply divided one. Predominantly market-driven North–South and East–West integration will lead to a permanent divide in economic structures and levels of development, while a 'business as usual' policy scenario that sticks the EU budget to present spending limits will be totally inadequate to deal with the realities in the East and in several cases in the South.

To a large degree, these disparities do not seem to have a transitory character, as they are affected by parametric factors such as the geographical co-ordinates of regions or countries. Especially for transition countries, differences in growth performance and success in reforming their economy seems to be affected – besides geography – by the seriousness of initial conditions. Aslund *et al.* (1996) and Krueger and Ciolko (1998) have claimed that initial conditions such as the legacy of central planning or the level of backwardness have had a relatively larger role in determining the severity of the output decline than policy choices. As Altvater (1998) suggests, transition is a path-dependent process where the point of arrival depends on the point of departure and where national, cultural and institutional legacies of the old system continue to exert a strong impact.

Undoubtedly, geography and initial conditions in time will become less important for transition countries and policy choices will become more important. However, it is unlikely that poorly designed policies have been responsible for the severity of the decline in output during the early years of transition (Krueger and Ciolko 1998). Similarly, economic success should not be always attributed to sound economic policies. Sachs (1997) observes that it is a mistake to attribute cross-country differences to economic policy, without taking into consideration other factors that might also account for the differential performance.

As well as the discussion on the relative importance of policy versus geography and initial conditions, another factor should also be taken into consideration. It is now a widely shared view that the market forces released by integration and transition leave winners and losers at all spatial levels, despite the fact that these processes are undoubtedly beneficial for the European economy at the aggregate level. These forces, which are associated with factor and commodity flows, are presently stronger than policy responses, especially those dealing with East–West and intra-East disparities. Moreover, while market forces tend to operate increasingly on a European level, spatial development policies are still often devised at national or regional level (ESDP 1997), explaining why spatial variations in welfare are so persistent and in several cases increasing.

Clearly, the EU has a double challenge to meet. The first is global competitiveness and the second is avoiding the risks and costs of widening disparities at all levels. Are these two goals complementary or in conflict with each other? Are growth and successful restructuring in the East and the South a threat or an asset for world competitiveness? Although clear answers have not been provided, most arguments point to the scarcity of resources available for development policies and the need for a sound macro-economic environment, to support a 'balanced' policy approach. The concern expressed is how to design development policies which, however, will not jeopardise the place of the EU in world markets. Less often one meets concerns about the implications of present disparities for the future of the European economy, despite the fact that the problems that arise from them are much more tangible, threatening and urgent.

How is the EU preparing to deal with the challenge of enlargement? The European Council in Berlin adopted Agenda 2000 and the policies proposed by the European Commission. In the introductory chapter of this volume it is shown that these policies are dominated by a 'balanced' budget consideration at the expense of solidarity and cohesion. A 4 per cent ceiling with respect to the new members' GDP is set as a maximum for the assistance provided, while pre-accession and accession funds are limited to 3.16 and 6.57 per cent respectively of the total EU budget (see Table 2.6). It is worth noting that, despite the dramatic changes that took place in the post-1989 Europe, the budget maintains the same financial perspective ceiling of 1.23 per cent of EU GDP. In actual payments, however, it is more likely to remain closer to 1.17 per cent of EU GDP, which was the 1997 level of expenditure.

Clearly, the reluctance of the European Commission to propose an – even slightly – increased budget is associated with its concern about deficits, interest rates, the euro and the competitiveness of the EU in world markets. It is also associated with the unwillingness of some wealthy EU-15 members to bear the cost that is associated with enlargement, despite the fact that they have already capitalised on the benefits.

What is the impact of this policy choice expected to be in the 2000–6 programming period? One answer is to look at previous experience in similar situations. The estimated impact of the 1994–9 Structural Funds on Greece and Portugal has been an annual increase of GDP by about 1 per cent (EC 1999). Note that the funds received by these two countries were much higher in per capita figures than those presently allocated to new members from the

Table 2.6 The EU-15 budget for the 2000–6 period

	Total	*%*
Agriculture	297,740	43.14
Structural operations	213,000	30.86
Structural funds	195,000	
Cohesion funds	18,000	
Internal Policies	42,350	6.13
External policies	32,060	4.64
Administration	33,660	4.87
Reserves	4,050	0.58
Pre-Accession aid	21,840	3.16
Phare	10,920	
Agriculture	3,640	
Structural	7,280	
Available for Accession	45,390	6.57
Total	690,100	100.00

Sources: EC (1997), EC (1999).

East. Even if the impact was the same – which is rather unlikely – what would be the convergence prospects of CEE countries?

Table 2.7 presents four scenarios about the years required for each transition country to converge to the 75 per cent of the EU-15 GDP per capita. The estimates are based on 1997 GDP per capita figures and are made under the assumption that the GDP per capita of the EU-15 grows at a constant annual rate of 2.5 per cent.[2] Under the first scenario, each country's GDP per capita grows at an annual rate that is 1 per cent higher than the average EU-15 rate. Under the second and third scenario it grows at a rate that is 2 and 3 per cent respectively higher than the EU GDP per capita rate, while under the fourth scenario the differential growth rate rises to 4 per cent. Besides the years required for each country to converge to the 75 per cent of EU-15 GDP per capita, Table 2.7 also shows estimated time periods for all CEE countries as well as three regional groups: Central Europe, the Baltic countries and the Balkans.

The figures presented reveal the magnitude of the problem. Even if we assume that CEE countries will converge in the post-1997 period towards the EU-15 – something that remains to be seen, as the 1989–97 period is characterised by clear divergence trends – this convergence will take an

Table 2.7 Convergence scenarios for CEE countries

Transition	*Years required to reach 75% of EU-15 GNP per capita*			
	g = 1%	*g = 2%*	*g = 3%*	*g = 4%*
Albania	321	161	108	81
Bosnia-Herzegovina	318	160	107	81
Bulgaria	277	139	93	70
Croatia	149	75	50	38
Czech	122	62	41	31
Estonia	168	85	57	43
Hungary	138	69	46	35
FYROM	283	142	95	72
Latvia	202	101	68	51
Lithuania	209	105	70	53
Poland	161	81	54	41
Romania	258	129	87	65
Slovakia	159	80	53	40
Slovenia	58	29	19	15
Yugoslavia	256	129	86	65
CE	146	73	49	37
Baltic	198	99	67	50
Balkans	267	134	90	68
Transition	181	91	61	46

Source: own estimates based on World Bank (1999) GDP data.

unsustainably long period of time to materialise. Depending on the scenario about growth rate differentials between the CEE and the EU-15 countries, it might take anything between 46 and 181 years for transition countries as a group to reach the 75 per cent of the EU-15 GDP per capita level. As expected, different countries and regions have a different pace of convergence. On the one extreme, backward countries like Albania might require more than three centuries in the less favourable scenario and something less than a century in the more favourable scenario. At the other extreme, more advanced transition countries like Slovenia might require something between 58 to 15 years to converge to the 75 per cent of the EU-15 GDP per capita.

Regional differences are also evident. In the best-case scenario of differential growth of $g = 4$ per cent, the Central European countries (including Slovenia) will require 37 years, the Baltic countries 50 years and the Balkan countries 68 years to reach 75 per cent of the EU-15 GDP per capita. In practice, the optimistic scenario is not very realistic, as it is unlikely for a transition country to maintain a growth rate that is 4 per cent greater than that of the EU for such a long period of time. Thus, the intermediate scenarios indicating a convergence period of 61–91 years for all transition countries as a group seem to be more realistic.

Is this period sustainable on political or – for that matter – any ground? Even if we deflate EU GDP per capita by nearly 20 per cent, to account for future accessions of CEE countries, it will still require half a century – or two generations – for the average CEE country to reach the 75 per cent threshold. Again, for some countries and regions it will take much longer.

If these figures indicate something, it is that present policies need to be re-examined as they lack the strength required by the magnitude of existing problems and macro-geographical imbalances. First, policies need to be more decisive and take the form of a more generously financed support framework that will deal with the problems of structural weaknesses and deficient infrastructure of the East and the South. Second, policies need to focus equally on the forerunners of the transition process (and the candidates of the first enlargement) and the laggards. That is, a new working balance must be found between maintaining a rational incentive structure between candidate states rewarding success and keeping the laggards in the race avoiding their further marginalisation. This of course implies that the allocation of funds among the three regional groups will have to be reconsidered.

This requires brave decisions on the part of the EU core countries that share a greater burden in the assistance programmes. These decisions, however, may be easier to take when the allocation of the costs and benefits of the integration–transition process and the implications of existing imbalances are examined in some depth. For example, the discussion of EU fiscal policy requires an understanding that the policy response problem for the East and the South, is to a large extent a problem of redistribution of the costs and benefits of economic integration. An examination of the geographical trade balances of each EU and CEE country reveals interesting aspects of the distribution of the costs and benefits of East–West and North–South integration. It also reveals the relative strength of market forces compared to policy responses, as the sums provided for structural funds seem rather inadequate, compared to income redistribution through market penetration. For example, the accumulated trade deficit of Greece with the other EU countries in the 1989–94 period is 9 trillion US dollars, a figure that is almost three times higher than the sum allocated to structural operations under the First Community Support Framework for Greece. However, these issues are not usually addressed. In economic thinking and policy-making, market self-regulation has received an axiomatic status, despite the poor record of market oriented policies in less advanced countries in the Third and most of the Second World (Taylor 1997).

A new synthesis of economic regulation is needed, that will take into consideration: (a) the creative, destructive and redistributive dynamics of the markets; (b) the realities of the economies under consideration with respect to structure, geography and initial conditions; and (c) the lessons of the 1950s and 1960s, when the post-war European economies adopted more interventionist approaches, having a task similar in magnitude to accomplish.

In addition, it should be clear that present European level imbalances in income levels cannot be maintained for long without generating severe pressures for population movements to the more affluent part of the continent. Given that the 'business as usual' policy scenario is unlikely to reduce substantially existing imbalances in levels of prosperity, in a foreseeable time horizon, this may upset demographic balances and labour markets. The Baltic and Balkan regions have a population of more than 60 million, the great majority of whom lives below the poverty line. Giving an opportunity to these people to stay, work and prosper at home may be easier, cheaper, more effective and more humanitarian than devoting effort and resources to keep them outside the national borders and the cities of Western Europe. Both options have a cost. The difference is that the first option may work, while the second (based on historic evidence) is unlikely to. Europe has already enough ethnic tensions and xenophobia, so that making the 'others' a target may seriously threaten solidarity, cohesion and the very essence of the European idea.

Notes

1 The term P_i has been added to equation (2) in order to take account of the distance of each country from its own market.

2 The estimated time period is derived from the formula: $Y_i\ (1+r+g)^t = .75(Y_{EU})(1+g)^t$, where Y_i is the GDP per capita of each country or region in 1997, Y_{EU} is the GDP per capita of the EU-15 in 1997, r is the annual growth rate of the EU-15, g is the differential growth rate of each country or region and t is the time required for the two sides of the equation to become equal.

References

Altvater, E. (1998) 'Theoretical deliberations on time and space in post-socialist transformation', *Regional Studies*, 32, 7: 591–605.

Amin, A., Charles D. and Howells, J. (1992) 'Corporate restructuring and cohesion in the New Europe', *Regional Studies*, 26, 4: 319–31.

Aslund, A., Boone, P. and Johnson, S. (1996) 'How to stabilise: lessons from post-communist countries', *Brookings Papers in Economic Activity*, 1: 217–91.

Bachtler, J. (1998) 'Reforming the Structural Funds: challenges for EU regional policy', *European Planning Studies*, 6, 6: 645–64.

Balaz, V. (1996) 'The wild East? Capital markets in the V4 countries', *European Urban and Regional Studies*, 3, 3: 251–66.

Barro, R.J. and Sala-i-Martin, X. (1991) 'Convergence across states and regions', *Brookings Papers on Economic Activity* I: 107–82.

Barro, R.J. and Sala-i-Martin, X. (1992) 'Convergence', *Journal of Political Economy* 100: 223–51.

Camagni, R. (1992) 'Development scenarios and policy guidelines for the lagging regions in the 1990s', *Regional Studies* 26, 4: 361–74.

CEC (1991) *The regions in the 1990s*, Fourth Periodic Report, Commission of the European Communities, Brussels: CEC.

CEC (1992a) *The Regions in the 1990s, Socioeconomic Situation and Development of the Regions in the Neighbouring countries of the Community*, Brussels: CEC.

CEC (1992b) *Urbanization and the Function of Cities in the European Community*, Regional Development Studies, No. 4, Brussels: CEC.

CEC (1993a) *New Location Factors for Mobile Investment in Europe*, Final Report, Regional Development Studies, No. 6, Brussels: CEC.

CEC (1993b) *Trade and Foreign Investment in the Community's Regions: The Impact of Economic Reform in Central and Eastern Europe*, Regional Development Studies, No. 7, Brussels: CEC.

Coffey, W. and Polese, M. (1987) 'Intrafirm trade in business services: implications for the location of office-based activities', *Papers of the Regional Science Association* 62: 71–80.

Cohen, R. (1981) 'The new international division of labour, multinational corporations and urban hierarchy', in M. Dear and A. Scott (eds) *Urbanization and Urban Planning in Capitalist Society*, London: Methuen.

Collis, C., Berkeley, N. and Noon, D. (1997) 'Attracting foreign direct investment to east European economies: can lessons be learned from the UK experience?' paper presented at the Regional Studies Association Regional Frontiers Conference in Frankfurt (Oder), September 1997.

Constantin, D. (1997) 'Institutions and regional development strategies and policies in the transition period: the case of Romania', paper presented at the 37th European Congress of the European Regional Science Association, Rome, 26–29 August 1997.

Downes, R. (1996) 'Economic transformation in Central and Eastern Europe: the role of regional development', *European Planning Studies* 4, 2: 217–24.

Dunford, M. and Perrons, D. (1993) 'Regional inequality as a cause and consequence of slower growth', *TOPOS* Special Edition, Athens: URDP.

EC (1997) *Agenda 2000*, Brussels: European Commission.

EC (1999) *Sixth Periodic Report on the Social and Economic Situation and*

Development of the Regions in the European Union, Brussels: European Commission, Directory General for Regional Policy and Cohesion.

ESDP (1997) *European Spatial Development Perspective: First Official Draft*, Brussels: European Commission.

European Council (1999) 'Presidency conclusions', Berlin European Council, 24 and 25 March 1999. Available HTTP: http://ue.eu.int/Newsroom.

Eurostat (1992) *External Trade and Balance of Payments*, Luxemburg: European Commission.

Faist, T. and Haubermann, H. (1996) 'Immigration, social citizenship and housing in Germany', *International Journal of Urban and Regional Research* 20, 1: 83–98.

Fazekas, K. (1996) 'Types of microregions, dispersion of unemployment and local employment development in Hungary', *Eastern European Economics*, 34, 3: 3–48.

Fournier, S. and Axelsson, S. (1993) 'The shift from manufacturing to services in Sweden', *Urban Studies* 30, 2: 285–98.

Gallup, J., Sachs, J. and Mellinger, A. (1999) *Geography and Economic Development, Working Papers*, No. 1, Center for International Development, Cambridge, MA: Harvard University.

Gorzelak, G. (1996) *Regional Dimension of Transformation in Central Europe*, London: Jessica Kingsley Publishers.

Haussermann, H. (1993) 'Regional perspectives of East Germany after the unification of the two Germanies', *TOPOS* special edition, Athens: URDP.

IMF (1998) *Direction of Trade Statistics Yearbook*, Washington, DC: IMF.

Ingham, M., Grime, K. and Kowalski, J. (1996) 'A geography of recent Polish unemployment', *European Urban and Regional Studies* 3, 4: 353–63.

Jackson, M. and Petrakos, G. (1996) 'The regional dimension of transition and the role of the new enterprise', *Eastern European Economics* 34: 2-4, (Guest Editors of a three issues special edition).

Jackson, M. and Petrakos, G. (1999) 'Regional differences in the impact of EU integration on the industrial structure and competitiveness of CEFTA countries', paper prepared for the Phare ACE P96-6071-R project: *Competitiveness of CEFTA countries: measurement and trends in the period of preparation to join the EU*.

Kratke, S. (1996) 'Where East meets West: the German-Polish border region in transformation', *European Planning Studies* 4, 6: 647–69.

Krueger, G. and Ciolko, M. (1998) 'A note on initial conditions and liberalization during transition', *Journal of Comparative Economics* 26: 718–34.

Landesmann, M. (1995) 'The patterns of East–West European integration: catching up or falling behind?', in R. Dobrinsky and M. Landesmann (eds) *Transforming Economies and European Integration*, Aldershot: Edward Elgar, pp. 116–40.

Landesmann, M. (1998) 'Features of East–West European integration: cost structures and patterns of specialization', paper presented in the international workshop on Competitiveness of the CEFTA countries: measurement and trends in the period of preparation to join the EU, Bratislava, 17–18 April.

Lever, W. (1993) 'Reurbanization: the policy implications', *Urban Studies* 30, 2: 267–84.

Mack, R. and Jacobson, D. (1996) 'The impact of peripherality upon trade patterns in the European Union', *European Urban and Regional Studies* 3, 4: 364–9.

Martin, R. and Steinen, M.S. (1997) 'State aid, regional policy and locational competition in the European Union', *European Urban and Regional Studies* 4, 1: 19–31.

Mertzanis, H. and Petrakos, G. (1998) 'Changing landscapes in Europe's economic structure', *Transition* 9, 2: 12–13, The World Bank.

Minassian, G. and Totev, S. (1996) 'The Bulgarian economy in transition: the regional after effect', *Eastern European Economics* 34, 3: 49–92.

Peschel, K. (1992) 'European integration and regional development in Northern Europe', *Regional Studies* 26, 4: 387–97.

Petrakos, G. (1996a) 'The regional dimension of transition in Eastern and Central European countries: an assessment', *Eastern European Economics* 34, 5: 5–38.

Petrakos, G. (1996b) 'The new geography of the Balkans: cross-border co-operation between Albania, Bulgaria and Greece', *Series of Transition in the Balkans*, Volume 1, Volos: University of Thessaly.

Petrakos, G. (1997a) 'Industrial structure and change in the European union: comparative analysis and implications for transition Economies', *Eastern European Economics* 35, 2: 41–63.

Petrakos, G. (1997b) 'A European macro-region in the making? The Balkan trade relations of Greece', *European Planning Studies* 5, 4: 515–33.

Petrakos, G. (1997c), 'The regional structure of Albania, Bulgaria and Greece: implications for cross-border co-operation and development', *European Urban and Regional Studies*, 4, 3: 193–208.

Petrakos, G. (1999) 'Patterns of regional inequality and convergence-divergence trends in transition economies', paper presented at international conference on Regional Potentials in an Integrating Europe, Regional Studies Association, 18–21 September, Bilbao, Spain.

Petrakos, G. and Brada, J. (1989) 'Metropolitan concentration in developing countries', *Kyklos* 42, 4: 557–78.

Petrakos, G. and Christodoulakis, N. (1997) *Economic Development in the Balkan Countries and the Role of Greece: From Bilateral Relations to the Challenge of Integration*, Discussion Paper Series No. 1620, London: University of London, CEPR.

Petrakos, G. and Totev, S. (2000) 'Economic structure and change in the Balkan Region: implications for integration, transition and economic co-operation', *International Journal of Urban and Regional Research* 24, 1: 95–113.

Petrakos, G. and Zikos, S. (1996) 'European integration and industrial structure in Greece, prospects and possibilities for convergence', in C. Paraskevopoulos, R. Grinspun and T. Georgakopoulos (eds) *Economic Integration and Public Policy*, London: Edward Elgar, pp. 247–59.

Raagmaa, G. (1996) 'Shifts in regional development in Estonia during the transition', *European Planning Studies* 4, 6: 683–703.

Ramboll (1996) *Regional Disparities in Romania*, Regional Policy Report, Phare Program, Ramboll-Consultants Group.

Richet, A. (1996) 'Transnational corporations, direct foreign investment and attractiveness of East European economies in transition', in M. Dimitrov and A. Todorov (eds) *Industrial Organization and Entrepreneurship in Transition*, Sofia: Informa, pp. 59–67.

Rosenblat, C. and Pumain, D. (1993) 'The location of multinational firms in the European urban system', *Urban Studies* 30, 10: 1691–709.

Sachs, J. (1997) *Geography and Economic Transition*, Working Paper, Centre for International Development, Cambridge, MA: Harvard University.

Taylor, L. (1997) 'Editorial: the revival of the liberal creed – the IMF and the World

Bank in a globalized economy', *World Development* 25, 2: 145–52.
UN (1996) *World Investment Report: Investment, Trade and International Arrangements*, Geneva: United Nations.
UN (1998) *World Investment Report: Trends and Determinants*, Geneva: United Nations.
UNCTAD (1996) *World Investment Report: Investment, Trade and International Arrangements*, Geneva: United Nations.
Williamson, J. (1965) 'Regional inequalities and the process of national development', *Economic Development and Cultural Change* 13, 2: 3–45.
Zinn, D.L. (1996) 'Adriatic brethren or black sheep? Migration in Italy and the Albanian crisis, 1991', *European Urban and Regional Studies* 3, 3: 241–9.

3 Regional disparities in the EU through the lens of official statistics[1]

Michael Dunford

Claims about the existence, quantification and size of regional disparities are the starting points for many analyses of the development of the European Union (EU). The analysis of these disparities does, however, raise a whole series of questions that are often taken for granted. The aim of this chapter is to identify and consider some of the problems associated with the measurement and comparison of disparities in the EC. Attention will be paid to the scale of inequality, the choice of indicators, the impact of different geographies on the measurement of inequality, the analysis of trends, and the determinants of inequality.

The measurement of regional inequality

In the EU analyses of inequalities rely most often on figures for Gross Domestic Product (GDP) per head. The data on GDP per head is provided at four levels of territorial aggregation: for the 15 member states, for 77 NUTS (Nomenclature of Statistical Territorial Units) Level I regions (European Community Regions), for 206 NUTS Level II regions (Basic Administrative Units) and for 1,031 Level III regions (Subdivisions of Basic Administrative Units). At present the time series are far from complete for all countries. In this chapter two different sets of REGIO data are used. A first data set for the period up to 1989 is for 63 Level I regions, 170 Level II regions (excluding the new East German *Länder*, the French overseas *départements* and Azores and Madeira), and for 686 Level III regions (as there was no GDP data in particular for Italian and Portuguese Level III areas) (see Dunford 1993b). The more recent series covering the period up to 1993 is more comprehensive, with 1993 data for all 77 Level I regions, 203 Level II regions (excluding 3 East German regions and the French overseas *départements* where 1991 figures were updated to 1993), and 734 Level III regions (as there was no NUTS Level III GDP data for Austria, the new German *Länder*, Italy, Republic of Ireland, some Spanish overseas dependencies and Portugal).[2]

This regional breakdown is the result of an attempt to integrate national regional administrative and statistical territorial structures. The national regional divisions are, however, not derived from a common set of criteria,

Table 3.1 The number and size of NUTS regions in EC Member States in 1993

	GDP (million ECU)				*GDP (million PPS)*				*Population (thousands)*			
	Maximum	*Minimum*	*Average*	*Number*	*Maximum*	*Minimum*	*Average*	*Number*	*Maximum*	*Minimum*	*Average*	*Number*
NUTS I												
Austria	72855	27046	51817	3	66355	24633	47194	3	3368	1768	2664	3
Belgium	105235	27439	60003	3	105803	27587	60327	3	5833	955	3362	3
Germany	368927	17850	101829	16	314784	15232	86885	16	17725	684	5074	16
Denmark	115473	115473	115473	1	92442	92442	92442	1	5189	5189	5189	1
Spain	126007	15481	58345	7	148903	18294	68946	7	10726	1526	5592	7
Finland	70990	491	35740	2	72384	501	36442	2	5041	25	2533	2
France	305590	59331	133572	8	285823	55493	124932	8	10853	3976	7166	8
Greece	29355	6597	19184	4	39634	8907	25902	4	3495	996	2591	4
Ireland	40365	40365	40365	1	45699	45699	45699	1	3563	3563	3563	1
Italy	168573	18554	77029	11	187541	20641	85697	11	9059	1618	5281	11
Luxembourg	10688	10688	10688	1	10118	10118	10118	1	398	398	398	1
Netherlands	133301	27599	66009	4	125887	26064	62337	4	7167	1617	3822	4
Portugal	70053	1067	24111	3	104588	1593	35998	3	9383	239	3292	3
Sweden	158108	158108	158108	1	135930	135930	135930	1	8719	8719	8719	1
UK	288479	18033	73160	11	327162	20451	82970	11	17733	1628	5279	11
NUTS II												
Austria	44389	3399	17272	9	40429	3095	15731	9	1585	275	888	9
Belgium	34775	3393	16365	11	34963	3412	16453	11	1622	237	917	11
Germany	120763	8288	45752	35	103040	7072	39037	35	5292	497	2246	35
Denmark	115473	115473	115473	1	92442	92442	92442	1	5189	5189	5189	1
Spain	77128	1129	22690	18	91142	1334	26813	18	7033	126	2175	18
Finland	23856	491	11913	6	24324	501	12147	6	1788	25	844	6
France	305590	3320	48569	22	285823	3105	45427	22	10853	252	2606	22
Greece	29355	1088	5903	13	39634	1469	7970	13	3495	188	797	13

Table 3.1 cont.

	GDP (million ECU)				*GDP (million PPS)*				*Population (thousands)*			
	Maximum	*Minimum*	*Average*	*Number*	*Maximum*	*Minimum*	*Average*	*Number*	*Maximum*	*Minimum*	*Average*	*Number*
Ireland	40365	40365	40365	1	45699	45699	45699	1	3563	3563	3563	1
Italy	168573	2213	42366	20	187541	2462	47133	20	9059	120	2905	20
Luxembourg	10688	10688	10688	1	10118	10118	10118	1	398	398	398	1
Netherlands	59367	3081	22003	12	56065	2910	20779	12	3307	240	1274	12
Portugal	33641	1067	10333	7	50226	1593	15428	7	3495	239	1411	7
Sweden	36879	7170	19763	8	31706	6164	16991	8	1740	397	1090	8
UK	139571	3423	22993	35	158287	3881	26076	35	6919	278	1659	35
NUTS III												
Austria	44389	44389	44389	1	40429	40429	40429	1	1585	1585	1585	1
Belgium	27439	544	4186	43	27587	547	4209	43	955	38	235	43
Germany	59885	665	4349	327	51097	568	3710	327	1700	36	193	327
Denmark	43303	824	9623	12	34666	660	7703	12	612	45	335	12
Spain	65547	987	8146	50	77457	1166	9626	50	5019	93	780	50
Finland	23653	491	3762	19	24117	501	3836	19	1286	25	267	19
France	108883	1011	11332	94	101840	946	10599	94	2538	73	607	94
Greece	29355	125	1505	51	39634	169	2032	51	3495	21	203	51
Ireland												
Italy	2213	2213	2213	1	2462	2462	2462	1	120	120	120	1
Luxembourg	10688	10688	10688	1	10118	10118	10118	1	398	398	398	1
Netherlands	27347	794	6601	40	25826	750	6234	40	1301	55	374	39
Portugal	2160	1067	1480	3	3225	1593	2210	3	343	239	279	3
Sweden	36879	903	6588	24	31706	777	5664	24	1678	58	363	24
UK	139571	899	12381	65	158287	1020	14041	65	6919	72	893	65

and so while an attempt was made to identify areas that are comparable in economic size the NUTS classification does not provide a harmonised set of regional units. As Table 3.1 for 1993 shows, the regions at each level vary significantly in size and number within and between member states. The 1993 Gross Domestic Product at Purchasing Power Standards of Level I regions varied from ECU 368,927 million in Nordrhein-Westfalen to ECU 491 million in Ahvenanmaa/Aaland in Finland, while population varied from 17,733 million in South East England to 25,000 in Ahvenanmaa/Aaland. At each level there was significant variation in the average size of the territorial units whether the indicator of size was GDP or population. These variations increased with the level of disaggregation. The greatest imbalance occurred at Level III between West Germany and the rest of the Community: in West Germany there were 328 *Kreise* whereas in France, Italy and the United Kingdom there were fewer than 100 areas (*départements*, provinces and counties).

The most common indicator of regional inequality is regional GDP per head which is a measure of the value of the goods and services produced in a region in a given period of time. Through the production of these goods and services, incomes are created, although the income that results does not necessarily accrue to a region's inhabitants: where the inhabitants of other regions have property rights in a region, there is an outflow of income, as there is if the human capital of other regions is used locally. As a comparison of GDP and GNP shows, in some cases these transfers are sometimes large and result in large differences between the wealth created and the wealth appropriated by the area's inhabitants. The most striking case at present is the Republic of Ireland where, by 1995, GDP was 15 per greater than GNP due to the presence of net factor outflows.

The distribution of original income is also modified by the redistributive transfers that result from government taxation, benefits and expenditures. As these transfers are often substantial, an appreciation of the impact of disparities in development on living standards and the distribution of wealth presupposes an explicit analysis of these and other mechanisms of redistribution.

GDP estimates do not, moreover, include the value of those goods and services that people produce for their own use which itself depends on the resources they control and can use and which in all probability varies significantly from one place to another. Also excluded are those economic activities in the informal and hidden economies which are not picked up through attempts to reconcile output, income and expenditure measure of GDP, which are particularly large in contemporary Europe and which also vary in importance from place to place.

There are, therefore, a number of shortcomings associated with approaches which confine their attention to official GDP estimates. As I shall show, however, variations in GDP are substantial and important – especially as indicators of the productive capacities of different economies – and provide at present one of the few EU-wide indicators of regional differences in economic prosperity.

The map of inequality

Inequalities in regional GDP per head can be measured in two ways. Measurements in European Currency Units (ECU) indicate the international value of the output of regional economies. The money value of regional output shows (1) what the output of the exposed sector can be sold for and can command on international markets; and (2) what the output of the protected sector can command directly on regional and indirectly on external markets. If a region's external trade is in equilibrium, this indicator reflects the 'quality' of its goods and services and its competitive strength. The 1993 figures for each NUTS Level II region are plotted in Figure 3.1(a). Measurements in purchasing power standards (PPS) make allowance for differences in the prices of goods and services in different areas: the quantity of goods and services that a given sum in ECU will exchange for is greater in a low cost than in a high cost region. The PPS measure allows for these differences in purchasing power and is therefore an index of the volume of goods and services that different local economies produce and the volume of output that their economic activities can command or exchange for in their own area. PPS measures are, in other words, indicator of differences in living standards.[3] 1993 PPS estimates are plotted in Figure 3.1(b). It is important to note, however, that this particular indicator is calculated using estimates of the average price level in each Member State. As price structures can differ quite sharply within Member States, this indicator can be somewhat misleading, overestimating GDP in high cost areas and underestimating it in low cost areas. This indicator is none the less one of the most important variables the EU uses to identify areas lagging in development. (Objective 1 areas are areas with a GDP per head less than 75 per cent of the Community average.) Also plotted in Figure 3.1(c) are the levels of GDP per head in Level III regions.

In 1993 output per head in NUTS Level II regions measured in PPS varied from 190 to 38 per cent of the EU-15 average, while in ECU the extreme values were 221 and 28. The ten per cent band or decile of the population of the Community that lived in the least prosperous areas had an average GDP per head of 58 (see Figure 3.2 which plots the average GDP per head per decile for 1993). A further 10 per cent lived in areas with an average of 71. More than 19 per cent of the population of the EU lived in (Objective 1) areas with a per capita GDP of less than 75 per cent of the Community average: included were all of Greece, Portugal outside of Lisbon, the French overseas *départements*, the former German Democratic Republic, 10 of 18 Spanish NUTS II regions, 5 of the regions of the Italian Mezzogiorno, Burgenland in Austria and South Yorkshire in the UK. Just outside were the Canaries, Merseyside, Corsica, Molise and Flevoland in The Netherlands

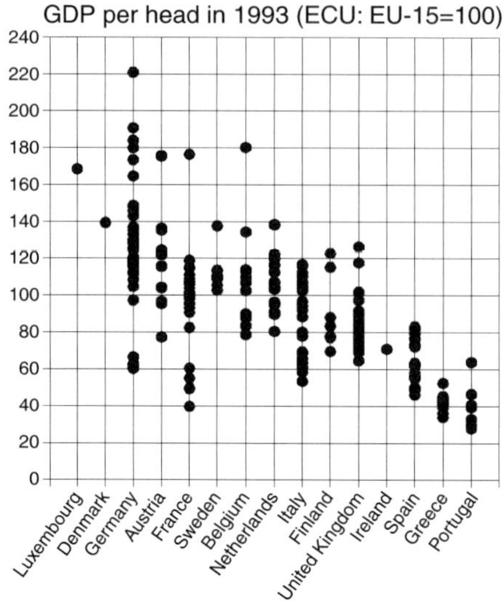

Figure 3.1 (a)

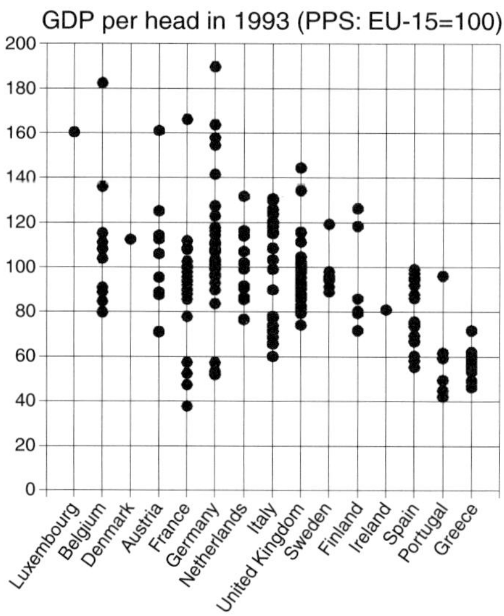

Figure 3.1 (b)

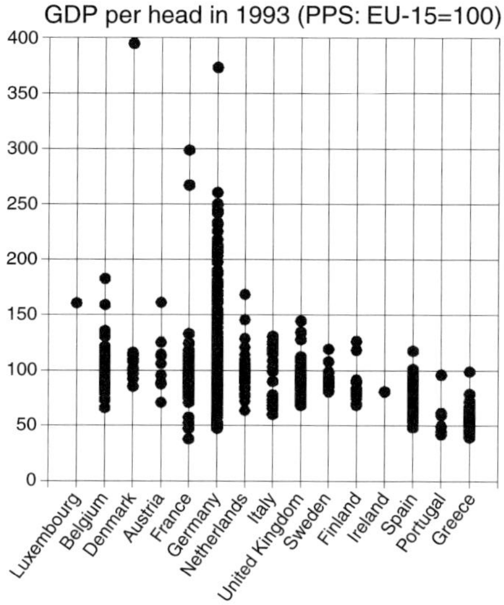

Figure 3.1 (c)

Figure 3.1 Disparities in regional per capita GDP in 1993.

Notes: (a) at current market prices in NUTS Level II regions (in ECU: EU-15 = 100), (b) at current market prices and purchasing power standards in NUTS Level II regions (in PPS: EU-15 = 100) and (c) at current market prices and purchasing power standards in NUTS Level III regions (in PPS: EU-15 = 100).

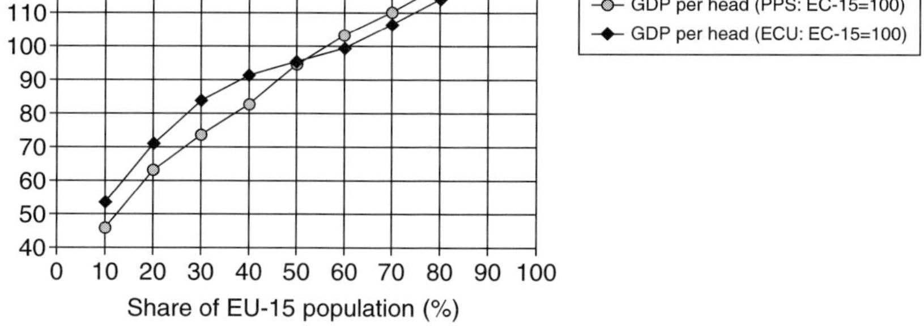

Figure 3.2 GDP per head for each decile of the EU population in NUTS level II regions in 1993

where a large proportion of the resident population works outside the area and which had been granted Objective 1 status. In most of these areas the share of income from low-productivity agricultural sectors was large, and unemployment was high. A further 36 per cent lived in areas with a per capita GDP of less than the Community average. Included are many rural areas and areas affected by the decline of employment in mining, steel, textiles and shipbuilding with above-average unemployment rates. At the other end of the spectrum 10 per cent of the population of the Community lived in areas with an average of 153. Included were Hamburg (190), Brussels (182), Ile de France (166), Darmstadt (164), Vienna (161), Luxembourg (160), Oberbayern (158), Bremen (154), Greater London (144), Stuttgart (141), Antwerp (136), Grampian (134) in Scotland, Groningen (132) and Lombardy (131). A large share of the regions in this group were West German, and most were metropolitan economies clustered around an axis (the so-called 'blue banana') that extended from Greater London southeastwards through Belgium and The Netherlands, that continued southwards along the Rhine into southern Germany, and that ended in Lombardy in the north of Italy.

To be in the 10 per cent band or decile that lives in the regions with the highest levels of per capita output does not imply, however, that a household or individual is rich: it is average output that is large, and household income depends, first, on whether the income associated with a region's output of goods and services accrues to the region's inhabitants, and, second, on the personal distribution of income within the region. Inequalities in wages and in personal incomes are in fact large and have increased in the late 1970s and 1980s. Social and spatial polarisation is found, therefore, not just at a regional and inter-urban level but also within ('multiply-divided') cities in core and less developed regions alike (see Krätke 1992). Greater intra-urban social polarisation is also a consequence of new job structures in advanced services and high-tech growth sectors which create relatively fewer middle-income jobs than in the 'golden age of Fordism'. High-level, high-status jobs are concentrated in metropolitan areas along Europe's major axes, while peripheral areas rely on low-level jobs. But the high-growth sectors also require a whole range of subordinate consumer service and low-level manufacturing activities characterised by part-time employment, short-term contracts, and informal work. What results is an intensification of social segregation in space and a differentiation and polarisation of lifestyles that has led to the use of the metaphor of the 'dual city' (Mayer 1992).

Measured inequality and territorial disaggregation

What happens as the level of territorial disaggregation increases? In Figure 3.1(c) 1993 GDP per head is plotted for Level III regions. With the increase in the number of areas the level of disparity increased within the Community with metropolitan cores in Denmark, Germany and France (Copenhagen 395, Frankfurt am Main 373, Paris 298, Hauts-de-Seine 267, Erlangen 260,

Wolfsburg 250, Stuttgart 250, Ludwigshafen am Rhein 245, Munich (*Kreisfreie Stadt*) 244, Munich (*Landkreis*) 243, Regensburg 243, Darmstadt 242, Ulm 233, Düsseldorf 232 Schweinfurt 226) standing out very sharply at one end of the spectrum. At the other end are once again areas in Greece which accounts for 19 of the 30 areas with the lowest GDP per head – the lowest scores are for Guadeloupe 38, Grevena 39, Thesprotia 41, Açores 42, Evrytania 43, Chios 44, Ioannina 45, Madeira 45, and Arta 46, though 6 German *Kreise* with predominantly residential functions lie at the upper end of this group. In the case of Level III regions the range in the Community (excluding French overseas *départements*) was from 395 (Copenhagen) to 39 (the Nomos of Grevena) in Greece. There were also wide gaps within each country. In West Germany there was an immense gulf between the *Kreis* of Frankfurt am Main (373) and *Landkreis* Schweinfurt (43) though the adjacent city of Schweinfurt (226) had the twelfth highest figure in the country. In France the dominance of Paris (298) and the adjacent *département* of Hauts de Seine (267) over the rest of the country appeared in a very dramatic form. The Rhône *département* (133) that contains Lyons came next. Setting aside the overseas *départements*, Creuse (71) in Limousin followed by Ariège (76) in Midi-Pyrénées were at the bottom of the list. In Britain, Greater London (144), which unlike Paris combines the central city, with Grampian (134), Berkshire (128), Lothian (112) and Buckinghamshire (112) scored highest, and Mid-Glamorgan (69), Dyfed (71) and the Isle of Wight (72) lowest. In Spain the Comunidades Autonomas of Tarragona (118) and Gerona (101) in Cataluña had a higher GDP per head than many areas in more advanced countries, while the weakest Spanish areas of Badajoz (48) in Extremadura, Granada (54), Juan (55) and Cordoba (56) in Andalucia, and Lugo (56) in Galicia lie in the south-west, south and north-west.

The fact that inequality increases with the level of territorial disaggregation is not unexpected. First, economic activities tend to agglomerate and are highly clustered. There are also strong forces of selection which concentrate key economic functions in core areas and force out those activities which are associated with lower levels of value added per head and are not required to service core metropolitan functions. Second, at high levels of aggregation workplaces, places of residence and rural zones are combined, and the differences between them are often averaged out. As the level of aggregation declines, regional economic space appears more differentiated.

To consider the implications of scale for the measurement of regional disparities there is a need to identify some summary measures of inequality. In this chapter I shall make use of a number of indicators centred on the standard deviation, the mean absolute deviation, and the Gini coefficient. As regional units vary significantly in size, however, all of these indicators are weighted by the region's share in the total population. If p_i denotes the population of the ith region ($i = 1,2, \dots n$) and y_i denotes its per capita GDP, and q_i denotes its GDP, the population-weighted standard deviation (WSD) is given by the equation

$$WSD = \sqrt{\sum_{i=1}^{n} (y_i - \bar{y})^2 \frac{p_i}{\sum_{i=1}^{n} p_i}}$$

the weighted absolute deviation (WAD) is given by the equation

$$WAD = \sum_{i=1}^{n} |y_i - \bar{y}| \frac{p_i}{\sum_{i=1}^{n} p_i}$$

the Gini coefficient (GC) is given by the equation

$$GC = \frac{1}{2n \sum_{i=1}^{n} y_i} \sum_{i=1}^{n} \sum_{j=1}^{n} |y_i - y_j|$$

and the Theil coefficient (TC) is given by the equation

$$TC = \sum_{i=1}^{n} \frac{q_i}{\sum_{i=1}^{n} q_i} \log \left(\frac{\frac{q_i}{\sum_{i=1}^{n} q_i}}{\frac{p_i}{\sum_{j=1}^{g} p_i}} \right)$$

As with the indicators based on the mean, the deviations from which the Gini coefficient was calculated were weighted by the product of the shares of the total population in each pair of regions. To facilitate comparisons the weighted standard deviation and the weighted mean absolute deviations are expressed as percentages of the mean to give a coefficient of variation (CV).

With these indicators it is simple to show how inequality increases with the level of spatial disaggregation. Suppose a country is divided into 16 areas (A1, A2, . . ., D4) with similar populations but different levels of GDP per head, and that these areas are grouped first into four and then into two regions (see Figure 3.3(a)). The standard deviation expressed as a percentage of the mean decreases from 38.5 per cent (16 areas) to 10.6 (4 areas: A1 ... B2, A3 ... B4, C1 ... D2 and C3 ... D4) and 3.22 (2 areas: A1 ... B4 and C1 ... D4). It is important to note, however, that the choice of regional boundaries can affect the result. If in Figure 3.3(a) the 16 areas are divided horizontally rather than vertically into two groups (A1 ... D2 and A3 ... D4) the indicator falls to 9.67 instead of 3.22. Alternatively, if four areas are identified in the

(a)

	A	B	C	D
1	5	10	10	5
2	10	10	10	10
3	10	15	20	10
4	5	10	10	5

(b)

	A	B	C	D
10	5	10	10	5
11	10	10	10	10
12	10	15	20	10
13	5	10	10	5

Figure 3.3 Measured inequality and regional division.

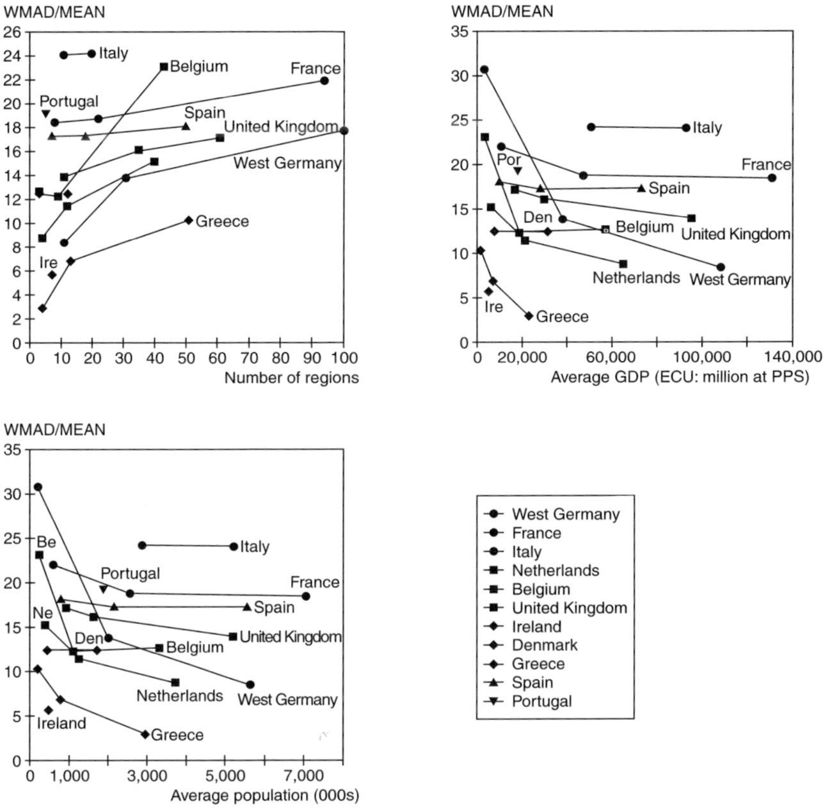

Figure 3.4 Disparities in per capita GDP (WMAD/MEAN) against (a) the number of regions, (b) average regional GDP and (c) average regional population in EU member states[a] in 1989.

Note: [a]In West Germany there were 328 Level III regions and the disparity index was 30.77. In order not to extend the x-axis, and to facilitate inter-Member State comparisons the equation of a straight line joining the West German Level II and III areas was estimated and is truncated in the diagram at an x-value of 100 regions.

manner indicated in Figure 3.3(b) the coefficient of variation will equal 24.7. Measured regional disparities depend, therefore, not just on the degree of spatial concentration of economic activities, but also on the regional division of the country: the number of areas and the choice of boundaries affect the measure of disparity, just as the delimitation of electoral districts shapes the outcome of elections. Clearly the ideal solution is to use functional economic areas which combine places of work with corresponding places of residence (Cheshire 1990), though disparities between politically identified areas are significant as determinants of the resources over which different communities can exercise political leverage.

To consider the implications of the size and number of regional units for the measurement of inequality, the degree of inequality in 1989 GDP per head was computed (WMAD as a percentage of the mean GDP per head) for each country for each of the three NUTS levels. The results are plotted in Figure 3.4. What is clear is that measured inequality increases as the number of regional units increases and as the size of the regional units decreases, whether size is measured by the GDP or the population of each region. The one exception to this rule is Belgium. In the Belgian case the WMAD/MEAN declines from 12.6 to 12.2, while the standard deviation measure which gives greater weight to extreme values declines from 20.8 to 14.8 as the number of areas increases from 3 to 9. The reason why is that the Level I regions are not divided into a whole number of Level II regions: the Brussels region, which is identified as a separate Level I area and accounts for 72 per cent of the variation in the WMAD, is only a part of the province of Brabant at NUTS Level II. As Brussels accounts for 60 per cent of GDP but just 43 per cent of the population of Brabant, its weight is concealed. At Level III, however, Brussels is once again a separate area. In Belgium therefore it makes sense to drop the intermediate level of disaggregation and compare directly Levels 1 and 3 at which point the Belgian case ceases to be aberrant.

With some control for the size and number of geographical areas in each Member State it is possible to compare the levels of inequality in each country. What emerges is that for regional divisions with areas with average populations of 2–5 million and average GDPs of ECU 35–100 billion there is a fairly clear hierarchy of inequalities. The most marked regional imbalances are in Italy where there is a deep-rooted north–south divide, followed by France where the the major cleavage is the divide between Paris and the rest of the country, Spain with its gap between the north-east and Madrid and the rest of the country, and the United Kingdom where the major division is between Greater London and the Home Counties, on the one hand, and the rest of the country on the other.

What Figure 3.4 also shows is that inequalities occur at different scales in different countries. In Italy, France and Spain there are substantial macro-geographical inequalities, while in West Germany and Belgium inequalities between large regions are smaller. As the size of areas increases, however, there is a much more pronounced growth in measured inequality in the last two countries. In West Germany, therefore, a comparatively equalised development of economic activities at the level of the *Länder* – required by the German federal *Grundgesetz* – and of large territorial units is associated with significant intraregional agglomerations of economic activities and significant intraregional inequalities.

Components of territorial disparities

To help identify the causes of disparities, differentials in development can be divided into two elements: an element that depends on productivity differentials; and an element that depends on differential in the employment rate (the percentage of the population in employment) (see Dunford 1993b). More formally:

$$\frac{\textit{Gross Domestic Product}}{\textit{Resident Population}} = \frac{\textit{Gross Domestic Product}}{\textit{Employed Population}} \times \frac{\textit{Employed Population}}{\textit{Resident Population}}$$

In order to identify the relative roles of variations in productivity and the employment rate the data for each region are plotted on a graph which records the value added per person employed on the vertical axis (measured in ECU and not at purchasing power standards) and the employment rate on the horizontal axis. Each variable is measured as a percentage of the EU average (see Figure 3.5). A score of 100 (or a logarithm of 2) is therefore equal to the EU average, a score of more than 100 is greater than average and a score of less than 100 denotes a less than average result. In Figure 3.5 a given GDP per head represented by a single curve can be achieved in a wide range of ways by trading off productivity and employment rates. (If the data were plotted using logarithms of the rates of productivity and employment the trade-off would be represented by a straight line sloping downwards from left to right). What the actual figures for 1986 plotted in Figure 3.5 make immediately clear is that the two determinants of regional GDP per head play quite different roles in different parts of western Europe. In most cases all the NUTS 1 regions in a particular Member State are clustered in a particular part of the graph, though there are exceptions.

In 1986 the areas with the lowest GDP per head were in the main in Greece and Portugal. (Data for this analysis were not available for the French overseas *départements* which also had particularly low levels of GDP per head.) What is clear in the case of Greece and Portugal, however, is the fact that their employment rates were close to the EU average (94 to 99 per cent). (Of the cohesion countries their unemployment rates were also comparatively low.) Yet their levels of productivity (measured in ECU without allowance for differences in price levels in different countries) were equal to 29 to 39 per cent of the EU average.

The situation in Spain and the Republic of Ireland was rather different. Generally speaking, employment rates were low varying from 86 per cent in North West Spain (S1) to 61 per cent in Andalucia (S6). In Ireland the employment rate stood at 78 per cent. The rates of productivity were below average but were much closer to it than in the cases of Greece and Portugal varying from 90 per cent in Madrid to 57 per cent in North West Spain but with most areas clustered in the upper half of this range. In the Republic of Ireland productivity was equal to 85 per cent of the EU average.

This cluster also included the regions of Southern Italy: Campania (I7); Puglia, Basilicata and Calabria (I9); Sicily (Ia); and Sardinia (Ib). In all of these areas productivity was between 82 and 89 per cent of the EU average, while employment rates were 79 to 84 per cent of the average. Abruzzo and

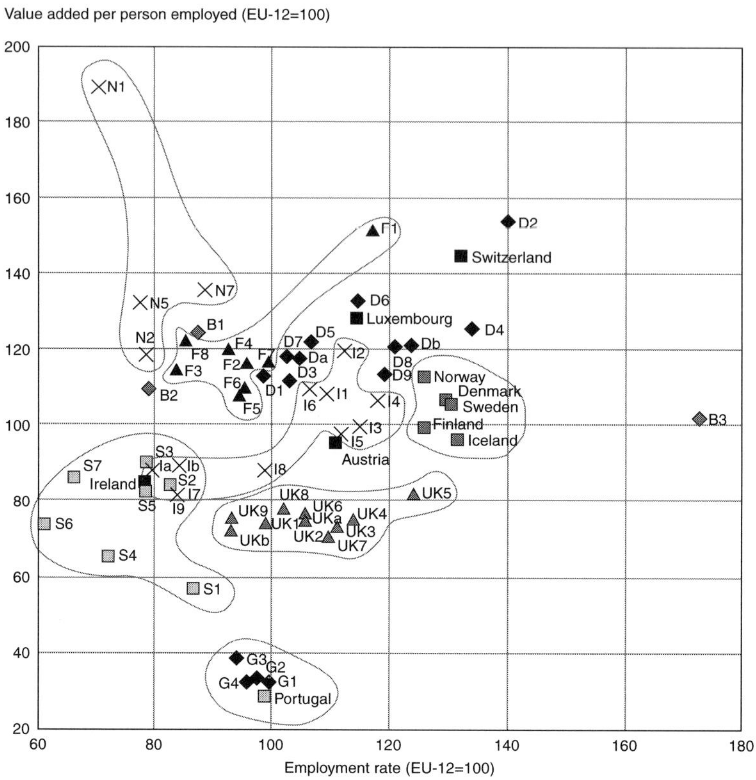

B1 Vlaams Gewest
B2 Region Wallonne
B3 Bruxelles-Brussel
R9 Danmark
D8 Baden-Württemberg
D9 Bayern
DB Berlin
DC Brandenburg
D4 Bremen
D2 Hamburg
D6 Hessen
DD Mecklenburg-Volpommern
D3 Niedersachsen
D5 Nordhein-Westfalen
D7 Rheinland-Pfalz
DA Saarnland
DE Sachsen
DF Sachsen-Anhalt
D1 Schleswig-Holstein
DG Thueringen
G1 Voreia Ellada
G2 Kentriki Ellada
G3 Attiki
G4 Nisia
S1 Noroeste
S2 Noreste
S3 Madrid
S4 Centro
S5 Este
S6 Sur
S7 Canarias
F1 Ile de France
F2 Bassin Parisien
F3 Nord-Pas-de-Calais
F4 Est
F5 Ouest
F6 Sud-Ouest
F7 Centre-Est
F8 Mediterranée
F9 Départements d'Outre-Mer
R8 Ireland
I1 Nord Ouest
I2 Lombardia
I3 Nord Est
I4 Emilia-Romagna
I5 Centro
I6 Lazio
I7 Campania
I8 Abruzzi-Molise
I9 Sud
IA Sicilia
IB Sardegna
R6 Luxembourg
N1 Noord-Nederland
N2 Oost-Nederland
N7 West-Nederland
N5 Zuid-Nederland
P1 Continente
P2 Açores
P3 Madeira
UK1 North
UK2 Yorkshire and Humberside
UK3 East Midlands
UK4 East Anglia
UK5 South East
UK6 South West
UK7 West Midlands
UK8 North West
UK9 Wales
UKA Scotland
UKB Northern Ireland

Figure 3.5 Employment and productivity rates in NUTS level I EU regions and Western Europe in 1986.

Source: elaborated from data from the REGIO database and OECD, National accounts of OECD countries, and Labour force statistics (various years).

Molise (I8) were somewhat detached from this group in that their employment rate (99 per cent) was just short of the average, although their productivity level (88 per cent) was quite close to the other parts of the Mezzogiorno. This region lay between the Mezzogiorno and the Centre-North. In the Centre-North productivity was close to and often greater than the EU average (varying from 97 per cent in the Central region to 119 per cent in Lombardia), while employment rates were 6 to 18 per cent higher. The differential positions of the two parts of the country graphically confirm the existence of two different economic and social worlds in Italy. Austria interestingly occupies a position that is close to that of the Centro region (I5) in Italy and the North East (I3) which in the past was under Austrian control.

The position of the United Kingdom is also particularly striking. Generally speaking, UK productivity is low, ranging from 72 to 82 per cent of the EU average. Employment rates were on the other hand much more varied and were in most cases in excess of 100 per cent: the lowest scores were 93 per cent in Northern Ireland and Wales, while the highest was 124 per cent in the South East, and the next highest was 114 in East Anglia. Overall, comparatively high rates of employment partially compensate for low productivity.

The Nordic countries are associated with substantially higher rates of employment: 131 per cent in Iceland, 130 per cent in Denmark and Sweden, and 126 per cent in Finland and Norway. In Iceland (96 per cent) and Finland (99 per cent) productivity lay just below the EU average, while in Norway (113 per cent), Denmark (106 per cent) and Sweden (106 per cent) it was above average. GDP per head seems therefore to have been high largely as a result of the high degree of mobilisation of the human potential of the Nordic countries.

Switzerland is a country with both a high rate of productivity (145 per cent) and a high employment rate (132 per cent). Hamburg (D2) in Germany is similar though its position along with that of Bremen (D4) is difficult to interpret due to the significance of commuting. In the rest of Germany employment rates are high in Berlin (DB) and Baden-Württemberg (D8) and Bayern (D9) in the south lying between 119 and 123 per cent. Rates of productivity in these two *Länder* are close to those in the northern Rhinelands and North Sea coast (112 to 122 per cent) but the latter are characterised by employment rates in the order of 98 to 107 per cent. Hessen which contains the city of Frankfurt is a little different in that productivity rates are higher (132 per cent) while its employment rate (115 per cent) lies in between the rates of the north and west which are close to the EU average and the higher rates in the south.

With the striking exception of Île de France, the French regions along with those in Belgium generally display above-average productivity rates but less than average employment rates. French provincial productivity rates range from 108 per cent in the Ouest to 122 per cent in the Mediterranée, while Belgian rates outside of Brussels equal 124 in Vlaams Gewest and 110 in the Région Wallonne. Employment rates are 87 and 79 per cent respectively in Flanders and Wallonia and range from 84 per cent in the old industrial region of Nord-Pas-de-Calais to 99 per cent in the Centre-Est (Rhône-Alpes and Auvergne) in provincial France. The Île de France stands out from the rest of France as a consequence of its higher employment rate (117 per cent) and in particular of its rate of productivity (151 per cent).

The Netherlands lies even more decisively in the top left quadrant of Figure 3.5. Rates of productivity range are 189 (Noord-Nederland), 135 (West-Nederland), 132 (Zuid-Nederland) and 119 per cent (Oost-Nederland), yet employment rates are low, ranging from 70 to 88 per cent of the EU figure. In The Netherlands therefore the strong positive impact of productivity on relative GDP per head is in part offset by the downward pressure exerted by comparatively low rates of employment.

The role of sectoral structures

Table 3.2 records the value added at factor per person employed for each of the single and two-digit NACE-CLIO sectors. (The data for Belgium are at market prices rather than at factor cost.) The range of variation is greater than for GDP per head as the figures are in ECUs and not in PPS. As the data show there are wide productivity differentials. The highest overall (adjusted) figures are recorded in The Netherlands (34,500 ECU per person) with France, Germany and Belgium bunched around 30,000 ECU. The lowest figures are for Portugal whose average productivity was just over one-fifth of the Dutch level and Greece which achieved just over one-quarter.

As Table 3.2 shows, these aggregate figures are underlain by a much more complex set of sectoral differentials. In agriculture, forestry and fishing productivity in Portugal is less than one-tenth of The Netherlands level. Greece and Spain are also areas of low agricultural productivity, while Italy (10,900 ECU) and Germany (14,900 ECU) which lie either side of the Republic of Ireland (13,400 ECU) achieve levels that are distinctly modest especially when compared with their relative performance in industry and services. Manufacturing productivity is greatest in Luxembourg and The Netherlands though the Dutch figure is boosted by its capital-intensive gas production. Portugal and Greece are outliers with particularly low productivity levels. The Republic of Ireland (28,100 ECU) and Spain (22,600) however compare well with the United Kingdom (24,600 ECU) in the industrial sector and in so far as can be discerned in manufacturing. Irish manufacturing performance is, however, critically dependent on the Republic's large wave of inward investment rather than the indigenous sector, and while the externally controlled branch plants do generate quite high levels of value added per employee, not all accrues to Ireland. A significant share of value added is translated into an outflow of repatriated profits, while in some sectors it is suspected that the low rate of Corporation Tax levied on inward investors encourages the use of transfer pricing practices which boost apparent levels of value added in Ireland and generate additional repatriated profits.

Table 3.2 Productivity differentials in EU Member States by sector in 1986 (in thousands of ECU)

	NACE-CLIO sectors									
			Industrial products				*Services*			
	Agriculture, forestry and fishery products	*Industrial products*	*Fuel and power products*	*Manufactured products*	*Building and construction*	*Services*	*Market services*	*Non-market services*	*Total*	*Total adjusted for imputed output of bank services*
Germany	14.9	30.9	65.6	30.2	25.2	33.6	39.2	23.4	31.7	30.3
France	18.3	32.1	76.3	31.3	25.3	34.1	36.5	29.0	32.3	30.8
Italy	10.9	28.8	80.8	28.7	22.8	28.3	32.4	19.1	26.5	25.3
Netherlands	27.4	43.3	223.5	36.7	27.0	33.7	35.9	27.2	36.0	34.5
Belgium	23.5	34.5	98.8	32.6	26.2	29.2	32.5	21.7	30.6	29.2
Luxembourg	18.1	33.3	81.1	36.9	19.3	35.0	36.9	28.5	33.8	27.0
United Kingdom	16.5	24.6	68.1	21.4	21.1	19.4	21.0	16.0	20.9	19.9
Ireland	13.4	28.1			17.1	21.9	26.4	16.0	22.3	21.3
Denmark	22.4	27.5	97.3	25.9	25.6	28.9	36.8	19.8	28.1	27.0
Greece	5.6	10.5				11.0				9.4
Spain	8.3	22.6	73.8	21.0	17.9	22.1	25.5	14.8	20.3	19.0
Portugal	2.6	8.9	27.7	9.6	5.1	9.2	11.3	6.0	7.5	7.1

Source: elaborated from data from the REGIO database.

In the service sector Germany, Luxembourg, France and The Netherlands lead the field. With about one-quarter and one-third respectively of French levels Portugal and Greece trail (though the recent revaluation of their GDP will have reduced the recorded disparities). The United Kingdom gets the next lowest score (19,400 ECU) due to the widespread existence of low-productivity jobs in its service sector.

These indications of the significance of sectoral structures suggest that it would make sense to develop further this analysis using in particular identities that enable the impact of disaggregations of output per head to be explored. Output per head can be expressed, for example, by the following equation:

$$\frac{GDP}{WAD} = \sum_{i=1}^{n} \left(\frac{GDP_i}{EMP_i}\right)\left(\frac{EMP_i}{POP}\right)$$

where *GDP* denotes Gross Domestic Product, *EMP* denotes employment and *POP* denotes population and where *i* denotes the sectors (i = 1,2, ... *n*).

Indicators of disparities and trends in inequality

Figure 3.6 shows how inequalities between the member of the EU have changed over the last thirty years. As far as trends in standards of living are concerned, the years after 1960 can be divided into two broad phases: in the 1960s and early 1970s the general trend was for national inequalities to diminish, whereas in 1976 this earlier trend came to an end. In Figure 3.6 indicators of inequalities between the fifteen members of the EU measured in PPS show how convergence gave way to divergence but with some further convergence/stabilisation of inequalities when growth temporarily accelerated in the late 1980s. More specifically, there was strong convergence until the mid-1970s. Convergence then gave way to divergence until the early to mid-1980s depending on the indicator used. From the mid-1980s until 1990 the Member States converged. At the start of the 1990s there was a further upturn in most measures of inequality with levels close to their 1974 level: over the period from 1974 to 1992 there was no overall reduction in disparities.

The early years of convergence were also years of unprecedentedly fast economic growth, while the years of divergence or non-convergence were years of slower growth.[4] As Table 3.3 shows, convergence in the first period was the result of a scissors movement in which the weakest economies and most of the strongest moved closer to the EU average – the United Kingdom moved from from 128 to 105, West Germany from 118 to 109, and so on – while divergence was a result of a stabilisation of the relative position of Spain, Portugal and Greece and a reinforcement of the position of West Germany.

These results are not very sensitive to the indicators used. As Figure 3.6 shows, the weighted mean absolute deviations, weighted standard deviations and the Theil coefficient indicate similar trends. There are usually, however,

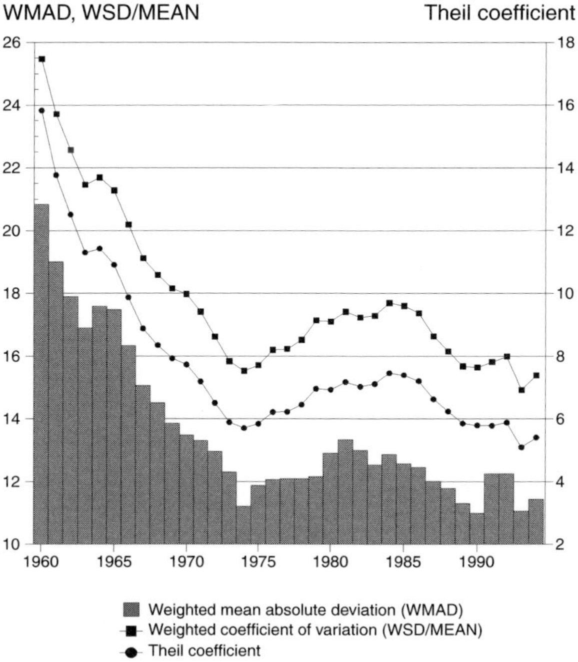

Figure 3.6 Indicators of disparities in per capita GDP in EU Member States in 1977–94.

Table 3.3 Changes in the relative economic strength of EU Member States in 1960–89

	GDP per head (in ECU: EC-12=100)				*GDP per head (in PPS: EC-12=100)*		
	1960	*1968*	*1979*	*1989*	*1960*	*1974*	*1989*
West Germany	122	119	143	129	118	109	112
France	126	134	125	115	102	109	109
Italy	80	93	76	101	91	100	104
Netherlands	96	110	129	101	119	114	102
Belgium	114	113	128	103	96	103	101
Luxembourg	158	130	131	126	131	127	130
United Kingdom	129	101	86	98	128	105	107
Ireland	60	54	55	65	62	60	67
Denmark	122	137	148	137	119	111	107
Greece	39	47	46	36	38	54	54
Spain	36	47	62	66	59	79	78
Portugal	28	31	25	31	38	54	55

Table 3.4 Trends in disparities in per capita GDP (WMAD) at current market prices and purchasing power standards between EU NUTS levels I and II regions and EU Member States in 1977–91

NUTS I	*Number of regions*	*1977*	*1978*	*1979*	*1980*	*1981*	*1982*	*1983*	*1984*	*1985*	*1986*	*1987*	*1988*	*1989*	*1990*	*1991*
Germany	11	7.8	7.6	7.5	7.5	7.5	7.6	8.0	8.2	8.4	8.5	8.8	9.1	9.6	10.0	10.3
France	8	15.6	15.8	15.3	15.5	15.9	16.9	17.7	17.2	18.1	17.7	18.5	18.8	18.7	18.6	18.6
Italy	11	22.1	22.6	21.8	22.6	22.3	22.1	20.7	20.8	21.9	22.4	22.3	22.8	23.0	22.9	23.0
Netherlands	4	11.1	10.5	10.7	11.5	13.2	13.4	13.3	13.6	13.5	10.7	8.6	9.0	8.0	7.3	6.8
Belgium	3	10.8	10.7	10.7	11.5	12.5	12.2	11.4	11.4	11.7	11.7	12.4	12.5	12.6	12.6	12.6
Luxembourg	1															0.0
United Kingdom	11	8.8	9.6	10.5	10.7	11.0	10.3	10.9	11.2	11.1	11.6	12.0	12.5	13.0	12.5	11.5
Republic of Ireland	1															0.0
Denmark	1															0.0
Greece	4			13.8	8.8	5.7	4.7	6.4	4.4	3.8	5.4	5.1	4.7	4.8	5.5	7.8
Spain	11				14.0	15.1	14.6	14.6	14.7	16.3	17.0	17.1	16.9	17.7	18.0	17.5
Portugal	3															0.0
EU	63				19.0	20.8	20.5	20.2	20.6	20.8	20.7	20.0	19.9	19.8	19.7	19.9

Table 3.4 cont.

NUTS II	*Number of regions*	*1977*	*1978*	*1979*	*1980*	*1981*	*1982*	*1983*	*1984*	*1985*	*1986*	*1987*	*1988*	*1989*	*1990*	*1991*
Germany	31				12.7	13.0	13.4	13.7	13.9	14.2	14.2	14.0	14.0	14.3	14.8	14.9
France	21/22 from 1982	15.9	16.1	15.8	15.8	15.9	17.0	17.7	17.3	18.1	18.0	18.8	18.9	18.8	18.8	18.7
Italy	20	22.5	23.0	22.0	22.6	22.4	22.1	20.7	20.9	22.0	22.6	22.5	22.9	23.1	23.1	23.1
Netherlands	9/12 from 1986	12.9	12.8	12.8	13.3	14.9	14.5	14.7	15.3	16.5	12.8	10.8	10.6	9.4	9.0	8.9
Belgium	9	13.4	12.8	12.7	13.3	13.4	13.4	12.1	13.0	13.2	12.2	12.4	12.3	12.2	12.2	12.2
Luxembourg	1															0.0
United Kingdom	34/35 from 1987	12.6		13.6		13.9			14.4			15.1	15.2	15.4	15.0	14.4
Republic of Ireland	1															0.0
Denmark	1															0.0
Greece	13			15.9	13.0	8.7	7.5	9.2	7.7	7.3	8.5	9.3	9.1	8.2	9.0	10.2
Spain	18				14.7	16.1	16.0	15.5	15.3	16.6	17.1	17.1	17.0	17.8	18.0	17.5
Portugal	5					23.2	23.8	23.2	22.6	22.0	24.8	28.3	24.4	24.2	25.5	25.5
EU	133/134 in 1982–3 and 1985/137 in 1986/ 165 in 1981 and 1984/170 from 1987				21.6	22.7	23.3	23.1	22.0	23.8	23.6	21.5	21.5	21.2	21.1	21.5

differences between weighted and unweighted indicators (Dunford 1993b). Unweighted indicators give equal weight to all geographical areas, notwithstanding the great variations in their size. Due to the scale of these differences, most of the evidence in this chapter will be centred on weighted indicators.

At an EU level it is difficult to measure trends due to discontinuities in the geographies and more importantly the absence of data for particular countries and/or regions in particular years. A far from ideal solution is to drop regions for which values are missing. The full available data show, however, that over the period as a whole there was little change in the scale of regional disparities. What do exist are longer-run data for individual countries. These series also show a clear reversal of trends in the early 1970s. The EU data, however, just cover the period since 1977, when national convergence had ended.

Ideally time series analyses should allow for the cyclical movements in economic behaviour: growth rates should be calculated for periods which run from a peak to a peak or a trough to a trough. Thus, 1989 was a peak in the economic cycle after which the European economies descended into recession; 1982 was a trough; 1979 was a peak as were 1976 and 1973. The problem is, however, that 1979 had few of the characteristics of the high point of an economic cycle, but was the end of a short oil-price shock upturn. Any rates of growth calculated from the regional time series data should therefore be treated with some caution, as the series runs from a low point in the economic cycle to an unsustainable peak. Similarly, as the timing of cycles and of troughs and peaks differed from one country to another, comparisons of regional performance should be made with great care. At the same time it is important to bear in mind that the last two turbulent decades are also decades of structural change, reflected in part in the changing relationships between the rate of profit and the rate of growth: while the years from 1960 to the early 1970s were years of high growth and high profits, the late 1970s were years of slow growth and lower profits, and the 1980s were characterised by a recovery of profits that outpaced output growth.

These qualifications must be remembered when the data for the regions of the EU are interpreted. Data on trends in inequality, set out in Table 3.4, show that at an EU level overall regional disparities changed little. At a NUTS I level the measure of disparity stood at 19.0 in 1980 and 19.9 in 1991. At a NUTS II level it did not change much after 1980, though changes in the number of regions for which data exist make it difficult to measure trends in inequality in the EU at this particular scale: for the 130 regions for which there is data for all years the index rose marginally from a value of 21.7 in 1980 to 22.5 in 1991 peaking at 24.1 in 1985.

Within Member States divergence predominated (see Table 3.4). There were two countries in which regional inequalities declined: Greece and Netherlands. In Greece there was a particularly sharp descent from 1979–81, after which disparities fluctuated around a lower level in the 1980s. In the early 1990s there was a renewed increase in disparities. In most Member States inequalities increased with particularly marked growth in Germany, France, Spain and the UK.

A disaggregation of trends in output per capita

To what extent are these changes in disparities a result of differences in changes in rates of productivity and in employment rates? Are inter-regional productivity differentials increasing or decreasing? Are variations in the employment rate increasing or decreasing? Are areas that are economically weaker comparatively unsuccessful in their attempts to redeploy people who lose their jobs as a result of structural change or to provide alternative employment possibilities for new generations entering the job market for the first time? Does interregional migration serve to adjust the changing regional supply of and demand for labour?

To answer some of these questions trends in the rates of productivity and employment were analysed. Table 3.5 records indicators of inequality at Member State, NUTS I and NUTS II levels, while Figure 3.7 plots the WMAD indicators for Member States and NUTS I areas. Figure 3.7 shows significant convergence in rates of productivity until 1987 or 1988. In so far as the same NUTS II areas are considered, there is evidence of significant reductions in disparities in productivity until 1990. Indicators centred on the standard deviation which gives particular weight to extreme values all show strong convergence from 1983 until 1990 or 1991 (see Table 3.5). The indicators plotted in Figure 3.7 also indicate, however, that disparities in the rate of employment increased.

The second feature of Figure 3.7 that warrants attention is the fact that disparities in the two constituent elements of differences in GDP per head (rates of productivity and employment) sometimes both increase as disparities in GDP per head decline and vice versa. This fact suggests that different areas are developing along different trajectories with some converging on EU rates of productivity while diverging on rates of employment and others changing in the opposite direction.

Figure 3.8 which records the trajectories of change of the twelve Member States lends some support to this notion. Of the cohesion countries, Ireland and Portugal both show significant convergence in rates of productivity but at the expense of divergence in rates of employment. Spain's overall position also improved but in different ways: until 1986 rates of productivity converged while rates of employment diverged, in 1986–90 the employment rate improved at the expense of divergence in rates of productivity, while in 1990–1 sharper convergence in rates of productivity coincided with a less pronounced loss of ground in employment rate terms.

Of the stronger economies Belgium and in particular France strengthened their position in rate of productivity terms but at the cost of a deterioration in their rates of employment. Italy, the former Federal Republic of Germany

Table 3.5 Trends in GDP per head, productivity rates and employment rates in 1980–91

		1980	*1981*	*1982*	*1983*	*1984*	*1985*	*1986*	*1987*	*1988*	*1989*	*1990*	*1991*
Member State													
GDP per head	WMAD	14.5	15.1	14.6	14.0	14.3	13.9	13.8	13.4	13.1	12.7	12.3	13.3
GDP per head	CV	19.0	19.4	19.1	19.1	19.5	19.3	19.1	18.4	18.1	17.6	17.5	17.6
GDP per person employed	WMAD	12.9	12.4	11.4	10.6	11.1	10.4	9.7	9.5	10.1	10.7	11.4	13.7
GDP per person employed	CV	15.4	15.3	14.8	14.5	14.9	14.5	13.9	13.7	14.0	14.3	14.6	16.7
Employment rate	WMAD	7.9	7.6	7.3	7.1	7.7	8.3	8.4	8.4	8.6	8.8	8.7	10.5
Employment rate	CV	10.1	10.1	10.1	10.0	11.2	11.9	12.0	11.5	11.2	11.0	10.4	12.5
NUTS 1													
GDP per head	WMAD	19.0	20.8	20.5	20.2	20.6	20.8	20.7	20.0	19.9	19.8	19.7	19.9
GDP per head	CV	24.4	26.5	26.4	26.3	26.6	26.9	26.7	26.3	26.3	26.1	26.1	26.2
GDP per person employed	WMAD	20.2	20.4	19.8	19.5	19.7	19.4	18.3	17.7	17.6	17.9	18.2	20.1
GDP per person employed	CV	45.4	44.9	44.8	46.3	46.0	44.3	41.9	40.6	38.3	37.7	37.0	37.4
Employment rate	WMAD	13.1	13.6	13.5	13.5	14.2	14.6	14.7	14.6	14.5	14.2	13.9	15.2
Employment rate	CV	18.3	18.4	18.4	18.4	19.2	19.5	19.4	19.1	18.8	18.5	18.0	19.3
NUTS 2													
GDP per head	WMAD	21.6	22.7	23.3	23.1	22.0	23.8	23.6	21.5	21.5	21.2	21.1	21.5
GDP per head	CV	27.4	28.8	29.8	29.8	28.8	30.7	30.1	28.4	28.4	28.1	28.1	28.3
GDP per person employed	WMAD	28.3	27.2	28.7	29.7	26.9	28.0	26.2	22.8	22.4	22.1	21.4	22.8
GDP per person employed	CV	79.5	74.1	80.2	86.2	78.4	78.5	70.6	61.1	56.5	52.7	46.3	43.2
Employment rate	WMAD	15.3	14.9	16.0	16.0	15.3	16.6	16.7	15.5	15.0	14.8	14.6	15.9
Employment rate	CV	23.1	22.3	23.6	23.6	22.9	23.5	23.4	22.2	21.6	21.4	20.8	22.0
Number		133	165	134	134	166	134	137	170	170	170	170	167

Table 3.5 cont.

		1980	*1981*	*1982*	*1983*	*1984*	*1985*	*1986*	*1987*	*1988*	*1989*	*1990*	*1991*
NUTS 2													
GDP per head	WMAD	21.7	23.9	23.5	23.3	23.7	24.1	23.9	23.3	23.3	22.9	22.7	22.5
GDP per head	CV	27.6	30.1	30.0	30.1	30.5	31.0	30.4	29.9	29.8	29.5	29.6	29.5
GDP per person employed	WMAD	28.2	28.7	28.8	29.8	29.1	28.1	26.4	25.1	24.4	23.6	22.4	21.4
GDP per person employed	CV	79.7	78.3	80.5	86.6	83.4	78.9	71.2	65.9	60.5	56.0	48.9	43.3
Employment rate	WMAD	15.3	15.9	16.0	16.0	16.3	16.6	16.8	16.3	15.4	15.0	14.8	15.3
Employment rate	CV	23.2	23.5	23.7	23.7	23.7	23.5	23.4	22.7	21.7	21.4	20.9	21.1
Number		130	130	130	130	130	130	130	130	130	130	130	130
NUTS 2													
GDP per head	WMAD		22.8			22.2			21.8	21.7	21.5	21.4	21.6
GDP per head	CV		29.0			29.0			28.6	28.6	28.4	28.4	28.4
GDP per person employed	WMAD		27.2			27.1			23.0	22.5	22.3	21.5	22.9
GDP per person employed	CV		74.3			78.7			61.6	56.9	53.1	46.7	43.3
Employment rate	WMAD		14.9			15.2			15.5	15.1	14.9	14.6	16.0
Employment rate	CV		22.4			22.9			22.2	21.6	21.5	21.0	22.1
Number			162			162			162	162	162	162	162

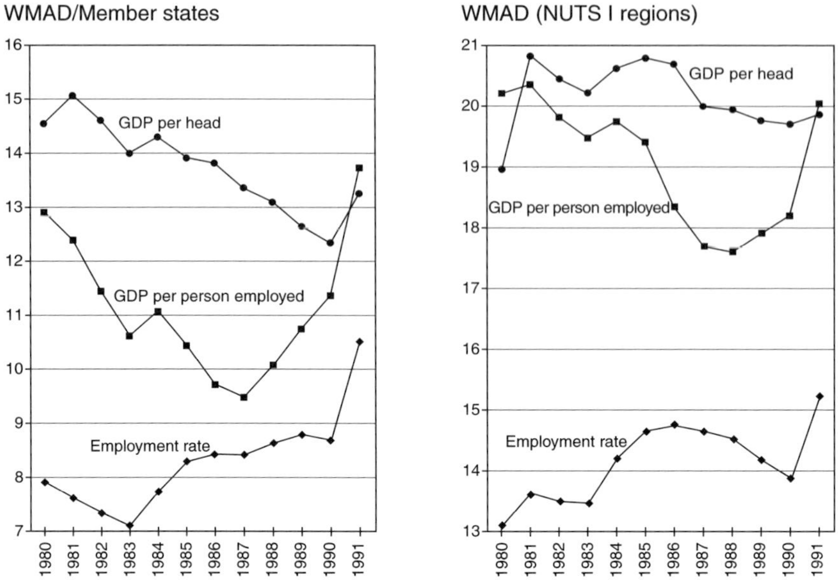

Figure 3.7 Trends in inequality in productivity and employment rates in 1980–81.

and to a lesser extent Denmark went through two phases returning in 1991 to a relative position close to the one occupied in 1980. In the case of the United Kingdom in 1987–91 an improved employment rate was achieved at the expense of a deterioration in its rate of productivity compared with the European average.

There are few signs of a virtuous cycle in which relative rates of productivity and employment increase. Instead there is some evidence of a trade-off with the achievement of gains in relative productivity rate the expense of employment and vice versa.

Conclusion and further research questions

The data on GDP per head provide a relief map of economic development. The variations they indicate are a result of several factors: differences in productivity levels, differences in the share of an area's population that is employed and differences in the prices an area's output commands on international and interregional markets (which depend on the inequalities in prices and exchange rates built into regional trade structures). A next step, therefore, is to identify the respective contributions of these factors. Clearly unemployment and variations in activity rates and dependency ratios play a major role through their impact on the mobilisation and use of the human potential of Europe's regions. The role of price, wage and exchange rate structures and their relation with the distribution of economic and political power are more difficult to measure but are at the heart of theories of unequal exchange, while productivity differentials are rooted in regional specialisation, production technologies and social relations which are the focus of theories of regulation. Theories that emphasise differences in price structures and in physical productivities are both relevant. An assessment of the relative importance of these two factors would, however, allow an evaluation of their relative significance.

The second task, however, is to consider why regional rates of growth have varied and what has made some regions more successful than others. The map of inequality is not simply reproduced. Its shape and intensity have changed, as networked metropolitan economies have reinforced their position, as formerly dominant economies have undergone relative decline and as new areas of growth have emerged. To answer this question, there is a need to

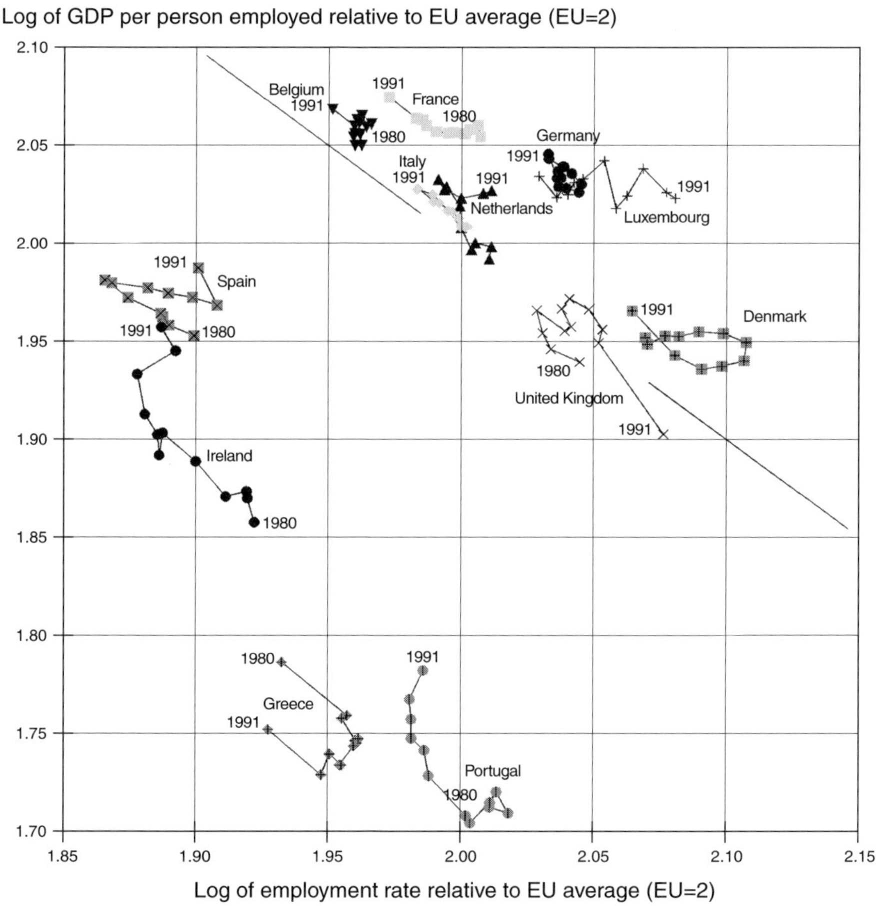

Figure 3.8 Trajectories in productivity and employment rates in Member States in 1980–91.

go behind differences in prices, productivities and resource mobilisation and to find out why they change, and there is a need to explore the role factors such as size, resource endowment, economic potential, centre–periphery relations and economic structure identified at the end of the last section. As an important first step attempts could be made to connect the structure of employment by oocupation and industry with the wage distribution to see to what extent the changing employment profiles of Europe's regions explain their relative performance. At the same time the fact that some regional economies are more successful than and stand out from the national territories of which they are a part – as in the case of the areas of the Third Italy or metropolitan cores – raise important questions about the role of their specialisations, their modes of productive organisation and their modes of regulation in shaping economic growth and development.

The third task is to explore the implications of the end of convergence and of its reversal in some cases. This reversal is inconsistent with the expectations of orthodox trade and regional growth theories, yet at present it is these views that are most influential and which underpin forecasts of the impact of closer integration: in the Cecchini Report, for example, it was argued that 'recent developments in trade theory and past experience with the removal of intra-EU tariff barriers indicate that redistributive effects in the wake of freer trade need not be excessive' (Cecchini *et al.* 1988: 105). The orthodox view is, of course, that if the expected consequences do not occur it is because markets are not allowed to work. What I would argue, however, is that the source of this reversal lies in a change in the model of development. In particular, there was a crisis in the model of accumulation (Fordism) which was at the root of western growth in the post-war golden age: rates of growth slowed down, and unemployment increased, as did inflation rates. At this point two of the mechanisms which had underpinned convergence ceased to operate: an earlier wave of productive investments in less developed areas came to an end, while the rise in unemployment in developed areas closed off the opportunities for emigration. At the same time there was an increase in conflict and competition between areas. What resulted was the adoption of defensive strategies of adjustment: in order to reduce its balance of payments deficit each nation sought larger wage reductions than its rivals, and to improve its capital account each nation introduced yet higher interest rates to attract international deposits (see Lipietz 1989). To the earlier supply-side problems were accordingly added a stagnation of internal and of world demand and the demand-side difficulties of the 'double-sided' crisis of Fordism. A way out of the current economic crisis in Europe would, in these circumstances, depend upon the identification of non-deflationary modes of economic adjustment and a convergence of Europe's regional economies. The Community itself is situated, however, in a wider Europe. Around it lie a series of zones. An inner circle of EFTA countries which are as if not more wealthy and socially advanced than Germany. To the south and east of the Community the situation is different. In the east there is a series of countries at very different levels of development, in some of which the collapse of Communism and the transition to capitalism carries with it the risk of extreme social polarisation. To the south a series of non-EU Mediterranean countries are confronted with deep economic, ecological and demographic crises. With the unification of Germany and the consequent devastation of the economy of the former German Democratic Republic the relationship between inequality and Europe's slow growth has assumed even more importance for Europe's future.

Notes

1 This chapter is a revised version of a paper published in the proceedings of a CEIES conference held in Rennes in January 1998 (see Dunford 1999). In part it updates and develops papers published in *Regional Studies* (Dunford 1993b, 1996). I would like to thank Herbert Allgeier for his detailed questions asked when he translated the CEIES conference paper into German. These questions helped clarify the argument. Any remaining errors are the responsibility of the author.

2 The data sets, which are large, were transferred into a relational database management system (INGRES/ORACLE) and the results were produced via the use of the SQL database query language.

3 Leborgne and Lipietz make a related distinction between quantitative and qualitative growth. Table 3.6 shows that in 1967–80 the share of Western Europe (the EU and EFTA) in world GDP fell significantly in volume and by a small amount in value terms. In the case of Japan, volume increased, and value increased even more sharply, while in Latin America an increase in volume was associated with a reduction in value. Two modes of integration can be distinguished: one which aims at the production of high-quality and high-value output, and one which aims at quantitative increases in the output of goods and services that command low prices on world markets. In relation to these paths Europe finds itself between Japan and Latin America (see Leborgne and Lipietz 1990: 5). The same differences are also found within Western Europe. In volume terms all the economies listed lost shares of world output except Southern Europe (Spain, Portugal and Greece). But just as in the case of Latin America the economies of Southern Europe

Table 3.6 The share of different areas in world output

	The share of world GDP			
	At purchasing power standards		At current exchange rates	
	1967	*1986*	*1967*	*1986*
United States	25.8	21.4	33.8	26.6
Western Europe	26.3	22.9	26.4	26.2
West Germany	5.0	4.2	5.1	5.7
France	3.8	3.4	4.9	4.6
Italy	3.9	3.5	3.6	3.8
Britain	4.8	3.5	4.8	3.6
Southern Europe	3.8	4.2	2.8	2.9
Japan	5.8	7.7	5.2	12.4
Latin America	6.9	7.9	5.1	4.6

increase their share more in volume than in value. West Germany and Italy lose in volume but gain in value. What emerges is an image of a northern Europe that is stagnant overall but with some zones whose position was strengthened in value terms, and a southern Europe where growth was rapid but where, with the exception of (northern) Italy, growth depended on increases in the volume of output rather than on increases in the value goods and services could command on global markets.

4 In several recent studies (see, for example, Dunford and Perrons 1993) it has been argued that while growth provided the resources required to finance the development of less developed countries, a causal relationship also ran in the opposite direction: the convergence of national (and regional) economies reinforced growth through its impact on the mobilisation of human resources, on the one hand, and increases in incomes in less developed areas, the widening of markets and the creation of outlets for the goods and services produced in the centre, on the other. After 1976, on the other hand, as neo-liberal doctrines started to hold sway, divergence occurred. Similar reversals occurred with respect to wage variations – where the change was called the great U-turn by Harrison and Bluestone (1988) and in unemployment disparities. Divergence and greater inequality were contributors to slower growth.

References

Castells, M. (1985) 'High-technology, space and society', in M. Castells (ed.) *High Technology, Space and Society*, Beverly Hills, CA: Sage.

Cecchini, P., Catinat, M. and Jacquemin, A.P. (1988) *1992: The European Challenge, 1992: The Benefits of a Single Market*, Cecchini Report, Aldershot: Wildwood House.

Cheshire, P. (1990) 'Explaining the recent performance of the European Community's major urban regions', *Urban Studies* 27, 3: 311–33.

Cheshire, P. (1991) 'Changing influences on the development of the European Community's major urban regions between 1971 and 1988', *Bulletin de la Société Belge d'Etudes Géographiques* 1, 1: 7–28.

Cutler, T., Haslam, C., Williams, J. and Williams, K. (1989) *1992 – The Struggle for Europe: A Critical Evaluation of the European Community*, Oxford: Berg.

Dunford, M. (1993a) 'Industrial decline and socio-spatial polarisation in a "market-led" society: the case of Britain', in the Proceedings of the *26th Deutscher Soziologentag on Lebensverhältnisse und soziale Konflikte im neuen Europa*, in press.

Dunford, M. (1993b) 'Regional disparities in the European Community: evidence from the REGIO databank', *Regional Studies* 27, 8: 727–43.

Dunford, M. (1996) 'Disparities in employment, productivity and output in the EU: the roles of labour market governance and welfare regimes', *Regional Studies* 30, 4: 339–57.

Dunford, M. (1999) 'Regional disparities through the lens of official statistics', in *Regional Information Serving Regional Policy in Europe*, Proceedings of the fourth CEIES seminar, Rennes, 30–31 January 1998, Luxembourg: Office for Official Publications of the European Communities, pp. 51–89.

Dunford, M. and Perrons, D. (1993) 'Regional inequality and economic growth in contemporary Europe', paper presented at the joint meeting of the ESRC Single European Market Initiative Group and European Policy Unit of the European University Institute at Villa Schifanoia, Florence, Italy, on 25–27 February 1993.

Harrison, B. and Bluestone, B. (1988) *The Great U-turn: Corporate Restructuring and the Polarizing of America*, New York: Basic Books.

Krätke, S. (1992) 'Cities in transformation', paper presented at the Spetses European workshop on Policies and institutions for the development of cities and regions in the single European market, held in Spetses, Greece, on 24–26 September 1992.

Leborgne, D. and Lipietz, A. (1990) 'Avoiding two-tiers Europe', *Labour and Society* 15, 2, April.

Lipietz, A. (1989) 'The debt problem, European integration and the new phase of the world crisis', *New Left Review* November–December, 178: 37–50.

Mayer, M. (1992) 'The shifting local political system in European cities', in M. Dunford, and G. Kafkalas (eds) *Cities and Regions in the New Europe: The Global–Local Interplay and Spatial Development Strategies*, London: Belhaven.

Statistical Office of the European Communities (EUROSTAT) (1989) *Regions: Nomenclature of Territorial Units for Statistics*, Luxembourg: EUROSTAT.

Statistical Office of the European Communities (EUROSTAT) (1991) *REGIO: Regional Data Bank Description of Contents*, Luxembourg: EUROSTAT.

4 Urban change in an integrating Europe[1]

Paul Cheshire and F.E. Ian Hamilton

Introduction

This chapter is more about urban change in Europe than it is about the impact of integration. The direct effects of integration are a significant force operating on Europe's cities but only one among many. The evidence from Western Europe (Cheshire and Carbonaro 1996; Cheshire and Magrini 1998) is that it is one of the less important. In the context of Central and Eastern European (CEE) cities it may be more important, at least in the short term. That is because the forces generated by integration have been at work in Western European cities since the 1950s but have quite suddenly arrived in those of the CEE. Albeit a special case, Berlin exemplifies how powerful these pent-up forces were. Led by the public sector it exhibits booming service sector expansion and downtown construction with sudden decentralisation and loss of manufacturing jobs to the hinterland now represented by Brandenburg. Change which has been bottled up over a protracted period can have substantial impacts in the short term when circumstances change.

Apart from integration there are a number of forces acting on Europe's cities. Some of these forces are changing their internal structures. Others influence the relative growth of different cities or in other ways operate at an inter-urban scale. These latter are changing the structure of Europe's urban system. Among them is, of course, the force of European integration itself.

An issue in relation to intra-urban change is sharpening patterns of residential segregation and polarisation associated, it is argued, with increasing social exclusion in cities (OECD 1998). There appears to be a strong link between changing patterns of income distribution in the wider society and changes in the intensity of social segregation in cities. Increasing evidence is emerging of how housing markets (even housing systems such as social housing (Maclennan 1993)) articulate in urban space the overall income distribution of urban society. There are locationally fixed amenities within cities (such as parks, views, good/bad schools) which command a price, in the sense that the value of access to them is capitalised into house/land prices.[2] The demand for such locationally fixed amenities is normal – households consume more of them as they become richer (Cheshire and Sheppard 1998). But in an urban context it is only possible for a household that becomes richer to consume more of such amenities if it moves closer to them. Thus, if income becomes more unequally distributed, richer households concentrate in neighbourhoods in which amenities (and richer households) are more abundant. Since the rich can always consume more of any good than the poor, the poor are squeezed into less amenity-rich neighbourhoods.

If one of the neighbourhood amenities which commands a price is simply a greater concentration of affluent households, then this spatial articulation of the distribution of household income in terms of residential segregation will be self-reinforcing. If the distribution of income in the 'society' which constitutes any city becomes more unequal then – since all residents are located somewhere – the physical intensity of residential segregation will become greater. Locationally fixed amenities are, by definition, the purest form of positional goods. If a family has to live within its catchment area to get its children to the best school in town and places are limited, then what determines whose children go to the school is not the level of income of the richest group in the city but which families are in the richest group. If the rich become richer compared to the poor, then this search for consumption of locationally fixed amenities and public goods simply means that the rich neighbourhoods become more exclusively rich.

Over the past fifteen years observers have been remarking on the widening income inequality in western societies (Adams *et al.* 1988; OECD 1993; Joseph Rowntree Foundation 1995) while other observers have been remarking on increasing social polarisation and social exclusion in Western cities (OECD 1998). But observers have not linked these changes when they are simply different aspects of the same process. Now that incomes are becoming more unequal in the countries of Central and Eastern Europe it must be expected that social polarisation will rapidly sharpen in CEE cities. Indeed, research summarised by the EBRD (1997) demonstrates the rise in poverty and income inequalities in all post-Communist states, although patterns and trends are differentiated internationally. The findings are further supported by data collected in household budget surveys by UNICEF (1997). These show divergent trends amongst three groups of countries. In the Czech and Slovak Republics, Hungary and Slovenia, where inequality was historically very low, poverty and inequality have risen, but only moderately. In Poland, Romania and the Baltic states, where it was somewhat higher at the start of the transition, inequality has since increased to levels at or above the OECD average. In Bulgaria, Russia and other CIS, however, inequality has risen dramatically to reach levels common in the more unequal developing countries.[3] The reasons are several, but lie essentially in the differential success of transition policies in achieving economic restructuring and transformation (Hamilton 1995; Hamilton 1999), unemployment trends, ethnic-related social exclusion (associated in part with immigration) and the presence or absence of welfare safety nets. While cities are becoming the main arenas for the development of inequalities, however, major interregional differences are also emerging between cities in the western areas of CEE where restructuring is faster and those in less developed more rural regions further east where poverty and unemployment are more serious problems.

The effects of integration on the European urban system are twofold. There are direct effects – some regions/cities gain relatively while some lose. The conventional view (and conventional views are not always wrong) is that these direct effects favour advanced urban economies in the core of Europe at the expense of backward urban economies on the periphery. The increasing integration of East and West Europe has shifted the 'core' towards the East. But still it is doubtful that there are many regions within the CEE that will be a part of the new extended core – at least in the medium term. Cities on the western fringes of the CEE, such as Bratislava or Prague, have benefited and will continue to do so. But part of that benefit reflects substantially lower costs. This cost advantage is likely to fall quite rapidly with EU entry. The CEE has been subject to a double effect, moreover. There is not only the impact of the current impact of integration with the West. There is also the impact of the disintegration of the previous period of integration with COMECON. Some cities – including Baltic ports in general but Gdansk as a shipbuilding centre in particular – grew in response to that previous wave of integration and are likely to lose from the current period of integration with Western Europe.

There are also indirect effects of integration. Integration generates the incentive for territorial competition;[4] that is a process through which groups, acting on behalf of regional or sub-regional economies (typically a city-region's), seek to promote it as a location for economic activity either implicitly or explicitly in competition with other areas. This competitive activity is often addressed to the attraction of mobile investment, sometimes with discrimination between more and less desirable activities. But it may equally be concerned with enhancing the share of existing local businesses in the markets they serve and generating new businesses and markets. There is evidence that territorially competitive policies do have some – albeit restricted – impact on differential rates of urban growth (Cheshire and Gordon 1998). In this sense the resulting patterns of urban change produced by territorially competitive policies can be thought of as indirect effects of European integration.

The analysis, however, has to be delimited somewhere and this chapter focuses on two other aspects of change within the European urban system. The first is in terms of processes of decentralisation and centralisation. Are cities likely to be increasingly at higher densities, with activity increasingly focused on the historic central city? Or are they decentralising, with an increasing degree of polycentricity and ex-urban residential 'villages', even ex-urban centres of economic activity, likely to become the norm? Will these processes of change make the cities of the CEE countries more or less like those of Western Europe?

In analysing these processes it will be argued that the built form of cities reflects underlying economic, social and demographic changes, articulated through markets and prices. Ultimately these disembodied, abstract forces determine what cities are like to live in; they determine our everyday experience of cities and the demands we make on cars or mass transit systems, and on land for urban purposes.

The period from the late 1950s until about 1980 in Western countries was one of increasing urban decentralisation. This led some observers to predict the virtual end of traditional cities or disurbanisation (see Champion 1989). One argument of this chapter is that the balance of forces causing such apparently regular patterns of decentralisation changed during the 1980s and that therefore more varied patterns of urban change should be expected in Europe in the future. Far from converging on a common pattern of decentralisation, this analysis suggests we should expect – indeed are beginning to observe – increasing variation between cities. Some cities (with identifiable characteristics) are likely to continue to decentralise and even decline. Other cities will experience new phases of centralisation and growth.

As was shown by French and Hamilton (1979) the main determinant of urban growth patterns in the CEE countries was centrally planned industrial growth. Those economic forces which led to such apparently unstoppable and remorseless processes of urban decentralisation in the West were dammed up for forty-five years. They are only now being released. As they begin to produce change in CEE cities, those cities may become more like those of the West just as the cities of the West themselves are becoming more varied.

The second aspect of urban change that is addressed is in terms of levels of economic activity: convergence and divergence. Many economists will be familiar with the recent literature on convergence of growth rates between countries and regions, (for example, Barro 1991; Barro and Sala-i-Martin 1992; Sala-i-Martin 1994). This chapter briefly examines this question at the level of urban regions. Do poorer urban areas have, on average, faster rates of growth than richer ones with the consequent implication of convergence of per capita incomes across Europe's urban system? Or are there instead (or in addition) mechanisms which systematically generate divergence? It should be obvious that the answer to these two implied questions: Are Europe's cities continuing (inevitably) to decentralise? Are Europe's cities tending (inevitably) to become more equal in terms of mean per capita incomes? Have fundamental and highly significant policy implications.

Some preliminaries

Before starting to attempt to answer these questions two preliminary points need to be clarified. The first relates to the question of definition. What is a city? As has been argued at much greater length elsewhere (e.g. Cheshire and Hay 1989), it is only possible to analyse cities empirically on the basis of a coherent definition. This is true even for individual cities: very different apparent patterns of residential segregation, mean per capita income, unemployment rates, population change or patterns of decentralisation will emerge, depending on how narrowly the city boundaries are drawn. This problem is multiplied manyfold if the analysis is of several or many cities, and even more if the analysis extends across countries – as any analysis of Europe's urban system necessarily must. Even such a simple question as whether there is population loss or gain from a particular city may have a different answer depending on whether it is broadly defined to include its suburban hinterland, or narrowly defined as the historic core city (as many cities are defined for political or administrative purposes).

In some countries, such as Germany or France, this problem is comparatively minor since there is a long-standing and relatively consistent definition of the 'city'. Even within single European countries definitions can vary wildly, however. The administrative cities of London, Brussels or Barcelona contain only small (in London's case, negligible[5]) fractions of the population of the built-up area. The administrative areas of Birmingham or Madrid are not much smaller than the built-up areas of those cities. In contrast, the administrative area of Zaragoza greatly exceeds the extent of Zaragoza's area of continuous urbanisation containing, as it does, several thousands of hectares of near desert. Thus for analytical studies of cities, and especially for an internationally comparative study, it is essential to have a consistent definition of 'city' and one which includes both the historic core city and the suburban residential hinterland. The definition adopted here relates to Functional Urban Regions (FURs). These are defined in terms of areas containing a concentration of jobs (the 'core') and then those areas from which more people commute to work in the core in question than to some other core (the 'hinterlands'). The data relate in most cases to the FURs defined in Hall and Hay (1980), although some very minor adjustments have been made (see Cheshire and Hay 1989). It unfortunately follows from this that the empirical analysis has largely to be confined to the city regions of Western Europe since it is only for those that data are available. Wherever possible, however, comparisons are drawn with developments in the CEE.

The second preliminary is that underlying the analysis is a conceptualisation of cities in terms of their economic and social functions. Traditional planners or urbanists tend to analyse cities as artefacts of design or intention, reflecting design norms of particular cultures or policy goals. Underlying the present analysis is the view that the overall characteristics and form of cities, if not the details of their design, are determined primarily by their functions and by economic forces. The economic forces reflect social and technical conditions as those determine, for example, relative prices and the volume of output. Economic forces are constrained by policy decisions and institutional factors as well as by natural limits on supply. The overall supply of land for urban purposes, for example, is determined by the laws of geometry, interacting with the costs of transport, the natural constraints imposed by topography and technology and also by land use planning policies which generate a non-price constraint on urban land supply. Together, these various factors determine the supply of land which, in interaction with demand, determines its price. Prices then influence the decision-making of all private – even public – actors. Prices thus influence densities of development, rates of renewal and conversion as well as the growth of one city compared to another. Such influences were tightly controlled but not entirely suppressed under the influence of Soviet-style central planning. But they did not disappear and their continued influence was one of the reasons underlying the collapse of the Soviet system.

In the context of changes in urban form and decentralisation it is helpful to start with how the functions of cities are changing. Historically, before the industrial revolution, cities served four primary functions. They were administrative, commercial and cultural centres and they acted as mechanisms of territorial and personal defence. This last function, identified with the walled city, in turn imposed a constraint on urban land supply and led to higher densities. In countries such as Britain, where a strong nation–state emerged early and which enjoyed the natural protection of being an island, city walls disappeared soonest, leading to a tradition of low density living. London had extensive and wealthy suburbs such as Highgate from the sixteenth century. Low density living is even more notable in the United States where cities effectively never had walls.

The industrial revolution radically transformed the functions of cities. Before then, with the exception of specialised, high value goods needing highly skilled labour, most goods had been produced where they were consumed (building materials, household goods or agricultural machinery, for example) and the great majority of the population was tied by low productivity peasant agriculture to the countryside. The industrial revolution was associated with a rapid lowering of the real cost of transport and, via the factory system, increasing economies of scale. This combination of changes transformed the functions of cities by making them pre-eminently the centres of goods production and distribution. The business of cities ceased so much to be business and became the making and distribution of things.

Various writers, for example Anas and Moses (1978) or more recently and in a much more formal way, Krugman (1991) have shown how falling transport costs for long-distance freight permitted the emergence of high density industrial cities. The canals and then railways of the eighteenth and nineteenth centuries produced very substantial reductions in the cost of shipping goods over long distances. This consequently extended the market that could be served from a single city or factory. But the early innovations had no effect of the costs of short haul transport. This continued to be by horse and cart,[6] by porters or on foot. Access points to the new transport systems were confined to a limited number of specific points – goods stations, wharves or ports – and so there was a strong incentive for a dense clustering of producers close to the access points. The enlarged markets that could be reached in turn allowed the exploitation of, and generated an incentive to extend, economies of scale. This provided the economic catalyst for the growth of the factory system and of mass employment in the new industrial cities. The large-scale population movement from the countryside to the cities this generated is well documented. In the words of Marx and Engels (1848) it 'freed the mass of the people from the idiocy of rural life'. Industrialisation was accompanied by 'de-agriculturalisation'.

In this system the housing of workers – who walked to work – was tightly packed around the employment centres. During the later nineteenth and early twentieth centuries residential suburbanisation was made possible by the development of public transport; first, horse trams and omnibuses, later suburban railways, metro systems and motor vehicles. Cities, however, remained strongly monocentric and employment remained focused on the access points to the railway system. Early lorries were for deliveries. They substituted for horses and carts, not goods trains. The key change was the development of modern highways and larger and reliable long-distance lorries. These did not emerge until the 1950s first in the US and a little later in Germany, the Benelux countries and Britain.

This development was catalytic because, within a very short space of time in Western Europe,[7] goods production became oriented to the road network for long haul as well as short haul transport. And not only was access to this network no longer restricted to a limited number of points – stations – but diffused throughout the network but the change in transport mode imposed a sharply increase congestion penalty on traditional, central factory locations. The cost advantage of the new system was not that it reduced the cost per kilometre of long haul freight[8] but that it eliminated two sets of transhipment costs as Figure 4.1 shows.

That it was the change in the structure of transport costs and technology which was the catalytic cause of the rapid decentralisation of goods production and bulk distribution (including in its later phase bulk retail) is confirmed by the observation that land costs had always been lower in decentralised locations. So, too, had labour costs. Labour had also been more flexible and less unionised in decentralised locations. Indeed, the process of urban decentralisation that began in the late 1950s significantly reduced the cost differential for labour and land between central city and ex-urban locations.

Thus in the late 1950s and early 1960s in Western Europe,[9] as rural–urban

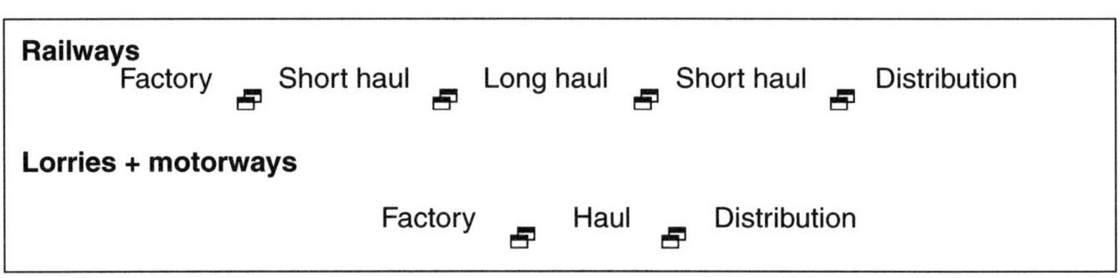

Note: = transhipment cost

Figure 4.1 Transhipment costs in alternative transport technologies.

migration was falling in absolute terms, there began a new process of urban–rural migration associated with the decentralisation of employment.[10] This interacted with rising incomes and falling real costs of commuting. These, coupled with the 'normal' family structure of a single earner and a larger number of children, encouraged residential suburbanisation in search of more space. Space was relatively cheaper in suburban locations as was access to green environmental goods. With only one worker per household and a stable labour market, access to urban labour markets was less critical. As goods transport transferred to lorries and motorways, and workers became increasingly dependent on cars for commuting, so this reinforced the demand for land in activities which handled good in bulk. Ratios of site to building areas increased.

This process of decentralisation of both jobs and people affecting the cities of northwestern Europe was further reinforced by the growth of air travel and air freight, and containerisation and RoRo ferries. Airports are land-extensive and cause environmental problems and therefore tended to be located on the urban fringe. Containerisation and roll-on roll-off ferries meant that port cities in a very short period of time lost their traditional locational attraction as sites for processing industries. A container could be unpacked anywhere that could be conveniently reached by lorry.

These forces causing decentralisation of both industrial jobs and workforces in the industrial economies of Western Europe in turn interacted with the process of economic transformation; that is the decline of employment in industry and the growth of service sector employment. Although the bulwark of state planning in socialist economies greatly retarded it there, this economic transformation (sometimes called 'deindustrialisation') has been a universal and predictable (see Rowthorne and Wells 1987) aspect of mature market-based industrial economies. It is associated with a number of interrelated changes. Production has been transferring to low labour cost, newly industrialising countries; there has been rapidly rising labour productivity in manufacturing (the change in composition is significantly less marked in output than it is in employment); and activities have been progressively reclassified, as large integrated plants including a range of functions (such as transport, marketing or administration) have given way to 'outsourcing' and more specialised units, each function in cost-minimising locations.

The pattern of decentralisation that this produced in Western Europe's larger cities is demonstrated in Tables 4.1 and 4.2. The data relate to the distribution of population between the city cores and hinterlands of all the large Functional Urban Regions (FURs)[11] in the EU of 12 for each decade from the 1950s to the 1980s. FURs are classified according to the relative rates of population growth in their cores and hinterlands, and in the urban region as a whole, into eight categories or 'stages'. Four of these stages – defined in Table 4.1 footnotes – relate to centralisation and four to decentralisation with the stages arrayed from left to right according to the extent of decentralisation. The final two columns summarise the data in a slightly

Table 4.1 The southward movement of decentralisation: all FURs over 330,000: frequency distribution (%)

	Stages of development of urban region[a]								*Urban cores*	
	1	*2*	*3*	*4*	*5*	*6*	*7*	*8*	*gaining*	*losing*
	Centralisation				*Decentralisation*				*2+3+4+5*	*1+6+7+8*
1951–1961										
N.W. Europe[b]	1	10	8	**37**	32	11	0	1	87	13
France + N. Italy	0	12	**48**	35	5	0	0	0	100	0
S. Europe[c]	0	**72**	7	22	0	0	0	0	100	0
1961–1971										
N.W. Europe[b]	1	1	3	14	**47**	26	5	1	65	35
France + N. Italy	0	1	18	**63**	17	0	0	0	100	0
S. Europe[c]	0	**67**	13	13	2	0	0	4	96	4
1971–75										
N.W. Europe[b]	7	0	2	10	26	**42**	12	1	38	62
France + N. Italy	0	1	5	35	**28**	27	3	0	70	30
S. Europe[c]	0	4	11	**46**	33	7	0	0	93	7

Table 4.1 cont.

	Stages of development of urban region[a]								*Urban cores*	
	1	*2*	*3*	*4*	*5*	*6*	*7*	*8*	*gaining*	*losing*
	Centralisation				*Decentralisation*				*2+3+4+5*	*1+6+7+8*
1975–81										
N.W. Europe[b]	15	0	1	3	17	**33**	27	4	22	78
France + N. Italy	3	1	1	7	30	**42**	12	3	40	60
S. Europe[c]	0	2	15	**48**	17	15	0	2	83	17
1981–91										
N.W. Europe	6	0	3	15	**30**	28	10	10	47	53
France + N. Italy	0	2	0	8	38	**32**	12	8	48	52
S. Europe	2	9	14	14	**19**	33	5	5	56	44

Notes: Cell indicated in **bold** contains the median.

a Stage 1 Core, hinterland and FUR losing; core rate of loss less than hinterland
Stage 2 Core gaining; hinterland and FUR losing
Stage 3 Core and FUR gaining; hinterland losing
Stage 4 All gaining; rate of core growth greater than that of hinterland
Stage 5 All gaining; rate of core growth less than that of hinterland
Stage 6 Core losing; hinterland and FUR gaining
Stage 7 Core and FUR losing; hinterland gaining
Stage 8 Core, hinterland and FUR losing; core rate of loss greater than hinterland.

b N.W. Europe = German Federal Republic, Benelux, Denmark and UK

c S. Europe = Italy south of Rome, Greece, Portugal and Spain

Table 4.2 Stages of development of FURS over ⅓ million population 1971–81 and 1981–91: frequency distribution for larger countries

			*Stages of development of urban region**										
			1 *Centralisation*	*2*	*3*	*4*	*5* *Decentralisation*	*6*	*7*	*8*	*Total*	*Urban cores* *gaining*	*losing*
Benelux	1971–81	n	0	0	0	0	10	**13**	1	1	25	10	15
NL+B		%	0	0	0	0	40	**52**	4	4		40	60
(not GdL)	1981–91	n	1	0	3	4	**8**	8	1	0	25	15	10
		%	4	0	12	16	**32**	32	4	0		60	40
FDR	1971–81	n	2	0	0	5	6	**25**	5	8	51	11	40
		%	3.9	0	0	9.8	11.8	**49.0**	9.8	15.7		22	78
	1981–91	n	2	0	0	7	**26**	14	0	2	51	33	18
		%	3.9	0	0	13.7	**51.0**	27.5	0	3.9		65	35
France	1971–81	n	0	1	1	6	**23**	6	1	0	38	31	7
		%	0	2.6	2.6	15.8	**60.5**	15.8	2.6	0		82	18
	1981–91	n	0	0	0	4	**23**	8	1	2	38	27	11
		%	0	0	0	10.5	**60.5**	21.0	2.6	5.3		71	29
Italy	1971–81	n	0	1	0	4	11	**15**	5	0	36	16	20
		%	0	2.8	0	11.1	30.6	**41.7**	13.9	0		44	56
	1981–91	n	0	1	1	3	1	**21**	6	3	36	6	30
		%	0	2.8	2.8	8.3	2.8	**58.6**	16.7	8.3		83	17
Spain	1971–81	n	0	4	14	**19**	4	0	0	0	41	41	0
		%	0	9.8	34.1	**46.3**	9.8	0	0	0		100	0
	1981–91	n	1	6	8	**6**	7	9	2	2	41	27	14
		%	2.4	14.6	19.5	**14.6**	17.1	22.0	4.9	4.9		66	34
UK	1971–81	n	2	0	0	0	3	**17**	11	3	36	3	33
		%	5.6	0	0	0	8.3	**47.2**	30.6	8.3		8	92
	1981–91	n	4	0	0	3	1	**10**	9	9	36	4	32
		%	11.1	0	0	8.3	2.8	**27.8**	25.0	25.0		11	89

Notes: Number in **bold** indicates cell containing the median.
**Notes:* As defined in Table 4.1

different way showing just the proportion of FUR cores gaining or losing population in each time period. Both tables present frequency distributions of FURs classified by stage of development for each time period. Table 4.1 shows the pattern for all FURs over one third of a million in population in 1981, classified by broad zones from northernwestern Europe to southern Europe. Table 4.2 subdivides the same set of Western Europe's largest FURs into two size classes, those that had a core city exceeding 200,000 at some date since 1951, and medium-sized urban region with core cities never exceeding 200,000.

What emerges is that from 1951 to 1981 there was a very regular pattern of change. Europe's cities moved steadily from stages of centralisation to decentralisation with decentralisation appearing first in the cities of northwestern European countries and spreading southwards; and spreading from the largest to smaller cities. This was the regular and apparently irreversible pattern of decentralisation that led commentators in the mid-1980s to start discussing it as one of 'disurbanisation' and the process as if it would inevitably continue for the indefinite future.

The problem with this projection of events is captured in the adage – 'a trend is a trend is a trend: the question is when will it bend'. Without an adequate underlying analysis of the reasons for the trend, predicting bends was impossible. In fact by the 1970s there were already indications of a bend. Empirically an examination of net migration flows from some major cities of northwestern Europe, such as Copenhagen or London, showed (Cheshire and Hay 1986) that net outmigration of people had peaked in the early 1970s and that by the early 1980s their core cities were in approximate migration balance.

Equally, just as the falling absolute numbers of workers in agriculture meant that, even though the rate of job loss continued approximately unaltered, the size of the associated rural–urban migration flow fell over time, so with industrial employment. Although the rate of loss of industrial jobs in traditional core city locations continued, as the urban employment base in manufacturing fell, the actual size of the outflow declined. For example, by 1981 manufacturing only accounted for 17 per cent of jobs in Greater London. In addition, unlike the declining manufacturing sector, the growing service sector was not forced by competitive pressures to locate in decentralised locations. Some of the fastest-growing service sub-sectors, such as finance, business services or the media, in fact, exhibited strong agglomeration economies and grew differentially in core city locations. The location of other sub-sectors, such as personal services, was mainly determined by the location of population; and sectors such as R&D, design or publishing, were relatively unconstrained. Compared to industry, their demand for space was low and they were not dependent on access to goods transport systems. More significant locational factors were access to high quality labour, intercity and international communications, and supporting services. Thus access to those factors which conditioned the preferred locations of their critical workforces – whether environmental amenities (such as mountains) or urban amenities (such as cultural facilities) – were more influential in determining the location of these new activities than was the traditional pull of transport access. The most significant exception to this is access to airports (and in the future, perhaps, high speed rail).

At the same time as the outflow of jobs was becoming less rapid there were parallel changes occurring in Western European societies and economies in the forces that conditioned residential choice. The typical household was changing. The number of children per family was falling and, with falling birth rates, the labour force participation rate of married women was rising, as was the proportion of households consisting only of adults or single people. This meant that the price of space was becoming relatively less important than access to the labour market in determining residential location. In addition, although demand for access to amenities rises with income, there are urban amenities, such as cultural, educational and entertainment facilities, as well as green amenities. There are households – particularly those without young children – which value such amenities and, if there was an incentive for such households to recentralise for labour market reasons, their presence as urban consumers would improve the range and quality of urban amenities.

Not all cities supply such urban amenities equally, however, nor do all cities have an equal relative supply of housing stock attractive to better paid and more skilled workers. The result was twofold. First, the underlying balance of forces changed so that by the early 1980s there was the potential for some cities to recentralise. Table 4.1 shows precisely this: during the 1980s the distribution of cities by stages of development within northwestern Europe showed a substantial reversion to core growth and centralisation. The median of the distribution moved 'back' a stage and the proportion of core cities gaining population increased from 22 to 47 per cent. In France and northern Italy there was some reversion. The movement towards decentralisation only continued to be obvious in southern European cities as a group. The second result was that, as a comparison of Tables 4.1 and 4.2 shows, this reversion was more marked in medium-sized cities than it was in the very largest.

Table 4.3 illustrates the reason for this last tendency. This presents an index of turnaround – the difference in the rate of decentralisation in the 1980s compared to the 1970s – for those cities with the largest absolute turnaround. They are not a random selection. There is a statistically significant (χ^2 = 4.74, significant at 5 per cent) tendency for them to be medium sized and they are mainly cities relatively abundant in urban amenities: Canterbury, Oxford, Cambridge, Ulm and Freiburg are not a random set of British and (West) German cities.

The comparative performance of Oxford and Reading is very illuminating. Both are medium-sized cities, of similar size, in South East England. Both are within 90 km of London, with Reading nearer by 25 km. Both experienced rapid economic and population growth during the 1970s and 1980s. The rate of population growth for their urban regions in those decades was 4.4 per

Table 4.3 Turnaround in Northwestern European FURs between the 1970s and the 1980s with rate of relative recentralisation of more than 1 per cent during the 1980s

Country/FUR	*Index of FUR turnaround*[a]	*% Change in core city population:1980s*	*Size group*[b]
Germany (West)			
Ulm	13.9	12.7	M
Krefeld	14.4	10.3	L
Freiburg	9.1	8.4	M
Benelux			
Maastricht	27.5	16.6	M
Brugge	14.3	–1.1	M
Zwolle	24.9	14.1	M
Groningen	25.3	3.5	M
Devente/Apeldoorn	4.4	4.9	M
UK			
Glasgow	24.2	–4.8	L
Canterbury	6.7	8.2	M
Oxford	23.2	10.6	M
Cambridge	33.2	11.7	M
Denmark			
Odense	10.7	6.1	M
Aarhus	17.1	9.1	M
Alborg	10.4	1.4	M

Notes: [a] Turnaround defined as: (%change in Hinterland_{70s}–%change in Core_{70s}) – (%change in Hinterland_{80s}–%change in Core_{80s})
[b] L = Largest, M = Medium.

cent and 8.9 per cent in Reading, and 5.0 per cent and 7.2 per cent in Oxford. During the 1970s both cities exhibited significant decentralisation; the differential between hinterland and core growth was 17.5 percentage points in Reading and 19.9 in Oxford. During the 1980s, however, while Reading continued to decentralise sharply, with hinterland growth exceeding core growth by 14.3 percentage points, Oxford showed not only turnaround, but significant recentralisation. The growth in the hinterland was 4.3 percentage points less than that in the core. As the Joseph Rowntree Foundation's study (1995) shows, unusually for Britain, Oxford is a city in which higher income and occupational groups are now concentrated in core areas, while low income and deprived households are in peripheral, mainly social, housing. Reading, although it also has a university, has an edge of town campus and has grown from a nineteenth-century industrial town. Its downtown area is dominated by high rise modern office buildings and it is poorly supplied – certainly relative to Oxford or London – with urban amenities. Many of its entertainment and recreational facilities, including restaurants and even nightclubs, are in its 'ex-urban' hinterland. The cities developed in mirror image of each other. Oxford was an ancient university city which during the first half of the twentieth century developed a major car manufacturing industry in its outskirts; Reading was a nineteenth-century industrial town which in the second half of the twentieth century developed a substantial campus-style university in its outskirts.

The experience of Oxford and Reading, and the evidence of Table 4.3, therefore, support the conclusion that while the balance of forces driving decentralisation has changed and weakened, even often reversed, recentralisation is far from inevitable. It is partly dependent on the functions a particular city performs. These in turn reflect the quality of its urban amenities and of its labour supply. There is an extent to which both decentralisation and recentralisation are self-reinforcing because of the demand for proximity to location-specific amenities, including the mean income of a neighbourhood's households, and the way in which in the production of urban amenities, demand creates supply, and increased supply feeds back to increased demand.

The conclusion would appear to be that while decentralisation is no longer a necessary fact of Europe's urban system, spreading with apparently remorseless regularity from northern to southern Europe and from larger to smaller cities, nor is recentralisation inevitable. The characteristics of particular cities will influence what happens. Because the supply of urban amenities, and the quality of life a city provides for its residents, are more capable of being influenced by policy than was the competitiveness of urban areas as locations for industry, once large lorries and motorways were available, there is also an enhanced role for urban policy.

In both Western Europe and CEE we should expect, therefore, a greater diversity both of patterns of urbanisation and of urban physical form in the future than in the recent past. Many cities, particularly the larger cities brought into existence by the industrial revolution and having restricted service functions, are likely to continue to decentralise and decline. This is even more likely if they are port cities. Thus we might anticipate cities like Liverpool, Duisburg, Rotterdam or Charleroi continuing to decentralise and decline; other cities, such as those identified in Table 4.3, may be likely to continue to grow and recentralise; while yet other cities, perhaps larger and with a strong service function might stabilise or recentralise. Table 4.4 shows that in the case of London this is already visible. The data relate to administrative units but Greater London corresponds quite closely to the core of the London FUR. Greater London lost population during the 1950s and the loss continued through to 1981. Since then there has been accelerating population gain with growth concentrated in the more central boroughs of Inner London. This is not an artefact of dockland redevelopment. Between 1981 and 1996 growth was systematically concentrated in the more central boroughs where it was concentrated on younger age groups living disproportionately in single person households. What has happened in London seems likely to happen in other cities with comparable characteristics such as Amsterdam or Copenhagen. In the CEE countries it may offset the

Table 4.4 Population of London: administrative definitions 1961–96

Unit	*1971*	*1981*	*1991*	*1996*	*% Change 1981–96*
Inner London	2771	2550	2627	2708	6.2
Outer London	4681	4255	4263	4367	2.6
Greater London	7452	6805	6890	7075	4.0
South East	17230	17011	17637	(16778)	(6.5)

Source: Regional Trends.

outflow from cities such as Prague or Budapest. Thus we should expect during the next twenty years a greater dispersion of centralisation/decentralisation than in the thirty years between 1950 and 1980.

There is one further factor which reinforces the conclusion that the experience of cities is likely to be more varied in the future than in the past; that is the development of high speed rail in Europe. Just as the development of air travel (and freight) acted as another factor in driving decentralisation, so high speed rail will tend to reinforce recentralisation. Access to airports is maximised in the urban hinterland (a recent study – Cheshire and Gordon 1995 – found that not only was access to Heathrow critical for their location but multinational companies rated Reading, 65 km west of London, as having better access to Heathrow than London itself) but with few exceptions, the limited access points to the emerging high speed rail network will be in traditional downtown areas. The evidence suggests that up to a distance of 500 km high speed rail dominates air travel, and that it continues to be competitive to a distance of 800 or 900 km. In so far as an increasing proportion of business travel in Europe is likely to be by high speed rail, therefore, those cities that are served will be subject to an additional recentralising factor. This will be absent from those cities (such as Toulouse or Dublin) which will not be connected to high speed rail. In contrast, the development of the underdeveloped motorway system in CEE countries is likely to provide a significant future boost to urban decentralisation.

This analysis, therefore, suggests not only will there be a greater variability in future patterns of decentralisation/recentralisation, particularly in the cities of Western Europe, but that there will be a degree of predictability in these patterns for individual cities, coupled with an enhanced capability of policy to influence outcomes. That it is only a degree of predictability is witnessed by the presence of Krefeld in Table 4.3, as one of the cities demonstrating the greatest relative turnaround towards recentralisation during the 1980s; the potential impact of policy is witnessed by the presence of Glasgow in the same list.

Convergence and divergence in urban economies

The EU's cities and regions have a well-established traditional pattern of disparities. The disadvantaged, problematic areas are the old, declining industrial cities and industrialised regions on the one hand, and the backward, agricultural regions, on the other. In fact, in both types of backward regions the problems of poverty and unemployment tend to be concentrated in the cities. In northwestern Europe they are concentrated in cities such as Liverpool, Belfast or Duisburg (or more recently – showing that we should not be too sweeping with phrases such as 'southern' and 'northwestern Europe' – places like Aviles/Gijon): in southern Europe the problems of cities such as Napoli, Palermo, Cordoba, Vigo, Thessaloniki or Dublin (again revealing the too simplistic definition of 'southern'), have been well documented. Conditions in such problem-growing cities are often worsening relative to the rural regions that surround them.

More recently observers have asserted that a new type of spatial disparity is emerging. For example, Bruce Millan, when European Commissioner for Regional Policy claimed that the traditional dichotomy of core and peripheral regions was becoming oversimplified, even outmoded:

> Dramatic contrasts such as those between the centre and the outlying regions are being overtaken by a more complex pattern of territorial organisation . . . This diversification of disparities is generating a patchwork in which privileged areas border directly on depressed areas.
>
> (Millan 1993)

At the same time there has been a lively debate between macroeconomists – most associated with Barro (e.g. Barro 1991) and Sala-i-Martin (e.g. Sala-i-Martin 1994) – which has spilled over into regional economics (see Armstrong and Vickerman 1995) on the issue of convergence of (regional) growth rates. Indeed, the focus has shifted in the analysis of regional growth rates from the traditional neo-Keynesian concern with cumulative divergence to convergence.

Recent studies (Cheshire and Carbonaro 1996; Cheshire and Magrini 1998) have examined processes of growth across the major city regions[12] of Europe. The results are summarised in Table 4.5. Underlying the approach adopted was the view that in principle the economic growth observed in a particular city or region over a given period is the outcome of the net influence of a large number of different factors. Growth models – particularly those analysing long-run underlying forces – necessarily simplify and concentrate on particular influences and relationships. Account has to be taken of such theoretical insights in applied work. But some influences are plausibly assumed to be long term and systematic while others are short-term shocks. There are, however, always short-term shocks; it is just that they are not necessarily the same ones.

The influence of some short-term mechanisms may persist over quite long periods in particular regions. Examples might be long-term loss of comparative advantage for established industries such, for example, as the slow elimination of shipbuilding or textile industries from Western Europe or – a rather different type of influence – the spatial effects of European integration. Other mechanisms – such as the response of factor flows to differential spatial opportunities – may be persistent and systematic influences on regional growth patterns although their influence on a particular region may change over time as actual patterns of spatial price differentials respond to emerging localised disequilibria. Factors may always tend to move to locations where rewards are relatively highest; but the locations with the highest rewards are not necessarily always the same. If economies of scale are not important, such factor movements will tend to be associated with convergence of regional growth rates; but if economies of scale are the norm, then factor flows may reinforce spatial disparities.

Labour flows are usually thought of as consisting of migration. In the densely urbanised parts of Europe, however, it is probable that there is a much more significant but less visible labour market adjustment mechanism. That is changes in commuting patterns. Job turnover is substantial. In the UK, for example, the annual flow of job changes amounted to about 20 per cent of the employment stock even in the relatively depressed labour market conditions of the 1980s. Even in the extreme and unlikely circumstance that all job search was spatially random, such job turnover would tend to equilibrate opportunities for labour of given characteristics between contiguous local labour markets linked by significant cross-commuting flows. This equilibration would be expected to be rapid both because of the volume of job turnover and because of the low cost of adjusting commuting patterns. Where a pair of local labour markets are not themselves contiguous but are linked by intermediate local labour markets, this process of equilibration will still take place via knock-on effects transmitted through those intermediate labour markets. The empirical evidence supporting the view that this is an important phenomenon is quite strong. For example, Gordon and Lamont (1982) found that local labour markets linked by 25 per cent cross-border commuting in the South East of England equilibrated quickly: the impact of additional employment opportunities in one such local labour market on local unemployment rates disappeared within one year.

Many regions of Europe consist of extensive and densely urbanised areas: examples include the whole of the Ruhrgebeit, nearly the whole of Belgium and The Netherlands, most of the South East, Midlands and the North West of England as well as north-eastern France and much of northern Italy. We should therefore expect that differential growth in one city within such a region would suck in commuters from surrounding cities. As Brussels expands, for example, so it will tend to attract increasing numbers of commuters from the relatively depressed cities of southern Belgium, such as Charleroi and Liége.

The result will be something of a paradox. The induced commuting will tend to equalise incomes for characteristic equivalent individuals across the set of interacting urban/regional economies but reinforce the divergence of mean per capita incomes. There are two reasons to expect this result. The first

Table 4.5 Convergence and divergence mechanisms in European urban growth, 1980–90

1. Constant	$\hat{\beta}$	26.6780
	t	(0.59)
	S.E.	45.2406
2. log of GDP p.c. : 1979–82		–4.3931
		(–0.93)
		4.7073
National factors		
3. % Income growth 1980–90 in national remainders		0.6991**
		(6.19)
		0.1130
4. Dummy for Northern Italy		4.8716*
		(1.97)
		2.4694
5. Dummy for Belgium and Germany		–4.2842*
		(–2.28)
		1.8812
European integration		
6. Change in economic potential resulting from European integration		12.4183*
		(1.89)
		6.5718
7. Change in Economic Potential resulting from European integration squared		–6.5880*
		(–1.85)
		3.5524
Objective 1 type variables		
8. % of L.F. in agriculture in 1975 in NUTS 2 region		0.5523*
		(2.20)
		0.2508
9. % of L.F. in agriculture in 1975 in NUTS 2 region squared		–0.0197**
		(–3.00)
		0.0066
Objective 2 type variables		
10. Historic influence of coal industry		–3.3911**
		(–2.99)
		1.1358
11. Historic influence of port industry		–1.6508**
		(–3.44)
		0.4805
12. % of L.F. in industry in 1975 in NUTS 2 region		–0.1649*
		(–1.69)
		(0.0977)

Table 4.5 cont.

Spatial processes	
13. Log of total population 1981	3.5551**
	(3.84)
	0.9254
14. Growth differential with neighbouring FURs 1979–82. 86 divided by distance	6.4082**
	(4.40)
	1.4560
15. Population density 1981	–0.0016*
	(–1.78)
	0.0009
Dynamic knowledge spillover effects	
16. Research and Development Establishments per million, 1988 raised to power of 4	0.0038**
	(3.92)
	0.0010
Adjusted R^2	0.60

Notes: for each independent variable the $\hat{\beta}$, t-statistic and Standard Errors are shown in order: ** significant at 1%; * significant at 10%. For theoretical explanation and full definition of variables and data see Cheshire and Carbonaro (1996).

is just a measurement phenomenon. The commuters attracted to work in the urban economy which has expanded will increase the measured output of that economy but not its resident population, thus further increasing its measured income per capita. Cheshire and Magrini (1998), however, show this is not an important contributor to the effect. It remains even when the model is estimated in terms of growth of GDP per worker rather than per resident.

There is also another implication. Since more highly skilled workers tend to commute further to work than less skilled, the effects are not likely to be neutral with respect to the skill structure of the urban labour forces. The more rapidly expanding city, attracting additional commuters will improve the composition and so, presumably the output, of its workforce. As a result, GDP per capita should rise even more rapidly relative to its slower growing neighbours. Table 4.5 provides evidence strongly supportive of this hypothesis.

This suggests that in the densely urbanised regions of Europe a systematic adjustment process generates a 'patchwork' of apparently more rapidly growing and declining urban economies. The divergence of mean per capita incomes (and total unemployment rates) between these interacting city economies is consistent, however, with a simultaneous convergence of characteristic specific incomes per capita or unemployment rates. In turn, this suggests that the welfare implications and so the appropriate policy response, to spatial disparities measured in mean per capita incomes, are very different if those disparities are between free-standing cities or between cities within densely urbanised regions.

The evidence presented in Table 4.5 is also strongly supportive of another mechanism generating divergence in per capita incomes between the city regions of the EU. Drawing on recent work on endogenous growth theory, and particularly that of Romer (1990), it was argued in Cheshire and Carbonaro (1996) that there were reasons for expecting rates of growth to be positively and exponentially associated with concentrations of R&D activity. This was because it was hypothesised that there were agglomeration economies in R&D activity and that a proportion of the output of R&D was converted into local growth (because some proportion of knowledge generated by R&D was applied locally both within the companies responsible for the R&D, and by new start-ups by R&D workers). Although the data used were imperfect, nevertheless the R&D variable proved highly significant.

The evidence, therefore, strongly supports the existence of increasing returns to concentration to R&D activity and a mechanism which transmits at least a proportion of such growth into the local economy. This implies that unless there are ultimately decreasing returns, R&D regions would form a 'club' of diverging regions, getting continually richer relative to other regions. This is consistent with the findings of Magrini (1999).

One further mechanism generating divergence, at least in the past, was the spatial impact of European integration itself. Most theoretical analysis of the spatial impact of integration has concluded that core regions gain relative to peripheral ones. This is the conclusion of analysts using a very wide range of theoretical approaches from formal economic models (Krugman and Venables 1990, 1993), economic analysis (Camagni 1992; Itaki and Waterson 1990), or economic geographers such as Clark *et al.*, 1969 or – in a very different approach – Amin *et al.* 1992. Dokopoulou and Hamilton (1988) combined theoretical insights with an analysis of empirical data relating to the mid-1980s and field survey work to suggest that, in general, the key nodal regions of Spain possessed the best potential to undergo dynamic restructuring in response to that country's full membership of the EU, although spillovers into adjacent regions were also likely (see also Hamilton 1996). Research by Rodríguez-Pose (1996) tends to confirm their predictions, particularly with respect to the influential role of the location of foreign investments. Although confined to one country, again the analysis suggested gains were concentrated in core regions.

Empirical analysis for all European regions together is scarcer but Cheshire and Carbonaro (1996) not only show that the evidence is consistent with the theoretical expectations but that the specific impact of integration has changed over time. In the earlier phases of integration, during the 1960s until the late 1970s, the evidence was consistent with integration being a quite powerful influence on the differential growth of regions with gains directly proportional to the calculated change in regional economic potential (see Clark *et al.* 1969) and the maximum gains right at the core of Europe in the Benelux countries. More recently the evidence suggested that not only was the impact of European integration as an influence on regional growth rates getting weaker but that the effects were spreading out to the 'near core' regions, even as comparatively remote as northeast Italy, southern Germany and south western France. To the extent to which these results are valid they would suggest that one mechanism which was generating strong regional divergence in a systematic way has evolved through time so that its impact is now much more mixed. This does not mean that it will continue to fade in the near future. European monetary union, unless accompanied by offsetting transfers to less competitive countries and regions, must be expected to reinforce the divergence effects of integration for a substantial period.

Working against these mechanisms generating divergence in regional growth rates there are others which must be expected to produce convergence. These, in the long run, should include European integration. Even in the presence of increasing returns to scale in manufacturing industry the 'Europeanisation' of institutional, cultural and legal systems, particularly of educational and training standards might in the long run generate convergence. Depending on the role and significance of increasing returns to scale so, too, might factor mobility. Above all, it might be argued, the policy responses triggered by European integration – specifically European regional policy – tend to produce convergence.

The implications of integration and adjustment for CEE cities

European integration – part of a wider process of globalisation – is one of the forces that are fostering more diversified trends in urban form (towards centralisation or decentralisation) and in levels of economic activity (towards convergence or divergence). Cities in CEE are no exception. Indeed, the differentiation emerging among them appears to be becoming sharper on account of marked cross-border, regional and local variations in (a) transition from centralised state management towards a market economy and levels of integration through foreign trade and foreign direct investment; (b) constraints or opportunities inherited from the socialist era; (c) cultural, economic and social conditions built-in from 'pre-socialist' periods; and (d) the responses of indigenous populations and decision-makers to the challenges and outcomes of the transition itself.

With the exception of the more urbanised former German Democratic Republic and Czech lands, which lost population after World War II, most of CEE experienced 'belated', but rapid, urbanisation during the socialist period, especially before the 1980s. The number of people living in cities almost doubled in the former Czechoslovakia and Hungary, and trebled in Poland, Bulgaria, Romania, the former Federal Socialist Republic of Yugoslavia, and Albania. The overwhelming trend was towards centralisation in core cities. This resulted from a combination of strong rural-to-urban migration, large- and medium-scale industrialisation, the predominant use of rail freight for hauling heavy industrial materials and products, national transport policies to restrict road transport to a feeder status to and from rail heads (see Figure 4.1), housing population growth in high-rise residential neighbourhoods, and the provision of highly-subsidised public transport. Industrial location policy in most CEE countries during the socialist era, however, also attempted to achieve greater interregional equality so that all regions shared in urbanisation. Thus cities located in less-developed or backward regions tended to exhibit faster relative growth, although often interregional rates of urban expansion varied as much as did the pattern, with urbanisation being more concentrated or 'monocentric' in some regions and more dispersed or 'polycentric' in other regions (Hamilton 1979a, 1982).

Of course, urban form and development in CEE were heavily influenced by political and economic integration with the Soviet Union. City planning incorporated or 'filtered' Soviet models of Milyutin's 'socialist city' and elements from the 1930s' Moscow city plan, yielding high levels of uniformity in socialist construction throughout Soviet bloc countries; any individuality was largely a product of cultural, economic and social differences inherited from the 'pre-socialist' past, local expediency or the relative and absolute scales of socialist urbanisation (French and Hamilton 1979).

Yet centralisation trends began to lose some momentum from the 1960s, particularly in the larger cities or urban-industrial regions, as a result of rising female participation rates in the labour force, increased housing and food shortages and congested public transport. In addition, active policies to restrict larger core-city growth were applied through administrative controls on work and residence and the diversion of new industries to new, or expanded small or medium towns in the hinterlands of Warsaw, Lódz, Kraków, Upper Silesia, Budapest or Prague and to designated 'growth centres' in more peripheral or rural regions (Hamilton 1982). Data are scarce, but evidence for Moscow, for instance, showed that already in the 1960s and early 1970s population growth in the outer suburban zone was accelerating towards the level of the central city, suggesting that decentralisation had become a forceful trend (Hamilton 1976). In addition, however, the phenomenon of second homes began to develop vigorously around capital and major provincial cities, so laying the preconditions for future decentralisation.

The current transition to a market economy is beginning to trigger more fundamental change, mainly towards decentralisation, although some recentralisation cannot be ruled out. The pattern appears to be complex and unclear in the continuing absence of statistical support. What *is* clear, however, is that the complicated process of privatisation – of enterprises, land and property – is creating differentiated conditions for change both within cities between the zones of the former socialist city (for an analysis, see Hamilton 1979b) and between cities. Economic restructuring is advancing more quickly and on a larger scale in the capital cities and key regional centres which enjoy greater international accessibility *vis-à-vis* Western Europe, while predominantly industrial (often single-industry) centres and cities in agricultural regions are suffering stagnation or decline. Conditions in the former group of cities suggest that at least an embryonic shift to decentralisation is beginning to occur, despite the rigidities imposed by the physical and structural legacies of socialism. These conditions are driving changes in land use and transport.

Land use is undergoing most rapid change in the historic core areas of leading cities as a result of escalating demand for space from local private enterprises and inward-investing foreign firms for consumer and producer services, causing rents to spiral (Hamilton 1995). Pressure has built up from foreign firms, too, for 'desirable' residential accommodation for their skilled foreign employees in the historic areas of Budapest, Prague and Moscow in particular. These trends appear to be having several effects: some displacement of the indigenous central-city population, expansion of service functions into the inner-city areas vacated by closed industrial enterprises, and a growing demand for suburban villa accommodation for foreign executives and their families. Furthermore, because of shortages of public land in the extensive socialist residential zones, new greenfield manufacturing, warehousing and shopping facilities are often being sited on the urban fringe.

Market reforms in the CEE are having major impacts on transport across the region, although the consequences for urban form are still rather embryonic and changes are more likely to be felt in the longer term. A sharp fall has occurred in the demand for rail freight transport (Dingsdale 1997), mainly because of the rapid contraction of the heavy materials-based and engineering sectors. On the other hand, there has been a significant relative shift to the use of road freight transport, despite large real cost increases (mainly associated with the removal of fuel-cost subsidies), as lighter modern sectors grow, the flexibility of the mode is better appreciated (especially by emergent new small firms), RoRo traffic develops, and inward-investing foreign multinational firms extend their use of modern truck and van fleets.

As happened in Western European cities from the 1960s, these trends are shifting comparative locational advantage to the urban fringe and suburban zones, especially in larger cities where road congestion is becoming a more serious problem. The rapid growth in private car ownership – reflecting both the legacy of pent-up demand from the socialist period and the emergence of the *nouveau riche* – is adding to the decentralisation trend through the construction of large new homes, villas, and even 'car-dependent' housing estates, on the urban fringe or in rural areas. This is particularly apparent in the metropolitan centres such as Budapest, Prague and Warsaw. These trends will accelerate in the twenty-first century as east–west and north–south limited-access highways are extended as an integral part of EU eastward enlargement. Already, Budapest is linked to Vienna by such an improved highway, funded by the EU PHARE programme (Dingsdale 1997). On the other hand, key cities in Hungary and Poland are enjoying the benefits of faster, regular inter-city rail passenger services. This, together with the planned future extension of the European high-speed train network in five links between Western Europe and CEE may well create some 'counter-trend' towards 'recentralisation' of population and producer services growth in the central areas of the main capital cities and selected western-located provincial centres in the future.

The speed with which conditions in some CEE countries are catching up with those in Western Europe means that there are even cases of trends which were sequential in Western Europe occurring simultaneously in some of the large CEE metropolitan centres. In Budapest, for example, decentralising and recentralising changes are occurring in this way. On the one hand, the forces of decentralisation are being boosted by the construction and improvement of a limited access road system radiating from the city and the construction of an orbital road. On the other, the construction of a technological park quite close to the city centre to the south by the Danube may produce a recentralising effect.

With respect to the development of their economic base, cities in CEE have been exposed since World War II to two quite distinctive phases of European integration. The first phase, of Soviet bloc integration[13] until the 1980s, saw urban development as a function, overwhelmingly, of state-directed and state owned industrialisation, with minimal daily consumer-service provision but substantial growth of education, training and medical facilities aimed at the creation of a more skilled, literate, healthy and productive labour force. From this perspective, therefore, the economy of CEE cities exhibited a significant level of convergence within the Soviet bloc but increasing divergence from trends in West European cities. This remained so, even though within CEE one could identify a certain level of divergence between the capital cities, on the one hand, which concentrated state administrative, managerial, planning and research functions, and the remainder of the urban system, on the other, which was highly specialised in resource-extraction, processing and manufacturing.

Nevertheless, it is also possible to identify two sub-periods of socialist economic development which are associated with rather different impacts of international integration on the economies of CEE cities. The Stalinist period of the 1950s was characterised by what might be termed 'horizontal integration'[14] within the Soviet bloc. This consisted in autarkic national economic development (import-substitution industrialisation) strategies which imitated the Soviet policy of 'socialism in one country' of the 1920s and the 1930s and essentially led to the cross-border duplication of industrial functions between CEE cities – underlining intra-bloc convergence. (This created a problem of contemporary international competition in the transition period, especially as post-1989 reforms exposed excess capacity in many key industries developed in the 1950s.)

A second sub-period, however, was initiated after 1958 when Khrushchev introduced policies for international division of labour within the Council for Mutual Economic Aid (or COMECON). This had two important consequences for CEE urban development in the 1960s and 1970s. First, a process of faster growth of selected cities occurred in association with their specialised development of (mainly) manufacturing to serve the wider

COMECON international market, e.g. shipbuilding in Gdansk (Poland), aluminium and buses in west-central Hungary and Budapest, or trams (street-cars) in Prague. And second, COMECON-wide management and research organisations were allocated among CEE capital and leading regional cities to foster international integration (e.g. of the electricity network) or develop new sectors (e.g. computing) (Linge and Hamilton 1981). This began to bolster the emergence of producer services in leading cities and hence contributed to some limited divergence in the urban system across CEE. The most important COMECON-wide functions, not surprisingly, were clustered in Moscow, the CMEA capital, which also by 1970 had 21 per cent of its workforce in scientific and R&D functions and concentrated 22 per cent of all employees in these sectors in the USSR (Hamilton 1976). By the 1970s, however, Brezhnev's policies for East–West *détente* and technological modernisation were also stimulating closer ties between West European and CEE cities, especially through Western technology transfer to new industries in Poland, Hungary and the Soviet Union itself (Linge and Hamilton 1981).

Trends in CEE cities become more divergent during the decade of transition following 1989 and are likely to continue to be so for the foreseeable future. The key to this lies in the differential speed and depth of reforms between states, regions and cities and their consequent greater or lesser integration into the spatial structure of the wider European economy. In broad terms a manifestation of the principle of distance decay factor is apparent. The interrelated processes of reform and integration are strongest in the nations and their regions closest to, or most accessible from, the EU core – Poland, Czech Republic, Slovakia, Hungary, Slovenia and Estonia – and weaken to the east and southeast with increasing distance (Hamilton 1995, 1999). Nevertheless, within that broad framework, individual cities range at one extreme from those, often of smaller or medium-size, which are still dominated by the remnants of state-owned industrial enterprise. Such cities are stagnating, declining or facing difficulties in restructuring their economic base. At the other extreme there are usually (but not always) larger cities and metropolitan areas where privatisation has penetrated their economic fabric more deeply and reform is fostering new-firm formation and entrepreneurship, spin-offs from larger enterprises, inward foreign-investment in existing or new facilities, or is leading to the closure of uncompetitive enterprises. Even cities in predominantly agricultural areas are experiencing divergent trends with some beginning to prosper from foreign investment in the deficit processed foods and beverages sectors while others stagnate under the impact of imported (sometimes dumped) EU food products.

The most striking and more universal trend, however, is the rapid growth of the urban service economy, which is beginning to put CEE cities on a more convergent trajectory towards their West European counterparts. This trend is a response to the underdevelopment of consumer-oriented services under socialism, the relatively small investments needed to start up new firms in services generally, and the lower risks of failure as a result of pent-up demand. Services growth is significantly more marked in cities in those states where real GDP per capita is now at or above the 1988 levels (Poland, the Czech and Slovak Republics, Hungary, Slovenia and Estonia) but is slower in Bulgaria, Romania and the CIS where GDP per capita remains far below 1988 levels or is still falling (EBRD 1997). Yet it is the expansion and new development of producer services – financial services, IT services, management consultancy, media, telecommunications or national and CEE regional sales and headquarters functions – that particularly differentiate the capital cities and more westerly provincial cities from the remainder of the urban system, especially in the advanced transition countries, and Moscow in the Russian Federation. Foreign investment, as well as local privatisation and marketisation, have been playing key roles in this process but it is one which is also fostering sharper international inter-city rivalry, too. In addition, attempts are under way, notably in Szczecin and Krakow (Poland) or Budapest (Hungary), to develop and attract R&D facilities to propel restructuring into a more dynamic mode and offset the effects of de-industrialisation of older sectors or outmoded enterprises. An important exception to this trend, however, appears to be Moscow where science and technology R&D has suffered severe decline following the collapse of Communism, the Soviet Union and Soviet military power, successive economic crises in the Russian Federation and a significant 'brain drain', mainly to the USA. This serves to underline the increasing diversity of experience among CEE cities.

Conclusion

An examination, then, both of the forces generating change in the spatial organisation and socio-economic and physical structure of European cities; and in their differential rates of economic growth suggests that we should not expect any uniform pattern of development in the foreseeable future. This is not to suggest that the patterns are random nor that each city is so individual that it has its own pattern of development. Indeed, the evidence suggests almost precisely the contrary. When data on a sufficiently large number of city regions are analysed, remarkably strong similarities and clear patterns emerge. Common forces and identifiable mechanisms are driving urban change in Europe. But cities have different inheritances and interact with specific environments in their wider regions and countries.

Those inheritances of, for example, economic specialisation, physical and architectural heritage, or patterns of residential segregation interact with changes such as those in transport and communications technology and cost, economic transformation and socio-economic trends (such as rising female labour force participation or falling family sizes) to determine the pattern of decentralisation or recentralisation in a particular city. Economic growth is similarly a multivariate process exhibiting strong and significant statistical patterns. The factors driving it at the urban level include both systematic long-term mechanism and short-term shocks of changes in the competitiveness of particular industries. Some of these mechanisms are consistent with growth rates diverging over extended periods. Two in particular have been identified although the way in which commuting flows adapt to changing patterns of opportunity between neighbouring cities means that the divergence is likely to be far greater in measured per capita income than in individual welfare.

Notes

1 Parts of this chapter have drawn on work being undertaken for a project 'The Implications of Interurban Income and Unemployment Divergences' within the ESRC's Cities Initiative under Award L 130251015.

2 That is we can estimate an hedonic price for such amenities – see Cheshire and Sheppard (1995).

3 For example, using the Gini coefficient as a measure of income inequality, it was found that Russia recorded a Gini coefficient in 1995 of 0.465 (as in Mexico or Thailand) compared with Hungary where it was 0.300 in the same year.

4 See, for example, Cheshire (1995); Cheshire and Gordon (1995); or Cheshire and Gordon (1996).

5 The City of London contained 4,230 people at the time of the 1991 Census of Population, compared to 6.4 million in Greater London, 8.1 million in the Functional Urban Region of London or some 20 million in Hall's (1989) Greater South East.

6 Right up to the early 1960s British Rail goods yards were so located that delivery and collection of goods could be done in one day by horse and cart.

7 These trends were held in check in the CEE countries both by the priority central planners gave to rail transport (with roads and lorries confined to a feeder role) and their concentration on heavy industries where rail had some continuing advantage.

8 Which is one reason why in the US rail freight remains a relatively profitable activity. The proposed 'freight freeways' in Europe, coupled with the Channel Tunnel and a fixed link between Sweden and Denmark, may, by increasing the proportion of journeys that can be made continuously in one goods train without transhipment or delays and labour costs at borders associated with paperwork and changing rolling stock, do more to transfer freight from road to rail than any environmental rhetoric.

9 Again there were differences between Western Europe and the CEE countries. Although the rural population was high in CEE countries, the housing shortages in cities from the 1960s on, coupled with the ability to grow some food on private plots in the countryside, slowed the rate of rural–urban migration but produced an increasingly numerous group of 'peasant-industrial workers' in countries like Poland and Yugoslavia. These peasant-industrial workers commuted to work from the countryside and rural fringe to the towns.

10 Interestingly, the proportionate rate of outflow of labour per annum from agriculture did not vary all that much across Europe. But since the proportion of the labour force working in agriculture varied from less than 10 per cent in the most agricultural of British regions to well over 50 per cent in the most agricultural regions of Spain, Italy or Greece, the absolute flows varied very considerably.

11 'Large' is defined as having a total population exceeding 1/3 of a million in 1981.

12 There are strong reasons for analysing the growth performance of city regions rather than the official NUTS regions of European policy and statistics (see Cheshire *et al.* 1996).

13 The federal (later Federal Socialist) Republic of Yugoslavia was something of an exception, however, as it was expelled from the Cominform in June 1948 and did not regain closer association with the Soviet bloc until 1960. Nevertheless, urban development in Yugoslavia until at least the 1970s bore considerable resemblance to that in the other socialist countries, despite greater decentralisation of management. Even so, economic development in Yugoslav cities was influenced more by wider international links with Western Europe and USA and, after 1960, also with Eastern Europe and the Third World or newly-industrialising countries.

14 The term 'horizontal integration' here is an analogy with the multinational corporation that develops identical or similar production in several host-country markets.

References

Adams, M., Maybury, R. and Smith W. (1988) Trends in the Distribution of Earnings, 1973–86', *Department of Employment Gazette*, 96, 75–82.

Alonso, W. (1964) 'Location theory', in J. Friedmann and W. Alonso (eds) *Regional Development and Planning,* Cambridge, MA: MIT Press, pp. 78–106.

Amin, A., Charles, D.R. and Howells, J. (1992) 'Corporate restructuring and cohesion in the new Europe', *Regional Studies* 25, 4: 319–32.

Anas, A. and Moses, L. (1978) 'Transportation and land use in the mature metropolis' in C.L. Leven (ed.) *The Mature Metropolis*, Lexington, MA: D.C. Heath.

Armstrong, H.W. and Vickerman, R.W. (eds) (1995) *Convergence and Divergence among European Regions*, London: Pion.

Barro, R.J. (1991) 'Economic growth in a cross section of countries', *Quarterly Journal of Economics* 106: 407–501.

Barro, R.J. and Sala-i-Martin X. (1991) 'Convergence across states and regions', *Brookings Papers on Economic Activity* I, 107–82.

Barro, R.J. and Sala-i-Martin X. (1992) 'Convergence', *Journal of Political Economy* 100: 223–51.

Camagni, R.P. (1992) 'Development scenarios and policy guidelines for the lagging regions in the 1990s', *Regional Studies* 25, 4: 361–74.

Champion, A.G. (1989) 'Counterurbanisation in Europe', *The Geographic Journal* 155, 1: 52–9.

Cheshire, P.C. (1979) 'Inner areas as spatial labour markets: a critique of the inner area studies', *Urban Studies* 16: 29–43.

Cheshire, P.C. (1995) 'A new phase of urban development in Western Europe? The evidence for the 1980s', *Urban Studies* 32: 1045–63.

Cheshire, P.C., and Carbonaro, G. (1996) 'Urban economic growth in Europe: testing theory and policy prescriptions', *Urban Studies* 33, 7: 1111–28.

Cheshire, P.C., Furtado, A. and Magrini, S. (1996) 'Analysis of European cities and regions: problems of quantitative comparisons', in L. Hantrais, and S. Mangen (eds) *Doing Cross-National Research: Techniques and Methods in the Social Sciences,* London: Pinter, pp. 39–50.

Cheshire, P.C. and Gordon, I.R. (1995) *Territorial Competition in an Integrating Europe: Local Impact and Public Policy,* Aldershot: Avebury.

Cheshire, P.C. and Gordon, I.R. (1996) 'Territorial competition and the predictability of collective (in)action', *International Journal of Urban and Regional Research* 20, 3: 383–99.

Cheshire, P.C. and Gordon, I.R. (1998) 'Territorial competition: some lessons for policy', *The Annals of Regional Science* 32, 3: 321–46.

Cheshire, P.C. and Hay, D.G. (1986) 'The development of the European urban system, 1971–81', in H.J. Ewers, J.B. Goddard, and H. Matzerath (eds) *The Future of the Metropolis: Economic Aspects*, Berlin: de Gruyter, pp. 149–69.

Cheshire, P.C. and Hay, D.G. (1989) *Urban Problems in Western Europe: An Economic Analysis,* London: Unwin Hyman.

Cheshire, P.C. and Magrini, S. (1998) 'The determinants of regional growth: some preliminary results', in *The Implications of Interurban Income and Unemployment Divergences Project*, Working Paper No. 2, London: LSE.

Cheshire, P. and Sheppard, S. (1995) 'On the price of land and the value of amenities', *Economica* 62: 247–67.

Cheshire, P. and Sheppard, S. (1998) 'Estimating the demand for housing, land and neighbourhood characteristics', *Oxford Bulletin of Economics and Statistics* 60, 3.

Clark, C., Wilson, F. and Bradley, J. (1969) 'Industrial location and economic potential in Western Europe', *Regional Studies* 3: 197–212.

Dingsdale, A. (ed.) (1997) 'Transport in transition: issues in the new Central and Eastern Europe', *Trent Geographical Papers* (The Nottingham Trent University) 1.

Dokopoulou, E. and Hamilton, F. E. I. (1988) 'Development potentials of the regions of Spain in the enlarged EC', unpublished Report to the Directorate-General for Regional Policy (DG XVI) Commission of the European Communities, Brussels: CEC, p. 320.

EBRD (1997), *Transition Report 1997: Enterprise Performance and Growth*, London: EBRD.

Evans, A.W. (1990) 'The assumption of equilibrium in the analysis of migration and interregional differences: a review of some recent research', *Journal of Regional Science* 30: 515–31.

French, R.A. and Hamilton, F.E.I. (eds) (1979) *The Socialist City: Spatial Structure and Urban Policy*, Chichester and New York: Wiley.

Gordon, I. and Lamont, D. (1982) 'A model of labour-market interdependencies in the London region', *Environment and Planning A,* 14: 238–64.

Hall, P.G. (1989) *London 2001*, London: Allen & Unwin.

Hall, P.G. and Hay, D.G. (1980) *Growth Centres in the European Urban System*, Heinemann Educational, London.

Hamilton, F.E.I. (1976) *The Moscow City Region*, Oxford: Oxford University Press.

Hamilton, F.E.I. (1979a) 'Urbanisation in Socialist Eastern Europe: the macro-environment of internal city structure', in R.A. French and F.E.I. Hamilton (eds) *The Socialist City*, Chichester and New York: Wiley. pp. 195–262.

Hamilton, F.E.I. (1979b) 'Spatial structure in East European cities', in R.A. French and F.E.I. Hamilton (eds) *The Socialist City*, Chichester and New York: pp. 195–262.

Hamilton, F.E.I. (1982) 'Regional policy in Poland: a search for equity', *Geoforum* 13, 2: 121–132.

Hamilton, F.E.I. (1995) 'Re-evaluating space: locational change and adjustment in Central and Eastern Europe', *Geographische Zeitschrift* 83, 2: 67–86.

Hamilton, F.E.I. (1996) 'European integration and regional capacities for manufacturing adjustment and change: the case of Spain', *Research Papers in Environmental and Spatial Analysis*, London: London School of Economics.

Hamilton, F.E.I. (1999) 'Transformation and space in Central and Eastern Europe',

Geographical Journal, July, forthcoming.
Itaki, M. and Waterson, M. (1990) *European Multinationals and 1992*, University of Reading Discussion Papers in Economics, Series B (141), Department of Economics, Reading: University of Reading Press.
Joseph Rowntree Foundation (1995) *Enquiry into Income and Wealth*, York: Joseph Rowntree Foundation.
Krugman, P. (1991) 'Increasing returns and economic geography', *Journal of Political Economy* 99: 483–99.
Krugman, P. (1993) 'On the number and location of cities', *European Economic Review* 37: 293–8.
Krugman, P.R. and Venables, A.J. (1990) *Integration and the Competitiveness of Peripheral Industry*, Discussion Paper Series 363, Centre for Economic Policy Research.
Krugman, P.R. and Venables, A.J. (1993) *Integration, Specialisation and Adjustment*, Discussion Paper Series 886, Centre for Economic Policy Research.
Linge, G.J.R. and Hamilton, F.E.I. (1981) 'International industrial Systems' in: F.E.I. Hamilton and G.J.R. Linge (eds.) *Spatial Analysis, Industry and the Industrial Environment:* Vol. 2: *International Industrial Systems*, Chichester and New York: Wiley, 1–112.
MacLennan, D. (1993) 'Decentralisation and residential choices in European cities: the role of state and market', in A.A. Summers, P.C. Cheshire and L. Senn (eds) *Urban Change in the United States and Western Europe: Comparative Analysis and Policy*, Washington, DC: The Urban Institute, pp. 529–51.
Magrini, S. (1999) 'The evolution of income disparities among the regions of the European Union', *Regional Science and Urban Economics* 29: 257–81.
Marx, K. and Engels, F. (1848) *Manifest des Kommunistischen Partei.*
Millan, B. (1993) *Memorandum to the Informal Council of Ministers Responsible for Regional Policy and Spatial Planning*, 11/93, mimeo.
OECD (1993), 'Earnings inequality: changes in the 80s', ch. 5 in OECD *Employment Outlook*, OECD, Paris.
OECD (1998), 'Integrating distressed urban areas', *Territorial Development*, OECD, Paris.
Rodríguez-Pose, A. (1996) 'Growth and institutional change: the influence of the Spanish regionalisation process on economic performance', *Environment & Planning C: Government and Policy* 14: 71–87.
Romer, P.M. (1990) 'Endogenous technological change', *Journal of Political Economy* 98: 71–101.
Rowthorne, R.E. and Wells, J.R. (1987) *De-industrialisation and Foreign Trade*, Cambridge: Cambridge University Press.
Sala-i-Martin, X. (1994) 'Cross-sectional regressions and the empirics of economic growth', *European Economic Review* 38: 739–41.
UNICEF (1997) 'Children at risk', *Regional Monitoring Report* 4, Geneva: UNICEF.
Wclawowicz, G. (1979) 'The structure of socio-economic space in Warsaw in 1931 and 1970: a study in factorial ecology', in R.A. French and F.E.I. Hamilton (eds) *The Socialist City*, Chichester and New York: Wiley, pp. 387–424.

5 The dilemmas of regional policy in the transition countries and the territorial organisation of the state

Grzegorz Gorzelak

Introduction

The East-Central European countries (E-CEC) discussed in this chapter (Bulgaria, the Czech Republic, Hungary, Poland, Romania and Slovakia) occupy an area of 883,000 sq kilometres and have a population of 94.4 million, thus being a great demographic and economic potential on the European scale. These countries entered upon the path of rapid socio-economic and political transformation about ten years ago. During this relatively short period of time very deep changes, involving all walks of life, have taken place there. The post-socialist transformation seems to be one of the most challenging experiments in modern economic history. The entire eastern part of Europe has begun its return to the global political and economic 'mainstream' – the market system and democracy.

Of particular importance is the fact that the political reforms of the post-socialist countries opened them to the global markets and to new – 'post-Fordist' – paradigms of socio-economic development. Thus the processes of economic restructuring, which in more developed countries have been for operation for two (in some cases even three) decades, were imposed on the post-socialist countries by the principles of global competition. These processes resulted in a deep – and fortunately for some of them rather short – recession, which was then replaced by an accelerated growth that took place in several cases (see Table 5.1).

The economic reforms that have been introduced in these countries since 1990 have assumed different models of transformation (Gorzelak *et al.* 1994). In Poland changes in the national economy implemented since January 1990 followed the pattern of a shock therapy, which resulted in deep recession and the breakdown of several branches of the Polish economy (see Balcerowicz 1997). Being the first country to enter the path of transformation, Poland was also the first to pay the economic and social costs incurred by this process. However, Poland was also the first to show, already in 1992, signs of economic recovery. By the end of 1995 the GDP in Poland had reached the 1989 level and in 1998 it exceeded it – as the only post-socialist country – by 15 per cent.

Table 5.1 Dynamics of GDP in the post-socialist countries, 1989–97

Countries	*1990*	*1991*	*1992*	*1993*	*1994*	*1995*	*1996*	*1997*	
	previous year =100								*1990 = 100*
Byelorussia			90	92	87	90	103	110	73
Bulgaria	91	99	93	99	102	102	89	94	73
Czech Republic	100	88	97	101	100	106	104	101	99
East Germany	84	89	108	106	109	109			110[b]
Hungary	97	88	97	99	103	100	101	105	96
Lithuania	93	87	48	76	101	103	104		34
Latvia	103	89	65	84	102	100	103	106	51[a]
Poland	**88**	**93**	**100**	**104**	**105**	**107**	**106**	**107**	**125**
Russia	97	95	86	91	87	96	97	100	61
Romania	94	87	91	102	104	107	104	94	89
Slovakia	98	85	94	96	105	107	107	106	98
Slovenia	92	92	95	103	105	104	103	104	104
Ukraine	96	88	83	83	77	88	90	98	38

Source: Statistical Yearbook 1998, Warsaw, table 96(662); also Jarosinski (1998).
Notes: [a]1996; [b]1995.

In spite of these successes, in the recent years Polish growth has slowed down considerably. Though still relatively high, according to several opinions this figure is too low for the needs and aspirations of the citizens. It is proposed that new structural economic reforms should be undertaken, which would lead to rationalisation of employment and would decrease the burden of inefficient state enterprises, located mostly in old industries (coal mining, steel, arms), agriculture and utilities (rail).

The two other central European countries – the Czech Republic and Hungary – have achieved some minor successes. Their transformation was more fragile, and recovery less durable. To some extent one may say that the reluctance to enter the recession phase resulted in smaller growth potential during the recovery phase. Only very recently has the Czech government prepared the principles of austerity policy and accelerated restructuring of the economy, which was retarded by the (wrong) conviction of the former prime minister that the Czech economy had already gone through the post-socialist restructuring and no further sacrifices were needed. Also Slovakia did not utilise all opportunities, which was due to the anti-reform attitude of the ruling political elites and their leaders. The Czech and Slovak republics, together with Hungary, are striving to reach the pre-transformation GDP level and their growth is still unsteady.

The situation of the other two less developed south-eastern countries, Bulgaria and Romania, demonstrates the negative results of a very inconsistent course of reforms, which have gone through ups and downs, parallel to the political changes in these countries. Both these countries are far below the 1989 level and there are no sound manifestations of recovery.

Table 5.2 Major economic categories in East-Central European countries

Countries	*Pop'n (mill.) 1997*	*GNP per capita PPP$ 1994*[a]	*Unemployment rate*	*Consumer price inflation* 1997	*Employment by sectors, 1996*			*Regional GDP per capita, EU = 100, 1995*	
					agriculture, forestry, fishing	*industry, construction*	*services*	*highest*	*lowest*
Bulgaria	8.3	4,000	12.5	123	22.1[b]	35.5[b]	42.4[b]	60	12
Poland	38.7	5,200	11.5	15	22.1	31.7	46.2	46	20
Hungary	10.2	6,100	10.5	18	8.3	32.6	59.1	63	24
Czech Rep.	10.3	8,100	3.0	9	6.2	41.6	52.2	61	43
Slovak Rep.	5.4	6,500	12.8	6[c]	9.2	37.4	53.4	39	30
Romania	22.6	3,100	7.8	155	38.0	31.5	30.5	27	16

Source: EPRC (1996); *Statistical Yearbook* 1998, Central Statistical Office, Warsaw.

Notes: [a] Averages of several estimates (World Bank, Economist Intelligence Unit, Eurostat, Wiener Institute);

[b] 1993;

[c] 1996.

The most dramatic situation exists in the post-Soviet republics, some of which have fallen to below half of GDP achieved at the end of the socialist era (in several cases the statistics, showing only 20–30 per cent fall, seem to be unrealistic). These countries are paying the highest costs of transition because of two reasons:

- the collapse of the Soviet Union deprived them of their traditional sources of supplies and of traditional markets;
- only in the Baltic republics have some traces remained of market economy – in the remaining post-Soviet republics (and also in Russia itself) seventy years of Communism have wiped out all direct experience different from real socialism.

Some comment should be made regarding the former GDR (East Germany). Its economic recovery should be mainly attributed to huge transfers from the western part of the country, which are estimated at around 1 billion DM. These transfers were allocated mostly in infrastructure, but were also used to ease the social costs of transition. However, parallel to the positive results of this assistance, several negative side-effects, like social demobilisation and split between the citizens from the western and eastern parts of the country, have also emerged.

Table 5.2 presents major economic categories in East-Central European countries during the transformation period. Table 5.2 shows that the Czech Republic is the most developed country in the group, and also the country with the most even regional distribution of GDP creation. To a large extent this is rooted in the history of this part of Europe, and this in turn is a product of the spatial differentiation of European economic development during the last few centuries. All six countries in Table 5.2 have been located on the European economic periphery throughout their history. The Czech Republic is the closest to one of the two main European economic axes: the 'old' northern one, extending from London to Rome (the 'European banana'). In fact, Bohemia used to be a part of the western European economic system well into the nineteenth century and the first half of the twentieth century. The whole of Eastern-Central Europe is far away from the new Mediterranean axis, extending from Milan to Barcelona. Only the Czech lands have experienced an advanced level of capitalist industrialisation.

At present, the economic situation of four East-Central European countries (Czech and Slovak Republics, Hungary and Poland) seems promising, though the chances for fast growth are varied within this group. Bulgaria and Romania are still striving to enter a stable path of growth and structural change.

The regional patterns of East-Central European transformation

The emerging regional profiles

Historical heritage, coupled with natural endowment of particular areas, have put the regions of East-Central Europe in very different positions at the start of transformation. The most general pattern of reaction of particular regions to this new situation is displayed in Table 5.3 (see Gorzelak 1995a). These four types of regional reaction to transformation processes manifested themselves in all East-Central European countries. Let us examine the four general types of regional reaction to the new economic, social, political and international situation.

The leaders (positive continuity)

All countries have their unquestionable leaders of transformation, which have already demonstrated the highest potential for restructuring and great capacity for adaptation to new conditions. These are their greatest agglomerations: Prague and Brno in the Czech Republic; Bratislava and to a lesser extent Košice in Slovakia; Budapest and the Balaton region in Hungary; Warsaw, Poznan, Wroclaw and Kraków in Poland; Sofia city and region, Bourgas and Haskovo, perhaps also Bucharest in Romania.

However, some of these nodes are not surrounded by innovative and progressive hinterlands. Warsaw is a kind of an island within the relatively poorly developed central part of Poland. Kraków borders on the west with one of the most difficult (if not the most difficult) regional cases in Europe (Upper Silesia, dominated by heavy and mining industries) and on the east with the Polish south-eastern periphery. Košice is a relatively small urban centre in a relatively backward Eastern Slovakia. An even more difficult situation exists in territories surrounding the Bulgarian and Romanian leading regions.

Table 5.3 Typology of regions under transformation

		Post-socialist transformation	
		positive	*negative*
Position in the socialist economy	Good	positive continuity (e.g. great urban agglomerations)	negative discontinuity (e.g. old industrial regions)
	Bad	positive discontinuity (e.g. Western regions)	negative continuity (e.g. the 'Eastern Wall')

On the other hand, the space between the remaining nodes is filled in by the regions which are in fact the core areas of the four 'Visegrad' countries (Czech and Slovak Republics, Hungary, Poland). For centuries, the main bulk of development and innovation has been concentrated in these regions. They have also proved to be natural candidates to become the final winners of transformation on the entire East-Central European scale.

The losers: old industrial regions (negative discontinuity)

The economic transformation was especially hard for the 'mammoths' of the old system: the big, state-owned enterprises operating in the traditional economic sectors (see Fazekas and Gorzelak 1995). There are several basins of old industries which are undergoing (or will have to undergo) very deep restructuring processes. One such concentration is of special importance: the big 'black hole' in the socio-economic space of East-Central Europe: Upper Silesia, a typical old industrial region. It is composed of the Polish Katowice *voivodship* and the Czech Ostrava-Karvina basin, and it constitutes the biggest regional problem in Europe. Until the beginning of the 1990s the Katowice region used to provide more than 20 per cent of Polish national GDP. Both parts of Upper Silesia (Czech and Polish) have to go through the painful process of massive restructuring and an increase in unemployment is probable; this process is more advanced in the Czech part of the basin. Coal mining, the most important branch in the regional economy, must undergo deep structural changes. Heavy and chemical industries, presently in decline, are the other dominating sectors of Upper Silesia and – if restructured – may produce unemployment and social tensions in the future, or – if still subsidised – these obsolete industries of the region will remain a heavy burden on the national economy.

It seems that the Czechs are much more successful in reconstructing their 'black basin'. The policies adopted in this country have not allowed subsidisation of the dying mines and factories, but the national funds allocated for industrial restructuring have been used to create new activities within the regions under restructuring. In Slovakia the decline has hit the regions specialising in heavy machinery and military industries – Bystrica, Zilina, Zvolen, Martin counties) – that were oriented to the Soviet markets.

In Hungary the heavy industry–mining region (Borsod-Abaúj-Zemplén) began its restructuring in the mid-1980s, which did not prevent a heavy recession in the 1990s. In Bulgaria the regions of Varna, Plovdiv and Russe are also in this group.

There is another group of regions which have lost out due to the post-socialist transformation: these are the regions of rapid decollectivisation of the socialised agriculture (see Halamska 1999). In Poland the northern and western regions, where this type of agriculture occupied around half of the arable land and gave work to some half a million people, the transformation resulted in structural unemployment up to over 50 per cent in several localities and around 25 per cent on the regional scale now. Several such regions have now gone through successful reconstruction of the former state or collective farms through privatisation.

The backward peripheries (negative continuity)

East-Central Europe has its very clearly marked external periphery, extending along the eastern borders of the countries under discussion. It extends from the north-eastern corner of Poland to the south-eastern part of Hungary, the eastern part of the Slovak–Hungarian border and then through Romania to Montana and Lovech in northern Bulgaria (although the Hungarian regions along the Romanian border are relatively well developed). These are the least developed, relatively sparsely populated rural areas with a poorly developed urban system and infrastructure. Some of these areas are crossed by main transportation routes going in the East–West direction and no major artery exists nor is envisaged which would connect them in the North–South direction. All of these regions are poorly integrated with the centres of their respective national systems. Transformation processes are slow there, the level of education low and they do not attract the attention of foreign investors.

For example, during the first two years of transformation, when the recession took place, the eastern regions of Poland noted smaller losses of GDP than the rest of the country, which led to the slight improvement of their relative situation compared to the national average. This was due to the fact that their backward, agriculture-dominated economies could not be restructured. However, after the recovery began, these regions displayed lower growth rates, and therefore the regional differences began to grow. Referring to the 'J-curve' concept (see for example Bradshaw and Stenning 1999), we may say that the relatively backward regions followed the shallow J-curve, while the more industrialised and urbanised regions followed the steep one. Also the external relations of the eastern regions of Central Europe cannot expect to receive inducement for transformation and recovery from their neighbours on the other side of the border (Lithuania, Byelorussia, Ukraine, Moldova).

In several countries – mostly notably in Romania (Sub-Carpathia and upland areas of Oltenia, Apuseni mountains, rural areas of Banat) – an internal periphery can also be noticed – like the Great Plains in Hungary and central part of Poland surrounding Warsaw and Lódz agglomerations.

The newcomers (positive discontinuity)

The western regions of East-Central Europe have become the new winners in the transformation processes. The negative impact of previous isolation of the western border regions has begun to be overcome as a result of collaboration with the more developed western neighbours in Austria and Germany.

Only the geographical location of the 'western belt' of the four countries bordering with Austria and Germany is its greatest potential. This is the region located centrally in Europe and the closest to the Western centres of economic activity. It is also the natural 'border market' for Germans and Austrians, who used to take advantage of price differences and increase the demand for basic commodities and services. It was estimated, for example, that in 1995 the German consumers spent some 4 billion DM per annum in western Polish regions, which became an important economic factor for the development of this area and covered part of the deficit of the Polish international 'official' trade (the Germans used to spend in Poland twice as much as the consumers from all the other countries neighbouring Poland).

However, these benefits for the price differential seem to be over, at least in Polish western regions. Constant appreciation of the Polish currency (which is an irreversible process, due to structural changes in Polish economy and its relatively fast growth) has led to price equalisation between Poland and Germany. More and more Poles go shopping in Germany, and only cigarettes and gas have remained the really cheap commodities on the Polish side of the border. It has now appeared that too few profits from previous 'bonanzas' were invested in production-oriented business – much of their share was transferred to central regions of Poland, and another large amount was spent on consumption and housing. After the boom of price differences is over, the Polish western belt will wake up without its huge profits and without a properly developed production base, which would utilise the proximity of the huge German market.

The western regions have advantages for investors from Austria and Germany who seek nearby cheaper labour and financial incentives for their production. The greatest agglomeration in Central Europe – Berlin – is just 80 kilometres from the Polish border and its positive (in economic terms) influence can already be noticed in the form of investment and other commercial contacts.[1] The impact of Vienna on Bratislava and also on the Hungarian western region can also be seen. Such development of manufacturing and service sectors may give jobs to many currently unemployed. The proximity of the Austrian and German markets will, no doubt, be a positive factor, too. The impact of Greek regions on their transborder partners in Bulgaria seems to be much smaller.

There is, however, another drawback, which relies on the uneven economic and technological potential between the two sides of the border. Too often Germany is the source of capital, technology, design and brand, and the Polish side provides labour, energy and natural environment. This results in the persistence of the 'low road of development' on the side of Poland and 'high road' on the side of Germany (Krätke 1997), which is manifested in constant technological and economic domination of the stronger partner over the weaker one.

There are a few more regions which demonstrate promising chances for development. These are the regions which are the European reservoirs of unspoiled environment. North-East Poland and the entire border region of Poland and Slovakia have extremely promising opportunities to become the basins for tourist services and recreation on the continental scale, providing, however, that these functions do not damage the purest nature in Europe, since conflicts between tourist services and environmental functions are possible. The shore of the Baltic Sea might also possibly attract tourists. The same applies to the tourist-recreational and spa centres with long European traditions.

Regional policies during transformation of East-Central Europe

The regional policies

During the entire transformation period no comprehensive regional policies were formulated in any of the East-Central European countries and the regional aspects of any social or economic policies (as weak as they are) are still almost non-existent. In fact (with the weak exception of Hungary) the national governments of all six countries – at least during the first period of the post-socialist transformation – have left the 'regional problems' to the so-called 'market forces', letting the new economic maps of their countries be reshaped by the sectoral processes. It was only recently that the institutional framework of regional policies appeared in some of these countries and some kind of legislation related to regional/spatial processes was passed.

In Bulgaria a government strategy for regional development has been prepared. It aims at alleviating regional differences through equalisation of public investment, implementation of regional restructuring strategies and strengthening of the positive impacts of transborder co-operation for development of border regions and localities. Studies and analysis of specific regions, as well as for the creation of national administrative and financial institutions (e.g. regional fund) directed towards regional development, are being carried out. A Council of Regional Policy, under the Council of Ministers, was established, and the regional/spatial policy as such lies within the responsibilities of the Ministry for Territorial Development, Housing and Construction. Most of these developments have occurred since 1994 and their real impact on socio-economic processes is severely limited due to the scarcity of financial resources.

In the Czech Republic the principles of regional policies were declared in 1992 and were oriented towards the so-called 'problem areas', mostly through financial incentives provided to the SMEs operating in specified parts of the country. The restructuring of the coal-mining Ostrava-Karvina basin, where the principle stating that not a single *koruna* from public sources can be spent on operating costs of coal mines and should be used only to create jobs outside this sector, for training and re-training of workers leaving mining or for early retirement etc., can be taken as a positive example of regional restructuring in post-socialist countries. In general, however, the neo-liberal doctrine has banned any regional intervention and only after the last elections in 1996 has a more balanced Parliament acknowledged the need for a regional policy. The Ministry for Local Development is responsible for spatial planning, which clearly indicated that this planning is limited to the local–urban scale (i.e. does not go beyond classical physical planning).

In the Slovak Republic no specific programmes or institutions have been created for regional policies. In 1994 the government commissioned the Slovak Ministry of the Environment and later on also the department for Strategy Development of Society and Technology to elaborate the state regional policy. No strategy or proposal has been published so far. Therefore, although it was argued that 'strong regional policy is needed' (OECD-CEET 1996), its presence can only be seen in the state assistance provided to a few areas dominated by military industries. Most of the funds directed at regional assistance programmes come from the PHARE sources. Partial conceptions of regional policies – non-obligatory – are being developed for some regions and regional associations. Spatial planning comes under the supervision of the Ministry for the Environment.

In Hungary the Ministry for the Environment and Regional Policy was established as early as 1990, the Regional Development Fund was reorganised in 1992 and assisted areas were designated and a number of regional programmes were established. Two major directions of regional policies were pursued: improving living conditions in less developed regions and alleviating the negative results of restructuring in regions dominated by traditional industries – a 'crisis management' approach was put in use in the case of the latter regions. The new law on Regional Development and Physical Planning was adopted in 1996, whose principles follow the regulation existing in the European Union (Regional 1998).

In Poland the importance of regional development and regional policies has been growing since 1995 (Gorzelak 1998b). There have been several initiatives undertaken both in the academic and governmental frameworks, which led to the very recent (August 1997) formulation of the principles of the spatial policy of the state (in accordance with the regulations of the Act on Physical Development of the Country, amended in 1994) and to the creation in January 1997 of the Committee for Regional Development within the Councils of Ministers. However, with the exception of three regional programmes directed towards 'old industrial regions' – Katowice, Lódz and Walbrzych – practical implementation of these principles is still a matter for the future, and the regional programmes have not been able to change the situation in these regions in any meaningful way. The PHARE-funded STRUDER programme, supporting these three regions parallel to a group of rural, peripheral ones, is of some importance for regional development and regional restructuring. Spatial planning is carried out at the local level (under the supervision of the newly created Committee for Housing) and on a regional and national level studies and concept of policies are being formulated. A slow, but clear shift from the equity-oriented regional policy to the efficiency-directed doctrine can be observed.

In Romania 'no clear programme for the development of regional policy is yet in existence . . . and no specific institutions have been created to take responsibility in this area' (EPRC 1996: 181). Some progress should be made as a result of a Green Paper on Regional Development, which is being prepared with the PHARE funding.

As can be seen from this concise presentation, only in three of the East-Central European countries out of six under discussion (i.e. in Hungary and Poland and in some way also in the Czech Republic) have regional policy and regional development received some attention. The other three countries seem to neglect the regional problem, which may be due to the fact that economic restructuring has not led, as yet, to durable positive effects in these countries. Moreover, in the majority of cases the regional policies – as weak as they were in all East-Central Europe – have been subordinated to the traditionally-oriented approaches, i.e. targeted to less developed, peripheral regions and to the regions undergoing deep industrial decline. None of the activities undertaken within the regional policies were directed towards enhancing the innovative environment in relatively more developed regions, which have displayed some potential for global competition. Only very recently (1998–9) have the discussions undertaken in Poland seemed to lead to the efficiency- and competition-driven regional policy which would replace the traditional doctrine of levelling out the interregional differences, though its practical implementation is still far off.

It seems that nowadays the two most important questions concerning the principles of regional policies in East-Central Europe are:

- can the East-Central European countries, needing rapid modernisation and growth, (which is a basic prerequisite for any restructuring) spend resources on alleviating regional differences which will necessarily grow, or should they concentrate on promoting development, investment, inflow of capital, which – necessarily – would be concentrated only in some regions and places?
- can these countries build modern, competitive economies and democratic societies in a centralised state, or should they enter the process of decentralisation by building strong regional units?

The traditional doctrine of regional policies has provided a direct answer to the first question: equality at the expense of efficiency. However, already five-year-old approaches to this dilemma seem to challenge this deeply rooted principle. In an OECD document we read:[2] 'a major objective of regional policy is to ensure that the spatial allocation of resources contributes to create economic growth, that is to promote competitiveness and to reduce unemployment.' The East-Central European countries have therefore a choice between traditional and rather ineffective policies which aim to decrease regional differences and the efficiency-oriented policies which can result in fast economic growth, deep economic restructuring and rapid technological advancement, at the expense of regional polarisation (which, in fact, is taking place in all post-socialist countries[3]). The first type of regional policies would be more rooted in the notion of 'social justice' – the second would lead to increased competitiveness of the leaders of transformation, and in this way of the entire national economies.

The decentralised or centralised state

The territorial organisation of the state is one of the most important aspects of the territorial development and regional policy. In a centralised state, in which the decisions are taken at the national level and in which the state budget has a strong redistributive function, the pro-efficiency regional policies are hard to implement, since the limits for development policies of the regions themselves are very narrow, indeed. In a decentralised state there are much richer possibilities for the regions to conduct their own policies that can be related to the specific situation of particular regions.

The reforms which moved the East-Central European countries from authoritarian rule to the democratic system have – paradoxically – in some cases led to increased centralisation on the territorial level. In the first 'shock of freedom' the process of fragmentation of the territorial units took place in Czecho-Slovakia and Hungary (Illner 1997). Hundreds of new municipalities were created, some of them with no more than fifty inhabitants. The regional level was abolished (only recently has it been reintroduced in the Czech Republic). In Hungary the attempts to create large regions (governed by the so-called 'Representatives of the Republic') were turned down and the bigger regional units are conceived to be built 'from below', by the decisions of the lower-level units, the counties. Even in Bulgaria, where the regional units seem to be sufficiently big, there are plans to reintroduce twenty-eight much smaller traditional territorial units. Only in Poland has a comprehensive reform which is aimed at creating large regions been conducted, though it was delayed for several years (it will be described later).

As a result, in most East-Central European countries self-government is limited to the very local level, composed of thousands of small municipalities (numbering more than 6,000 in the case of the Czech Republic). With the exception of Poland, the regional level either does not exist, or is subordinated to the central government. Where the highest level is composed of small sub-regional units, their size does not allow for own development policies of the regional administration.

As can be seen from Table 5.4, the territorial organisation of the six states differs considerably. In terms of average area the new Polish *voivodships* are by far the biggest regional units. Next come Bulgarian regions. Polish old regions (*voivodships*) were similar in size to Hungarian counties (*megye*) and both these units are bigger than the Czech and Slovak districts – in the Czech part of the former Czechoslovakia the truly regional units were destroyed and very recently in the Slovak Republic the large regions were split into smaller

Table 5.4 Territories and administrative structures in East-Central Europe

Countries	*Total area, 1,000 km²*	*Number and status of administrative units*		
		regional	*county/district*	*local*
Bulgaria	111,0	9 governmental		249 self-governmental
Czech Republic	78.9	– (8 plus 1 urban abolished in 1991)	77 plus Prague governmental	6,233 self-governmental
Hungary	93.0	– (creation of 6 Representatives of the Republic stopped in 1995)	19 self-governmental/ governmental, 22 cities of county status	2,920 rural, 173 towns, self-governmental
Poland until 31 December 1998	312.7	49 governmental/ indirectly self-governmental	267 purely governmental	315 urban 1613 rural 555 urban–rural, self-governmental
Poland after 1 January 1999		16 self-governmental/ governmental	308 rural, 65 urban, purely self-governmental	
Romania	238.4	40 governmental 1 municipality (Bucharest)		
Slovak Republic	49.0	8	79 governmental	2,679 rural 135 towns self-governmental

ones. With the exception of Poland, in all countries the government controls the tier(s) of territorial division above the local level.

The self-governmental commune (municipality) is the biggest in Bulgaria – its average size is 430 sq. kilometres and average population 30,000. Then comes Poland, where only twenty-seven (i.e. 1 per cent) communes have less than 2,500 inhabitants. In Hungary one-third of municipalities have a population of fewer than 500 inhabitants. In the Czech Republic some 80 per cent of the municipalities have a population of fewer than 1,000.

There are also differences in the powers and competencies of local governments. Polish municipalities seem to be the strongest economic and legal entities. Although the size of Bulgarian communes is the greatest, they

Table 5.5 Expenditure of local budgets within national public finances, 1993

Countries	*Local expenditure as per cent of:*	
	all public expenditure	*GDP*
Bulgaria	19.8	8.6
Czech Republic	25.2	9.8
Hungary	26.1	18.7
Poland	19.0	6.2
Romania	–	3.3
Slovak Republic	13.2	6.7

do not have sufficient competencies and sources of revenues (Stoyanovska *et al.* 1993). Table 5.5 presents the positions of local budgets within the national systems of public finance (Gilowska and Misiag 1995, Table 4).

As can be seen from Table 5.5, only in Hungary can the system of public finances be labelled as decentralised. Romania and Slovak Republic displayed much higher levels of centralisation than other countries.

The powers allocated to local authorities in the post-socialist countries allow them to enter into international co-operation. With the involvement of national authorities, the local/regional units of the six countries have established several EUROREGIONS, which embrace territorial units from the six post-socialist countries and their neighbours. Through PHARE-CROSSBORDER several projects of transborder co-operation are being financed, which pave the way for the future integration of these countries with the European Union. It should be stated, however, that either the transborder co-operation is unevenly supported financially with the dominance of one partner only (as in the case of Polish-German and Polish-Czech-German Euroregions) or this co-operation is weak and anticipates further problems, as in the case of Polish–Lithuanian and Polish–Ukrainian–Slovak–Hungarian Euroregion Carpathia, for example.

The Polish decentralisation reform was conducted in two steps: the first one was taken in 1990, when true self-government was reintroduced on the local level. The second step was taken in 1999 by reintroducing self-government on the mezzo- and regional levels. The territorial structure of public authorities in Poland is the following:

- 16 regional units (*voivodships*), equipped with the self-government elected in direct elections and presided over by a marshal. In theory, the self-government authorities are responsible for all development matters in their region, though in practice their financial resources (coming from a 5 per cent share in state personal income tax and state subsidies) are far too scarce to implement these tasks. Parallel to the self-government authorities there is the governmental administration, headed by the *voivod*, who is nominated by the prime minister and is responsible for implementing state policies (which should be limited to 'police-like' duties, i.e. maintenance of national standards etc.) Big *voivodships* have to assume many of the responsibilities of the national government, which should make the central government smaller, but stronger. Along with the process of decentralisation they will also be able to undertake new tasks which at present are not carried out at all (such as the creation of regional systems of innovation, technology transfer centres, international promotion, etc.).

- 308 fully self-government districts (although only 200 would be economically viable). The *powiat* councils are elected by direct vote. They have assumed some responsibilities previously performed by the former *voivodships* (such as the administration of hospitals, secondary schools, roads, etc.). The *powiats* provide these services which are too 'big' for the local units – the *gminas*. No functions of the *gminas* were transferred up to the districts. In the first year of their activities the *powiats* appear to be underfinanced, and there is a need to add extra resources to the current 1.5 per cent share in state personal income tax plus state subsidies for services performed by the powiats.
- *Gminas*, numbering around 2,500, which remain the basic self-government territorial structure and which are the main creator of the local business climate and local economic development.

Polish experience clearly indicates that territorial decentralisation releases new potential for development. The success of Polish transformation is often rightly attributed to two main factors: the private entrepreneurs and local self-governments. The creation of additional levels of the territorial self-government should release still new reserves of social and institutional initiative and activity.

European integration and the Central European transformation

Becoming full members of the European Union is for the Central European countries a strategic goal of the highest importance. This membership should be considered in several dimensions:

- *political*: joining the European structure would unambiguously introduce the CEC into the Western sphere of influence, thus ending their 'hung' position between East and West;[4]
- *economic*: the mutual exchange with the European Union markets is the major direction of foreign trade of the CEC; the vast majority of foreign investment arrives to the CEC from the EU countries, increasing the possibilities of fixed capital formation and structural change;
- *social*: common cultural heritage, current cultural and social ties, point to the European Union as the most natural direction for personal contacts, cultural interrelations, tourist movements, etc.;
- *technological*: achieving technological advancement is a condition for

the economic and social restructuring of the CEC. The European Union, as the main supplier of foreign capital and the greatest investor, is of crucial importance in this process.

Achieving access to the common policies of the European Union and the Structural Funds is an important, though often exaggerated, advantage of future membership. Currently, the weakest national economies may receive as much as up to 4 per cent of their GDP in the form of payments from the Structural Funds (this is a gross figure – net transfer is half the size, since the contribution of a given country to the common budget should be deducted).

Table 5.6 The balance-sheets for accessing the European Union by the Central European countries

The Central European perspective	*The European Union perspective*
+	+
1. Direct access to the largest single market in the world.	1. Getting access to an additional market of over 60 million consumers.
2. Access to sources of capital, new technologies, new organisational skills.	2. Securing political and military stability on Eastern side of the Union and thus achieving better control of a 'buffer zone' between the Western European 'core' and the potentially unstable post-Soviet republics.
3. Taking advantage of the structural funds and other forms of assistance for the poorer member states, regions and individuals.	3. Proceeding on the economic and political paths of integration that have strong ideological underpinnings.
4. Modernising the administrative structures, legislation, norms and rules.	4. Broadening access to new land acquisitions, locations for retirement, to rich natural environment, etc.
5. Taking advantage of political and military integration with the strong partner.	5. Opening new opportunities for the regions bordering the new member states.
–	–
1. Necessity of a general economic, social, technical and legislative adaptation to common regulations within the EU.	1. Admitting competition on the 'sensitive' markets.
2. Entering into an open competition with the more technologically advanced producers on all markets.	2. Enlarging the scope of assistance directed to poorer countries, regions, institutions and individuals.
3. Opening of the Central European economies to the intervention of international economic agents, which may result in permanent subordination of the CEC to international capital.	3. Moving of some less developed regions below the threshold of 75 per cent of the new, lower EU average of GDP/person.
4. Allowing for land ownership by foreigners, which may meet with some resentments of historical background.	

It is obvious that present architecture of the common structural policies could not be maintained after enlarging the EU with new members. It appears that the reforms of the common agricultural policy and the structural policy of the European Union are rather shallow, which does not create many opportunities for the potential members. This will not allow the pursuit of the traditional course of generous assistance directed to the backward and poor regions and countries and will make the structural policy more selective and efficiency-oriented than before.

There is also another factor that may slow down the association process – the competition on several 'sensitive' markets that the CEC may enter into with the producers in the EU. Free exports of agricultural products, coal, steel, textiles – these products in which the CEC may have an advantage due to their lower labour costs – are considered as dangerous for EU producers. This is why, despite numerous declarations of support for Central European countries in their attempts at integration with the EU, the reality has proved to be different. In particular, the trade restrictions practised by the EU give grounds to suggest that some EU countries are in fact opposed to a full integration of Central and Eastern European countries since they are afraid of their competition in the particularly sensitive segments of the market.

The balance-sheets of enlargement (Gorzelak 1998a) reveal positive results for both the European Union and the Central European countries, though the 'red' (negative) side of these balance-sheets is not blank (see Table 5.6). On the whole, from both perspectives the enlargement of the European Union seems to lead to positive results and one may hope that this process will proceed in a smooth and uninterrupted way.

Conclusion

The Central European countries need a breakthrough in their approach to spatial/regional problems of their development. It can be advocated that the foundations of regional policies should assume the following principles. First, regional policies should be subordinated to the strategic objectives of a given country as a whole. These objectives can be formulated as the need to catch up with the more advanced countries in socio-economic development by promoting a high rate of economic growth and deep structural changes, which is a prerequisite for joining the European Union.

Second, since the pattern of polarised regional development has to be acknowledged as a real and inevitable way of national development, the regional policy at the turn of the century should be oriented towards efficiency, because this principle allows for accelerated growth and increase of new capital formation, which is necessary for changing obsolete economic structures of the countries of Central and Eastern Europe. Therefore, the regional policies should not – at least during the next 10–15 years – be oriented towards equalisation of regional differences.

Third, the regional policies of the Central and Eastern European states should concentrate on these undertakings which are crucial for the spatial-functional structure of their entire countries, in particular those that are connected with their international relations. The state authorities should be – along with the regional authorities – jointly responsible for the development (with the growing participation of the private sector) of basic transport and telecommunications infrastructure, border crossings, sea harbours, air traffic facilities, etc.

Fourth, the regional policies of the states should prioritise assistance for regional restructuring of the areas dominated by traditional industries. This objective has to be undertaken for both economic and political reasons.

Fifth, since the tasks of equalising some of the regional differences should not be totally neglected as they could lead to irreversible divisions in some of the Central and eastern European countries and the permanent marginalisation of some territories and their communities, a principle of 'balancing regional development' should be adopted, which means that nobody would aim at 'balanced' meaning 'levelled' regional structure of the country, although alleviating those differences which could permanently distort the development potential in the depressed or backward regions should be one of the explicit goals of such a policy.

Finally, decentralisation of the territorial organisation of the states should be performed; the territorial self-governmental units should be responsible for most of the duties and tasks that are currently performed by the governmental administration at the central and territorial levels.

Notes

1 For example, a Polish rural commune Tarnowo Podgórne – just west of Poznan – attracted over 400 million US dollars of Western – mostly German – investment, which is due to the ability of local authorities to take advantage of a favourable location close to a big city and to an international road.

2 Themes for discussion, 3rd informal meeting of OECD Ministers responsible for Regional Policies, Vienna 1994 (mimeo).

3 And is part reality in the European Union – see EC (1996), which openly states that the policies aiming at decreasing the regional policies proved to be ineffective, as least in the decade 1983–93.

4 There is a famous saying by a Polish playwright, Slawomir Mrocek: '*Poland is a country located east to West and west to East.*' The Czechs, as the only ones from Eastern-Central Europe, would not have such problems with self-affiliation, since they have belonged to the West for most of their modern history, in spite of their Slavic origins.

References

Balcerowicz, L. (1997) *Szkice z prze omu epok* (*Essays from the Change of Epoques*), Warszawa: PWN.

Bradshaw, M. and Stenning, A. (1999) 'The progress of transition in East Central Europe', in J. Bachtler, R. Downs and G. Gorzelak (eds) *EU Enlargement: Cohesion and Regional Policy,* Dartmouth (forthcoming).

EC (1996) *First Report on Economic and Social Cohesion*, Luxembourg: European Commission.

EPRC (1996) *Draft Final Report to the European Commission (DGXVI)*, Glasgow: University of Strathclyde: EPRC.

Fazekas, K. and Gorzelak, G. (1995) 'Restructuring and the labour market in regions dominated by heavy industry in Central and Eastern Europe', in *The Regional Dimension of Unemployment in Transition Countries*, Paris: OECD.

Gilowska, Z. and Misiag, W. (1995) *Decentralizacja polskiego systemu budzetowego (Decentralisation of the Polish Budgetary System*), Gdansk-Lublin: Instytut Badan nad Gospodarka Rynkowa.

Gorzelak, G. (1995a) *Transformacja systemowa a restrukturyzacja regionalna (Systemic Transformation and Regional Restructuring*), Warszawa: EUROREG.

Gorzelak, G. (1995b) *Regional Dimension of Transformation in Central Europe*, London and Bristol, Pennsylvania: Jessica Kingsley Publishers.

Gorzelak, G. (1998a) 'Europäische Integration und Regionalpolitik in den Transformationländer', in H.-J. Wagener and H. Fritz (eds) *Im Osten was Neues*, Bonn: Dietz.

Gorzelak G. (1998b): *The Regional and Local Potential for Transformation in Poland*, Warszawa: EUROREG.

Gorzelak, G., Jalowiecki, B., Kukliski, A. and Zienkowski, L. (1994) *Eastern and Central Europe 2000. Final Report,* Luxembourg: Commission of the EC.

Halamska, M. (1999) *Dekolektywizacja rolnictwa w Europie Srodkowej i jej spoleczne konsekwencje (Decollectivisation of Agriculture in Central Europe and Its Social Consequences)*, Warsaw: Polish Academy of Sciences.

Illner, M. (1997) *The Territorial Dimension of Public Administration Reforms in East Central Europe,* Working Papers Institute of Sociology, Prague: Academy of Sciences of the Czech Republic.

Jarosinski, W. (1998) 'Rozwój gospodarczy Polski na tle krajów Europy Srodkowo-Wschodniej', ('Development of Poland among other Central European Countries'), *Z Prac ZBSE*, z. 253, Warsaw: GUS.

Krätke, S. (1997) 'Regional integration of Fragmentation? The German-polish border region in a new Europe', paper presented at the Regional Studies Association Conference, Frankfurt (Oder).

OECD-CEET (1996) *Regional Problems and Policies in the Czech Republic and the Slovak Republic*, Paris: OECD.

Regional (1998) *Regional Development in Hungary,* Budapest: Ministry of Agriculture and Regional Development.

Stoyanovska, A., Lukanova, P. and Spirydonova, J. (1993) *Bulgaria – Country Report for the LEDA Programme*, Sofia-Brussels (mimeo).

6 Regional labour market differentials during transition in Hungary[1]

Károly Fazekas

Introduction

This chapter presents results of an attempt to classify Hungarian local labour markets by the most important determinants of regional unemployment rate differences. First, four prominent features of the Hungarian regional unemployment dispersion are discussed. The second section presents a taxonomy of the Hungarian local labour markets according to the determinants of regional unemployment rates differentials, and then we sum up policy implications based on the classification presented in this chapter.

Major characteristics of regional unemployment rate differences in Hungary

The harsh emergence of open unemployment has been accompanied by wide regional differences in the labour market in Hungary since 1990. Traditional regional inequalities acquired a new dimension with the appearance of open unemployment. The incidence of regional unemployment differences has had four important features during transition: (a) relatively wide range and persistence of regional dispersion; (b) high stability of the position of local labour markets in the rank of unemployment rates; (c) high degree of spatial fragmentation of labour markets; and (d) substantial accumulation of labour market tensions in hard-hit regions.

Regional differences of unemployment in transitional countries are usually examined by regional indicators aggregated at the level of counties, macro regions or given types of settlements.[2] (Dorenbos 1999; Laky 1998; Scarpetta 1995). These aggregates, however, conceal or fail to reveal the existing differences between various types of local labour markets. Although county or regional level indicators show a relatively wide range of unemployment differences, a considerably greater regional alteration can be observed if regional unemployment ratios are examined on the level of sub-regions[3] or on the level of employment district,[4] which are more adequate to actual local labour markets.

Range and persistence of regional dispersion of unemployment

In March 1993 – at the peak of the time path of the unemployment rate between 1990–8 – the difference between the bottom and top quarters of employment districts was more than 50 per cent higher than that between the bottom and top quarters of the counties. The rate of unemployment in the lowest quartile of the 170 employment districts peaked at 8 per cent in March 1993. In the upper quartile, the average rate approached 25 per cent and failed to drop below 20 per cent at the end of 1996 while the rate of the lowest and upper quartiles was less than 8 per cent in the last two years. The Evans (1985) or Jackman–Roper (1987) index measuring the degree of regional mismatch of labour demand and supply[5] while having increased until the end of 1992, then fell from 2.0 to 1.8 in 1994 (Fazekas and Ozsvald 1998).

Figures 6.1, 6.2 and 6.3 show the time path of regional differences of registered unemployment at the level of sub-regions measured by the average unemployment ratios of deciles of the 150 sub-regions. Note the extremely wide relative differences, which emerged in the first few months of transition. After that the relative position of top and bottom deciles started to shrink rapidly until 1993. Figures show a substantial increase in regional differences of registered unemployment ratios between 1993–8.

The measured rate of unemployment, however, is influenced by the cost of and benefit from looking for a job: in regions with low demand for labour, workers may give up the job search entirely and may be counted in surveys as inactive. The rate of non-participation correlates with the rate of unemployment. In the first quartile employment districts (by unemployment in rate March 1993) the rate of inactivity was 45 per cent in 1993 and had risen by less than 1 per cent by the end of 1994. In the fourth quartile the rate was 46 per cent and raised by 2.5 per cent in the same period (Fazekas and Köllõ 1998).

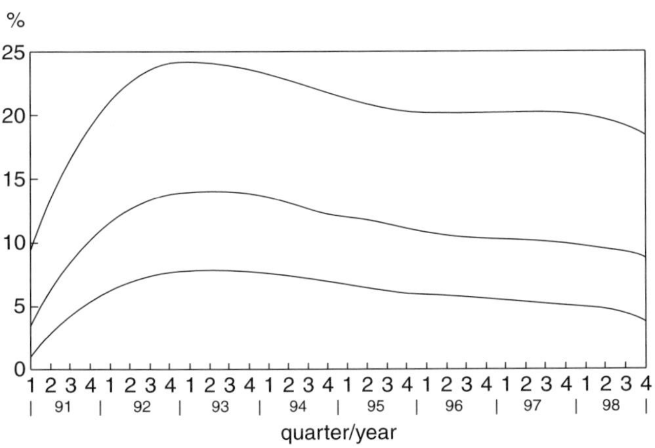

Figure 6.1 Time path of the average unemployment rates in the lowest and upper quintiles and the median of sub-regions.

Source: IE-HAS Regional Database.

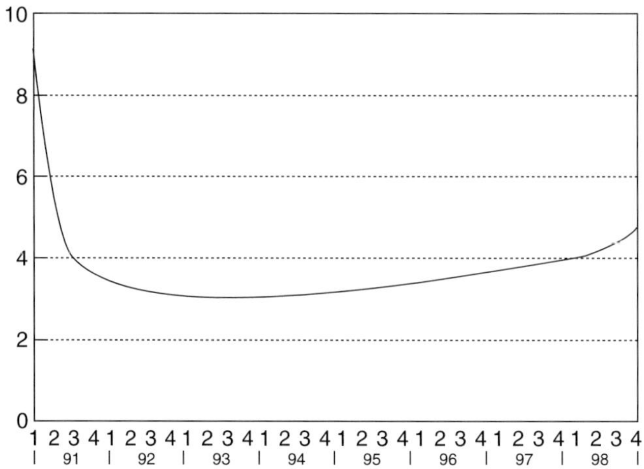

Figure 6.2 Time path of the ratio of average unemployment rates in the lowest and upper quintiles of sub-regions.

Source: IE-HAS Regional Database.

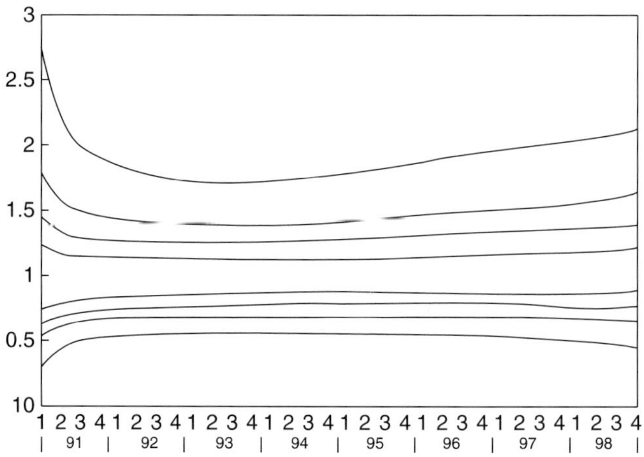

Figure 6.3 Relative regional unemployment rate differentials (from above: mean unemployment rate of the 10th, 9th, 8th, 7th, 4th, 3rd, 2nd, 1st decile divided by the median unemployment rate).

Source: IE-HAS Regional Database.

Expressing the mean unemployment rates of the different deciles in percentages of the median (fiftieth centime) at each period of time, a more sophisticated picture of the time path of the relative unemployment rate differentials emerges. This measure of relative differential is, by definition, independent of the current levels. Figure 6.3 shows that the very large relative inequalities in the early phase are almost entirely due to the extremely high relative unemployment rates of some sub-regions which had the highest unemployment rates at the starting period. Ábrahám and Kertesi attribute these peculiarities of the first phases to the changing composition of factors having decisive influence on relative regional differences. 'Certain factors which at the start might have had temporarily decisive influence on relative regional differences are losing their importance, and are being replaced gradually by some more basic factors that in the long run shape regional inequalities' (Ábrahám and Kertesi 1998). Figure 6.3 shows that after 1993 – parallel to the decrease in the unemployment rate – there is a substantial increase in regional unemployment rate differences at the level of sub-regions, mostly due to the relative deterioration in position of the sub-regions which had the highest unemployment rates.

Stability of the relative position of sub-regions with respect to unemployment rates

One could predict considerable changes in the relative position of individual sub-regions with respect to their actual unemployment rates over time. As different factors may determine relative differentials in the early and in the later phases of transition, it seems reasonable to compare relative positions at the start and at the end of the 1990–6 period. Nevertheless, figures show significant stability among relative positions. Correlation coefficients between the unemployment rates registered in December 1998 and quartiles between March 1991 and September 1998 are higher than 0.8. This is a relatively high value if we consider that the average sub-region has a labour force of about 26,000:[6] thus, the market is small enough to be exposed to random fluctuations (see Figure 6.4).

Table 6.1 shows inter-quartile unemployment rate transitions between December 1992 and December 1998. Most of the cases are to be found in the neighbourhood of the main diagonal. Only eight sub-regions (5.3 per cent) changed their position by more than one quartile in six years. Figure 6.5 shows the time path of percentages of regions which did not perform inter-quartile transition from March 1991 to March 1993 and from March 1993 to December 1998. This figure gives information on the time path of the intensity of inter-quartile transition. One can see that the bulk of the changes took place in the first four turbulent years of transition. Actually there were no changes in the position of sub-regions after 1994. The winners of the first years remained winners and the losers remained losers, see Figure 6.6.

Spatial fragmentation

There are large differences between the employment districts or the sub-regions of each county in terms of development, wages and unemployment in particular. It is easy to illustrate the latter by the analysis of variance. In

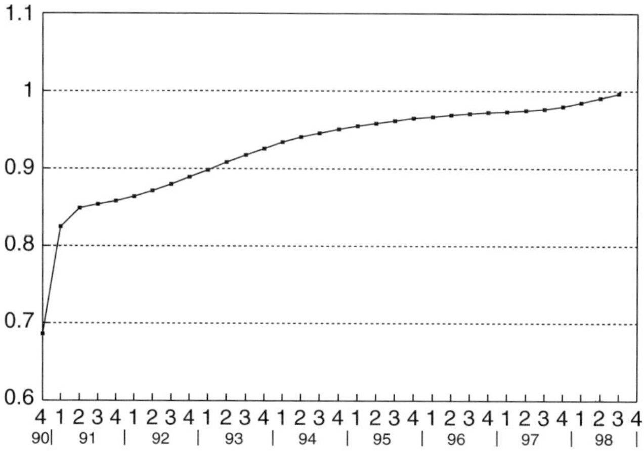

Figure 6.4 Correlation coefficients between sub-regional unemployment rates (Dec. 1990–Sept. 1998) and unemployment rate Dec. 1998.

Source: IE-HAS Regional Database.

Table 6.1 Inter-quartile unemployment rate transitions (December 1992–December 1998)

Unemployment rate in Dec. 1992	*Unemployment rate in December 1998 (quartiles)*				*Number of sub-regions*
	lowest	*second*	*third*	*highest*	
Lowest quartile	**25**	11	2		38
Second quartile	11	**14**	9	3	37
Third quartile	2	11	**15**	9	37
Highest quartile		1	11	**26**	38
Number of sub-regions	38	37	37	38	**150**

Source: IE-HAS Regional Database.

March 1993, for instance, the standard deviation of the unemployment rates of the 170 employment districts amounted to 5.04 per cent with between-county variance and within-county variance. The county-level classification could capture half of the employment district variation of unemployment rates (F = 9.84 (0.000), $r^2 = 0.4985$) (for an overview of the employment district level regional differences of unemployment rates see Map 6.1).

Accumulation of labour market tensions in hard-hit regions

The unemployment rate is an important though by no means the only indicator of employment tensions. Table 6.2 shows substantial accumulation of employment tensions in regions hit by a high rate of unemployment. In hard-

Figure 6.5 Percentages of sub-regions being in the same quartiles as in March 1993.

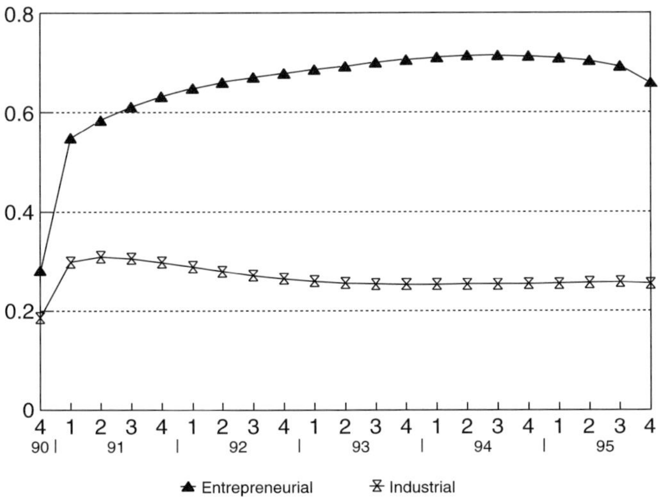

Figure 6.6 Time path of standardised parameters of factor 1 and factor 2 in the pre-transitional model.

hit regions one could observe a higher ratio of hard-to-place (low educated, long-term) unemployed. High unemployment is accompanied by a higher outflow from the labour market. In the top quartiles the ratio of working age inactive population is substantially higher than in the bottom quartile.

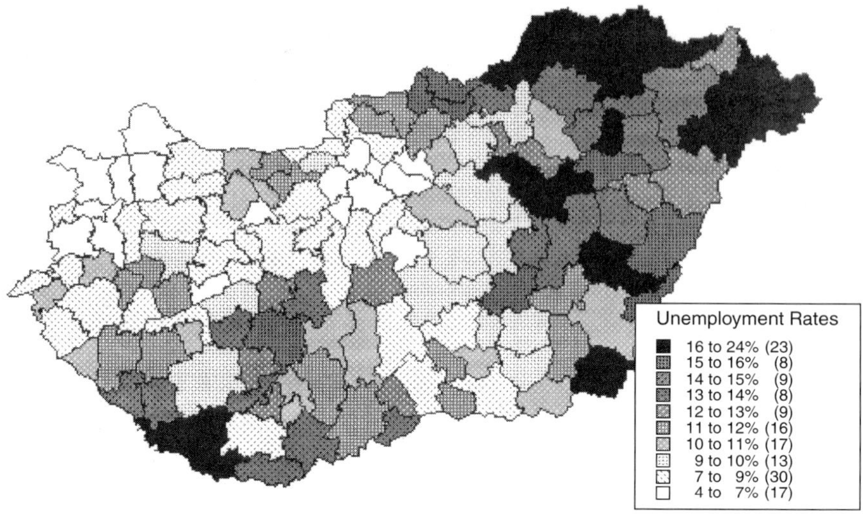

Map 6.1 Sub-region level unemployment rates in 1997.

Table 6.2 Characteristics of registered unemployed (December 1996)

	Entire population	*Top quartile*	*Button quartiles*
Level of education[a]			
Max. 8 classes	41.8	37.1	47.8
University	2.7	4.3	1.2
Lengths of unemployment[a]			
less than 3 months	5.0	7.3	2.9
more than 1 year	4.76	30.3	42.5
Labour market status of active age population[b]			
employed	44.4	37.1	50.3
unemployed	5.4	6.6	4.2
out of labour force	50.2	56.3	45.5
Ratio of unemployed received social unemployment benefit[a]	44.3	33.8	56.8

Sources: [a] OMK database
[b] HCSO Labour Force Survey.

Typology of the Hungarian local labour markets according to determinants of regional unemployment rate differentials

Pre-transitional classification of sub-regions

Spatial dispersions of unemployment in transitional countries are often traced to a higher regional concentration of industrial plants established in the pre-transition period (Jackman and Rutkowski 1994). As far as Hungary is concerned, regional analyses challenge this explanation. Analysis of employment districts and HCSO sub-regions (Fazekas 1996; HCSO 1995) has shown how unemployment rate differentials in cross section can be tracked down mainly to two key factors: differences in the entrepreneurial and industrial capacity of regions at the starting point of transition.

A common experience with various attempts along these lines (but using different sets of variables or factor techniques) is that unemployment rates have little to do with either industrialisation or with the often-used Herfindahl index measuring the degree of diversification in a region's economy (Scarpetta 1995; Simon 1988). Although the collapse of large industrial firms did generate high unemployment in some regions, especially in single-employer towns like in the infamous case of Ózd (Fazekas 1990), this and similar cases are more an exception than a rule. Unemployment is typically high in remote agricultural regions with poor infrastructure, low educational levels, no tourism, poorly developed services and trade, with large Gypsy communities and location far from the affluent centres of the country (Ábrahám and Kertesi 1998; Fazekas and Köllõ 1998).

The first classification of Hungarian local labour markets based on pre-transitional determinants of regional unemployment differences was carried out in 1993 (Fazekas 1996; HCSO 1995.) Correlation between regional unemployment rates and the state and structure of the local economy were examined in four steps:

1 A large number of regional indicators were considered to cover physical and human infrastructure (water, sewage, gas and phone supply, schooling levels), structure of the local economy (ratio of industry, agriculture, self-employment), wealth (cars, tax base, land quality). The correlation between these variables and regional rates of unemployment was explored.
2 Variables found relevant were factor-analysed in order to achieve a relatively small set of uncorrelated dimensions.
3 Local unemployment rates were regressed on the factors to assess their relative importance.
4 Finally, employment districts were classified according to the two most important factors.

Fazekas' model identified two factors determining the bulk of regional differences in unemployment at sub-region level.

Factor 1 Entrepreneurial capacity

This factor quantifies the extent to which infrastructure and social conditions of economic development were in place in the sub-region in 1990–1, at the starting point of the transition. The factor takes a high positive score in a region with a higher than average: ratio of self-employed persons; number of cars per thousand inhabitants, per capita PIT; ratio of households connected to water supply network; number of telephones per thousand inhabitants; level of education of inhabitants; positive balance of migration; and the average activity of inhabitants; and with a lower than the country average of people employed in agriculture.

Factor 2 Industrial capacity

This factor could be used to characterise the dominance of state-owned, capital-intensive industries in the local economy. The factor had high positive scores in regions where the ratio of those employed in industrial companies with more than 50 employees was higher than the average; the per capita capital stock of industrial companies was higher than the average and the ratio of those employed in agriculture was lower than the average.

Multivariate regression equations were calculated using factor values as independent variables and regional unemployment rates as dependent variables with a result of very good estimations of regional unemployment rates. Four types of regions were classified by the combination of the two factors:

- entrepreneurial – industrial regions,
- entrepreneurial – non-industrial regions,
- non-entrepreneurial – industrial regions,
- non-entrepreneurial – non-industrial regions.

Industrial regions with relatively good entrepreneurial capacities are situated along the western border of the country, at the centre of the Trans-Danubian region, and around the largest cities of the country. Non-industrial regions with relatively good entrepreneurial capacities are located around Lake Balaton, Budapest, and in the southern part of the Hungarian Plain. Industrial regions with relatively poor entrepreneurial capacities are situated along the north-eastern border of the country while non-industrial sub-regions of unfavourable entrepreneurial capacities are located in the central and eastern parts of the Great Hungarian Plain (see Map 6.2).

Hungarian data indicate that the dominance of the state-run large-scale industry on its own is in a negative relationship with the level of unemployment emerging in a given local economy. The dominance of big state industry has led to higher unemployment only in those regions where this dominance was coupled with a less favourable entrepreneurial capacity. This means that job/enterprise destruction seems to be less important than job creation in determining regional unemployment rates.

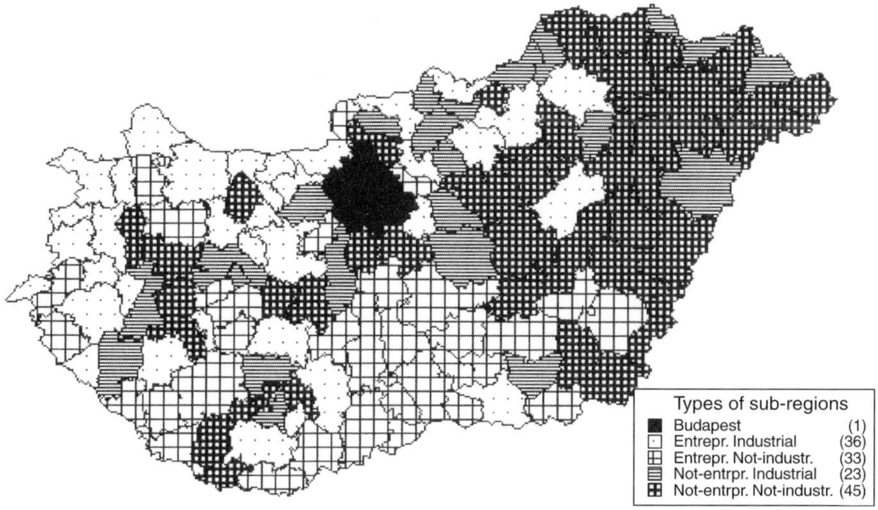

Map 6.2 Pre-transitional typology of sub-regions.

As most of the variables in the pre-transitional set are either constant over time or change little (in relative terms) during the transition one may try to study their effect on unemployment over time. Figure 6.5 shows the time path of standardised parameters of the two most powerful factors in multivariate regression equations where the four factors were used as independent variables and employment district level unemployment rates between quarters of 1990–6 were used as dependent variables. The explanatory power of the model rises fast to a level of a $R^2 = 0.6–0.7$ as we move from 1990 to 1996 (and it is very stable after 1992). Both factors are significant at least from mid-1992 onwards. Over time it is the entrepreneurial capacity that has stronger and increasing explanatory power. Industrial capacity has a weaker but significant effect in the period investigated.

Post-transitional classification of sub-regions

The pre-transitional model attached great importance to the weight of pre-transitional industrial employment and to the level of entrepreneurial capacity. These factors reflect the regions' potential to react to the enormous challenges of transition. Although this model gave good estimations on regional unemployment differences over the years of transition, we have found good reasons to modify it. Part of this potential manifested itself directly in the original variables of the factors (level of education, level of development of infrastructure) but some of the crucial indicators of adaptability were not represented directly in the old model.

In this chapter an updated version of the pre-transitional classification of sub-regions will be presented. Recent tendencies of regional unemployment rate differentials will be explained by a set of independent factors representing some stable and some dynamic post-transitional characteristics of Hungarian local labour markets. As we are concentrating on sub-regional differences in unemployment, Budapest will be excluded from the analysis.

The chapter will follow four steps:

- Selection of sub-regional level variables reflecting determinants of regional unemployment rate differentials.
- Identifying factors of independent groups of variables accounting for the largest amount of variance in the sample.
- Measurement of explanatory power of factors by cross-sectional multivariate regressions.
- Classification of sub-regions based on the most powerful factors.

Selection of regional variables

High stability in the explanatory power of factors representing regional characteristics at the starting point could be explained by three main causes:

- A part of the pre-transitional regional variables did not change much over the years of transition (level of education, transport networks, entrepreneurial tradition).
- Behind the factors there are very stable latent variables (such as geographical position, ethnic composition of the regions).
- There is a strong correlation between the 1990 and 1998 values of dynamic variables (indicators of infrastructure development or intensity of enterprise creations, income, industrial employment) (see Table 6.3).

Table 6.3 Correlation coefficients between some pre- and post-transitional sub-regional variables

Variables	*PHONE 1997*	*CARS 1997*	*ENTDENS 1997*	*INCTAX 1996*	*INDUSTRY 1997*	*SELFEMP 1997*
PHONE 1991	.6334	.5153	.6586	.5193	.1806	.5504
CARS 1991	.7199	.8929	.6606	.5477	.1971	.6597
ENTDENS 1992	.7716	.7776	.9803	.7464	.0444	.5941
INCTAX 1991	.6862	.6349	.7770	.9416	.3571	.3679
INDUSTRY 1990	.2537	.1704	.2234	.5178	.8049	.0177
SELFEMP 1990	.7165	.6738	.6031	.3989	–.0267	.9768

Source: IE-HAS Regional Database.

When updating the model we used three new regional variables reflecting geographical position, ethnic composition and the results of enterprise creation in sub-regions, namely, DISTANCE: distance from the important innovation centres of the transition (Budapest, northern and southern part of the Austrian border) measured by average travelling time on road;[7] GYPSY92: estimation ratio of Gypsy population in the region in 1992;[8] ENTDENS: density of enterprises in the region (t = 1992–7). Updating the original variables in most cases we used variables from the HCSO/ TSTAR community level data base for the years 1990–7. Unfortunately, in the case of some variables (ratio of active population employed in agriculture, level of education) at settlement level there are no other sources than the HCSO/Census-1990. Sub-regional level unemployment rates and regional characteristics of the registered unemployed were calculated from the OMK-Unemployment Register. Register data were available for four months in each year between 1990–8 (March, June, September and December). Table 6.4 shows sets of regional variables used in the following steps of analysis. Table 6.5 shows correlation coefficients between regional variables and sub-regional level unemployment rates between 1991 and 1997. One could observe strong significant correlation in all cases of the new and the updated variables.

Table 6.4 Content and source of variables used in the post-transitional model

Variable	*Content of the variable*
$UNEMPL_t$	Seasonally adjusted quarterly unemployment rates t = 1-33, 1 = 1990 December, 33=1998 December[c]
FARMSt	Number of employees in private farms per 1000 person of population (t = 1991 and 1994)[b]
$INDUSTRY_t$	Ratio of employees in industry in the active age population (t = 1991–7)[b]
INDSIZEt	Average number of employees of industrial plants in the su-region (t= 1991–7)
$CARS_t$	Number of cars per 1000 person of population (t = 1991–1997)[b]
$INCTAX_t$	Personal income tax per 1000 person of population (t = 1990–6)[e]
$PHONE_t$	Number of telephone lines per 1000 person of population (t = 1991–7)[b]
EDUC90	Average number of completed classes per capita for population being older than 7 years in 1990[b]
GYPSY92	Ratio of Gypsy as a percentage of population in 1992[c]
DISTANCE	Minimum travelling distance from the region centre to Budapest or to Hegyeshalom or to Rábafüzes on road (km) [d]
ENTDENSt	Number of companies with or without legal entities per 1000 person of population (t = 1992–7)[b]

Notes: [a] Unemployment register of the National Labour Centre
[b] Central Statistical Office 'T-star' community level data base
[c] Ministry of Education
[d] ® androute
[e] IE-HAS Regional Database.

Table 6.5 Correlation coefficients between regional unemployment rates and the original explanatory variables

	UNEMPL *t = 1991*	*UNEMPL* *t = 1992*	*UNEMPL* *t = 1993*	*UNEMPL* *t = 1994*	*UNEMPL* *t = 1995*	*UNEMPL* *t = 1996*	*UNEMPL* *t = 1997*
EDU90	–.6707	–.7069	–.7115	–.7101	–.6906	–.6863	–.6710
PHONEt	–.3380	–.3803	–.4030	–.4777	–.4600	–.6042	–.7222
ENTDENSt	–.5018	–.5356	–.5475	–.5736	–.5719	–.5725	–.5606
SELFEMPt	–.4329	–.5022	–.5415	–.5415	–.5310	–.5132	–.4557
INDUSTRYt	–.2705	–.3221	–.3323	–.2902	–.3006	–.3181	–.3302
INDSIZEt	–.3145	–.3053	–.3180	–.2580	–.2710	–.2382 *	.2388 *
INTAXt	–.6004	–.6648	–.6859	–.6924	–.6740	–.6851	–.6721
FARMSt	.5008	.5222	.5203	.4974	.4640	.4509	.4294
CARSt	–.6464	–.6958	–.7138	–.7486	–.7548	–.7644	–.7598
GYPSY92	.7495	.7406	.7527	.7249	.7669	.7967 .	8014
DISTANCE	.6651	.6288	.6477	.6973	.7162	.7194 .	7544

Source: IE-HAS Regional Database.

Note: All of the variables are significant at 1 per cent level, * significant at 5 per cent level.

Table 6.6 Final statistics of principal component analysis, 1997

Proportion of variance explained by the factors

Factors	Eigenvalue	Pct of Var	Cum Pct
1	6.19815	56.3	56.3
2	1.90571	17.3	73.7
3	1.02686	9.3	83.0

Rotated Factor Matrix:

	FACTOR 1 URBANISATION	FACTOR 2 INDUSTRY	FACTOR 3 DISTANCE
EDU90	0.75767	0.43726	.32007
PHONE97	0.80486	0.09827	.44679
ENTDENS97	0.89655	0.07602	.22884
SELFEMP97	0.79237	–0.20020	.15557
INDUSTRY97	–0.02121	0.90079	.21641
INDSIZE97	0.13197	0.94801	.01908
INTAX96	0.67199	0.48324	.39952
FARMS94	–0.80339	–0.49382	.01334
CARS97	0.76077	0.01654	.51491
GYPSI92	–0.32618	–0.12776	–.76390
DISTANCE	–0.18770	–0.12468	–.86097

Results of the principal component analysis of selected regional variables

Using factor analysis (principal component analysis) we could condense criteria found to be in a significant correlation with regional unemployment rate differences into a reduced number of independent factors. Table 6.6 shows the final results of the process for the year 1997. The three factors could capture more than 75 per cent of the variance of the original variables.[9] Based on the correlation coefficients (factor loadings) between the original variables and the new factors we gave the following interpretation of the factors:

- Factor 1 – Urbanisation. This factor can be used to characterise the level of urbanisation in the region. The factor takes a high positive score in regions with a higher than average tax base income per 1,000 taxpayers; a higher than average level of education of inhabitants; a higher than average density of companies; a higher than average number of telephone lines per 1,000 inhabitants; and with a smaller than average ratio of habitants working in agricultural private farms and a smaller than average ratio of habitants employed in agriculture.
- Factor 2 – Industry. The factor takes a high positive score in sub-regions where the ratio of employees in industry in the active age population is higher than average.
- Factor 3 – Distance. This factor can quantify some geographical, social and ethnic characteristics of the region. The factor has high negative scores in regions where the minimum distance of the region from Budapest or the southern or northern part of the Austrian border, and the ratio of the Gypsy population is larger than the average. The factor takes a high positive score in sub-regions where the positive balance of migration between 1990–5 and the number of cars per thousand inhabitants is higher than average.

Measuring explanatory power of the factors by cross-sectional multivariate regressions

A multivariate regression equation provides us with a means of analysing the relation of the three factors to the regional unemployment rates. In the fourth step of the analysis the three factors were regressed with the average of sub-regional level unemployment rates in 1997. Table 6.7 shows the results of the regression analysis. One can see that the computed functions give very good estimations of the sub-regional level unemployment rates explaining 83 per cent of the variance. All factors are significant at the 1 per cent level. The strongest effect is that of Factor 3 (DISTANCE) referring to the geographical disadvantages or advantages of the region. Considerably weaker but still strong is the effect of the first factor (URBANISATION) expressing the level

Table 6.7 Results of multivariate regressions between regional unemployment rates and factor values (1997)

		Variables in the Equation			
Variable	*B*	*SE*	*Beta*	*T-value*	*Significance*
DISTANCE	–.306646	.135355	–.790069	–24.429	.0000
INDUSTRY	–.727598	.135355	–.173848	–5.375	.0000
URBANISATION	–.837995	.135355	–.439159	–13.579	.0000

Analysis of Variance

Multiple R	.92049
R Square	.84729
Adjusted R Square	.84416
Standard Error	1.65222
F	270.02664
N	150

of human and physical infrastructure and the development of enterprise creation in the region. The dominance of industry in local economy represented by Factor 2 (INDUSTRY) has a weak but significant negative effect on unemployment rates.

As most of the variables in the set are either constant over time or have changed little in the last two years one may try to study their effect on regional unemployment rates in 1995–6. There is a slight increase of explanatory power of the third factor (DISTANCE), while parameters of the first and second factors (URBANISATION, INDUSTRY) decreased over the last two years. These tendencies may refer to the changing characteristics of registered unemployment in Hungary. Parallel with the increasing ratio of long-term unemployed in the unemployment stock there is an increasing ratio of unemployed living in remote regions.

An attempt to classify sub-regions on the basis of the two main factors

Pre-transitional classification of sub-regions was based on the combination of the two most important factors comprising entrepreneurial and industrial capacity of the regions in 1990. Based on the results of the principal component analysis we must change the key factors of the classification as well. The explanatory power of Factor 2 representing industrial capacity of sub-regions has decreased to almost under the significance level while Factor 3 representing the geographical backwardness or advantages of regions has had crucial effects on regional unemployment rates. Updating the pre transitional typology the new classification of regions will be based on the combination of the two most powerful factors: URBANISATION and DISTANCE in the following way:

- Type 1 urbanised–central regions. This group of sub-regions has a better than average level of urbanisation and a better than average geographical situation: (Factor 1 ≤ 0; Factor 3 ≤ 0).
- Type 2 urbanised–remote regions. This group of sub-regions has a better than average level of urbanisation and a worse than average geographical situation: (Factor 1 ≤ 0; Factor 3 ≤ 0).
- Type 3 rural–central regions. This group of sub-regions has a lower than average level of urbanisation and a better than average geographical situation: (Factor 1 ≤ 0; Factor 2 ≤ 0).
- Type 4 rural–remote regions. This group of sub-regions has a lower than average level of urbanisation and a worse than average geographical situation: (Factor 1 ≤ 0 ; Factor 3 ≤ 0).

The taxonomy is described in Table 6.7.

	Factor 1 ≤ 0	Factor 1 ≤ 0
Factor 3 ≤ 0	urbanised central	rural central
Factor 3 ≤ 0	urbanised remote	rural remote

Figure 6.7 Factor taxonomy.

Table 6.8 shows the average values of the original variables included in the analysis in the four types of regions, as well as values of these variables in Budapest. Table 6.9 shows the results of the regression functions between regional unemployment rates and factor values, 1991–7. The four types of sub-regions are depicted in Map 6.3. Table 6.10 summarises some characteristics of the labour market in the four types of regions. One could see that beside the sub-regional level unemployment rates there are substantial differences in the composition of the unemployed stock as well. Urbanised–central regions have the lowest, rural–remote regions have the highest percentages of hard-to-place unemployed. This type of region has the highest ratio of long-term unemployed, the highest ratio of unemployed receiving social unemployment benefit, the highest ratio of unemployed with

Table 6.8 Average values of variables included in the analysis in the four types of sub-regions in 1997

	Country *N=150*	*Budapest* *N=1*	*Urbanised Central* *N= 26*	*Urbanised Remote* *N=24*	*Rural Central* *N=56*	*Rural Remote* *N=43*
$EDUC_{90}$	8.58	9.64	8.66	8.67	8.08	7.82
$PHONE_{97}$	.30	.48	.31	.28	.24	.19
$ENTDENS_{97}$	.01	.04	.01	.01	.01	.01
$SELFEMP_{97}$	.06	.09	.07	.07	.05	.04
$INDUSTRY_{97}$	11.91	8.89	4.02	12.61	12.87	10.25
$INDSIZE_{97}$	98.59	108.38	106.46	111.77	84.00	76.64
$INCTAX_{96}$	42650.00	78734.00	46495.00	36400.00	29005.00	21959.00
$FARMS_{94}$	.16	.01	.15	.14	.26	.26
$CARS_{97}$	.22	.32	.25	.21	.19	.14
$GYPSY_{92}$	4.23	1.60	2.02	4.21	3.69	10.43
DISTANCE	108.43	.00	58.93	179.53	92.51	201.10

Table 6.9 Results of regression functions between regional unemployment rates and factor values (1991–7)

Years	R^2	*F-stat*	*Factor 3* *DISTANCE*	*Factor 2* *INDUSTRY*	*Factor 1* *URBANISATION*
1991	0.71	115.69	–.7297	–.2355	–.3427
1992	0.70	112.14	–.6852	–.2223	–.4244
1993	0.74	141.01	–.7092	–.2250	–.4372
1994	0.77	164.68	–.7188	–.1819	–.4725
1995	0.81	204.88	–.7507	–.1872	–.4585
1996	0.83	236.84	–.7502	–.1816	–.4845
1997	0.85	270.03	–.7901	–.1738	–.4392

a maximum of 8 years or less elementary school education, and the highest ratio of unemployed looking for unskilled manual jobs.

Policy implications of the post-transitional model

In interpreting the above or similar models a researcher obviously faces a chicken and egg problem: the causality link between the variables is not entirely clear and the search for a meaningful explanation may take us very far from labour market issues. The message for research and policy, however, is not that uncertain. As a result of substantial changes in the economic structure of local labour markets, industrial job destruction or job creation does not seem to play a major role in the intensity of regional employment tensions. The long-lasting, stable differences in unemployment rates can be traced back to other factors related to historical and cultural traditions, economic development and hard-to-change endowments rather than to events occurring in the first five years of transition.

Table 6.10 Characteristics of the registered unemployed in December 1997

	Registered Unemployed Total	*Budapest*	*Urbanised Central sub-regions*	*Urbanised Remote sub-regions*	*Rural Central sub-regions*	*Rural Remote sub-regions*
Unemployment rate	11.1	4.4	7.5	10.2	9.5	16.1
Unemployment spell						
< 1 months	2.3	4.0	3.0	2.3	2.5	1.5
< 3 months	29.6	28.0	31.3	30.9	30.2	27.2
> 1 year	35.3	20.0	28.6	34.0	33.4	43.0
Ratio of reg. unemployed. receiving social unempl. benefit	40.4	36.2	32.7	39.4	38.7	48.0
Ratio of females	42.5	55.2	49.0	44.8	42.3	37.3
Schooling:						
< 8 classes	6.6	2.5	4.4	5.4	6.6	8.7
8 classes	35.9	30.4	32.0	33.1	37.1	38.5
University	2.2	6.0	3.5	2.9	1.9	1.3
Desired job:						
Unskilled manual	22.5	12.0	16.6	21.3	22.0	28.8
Non-manual	15.4	40.0	21.6	18.6	14.0	11.1

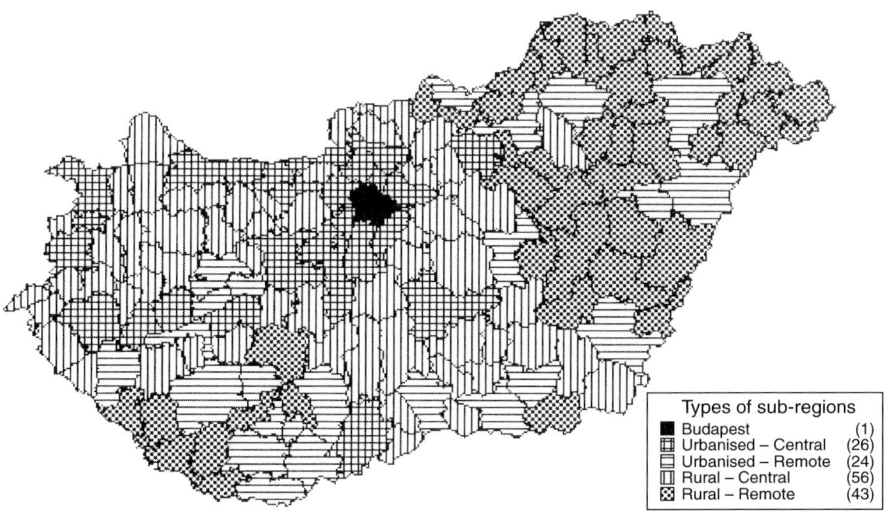

Map 6.3 Post-transitional typology of sub-regions.

The most serious problem of the existing practice of regional development is that it does not provide clear guidelines for decision-makers at the national, regional, or local level. For example, if the reduction of regional unemployment differences is high on the priority list of regional development and differences in unemployment are mostly determined by the degree of urbanisation, distance from economic centres and the ethnic composition of regions, then the central or local officials responsible for regional development should be encouraged to prefer: (a) development of the traffic and transport system; (b) investment in decisive fields of urbanisation to prevent the country from regional segregation; (c) special programmes for the Gypsy minority to raise their prospects in local labour markets. Similarly, if the level of education is the crucial factor of the entrepreneurial capacity of regions, policy-makers should concentrate on the long-term development of the educational system in backward regions.

Notes

1 The author acknowledges the financial support of the National Scientific Research Fund of Hungary (OTKA): project number: T 026113. The first version of this chapter was presented at the International Conference 'Integration and Transition in Europe: the Economic Geography of Interaction' supported by The European Union's Phare ACE Program, Budapest, 12–14 September 1997.
2 On the regional profile of Hungarian labour market in transition see Fazekas and Ozsvald (1998).
3 'Sub-regions' refers to the NUTS-IV level, in EU statistical terms. There are 20 county level regions (19 counties + Budapest) and 150 sub-regions in Hungary according to the latest nomenclature of Hungarian Central Statistical Office (HCSO).
4 'Employment district' means the service areas of Employment Offices under the County Labour Centres. With the organisational changes, the number of employment districts rose from 170 to 190 between 1990 and 1998.
5 The index is defined as $I = \Sigma Li [(Ui-Vi)-(U-V)]$ where U and V are unemployment and vacancy rates, L is the share of a region in labour force and i stands for regions.
6 The average size of the labour force of sub-regions is 21,000 if Budapest is excluded.
7 Variable DISTANCE measures minimum travel distance between the centre of sub-region, Budapest or Austrian border on road. Calculations were made by ANDRUTE®.
8 Variable GYPSY: estimation was based on the ratio of Gypsy pupils to the total number of children attending primary schools in the 1992–3 school years. Source: Ministry of Education. Regional consequences of the exclusion of Gypsy community from employment during the transition are discussed in Ábrahám and Keretesi (1998).
9 Principal component analyses produce linear combination of original variables that are independent of each other and that explain most of the variance of the variables. In the rotated factor matrix obtained as a result of the process, the various factor loadings associated with the variables refer to the extent to which a given variable contributes to the composition of the factor.

References

Ábrahám, Á. and Kertesi, G. (1998) 'Regional Unemployment Rate Differentials in Hungary, 1990–1995: the changing role of race and human capital', in L. Halpern and C. Wyplosz (eds) *Hungary: Towards a Market Economy*, Cambridge: Cambridge University Press.

Blanchard, O. and Katz, L. (1993) 'Regional issues', *Brookings Papers on Economic Activity* 1.

Dorenbos, R. (1999) *Labour Market Adjustments in Hungary and Poland: Theses on Systems, Organisation and Management*, Graduate School/Research Institute Systems, Organisation and Management, AR Capelle a/d, Ijsell: Labirint Publications.

Evans, G. (1985) *A Cyclically Adjusted Index of Structural Imbalances*, London: London School of Economics, mimeo.

Fazekas, K. (1990) 'Crise d'Entreprise et crise locale dans deux bassins industriels: Étude comparative: Ózd (Hongrie), Le Creusot (France)', in *Innovation et emploi à l'est et à l'ouest*, Paris: l'Harmattan.

Fazekas, K. (1996) 'Types of micro regions dispersion of unemployment and local development in Hungary', *Eastern European Economics* 34, 3: 3–48.

Fazekas, K. and Köllõ, J. (1998) *Regional Wage Curves in the Quasi-Experimental Setting of Transition: The Case of Hungary 1986–95*, IFO discussion papers 47, Münich: IFO Institute.

Fazekas, K. and Ozsvald, E. (1998) 'Transition and regional policies: the case of Hungary', in. M. Keune, *Regional Development and Employment Policy, Lessons from Central and Eastern Europe*, Geneva: International Labour Office.

Hungarian Central Statistical Office (HCSO) (1995) Kistérségi Vonzáskörzetek. A regionális térszerkezet jellemzõi az átmenet éveiben (Characteristics of Sub-Regions in the Years of Transition), Budapest: Központi Statisztikai Hivatal (Hungarian Central statistical Office – HCSO).

Jackman, R. and Roper, S. (1987) 'Structural unemployment', *Oxford Bulletin of Economics and Statistics* 49, 1.

Jackman, R. and Rutkowski, M. (1994) 'Labour markets: wages and employment', in N. Barr (eds) *Labour and Social Policy in Central and Eastern Europe*, World Bank and London School of Economics, Oxford: Oxford University Press.

Laky, T. (ed.) (1998) *Main Trends in Labour Demand and Supply*, Budapest: Labour Research Institute.

Scarpetta, S. (1995) 'Spatial variations in unemployment in Central and Eastern Europe: underlying reasons and labour market policy options', in *The Regional Dimension of Unemployment in Transition Countries*, Paris: OECD.

Simon, C.J. (1988) 'Frictional unemployment and the role of industrial diversity', *Quarterly Journal of Economics* 103(4), November: 715–28.

7 The new regional structure in Hungary

József Nemes-Nagy

In Hungary, the basic socio-economic changes launched by the political transition of 1989 have more or less been completed: the institutions of political democracy and market economy have been established. As a result of these processes, a new regional pattern has emerged, being substantially different from that of the socialist period. This study presents some important features of this altered regional pattern using basically county-level regional data, although attention is also paid to disparities at the micro-regional and settlement level. The spatial levels and units of the analysis are the following: (a) seven planning-statistical regions (the proposed NUTS 2 units); (b) nineteen counties and the capital, Budapest (NUTS 3 units, actual regional authorities); (c) 150 statistical microregions (without any administrative institutions); and (d) 3,100 settlements (local authorities). In this chapter we review the most significant quantitative features of regional development and spatial inequalities (e.g. the variation in employment structure, income, and foreign capital investment) and analyse the new spatial pattern of Hungary with the use of appropriate mathematical-statistical methods and indices.

Building a multi-party democratic constitutional state and a market economy in the 1990s has had far-reaching consequences for all levels of Hungarian society. As a result of these comprehensive changes in such a short period of time, radical regroupings within the socio-economic spatial structure have taken place as well (Enyedi 1996a; Turnock 1998).

The most fundamental change has taken place in the ownership structure. Following privatisation (Rechnitzer 1998), land ownership compensation and new capital investments (especially foreign capital, amounting to 16 billion US dollars by 1997), private ownership had become dominant by the mid-1990s. In 1996, more than half of all wage earners in every county worked for private or at least partly-private enterprises. Today there are some 700,000 individual entrepreneurs as well as over 300,000 business enterprises in Hungary. The role of the state is now dominant only in the field of education, health services, and public administration. At the same time, the number of actual wage earners decreased from 4.8 to 3.6 million between 1990 and 1995, and unemployment figures peaked at over 700,000 in 1993, dropping to less than 400,000 by 1998.

Hungary was compelled to undergo a complete reorientation of its external economic ties, with a subsequent deepening of the regional crisis in the manufacturing and agricultural industries which had been producing for the Soviet market. The complete opening of borders served as a catalyst for changes in the spatial structure. The system of state-monopoly and centrally organised international relations began to give way to cross-border co-operation. Previously acting as barriers and filters, being closed to economic ties, some border regions soon became zones of dynamic activity. It is true, however, that at different sections of the border this process varied widely, and was full of contradictions. At the Austrian border, there was large-scale investment while at the southern border, there was only a controversial business boom fuelled by the Balkan crisis, based on activities only some of which were partly legitimate. On the eastern borders a network of illegal businesses sprang up. Therefore the geographic periphery of the country cannot be considered an economic and social whole. On the contrary, the western border region rather should be considered the dynamic region of the country.

Macroregional pattern of development

Following the change in the system, radical changes occurred in the Hungarian regional socio-economic pattern, which significantly altered the spatial structure that had evolved during the former decades. The most significant economic indicators available (see Table 7.1) give almost an identical picture of the country's spatial economic structure. Population, income, employment structure, unemployment and indicators of foreign capital show the outstanding importance of Budapest and the relatively favourable position of the West compared to the eastern and northern regions.

This basic structure was a characteristic of Hungary in the early 1990s as well, which also means that regions in the most favourable positions today are those which had the initial advantages. This point has been clearly demonstrated by several other studies; Fazekas and Köll (1998) for instance, arrived at the same conclusion after examining the labour market.

Foreign capital, which undoubtedly has shown a strong preference for the western region and the capital, has played a significant role in the radical transformation of the regional pattern of Hungary (Cséfalvay 1995; Enyedi 1996b; Hastenberg 1996; Swain1998). It was only in 1998 that there was some evidence of foreign capital crossing the Danube, as new industrial and commercial projects were launched in a number of eastern and northern towns by multinational companies. However, the effect of these developments cannot be shown on the spatial pattern of development.

On the basis of taxable income, we can examine the change in the dispersion of income in various levels of spatial aggregation (see Table 7.2). The calculations provide clear evidence of the main tendencies in regional development in the 1990s: income dispersion increased at all levels of aggregation

Table 7.1 Indicators of the regional transformation in Hungary in the mid-1990s

Regions, counties	*Population (th.)*	*Number of joint ventures*	*Foreign direct investment*[a]	*Employment by sectors(%)*[b]			*Unemployment rate (%)*			*Personal income per capita (%)*	*GDP by sectors(%)*[b]		
				I.	*II.*	*III.*					*I.*	*II.*	*III.*
	1997	*1996*	*1996*		*1996*		*1990*	*1993*	*1997*	*1995*		*1996*	
Central Hungary	2881	14560	1402.8				0.4	7.2	5.4				
Budapest	1886	12921	1237.1	0.7	23.7	75.7	0.3	6.2	4.7	126	0.5	21.8	77.7
Pest	995	1639	165.7	6.0	31.9	62.1	0.6	9.3	6.9	97	6.1	38.3	55.5
Central Transdanubia	1114	1815	150.4				1.4	12.7	9.7				
Fejér	426	529	60.6	10.4	41.1	48.5	1.6	12.4	9.4	100	7.5	47.0	45.5
Komárom-Esztergom	311	528	60.3	7.0	40.6	52.4	1.0	13.9	10.9	96	7.0	43.4	49.6
Veszprém	377	758	29.5	8.2	36.9	54.8	1.4	12.1	9.1	93	6.3	38.7	55.0
Western Transdanubia	995	2955	197.0				0.8	9.3	6.8				
Gy r-Moson-Sopron	425	1274	120.0	7.8	37.7	54.5	0.9	8.7	5.8	100	7.8	38.0	54.2
Vas	270	678	46.8	8.1	42.2	49.8	0.5	9.1	6.2	104	6.4	48.5	45.1
Zala	299	1003	30.2	6.3	39.9	53.9	1.1	10.3	8.8	100	7.5	38.4	54.1
Southern Transdanubia	990	1943	87.2				1.9	13.1	13.0				
Baranya	407	994	62.1	11.4	33.1	55.4	1.8	12.5	13.0	102	9.3	26.2	64.6
Somogy	336	679	17.0	12.5	25.4	62.1	2.0	12.6	12.5	94	13.2	26.7	60.1
Tolna	248	270	8.1	14.2	36.0	49.9	2.1	14.7	13.5	104	14.1	39.1	46.8

Table 7.1 cont.

Regions, counties	*Population (th.)* 1997	*Number of joint ventures* 1996	*Foreign direct investment*[a] 1996	*Employment by sectors(%)*[b] I. 1996	II. 1996	III. 1996	*Unemployment rate (%)* 1990	1993	1997	*Personal income per capita (%)* 1995	*GDP by sectors(%)*[b] I. 1996	II. 1996	III. 1996
Northern Hungary	1291	787	206.1				3.0	19.4	16.6				
Borsod-Abaúj-Zemplén	743	352	143.1	5.7	37.3	57.0	3.2	21.1	18.8	88	6.3	39.3	54.4
Heves	327	270	51.7	6.9	38.4	54.7	2.3	15.3	12.0	91	9.2	32.3	58.4
Nógrád	221	165	11.3	5.6	39.8	54.6	3.4	19.5	15.7	88	7.2	32.2	60.6
Northern Great Plain	1539	1018	122.4				2.4	18.1	16.4				
Hajdú-Bihar	546	407	83.9	12.3	31.6	56.0	1.3	16.6	15.1	86	13.6	27.7	58.7
Jász-Nagykun-Szolnok	419	272	22.5	12.3	34.2	53.5	2.0	17.1	14.3	92	12.6	34.3	53.1
Szabolcs-Szatmár-Bereg	572	339	16.0	10.0	34.8	55.2	3.8	20.3	19.3	81	12.0	28.8	59.3
Southern Great Plain	1364	3052	114.2				1.4	14.7	11.1				
Bács-Kiskun	539	1075	25.4	15.8	31.5	52.6	1.3	15.6	10.5	93	15.6	27.8	56.6
Békés	401	273	17.7	16.2	32.5	51.3	1.8	17.2	14.2	93	17.4	30.4	52.3
Csongrád	425	1704	71.1	15.3	28.9	55.7	1.3	11.5	9.2	102	12.0	29.7	58.3
Hungary	10174	26130	2280.1	8.0	32.7	59.3	1.4	12.6	10.4	100	6.6	30.7	62.7

Source: CSO of Hungary, different publications

Notes: [a]by 1996, billion HUF,
[b]I: Agriculture, II: Mining, manufacturing, building, III. Tertiary and Quaternary branches.

Table 7.2 Inequalities in taxable income per capita within the main spatial levels

Years	*Weighted standard deviation (%)*			
	Settlements	*Microregions*	*Counties*	*Regions*
1988	25.4	22.2	19.6	17.3
1989	27.6	24.0	21.2	18.5
1990	30.2	26.1	23.1	19.9
1991	30.8	25.5	21.2	17.9
1992	34.6	29.8	26.4	22.1
1993	35.6	30.8	27.1	22.7
1994	36.5	31.5	27.7	23.5
1995	35.9	30.7	26.7	22.6
1996	35.7	30.5	26.4	22.3

between 1988 and 1996, while the figures of the last two years show a relative stability in the income inequalities at a significantly higher level compared with the starting point. These movements, however, have not caused an 'inversion' in the spatial pattern of income. This is indicated by the fact that the Spearman Rank Correlation value on the basis of total income data for the years 1987 and 1995 is 0.61. This figure substantiates the view that although there have been some changes in the counties' relative positions, the regions which originally had higher incomes are still leading the list, and the traditionally more backward counties have not been able to achieve improvement to a substantial degree.

At this point, it is worth examining the differences in the changing development levels with the help of two indicators. The transformation of the spatial pattern of development can be shown on the one hand by means of the per capita GDP values, and on the other, by the so-called 'economic health indicator', which is an index obtained by factor analysis. With the help of these two indices, it becomes possible to distinguish a contrast between both long- and short-term changes.

With the use of GDP per capita data, which have been estimated at the county level since 1994 by the Hungarian Central Statistical Office (HCSO), it is possible to make comparisons with the proportions existing in 1975 that indicate the typical spatial pattern of the socialist period. The regional data of GDP for 1975 have been estimated by the author based on official statistical information and data from Barta (1977).

In the case of the 'economic health' indicator formed by factor analysis, we could make calculations for the years 1990 and 1996. This index comprises the elements of crisis and relative dynamism symptoms characterising this decade. Entrepreneur activity measured by firm density, employees' taxable incomes, unemployment rate and the proportion of joint ventures to the total number of firms are merged resulting in a single factor (with common high – over 0.8 – factor weights, and with 72 per cent of variation). High positive figures mean relatively high levels of income, low rates of unemployment, a great number of business ventures, and a large amount of foreign capital investment. In contrast, high negative figures indicate counties where the signs of crisis are dominant, while figures close to 0 represent the average. In Table 7.3 GDP per capita data reflect considerable changes in the relative positions of the counties since 1975.

From among the positive shifts, the position of the capital city with its outstandingly high level of development deserves particular attention. Budapest, with regard to its dynamics and to the features of its economic development, has not only retained its advantage over the rest of the country, but has further increased it. The 'economic health indicator' calls attention to the fact that in the transition process the initial position of the capital was already very favourable as compared to other regions of the country. Here, the factor for the year 1990 was prominently high, and although this structural advantage had decreased to some extent by the middle of the decade, it is still significant today.[1]

Table 7.3 The dynamics of county-level differences in economic development

Regions, counties	*GDP per capita (National average = 100)*			*'Economic health' (factor values)*		
	1975	*1996*	*Change*	*1990*	*1996*	*Change*
Central Hungary						
Budapest	139	186	47	3.22	2.80	–0.42
Pest	61	74	13	0.72	0.48	–0.23
C. Transdanubia						
Fejér	106	102	–4	0.24	0.40	0.15
Komárom–Esztergom	131	89	–42	0.53	0.11	–0.42
Veszprém	116	80	–36	0.23	0.39	0.16
W. Transdanubia						
Gyr-Moson-Sopron	111	110	–1	0.92	1.01	0.09
Vas	82	109	27	0.46	0.89	0.43
Zala	88	93	5	0.09	0.73	0.63
S. Transdanubia						
Baranya	108	77	–31	0.27	0.01	–0.26
Somogy	71	75	4	–0.37	–0.22	0.15
Tolna	77	90	13	–0.24	–0.43	–0.20
N. Hungary						
Borsod-Abaúj-Zemplén	111	70	–41	–1.01	–1.29	–0.29
Heves	100	73	–27	–0.82	–0.50	0.33
Nógrád	77	57	–20	–0.95	–1.01	–0.06
N. Great Plain						
Hajdú-Bihar	83	78	–5	–0.44	–0.87	–0.42
Jász-Nagykun-Szolnok	93	76	–17	–0.69	–0.80	–0.12
Szabolcs-Szatmár-Bereg	59	59	0	–1.65	–1.56	0.08
S. Great Plain						
Bács–Kiskun	79	76	–3	0.00	–0.15	–0.15
Békés	89	76	–13	–0.65	–0.77	–0.12
Csongrád	109	93	–16	0.13	0.78	0.66
Hungary	100	100		0.00	0.00	

Outside the capital, it is only in the western, Transdanubian (Dunántúl) part of the country where counties with steadily improving positions can be found. The advance of Vas County is the most spectacular. Also, Gyr-Moson-Sopron has a development level firmly above the average, and is still improving its position. These two western counties are, in the economic sense, the winners in the economic-political transition.

The present dynamics of the western regions is primarily due to their favourable geographic location. The prime beneficiaries of this external impact are the three counties mentioned above (for details see Chapter 3). Another unique advantage for this area is that the western border zone (for political-military reasons) was neglected during the heavy industrial stage of socialist industrialisation, therefore it reached the threshold of transition with a less obsolete and more flexible structure of economy and professional culture. This area is connected by a system of massive daily links to the adjacent Austrian regions. These factors strengthen the advantages due to a common mentality built upon the socio-psychological heritage of remote historical times.

While there has been significant development in the two western counties, we are witnessing a radical decline in the North Hungarian region. Borsod-Abaúj-Zemplén county has gone through a long period of depression, and also Nógrád, which has now fallen to the bottom of the hierarchy in economic development. It is only Heves where the results of our calculations show some positive turn in the first part of this decade. North Hungary is a typical example of a once developed region suffering depression and struggling with the crisis of its obsolete heavy industrial base. The level of development in North Hungary, due to its economic demise, no longer differs greatly from the Great Plain (Alföld).

Nor do the development indicators of the traditionally less developed macroregion, the agrarian Great Plain, give any reason for optimism. It is only Csongrád that exceeds the average level of development in the Great Plain. Among the main reasons for Csongrád's relatively better position is the attraction of the city of Szeged, and the outstandingly high density of small-scale entrepreneurship, which has evolved due to immigration and an influx of capital escaping from Yugoslavia, which was heavily interwoven by 'black and grey' elements as well.

The causes of the depression and crisis (sharp decrease in production, high unemployment rates) in the first half of the 1990s in the eastern counties were many. First of all, one has to look for them not only in local features, but in the peculiar mechanism enabling the economy of the more developed regions (the capital in particular) to react to the difficulties by passing most of the burden of depression onto the peripheries: the commuters were the first in the labour force to be dismissed, and the small plants in the countryside were the first to be closed down. The high unemployment rate in the county of Szabolcs-Szatmár-Bereg was actually the result of the capital's ability to react fast. Second, another cause of depression in the east was that the northeastern counties were those hit most severely by the crisis of heavy industry and agricultural mass production oriented towards the collapsing Soviet market. Third, as a consequence of the insufficient macroregional infrastructure, the incoming foreign capital remained in the western part of the country and in Budapest, while in the east, it picked out and acquired through privatisation, only those few companies with the most promising markets.

The central part of the country is also strongly divided on the county level owing to its rather unstable transitional character. On the one hand, there is the county of Komárom-Esztergom, having suffered the greatest loss of position during the last twenty years, and Veszprém, a county facing similar problems. On the other hand, directly adjoining the latter is the county of Fejér, which has experienced a spectacular development since 1990. The reason for the present high GDP in Tolna (the county that has been second best in achieving a lasting development after Vas) is chiefly the great production potential of the Paks Nuclear Power Plant completed in the early 1980s. Thus Tolna's relatively favourable position has nothing to do with the post-transition processes. This is also evident in the fact that Tolna is not among the highest ranked counties according to the index of economic health. Considering the GDP indicator, in the county of Pest, closely tied with the administratively separated capital city, the improvement is also remarkable, although the GDP per capita allocated according to the actual place of production, certainly underestimates Pest's position. According to the economic health indicator Pest ranks among the counties' average, and that is quite realistic. Finally, the county of Bács-Kiskun is also part of this heterogenous and unstable middle zone. Although it is located east of the Danube, Bács-Kiskun does not share the sluggish character of most other counties in the Great Plain, but boasts a vigorous small enterprise activity.

Microregional inequalities: 'winners' and 'losers'

Examining smaller spatial units, the picture is more mosaic-like. As we have no small-region level GDP data, regions can only be evaluated on the basis of a cumulative index.[2] This index is constructed for the 150 microregions for the years 1995–6 on the basis of the following seven indicators:

1 taxable income per capita;
2 unemployment rate;
3 sole proprietors per 1,000 inhabitants;
4 personal car per 1,000 inhabitants;
5 telephone lines per 1,000 inhabitants;
6 foreign capital per inhabitant;
7 share of joint ventures within the firms.

On the basis of these indicators, we distinguished four aggregated categories of regions:

1 'Winner' regions are those where the values of at least 6 indicators are higher than the rural average (i.e. the country average without the capital).
2 'Starting-up' regions are those where 4–5 indicators result in figures above the rural average.
3 'Stagnating' are those regions which have only 2–3 indicators above the rural average.
4 'Losers' are regions where the value of not more than one indicator is higher than the rural average.

It is necessary to use the rural average as the basis for comparisons because of the disproportionately great economic weight and high development level of the capital. This raises the country averages so much in the case of most of the economic and social indicators that, with the exception of some really dynamic regions or towns, such as for instance Gyr, Sopron, Székesfehérvár and a few towns in the capital's agglomeration, almost all the other regions are below the average.

Mapping the results of the calculation clearly shows the change already mentioned: change in the spatial structure – the collapse of the northeast–southwest-oriented heavy industrial axis which was located in the mountain region (see Map 7.1). Among the different branches of industry, it was only the chemical industry that was able to revive after the shock caused by the transition into a market economy. A number of industrial cities in this region are today the archetypes of settlements facing environmental and social disaster. (Ózd, in the Northeastern Slovakian border zone is one of the cities in the worst position.) At the same time, there are some cities in the industrial axis (Székesfehérvár, and most recently, Tatabánya) where there is

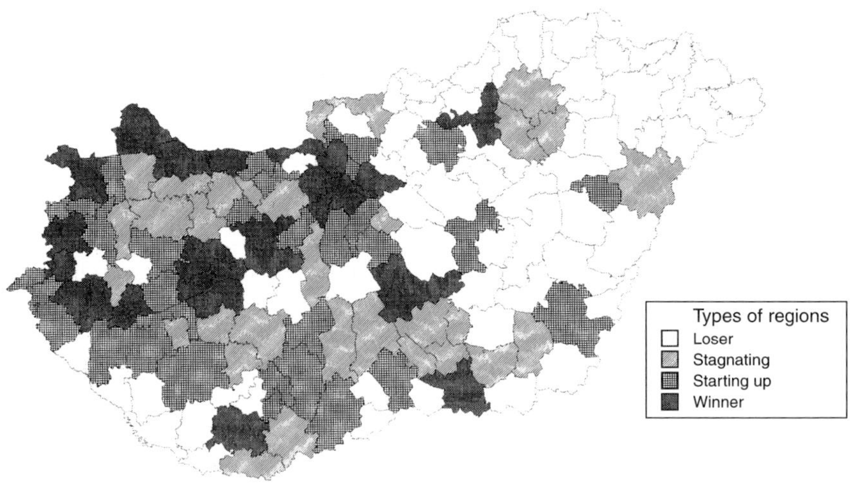

Map 7.1 Microregional disparities in Hungary, 1995.

a dynamic revival based on the most modern processing industries (machine industry, electronics).

The more stable western (northwestern) and the depressed eastern (northeastern) parts of the country are well separated in the new pattern shaped at the level of smaller spatial units. The dynamic axes in the western part of the country are easily recognisable: the Budapest–Gyr–Mosonmagyaróvár–Sopron (Bratislava–Vienna) axis, and the Budapest–Székesfehérvár–Balaton axis. These two axes branching out from the capital are linked by the 'starting-out' zone along the Austrian border, where both the areas of bigger cities and smaller centres have entered the group of regions having the most favourable position. The most significant factors of development in this border region were obviously the external impacts, especially the activating effects of the relatively close, economically powerful South German, North Italian and Austrian regions. The Balaton region has grown primarily due to the concentration of small entrepreneurship, and therefore, it depends strongly on the ups and downs of tourism.

However, there are some characteristically agrarian 'shadowy regions', once prosperous, but today depressed smaller industrial districts in between the Transdanubian development axes. Probably the most problematic contiguous area here is the southern peripheral border zone, since it was also affected indirectly by the Croatian war in the first part of the 1990s, which had an debilitating effect on economic relations.

It is true in the case of both the southern and eastern parts of Hungary that almost all of the county capital cities have emerged from their environment, forming local dynamic centres. The big cities attract commercial functions since they provide suitable markets. They also act as organisational centres, and attract the reformed financial and economic service activities as well.

Pest and Bács-Kiskun form a transitional zone on the eastern bank of the Danube. This region being close to the capital, it benefits from its economic attraction; it has also relatively favourable transportation connections, and small-scale agricultural production as a stabilising element. Nevertheless, foreign capital has reached only the biggest cities (Kecskemét, Szeged) so far. The more distant northern and eastern regions form almost a contiguous 'loser-zone', with massive permanent unemployment. Compared to the whole country, the relatively positive economic features appear only in the county city centres and a few stable industrial cities of strategic importance (such as Tiszaújváros).

Similarly to the classification of microregions, using the same indicators, we have distinguished 'winning', 'starting-up', 'stagnating', and 'loser' settlements. A further division within microregions can in this way uncover the main characteristic of the whole country, i.e. that cities are in much more favourable positions than villages. This calculation makes it possible to determine the proportions of population living in the four types of settlements in each region, and in the whole country (see Table 7.4).

Table 7.4 The distribution of the population (1996) between characteristic categories of transition

Spatial units, regions	Distribution of population living in different types of settlements				
	Total	*Winners*	*Starting-up*	*Stagnating*	*Losers*
Hungary	10174	40.1	19.3	17.8	22.8
Budapest		100.0	0.0	0.0	0.0
Countryside	8287	26.4	23.7	21.9	28.0
C-Hungary	2880	77.2	10.4	9.9	2.5
C-Transdanubia	1113	28.6	32.8	24.8	13.8
W-Transdanubia	994	52.5	17.0	22.6	7.8
S-Transdanubia	991	25.6	32.8	18.0	23.5
N- Hungary	1290	18.6	14.8	21.2	45.4
N. Great Plain	1539	13.5	19.3	13.2	54.0
S. Great Plain	1364	22.7	23.3	27.0	27.0

In the country (attributable chiefly to the capital), the share of the two more favourable categories is about 60 per cent, and so about 40 per cent of the population fall into the two unfavourable groups. Considering just the country without the capital, the shares are 50–50 per cent, and it becomes evident that the two favourable groups comprise mainly the large and medium-sized cities. Regional inequalities are quite evident here: in the case of the Central Region and Western Hungary, development spreads outside the cities as well, while the proportion of those people living in the 'loser' settlements is the highest in the northeastern regions of the country.[3]

Assessing the influence of geographic location by means of the potential model

We have examined the key role of geographic location in the new spatial structure (already justified above by the most important economic indicators) using a peculiarly modified version of the so-called potential model, a traditional instrument of economic-geographical analyses.

In the spatial structuring of economy and society, as a result of relationships and interactions (just as in the systems of relations in physics), force fields are created in the various points where 'field intensity' differs. Socio-economic field intensity, analogous to electric and magnetic fields, can be approached by potential models. At a certain point of geographical space *i*, 'field intensity', economic-geographical potential is given by the following formula:

$$P_i = \sum_j \frac{Wj}{dij}$$

where W_j is the active weight given to point j (in economic analyses, the volumes of GDP or other income indicators, characteristically), d_{ij} is the distance between points *i* and *j* ($i \neq j$). The assumption behind this formula is that field intensity in social space as well, is the greatest near the biggest 'masses'.

The course of calculating potentials

The peculiarity of our study were that its basic units were not settlements but *regions* (182 microregions in Hungary distinguished by the author). The economic potentials of these microregions were calculated. Potential in our model is made up of three elements:

$$P_{total} = P_{proper} + P_{domestic} + P_{external}$$

From among these three, calculating domestic and external potentials are actually without any difficulties. The domestic potential of a region is determined by consideration of the other 181 regions in Hungary, the external potential measures the influence of the economic weights of regions outside Hungary in a way that the country is placed in a Central European context during calculation.

It requires an estimation procedure of several steps to specify the 'mass' used in the model. 'Mass', in our case, was the estimated GDP for the individual regions in the year 1994, on the basis of regional GDP – and income – data, which we took from various national and international sources (see more details in Nemes-Nagy 1998). The distance between microregions was the 'bee-line' distance between regional centres (towns).

However, the original potential model does not include the income masses of the basic points themselves (the proper masses; in our case, that of the Hungarian regions), because, considering their own area, the distance would be $d_{ii} = 0$. This consequently leads to a relatively low income potential for regions concentrating outstandingly great income masses (e.g. Budapest), and distinctively higher potentials for the neighbouring regions. In order to have a more realistic model, it is necessary to consider the proper masses. This element appears in the definition of proper potential. The main question here is how to specify the 'distance' belonging to the region itself. From among the theoretically possible and accepted methods, we chose the following: knowing the area of each region (T_i), we determined the radius of the circle that is equal in area to the given region, and considered this radius (r_i) as the distance belonging to the region's own income mass. The value calculated from the above elements is the proper potential of the region.

Two maps present the final results of our calculations. In Map 7.2, the sums of proper and domestic potentials are mapped. Here, the basic spatial pattern is clearly determined by the dominance of Budapest. The potential decreases in a concentric ring-like pattern with the increase of distance from the capital, although regions with higher income potentials are a little shifted to the west as compared to the proportions in distance. This spatial structure

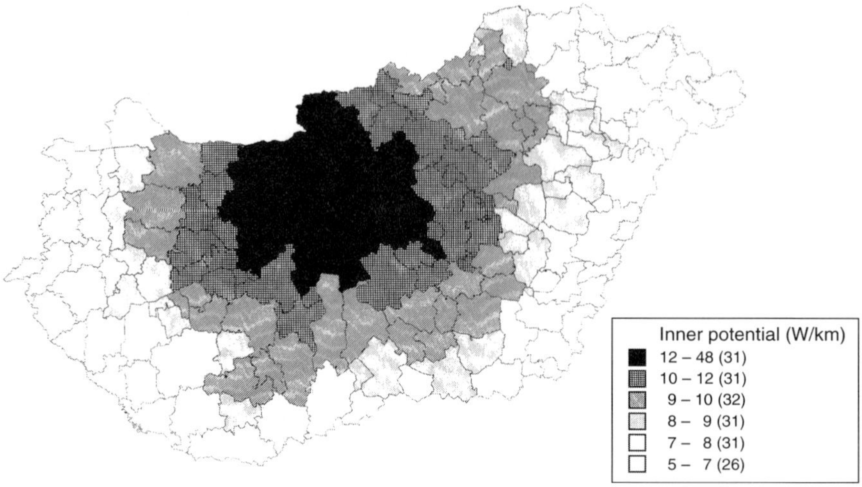

Map 7.2 Pattern of inner economic potential of the microregions in Hungary.

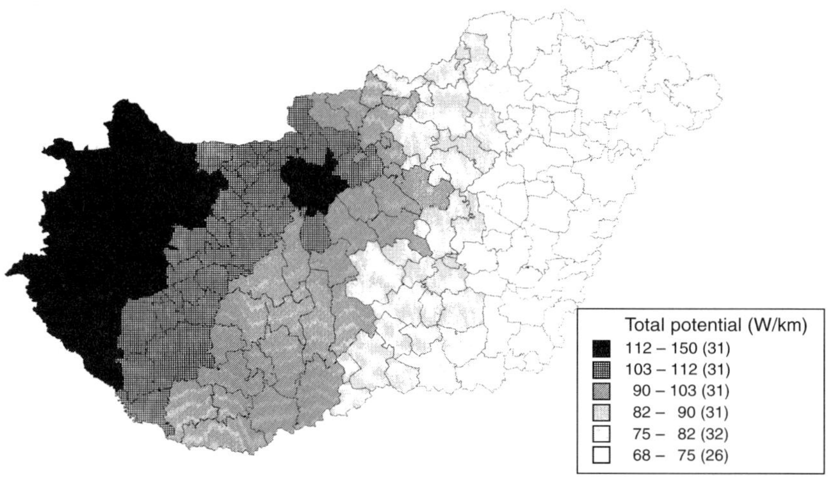

Map 7.3 Pattern of total economic potential of the microregions in Hungary.

represents an economy existing only theoretically, which is completely self-contained, and without external connections, and it shows almost no relevance to the spatial pattern of today, except for the dominance of the capital. The concentric nature of this pattern also draws attention to the fact that the relatively favourable present position of the western regions, which does not appear here at all, has emerged definitely not because of the economic force field created by Budapest, 'within the country'.

At the same time, if we draw the map of total (proper + domestic + external) potentials (Map 7.3) we might almost have the feeling that we have mapped a development indicator of the present situation (see the next chapter), and not the results of a theoretical model. The definite spatial structure presented by the map shows a northwest–southeast slope with just one exception, the region of the capital. This spatial pattern is undoubtedly due to the western – Austrian, South German, and North Italian – regions of great economic power. The calculations also showed that external potential measuring the indicated western influence has a dominant share within the total potential in each region in Hungary (in the capital, as well). The low potentials of the eastern and northern parts of the country can be attributed *inter alia* to the fact that the economic strength of the other (eastern, southern, and northern) neighbours of Hungary is so small that it has virtually no effect on the potential.

The future of regional development

So how permanent is the spatial pattern that has evolved in Hungary by the end of the twentieth century and to what extent is it transitional? Considering the most significant types of regions found in the new spatial structure, on the basis of the above analyses, we can claim that not only their present situations vary, but their future courses of development (for the coming decades) will most probably be different (Ehrlich and Révész 1995; Enyedi 1994)

The dynamic regions of the country (the capital and its surroundings, the western counties) and some bigger and medium-sized cities (Nemes-Nagy 1995a) have built by now the basis of those economic and social structures, which will be able to utilise the increased indigenous potentials of these zones (the advantages of location, the attraction and weight on the market, innovative powers). Budapest, ranked a second or third level city in the European 'city-competition' (Barta, and Conti 1994), is undergoing an extremely dynamic transformation. The lead of the 'central core' formed by the capital, and the 'dynamic edge' by the Austrian border over the rest of the country seems lasting, although the positive prospects in the case of some smaller towns, where sudden development was exclusively due to large foreign capital investments and thus lacked domestic links, are not certain: the multinational company might change profile, close down its plant or move further to the east. Because of the spread of capital-intensive improvements, and the low mobility of the Hungarian labour force, the massive migration into the dynamic regions expected by several analysts has not taken place. This has resulted in a relative lack of labour in certain dynamic regions (for example, the city of Gyr), yet it also makes it possible to maintain stable social structures.

Extensive regions of the country (especially the regions east of the River Tisza, North Hungary, and the border zone of southern Transdanubia) are still struggling with deep-rooted and new difficulties (they are 'problematic regions'), as the decentralising regional development policy, though reformed in its institutions, has not been able to improve their situation yet (Horváth and Illés 1997).

Whether these regions will catch up is the crucial question in the positive transformation of regional proportions. Besides the inner factors, the development of the neighbouring countries (Slovakia, Ukraine, Rumania, and the Balkan states) is of crucial importance. Via Southern and Eastern Europe, the great cities near the borders (Pécs, Szeged, Debrecen, Nyíregyháza) may act as 'gates', and thus their logistic importance may grow. However, this role is made uncertain by instability over the borders. It would be a much more favourable scenario if the economy of the neighbouring countries stabilised, for co-operation could be much more extended (Süli-Zakar 1997). The influx of regional development funds which are expected from Hungary's European Union membership (and which are very much looked forward to) can play a great part in the improvement of these regions (Horváth 1997).

We must not forget the fact that there are millions of people living in regions of unstable transitional economic and social conditions (first of all in the South-Central part of the country), besides the dynamic core and the problematic peripheries we have already discussed above. Mobilised socio-economic resources have been enough to create relative stability here, but were insufficient for further advancement. Local innovative power is particularly significant in the development of these regions, since a spontaneous and fast increase cannot be expected either from international resources, or from the central governmental funds: foreign capital still prefers the western part of the country, and the national regional development grants aim at the improvement of the most backward eastern regions.

The hardening of the most fundamental elements of today's spatial pattern (the capital–countryside dualism, the west–east divide and the urban–rural economic disparities) is confirmed by the fact that the intensity of interactive links *within* the country is low, the positive poles are of no considerable interest to the other regions, and they use their own potentials basically, while they receive the missing resources from abroad. However, the increasing speed of economic growth since 1996–7 hopefully will put an end to the trend of increasing differences on the regional and settlement levels, and its positive effects will reach the stagnating and backward regions as well. Still, the evolution of a 'newer new spatial pattern', more stable than the present one, is only likely in the long run, even if a constantly high (3–5 per cent) rate of economic growth is achieved.

Notes

1 However, without intending to reduce the economic and social potential of Budapest, we have to note that the Central Statistical Office has estimated the per capita GDP in Hungary in proportion to the European Union average, and has

come up with 37 per cent for 1994. This means that the outstandingly high figure calculated for Budapest hardly exceeds half of the EU average. Therefore, if measured according to 'European' criteria (the famous 75 per cent GDP per capita 'underdevelopment limit' in the EU), not only the countryside, but the capital city as well is in need of support, still being far from achieving the 75 per cent of the EU per capita GDP level.

2 The methodology used in this section is only one of several available for microregional analysis. Several authors (Csatári 1996; KSH 1995; Nemes-Nagy 1995b) have used other methods and indicators of multivariate analysis, but the main results are very similar.

3 Of course, there are 'loser' social groups living in 'winner' settlements, and 'winner' groups of people in 'loser' villages. The population figures in Table 7.4 describe the settlement level only.

References

Barta, G. (1977) 'A területi gazdasági különbségek változása 1960–75 között' ('Changes of regional economic inequalitities between 1960–75'), *Területi Statisztika* 2, pp. 522–37.

Barta, G. and Conti, S. (1994) 'Budapest's changing position in Europe and Hungary', in Z. Hajdú and Gy. Horváth (eds) *European Challenges and Hungarian Responses in Regional Policy*, Pécs: MTA RKK, 170–82.

Csatári, B. (1996) *A magyarországi kistérségek néhány jellegzetssége (Some Characteristic Features of Hungarian Microregions)*, PHARE Iroda, Kecskemét: MTA RKK-KTM.

Cséfalvay, Z. (1995) 'Raum und Gesellschaft Ungarns in der Übergangsphase zur Marktwirtsch', in P. Mesburger and A. Klinger (eds) *Von Plan zum Markt. Eine Untersuchung am Beispiel Ungarns*, Heidelberg: Physica-Verlag, pp. 80–98.

Ehrlich, É. and Révész, G. (1995) *Hungary and its Prospects 1985–2005* Budapest: Akadémiai K.

Enyedi, G. (1994) 'Regional and urban development in Hungary until 2005', in Z. Hajdú and G. Horváth (eds) *European Challenges and Hungarian Responses in Regional Policy*, Pécs: MTA RKK, pp. 239–53.

Enyedi, G. (1996a) *Regionális folyamatok Magyarországon az átmenet id szakában (Regional Processes in Hungary in the Transition Period)*, Budapest: Hilscher Rezs Szociálpolitikai Egyesület.

Enyedi, G. (1996b) 'Külföldi müködtke befektetések hatása a regionális fejldésre Magyarországon' ('Direct foreign investment and the regional development in Hungary'), in Z. Dövényicszerk, *Tér – Gazdaság – Társadalom*, Budapest: MTA FKI, pp. 247–56.

Fazekas, K. and Köll, M. (1998) 'A külföldi érdekeltség vállalatok munkaerkeresletének jellemzi Magyarországon 1995-ben' ('Labour market of the joint ventures in Hungary'), paper presented at the conference *Labour Market and Regionalism*, MTA KK KI, Bp., pp. 29–57.

Hastenberg, H. van (1996) 'Regional and sectoral characteristics of foreign direct investment in Hungary', in *Workshop Transition Processes in Eastern Europem*, The Hague: ESR, pp. 121–36.

Horváth, G (1997) 'Európai integráció, keleti bvítés és a magyar regionális politika' ('European integration, enlargement and the Hungarian regional policy'), *Tér és Társadalom* 3: 17–56.

Horváth, G. and Illés, I. (1997) 'Regionális fejldés és politika' ('Regional development and policy') *Európai Tükör 16,* Budapest: ISM.

KSH (1995) *Kistérségi vonzáskörzetek. A regionális térszerkezet jellemzi az átmenet éveiben* (*Microregions: The Regional Structure in the Transition*), CSO Bp.

Nemes-Nagy, J. (1995a) 'Soprontól Nyíradonyig (városok a piacgazdasági átmenetben)' ('The Hungarian cities in the economic transition') *Comitatus* 8–9: 15–22.

Nemes-Nagy, J. (1995b) 'A piacgazdasági átmenet terei' ('Spaces of the transition in Hungary'), *Falu–Város–Régió* 7–8: 6–11.

Nemes-Nagy, J. (1998) 'A fekvés szerepe a regionális tagoltságban' ('Importance of location in regional disparities'), paper presented at the conference Labour Market and Regionalism, Budapest: MTA KK KI, pp.147–65.

Rechnitzer, J. (1998) *A privatizáció regionális összefüggései* (*Privatisation in Regional Context*), Budapest: ÁVÜ.

Süli-Zakar, I. (1997) 'A Kárpátok Eurorégió a régiók Európájában' ('The Carpathian Euroregion in the Europe of the regions') *Educatio* 3: 438–52.

Swain, A. (1998) 'Governing the workplace: the workplace and regional development implications of automotive foreign direct investment in Hungary', *Regional Studies* 7: 653–71.

Turnock, D. (1998) 'Socio-economic stress, spatial imbalance and policy responses in the new democracies', in D. Pinder (ed.) *The New Europe,* Chichester: John Wiley & Sons, pp. 323–39.

8 Employment problems and regional differences in Central and Eastern Europe

The need for local development initiatives[1]

Maarten Keune

Introduction

Since the end of the socialist era, the Central and Eastern European countries (CEECs) have been suffering from declining employment and growing unemployment. One of the peculiarities of the transformation period has been the geographical concentration of employment problems, resulting in strong intra-country regional differences (Keune 1998b). On the one hand, most countries have a group of thriving regions or cities where unemployment hardly exists and where wages and incomes are far above the national average. On the other hand, in all countries in certain regions decline has been much deeper than in others, resulting in a depressed labour market and ultimately in poverty. The former have demonstrated a great capability for restructuring and adaptating to new conditions although their dynamism has generally not been sufficient to pull their respective country out of the transition crisis. Very little success has been achieved in improving the situation in the latter group of regions.

In this chapter, employment problems in the CEE countries and their regional dimension will be explored. In the first section, recent developments concerning employment and unemployment and their relationship with economic growth are examined. The second section explores regional differences, their causes and determinants. In the final section it will be argued that the present economic strategies in most CEECs are incomplete and that they should be complemented by a decentralised, bottom-up approach to economic and employment policy. A number of issues important for the design and implementation of related policies will be considered here.

GDP and employment in the 1989–97 period

The change from a centrally planned to a market-based economic system in Central and Eastern Europe resulted in a severe economic crisis – expressed first of all in a drastic decline in GDP (see Table 8.1). In 1992, Poland was the first country to experience recovery from this crisis and achieve economic

Table 8.1 Real GDP and total employment in selected countries in Central and Eastern Europe, 1989–97

Country	*GDP (1989=100)*		*Employment (1989=100)*	
	1993	*1997*	*1993*	*1997*
	Central and South-eastern Europe			
Bulgaria	76.1	66.6	73.8	73.3
Czech Rep.	85.0	97.5	89.7	92.4
Hungary	81.9	90.4	75.6	72.8
Poland	87.6	111.8	84.3	90.0
Romania	76.2	82.3	91.9	82.4
Slovakia	75.1	95.6	84.6	82.2
Slovenia	81.4	95.5	81.3	78.6
	Former USSR			
Estonia	65.0	77.1	84.5	77.4
Latvia	51.1	56.2	85.6	73.7
Lithuania	60.2	62.3	93.4	87.7
Russia	72.0	58.6	93.7	85.5
Ukraine	68.0	40.1	94.1	88.8

Sources: Economic Survey of Europe 1998 – No. 3, UN-ECE, New York and Geneva.

growth. In the following years, Poland was followed by most other Central and Southeastern European countries, and by the Baltic States.[2] Meanwhile, Russia, Ukraine and most other CIS countries are still caught in a negative spiral. In 1996, Poland was the first (and so far only) country to surpass its 1989 level of GDP.

The fall in GDP has been accompanied by an enormous decline in employment, growing unemployment (both open and hidden) and falling participation rates. Employment decreased strongly in the period through 1997 in all CEE countries, with decline ranging from 7.6 per cent in the Czech Republic to 27.2 per cent in Hungary. There is no straightforward relationship between GDP and employment as it differs from country to country. In four countries the decline in employment has been substantially stronger than the fall in GDP (Hungary, Poland, Slovakia and Slovenia – see Table 8.1) while especially in the countries of the former Soviet Union, GDP declined much more sharply than employment. The former countries appear to have undergone more profound economic restructuring in recent years while in the latter restructuring has often been avoided or postponed, frequently resulting in increased labour hoarding and declining labour productivity. Recent developments show that labour shedding is now accelerating in these countries.

After the initial economic decline, most countries of Central and Southeastern Europe and the Baltic region have achieved growth since 1993. Economic growth has, however, generally not led to comparable growth in (formal) employment. In fact, with the exception of Poland and the Czech Republic, after 1993 employment continues to decline everywhere despite the achieved economic growth. Nesporova (1997) therefore argues that growth in most transition countries has had a labour-saving character. A clear example is Hungary where employment declined continuously in the period 1989–94 to stabilise in 1995 despite (modest) economic growth since 1994. While in 1997 GDP was 10.4 per cent higher than in 1993, employment was 3.8 per cent lower. In Poland, employment has been growing but is nothing compared to GDP. In 1997, the Polish GDP was 27.6 per cent higher than in 1993, but employment grew by only 6.8 per cent in the same period. On the one hand, this is a positive development, as labour productivity is increasing. Apart from this, these figures do not take into account the informal labour market, and it may also simply be unrealistic to expect the former socialist countries to re-attain their former high employment levels. On the other hand, the extent of the employment losses and the inability of growth to stimulate sufficient job creation raise questions about the level or type of economic growth needed to induce recovery on the CEE labour market. This points to a need to evaluate what type of economic development is favourable for the labour market and how employment promotion can be strengthened.

The decline in formal employment has resulted in unemployment, declining participation rates and growing informal employment. An overview of the evolution of registered unemployment is provided in Table 8.2. Unemployment increased rapidly after 1989 in the Central and Southeastern European countries (with the exception of the Czech Republic) and reached its peak in 1993–4. Although in 1997 unemployment is below its 1993 level in all these countries (again with the exception of the Czech Republic) in several countries it shows an increasing tendency.

Table 8.2 Registered unemployment in Central and Eastern Europe 1991–6 (end-of-year rates, per cent of labour force)

Country	*1991*	*1993*	*1995*	*1997*
	Central and South-eastern Europe			
Bulgaria	11.5	16.4	11.1	13.7
Czech Rep.	4.1	3.5	2.9	5.2
Hungary	7.4	12.1	10.4	10.4
Poland	11.8	16.4	14.9	10.3
Romania	3.1	10.4	8.9	8.8
Slovakia	11.8	14.4	13.1	12.5
Slovenia	10.1	15.5	14.5	14.8
	Former USSR			
Estonia	n.a.	5.0	5.0	4.6
Latvia	n.a.	5.8	6.5	6.7
Lithuania	n.a.	3.4	7.3	6.7
Russia	0.0	1.0	3.2	3.4 *
Ukraine	0.0	0.3	0.6	2.8

Sources: Economic Bulletin for Europe, Volume 48, Geneva: UN-ECE, 1996. Economic Survey of Europe 1998 – No. 3, UN-ECE, New York and Geneva.

Note: * 1996.

In the countries of the former Soviet Union, registered unemployment has grown only very slowly. This is mainly because rather than being dismissed, many workers have been placed on part-time work or on (often unpaid) administrative leave.[3] For example, in 1996, 24.5 per cent of all employed people in Ukraine were sent on administrative leave for a certain period of time, while 8.6 per cent were put on part-time work.[4] As a result, hidden unemployment is very high. If hidden unemployment were to become open in countries of the former Soviet Union, the unemployment rates would be much higher and far above those in Central Europe. Moreover, registration data in these countries do not reveal the true extent of open unemployment. The unemployed often do not register due to a lack of incentives, difficulties in registration, or other reasons. This is clearly seen when registration data are compared to Labour Force Survey (LFS) data. For example, in Ukraine registered unemployment was 1.0 per cent in October 1996, while LFS unemployment was 7.6 per cent; in Russia in 1996, LFS unemployment was almost three times the registered rate.[5]

Apart from increasing open and hidden unemployment, participation rates have been declining strongly in most CEE countries, with the effect that employment losses have only partly been reflected in unemployment. For example, the participation rate in Hungary fell continuously between 1989 and 1996, from 85.3 per cent to 71.9 per cent. In Poland, although economic growth began in 1992, participation declined by 4.4 per cent in the period 1992–4, from 83.2 per cent to 78.8 per cent (Keune 1998c). Finally, informal employment of all categories has been increasing rapidly. While very little reliable data is available on the extent of informal employment, without a doubt it plays an important part.

Regional differences and their causes

The deterioration of the general labour market situation has been characterised by strong intra-country differences. Within all CEE countries, certain regions or cities are performing far better than the national average, with very low unemployment rates and positive employment growth. Others are far behind, suffering from huge employment losses, persistently high (open or

Table 8.3 Unemployment rates in selected regions, Poland 1990–6

Region	*1990*	*1996*
Warszawskie	2.1	4.3
Krakowskie	3.4	6.4
Poznanskie	3.5	6.2
Koszalinskie	9.5	25.1
Olsztynskie	10.2	23.8
Suwalskie	11.5	25.4
Poland	6.1	13.6

Source: National Labour Office.

hidden) unemployment, and limited employment creation.[6] Regional differences in open unemployment tend to be quite large and get larger the smaller the units observed. For example, in Poland, in 1996, the highest regional rate of registered unemployment was 21.1 percentage points higher than the lowest regional rate (Table 8.3). In the same year, the lowest regional rate was only one-third of the national average, while the highest was almost twice as high as the national average. Other CEE countries show similar characteristics, although in some countries of the former USSR regional differences in unemployment still appear limited because of the artificially low level of open unemployment. Here regional employment differences are sometimes expressed in hidden rather than in open unemployment.

Regional differences tend to be rather stable, or even increasing. Table 8.3 again clearly illustrates this point for Poland. The regions with the highest unemployment in 1990 still show very high rates in 1996, while rates in low-unemployment regions have remained low.[7] Moreover, the gap between the two categories has increased substantially. In general terms, we can say that in all CEE countries, the regions and cities that were in better shape in the first years of transition have tended to continue their above-average performance today, while most regions that were lagging at the beginning have not been able to close the gap. The latter suffer from an accumulation of negative consequences of economic change, and the existence of regions with profound employment problems has become a structural feature of transition. This has led to a spatial concentration of those who bear the cost of the move to a market economy (OECD 1996). Still, there are also regions that have been able to improve their relative position – notably certain regions bordering EU countries.

The large and persistent regional differences reflect uneven regional development, and show that local units have an economic life of their own. They also serve to emphasise that national economic and social outcomes are the result of numerous local achievements, rather than the result of national strengths or weaknesses. Finally, they underline the importance of the local labour market, which plays a key role in determining employment opportunities for the population, often to a greater extent than the national labour market.

The causes of regional differences in employment and unemployment are many. Most analyses concerning such differences in transition countries have focused on long-term development characteristics like pre-1989 industrial structure, skill profiles, infrastructural development, and educational levels, or on geographical factors like proximity to the large urban centres or to the borders of the European Union (e.g. Fazekas and Ozsvald 1998; Scarpetta 1995; UNDP 1997). Capital cities and western regions (in the case of Central Europe) have generally been quite successful, while many agricultural regions are lagging. It seems that the advantage of the relatively more developed regions has not only been that they could limit their employment losses, but rather that they have been far better at developing new productive activities and creating new employment. They have demonstrated a comparatively high capacity to overcome the transition crisis and to adapt to the new circumstances.

In particular the type of industrial development promoted during the centrally planned era has frequently been cited as an important factor with respect to regional development. Many regions previously specialised in (and depended on) one or very few industries. Where these industries were hit by major crises during transition, the respective regions have often suffered severe employment losses or accumulated high levels of hidden unemployment. Typical examples of such regions in crisis are those with concentrations in mining and steel, arms production, or certain textile regions (see e.g. Keune 1998a; Kiss 1997). The reasons for the poor performance of these monostructured regions are partly found in their lack of competitiveness or, in some cases, because foreign markets (e.g. the EU steel market) are hardly accessible for CEE enterprises. More importantly, they are generally ill prepared for the creation of new enterprises and employment in new sectors. Often the entire local economic and social infrastructure was rigidly focused on one industry, including educational institutions, supporting industries, transport facilities, etc. This has made these regions vulnerable to decline and has severely limited their employment-creating capacity.

Apart from the above-mentioned long-term development and geographical factors, institutional factors have played an important role in recent regional success or failure as well. According to Hudson (1998), in recent research there has been a convergence upon the significance of endogenously produced features as sources of competitive advantages. It is claimed that, at least in part, 'successful' regional economies are dependent upon conditions and processes internal to the region and are not simply dependent upon external conditions and broader processes as the basis for their success. Recent case studies increasingly underline the importance of endogenous, socially produced factors in understanding developments in the Central and Eastern European regions (e.g. Nesporova 1998; Swain 1998). They include the local policy-making capacity, the supply of collective goods by local institutions, inter-firm co-operation, and the ability of local actors to co-ordinate development policies and initiatives.

The above implies that the regions can do something themselves to improve their economic fortune, that there is scope for regional action and initiatives within the parameters of a global political economy (Hudson 1998). Development opportunities are of little value if they are not acted upon. Also, while obstacles to development may be high, they may be overcome with proactive policies combined with adequate resources. Especially in the more problematic regions 'spontaneous' development can hardly be expected. Even if the national economy manages to get on a path of growth, this does not automatically trickle down to a country's problem regions (Keune 1998a). Here, comprehensive local development strategies, backed by appropriate financial means, are necessary to start recovery and generate employment.

But also in the more advantaged regions, locally based development policies and programmes can play an important role in developing a region's productive power and competitive strength to its fullest extent, and in creating employment opportunities. They can speed up the restructuring and revitalisation of the local economy and explicitly aim to improve the employment situation in the region.

Promoting local development

In spite of their potential importance, local policies and initiatives aimed at economic growth and employment creation have so far received limited attention in Central and Eastern Europe. Especially in the initial years of transition, the emphasis of economic policy in most CEECs was on macroeconomic objectives, including price and trade liberalisation, restraining inflation and limiting budget deficits. It was expected that under the right macroeconomic conditions, market forces would create the necessary economic dynamism. However, as demonstrated above, with few exceptions, the present economic strategies do not seem to be able to create sufficient and sustainable economic growth, nor does economic growth necessarily lead to net employment creation. Experience of the past thirty years in Western Europe and the United States, and more recently also in the CEE countries, demonstrates that strengthening economic growth and employment creation requires that national-level policies be complemented by a decentralised, bottom-up approach to economic and employment policy taking into account the particular problems of local areas, and exploring their specific advantages or opportunities (see e.g. Sengenberger and Keune 1996; Vignon 1996). As discussed in the remainder of this section, several policy areas need attention if such an approach is to be facilitated.

Strengthening national regional development policy

National governments can play an important role in promoting development at the local or regional level, through regional development policies and through initiatives in related policy areas. However, little has been done thus far to this end in the transition countries. As observed by Gorzelak (1998), no CEE government (with the possible exception of Hungary) has developed a comprehensive regional development policy, and regional considerations are almost non-existent in the current social and economic programmes. Although good intentions in this direction have been announced in several countries, little has been achieved in practice. To fill this gap, several steps could be taken.

First of all, national governments have to clearly define the objectives of regional development policies. There are two commonly defined but potentially conflicting aims of regional policy (Van Dijk and Oosterhaven 1994). One of these is increased *equity*, meaning the achievement of a geographically more balanced development of economic activities, generally pursued by support measures for lagging regions. The other is increased *efficiency*, aimed at facilitating local development in general, by achieving the maximum contribution of each region to national welfare. Both aims may be highly relevant, and the question of which objective can or should be emphasised most depends on the particular national situation. Because of the significant regional differences in Central and Eastern Europe, the equity objective should have a prominent place in most countries, with the most problematic regions receiving special assistance. Large regional differences create social tensions, and the further less developed regions lag behind the national average, the harder it is to close the gap. However, a general promotion of local development seems to be equally or even more important. Reducing regional differences in the level of economic development may be less urgent than the challenge of rebuilding the economy as a whole.

Promoting general local development from a national perspective may have many components and is not limited only to regional development policy. The main objective in this regard would be to provide local actors with the necessary capacity and means to develop and implement local development initiatives. This may include many specific measures, such as:

- decentralising responsibilities from the central government to regional or local governments;
- strengthening the role of local and regional labour offices;
- decentralising decision-making power on the use of regional development funds, employment funds or social funds;
- promoting the establishment of institutions that may play a role in local development (e.g. local and regional development councils and agencies or enterprise promotion agencies);
- promoting co-operation between the social partners at the local level;
- capacity-building for local actors.

When special assistance is offered to regions, it should be clearly determined on what criteria this assistance is based. Regional disparities regarding a number of social and economic indicators (e.g. GDP per capita, employment and unemployment figures, participation rates, etc.) may be used as criteria. Reducing these disparities is closely linked to the equity objective. On the other hand, funds can be made available on the basis of competition, with support going to the region(s) presenting the best projects in certain areas – such an assistance scheme would be aimed primarily at increased efficiency. There can also be solutions that seek to serve a combination of these two objectives. Moreover, assistance criteria can be important in directing the course of development. For example, considering the unfavourable employment situation prevailing in the CEE countries, economic assistance may be explicitly based on employment-related disparities or on the expected employment-creating capacity of development initiatives presented for support.

Interesting in this respect is the EU Territorial Employment Pact programme, started in 1996. The programme gives financial support to local initiatives aimed at creating employment, on the condition that they are based on a bottom-up perspective and partnership between the involved local actors, that they take an integrated approach based on a detailed analysis of the local situation, and that they seek to develop an integrated strategy with innovative measures (a so-called Employment Action Plan) (Pyke 1998).

However, EU experience shows that central government should not play too dominant a role in regional development. The type of projects and their execution should be left to the discretion of the regions themselves, as long as it is likely that they will lead to satisfactory results. Development strategies imposed from the centre are likely to have limited success, and decentralisation of responsibility for policy-making and implementation should be part and parcel of regional development policies.

Towards endogenous local development strategies

Effective local development policies aimed at the promotion of economic and employment growth take a multi-sectoral perspective and co-ordinate between various policy areas to come to a comprehensive local development strategy. As observed by the OECD (1995: 76), 'local development is an attempt to combine a range of policy responses originating from many sources into a cohesive programme tailored closely to local needs and characteristics'. It facilitates reinforcement between a variety of policy areas (e.g. the labour market, enterprise development or education) based on shared goals, rather than operating in a vacuum. The formulation of a local development strategy allows for the identification of specific objectives, such as full and balanced employment, improving the environment, or attaining diversity of economic activities in the region in order to reduce its vulnerability and dependence on particular industries. A local development strategy includes both short- and longer-term considerations, and is based on a thorough analysis of the region's strengths and weaknesses, obstacles to development, and opportunities for economic growth and employment creation. It identifies necessary actions and determines the role of the relevant actors in policy design and implementation. Most importantly, it should specify how proposed actions will be financed.

Sustainable local development is above all endogenous in nature. Its primary aim is to improve the local economic and social infrastructure, develop the area's own resources, and create a high-quality 'enabling environment' that stimulates economic activity and employment growth (Sengenberger and Keune 1996). Local development initiatives and projects include both public and private investment in the physical infrastructure, education and training of workers, innovation, information and marketing, the financial infrastructure, and other elements that improve the capacity for economic activity. Creating an enabling environment often implies assistance for the supply of collective goods and the establishment or strengthening of local support institutions, such as business and technology centres, education and training institutions, labour offices, or chambers of commerce. Endogenous development does not exclude external inputs like outside (foreign) investment, on the contrary. However, attracting such investment should fit into an area's development objectives and should be mainly based on offering high-quality resources, rather than on providing cheap labour or financial incentives.

For the time being it appears few regions or localities in Central and Eastern Europe have managed to develop comprehensive and realistic development strategies. Many development plans have been drawn up, often with international assistance, but few have resisted the test of reality. Often funding is lacking and too much is expected from foreign investors or tourism. The strengthening of the local policy-making capacity therefore seems to be an urgent matter.

Co-ordinating development efforts and capacity building

To develop an effective local development strategy and identify development objectives is not something for a small elite group of experts; rather, it requires strong involvement and the intervention of many regional and local actors. Economic and employment policies need the support of local leaders and interest groups, and success often depends on the strength of these actors and their input in the policy-making and implementation process. This kind of participation, based on social partnership, may be channelled through bodies such as regional social and economic councils or other 'regional forums of strategic choice and action' (Scott 1995).[8] All relevant local actors with an interest and role in socio-economic development should ideally participate in the design and implementation of such policies, including representatives of the regional and local governments, universities, enterprises, trade unions and employers' organisations, private entrepreneurs, or labour offices (ILO-CEET 1996). This would secure the support from the relevant actors and institutions, help to build consensus, and facilitate lobbying outside institutions (e.g. the central government). Local development activities may be channelled through professional bodies such as local or regional development agencies, often indispensable to ensure that regional strategies are in fact translated into practical action. However, the objectives and actions themselves should have the support of a broadly based coalition of local socio-economic actors and interest groups. This would also provide the required co-ordination of activities and ensure that 'all noses are pointed in the same direction'. This kind of structured co-operation often requires the participants to step outside the borders of their traditional activities. A number of interesting examples of effective local co-operation can be found in CEE countries (see e.g. Nesporova 1998; Sengenberger and Keune 1996; Szczepanski Cybula 1998) showing its value in preventing or overcoming local economic and employment crises.

Conclusion

In the past ten years the countries of Central and Eastern Europe have been experiencing a deep fall in employment, resulting in high open and hidden unemployment, declining participation rates and a growing informal sector. Even in countries where the economy has been growing in recent years, employment has not followed this tendency and in 1997 in all CEECs employment remained far below its 1989 level. These developments have been characterised by large and persisting intra-country regional differences, which underline the fact that local units have an economic life of their own and emphasise the importance of local labour markets.

For the time being, in most CEECs, social and economic policies have failed to take this local dimension sufficiently into account. The comprehensive promotion of endogenous local development as a vehicle for economic advancement and employment creation is generally missing from the policy package. Strengthening this dimension seems indispensable to improve the overall situation on the labour market and especially in the CEE problem regions. Particular attention should be given to the formulation and implementation of a comprehensive regional development policy, the promotion of endogenous local development, the co-ordination of development efforts and capacity building for local actors.

Notes

1 This article is a substantially revised and updated version of the introduction published in M. Keune (1998) (ed.) *Regional Development and Employment Policy: Lessons from Central and Eastern Europe*, Budapest and Geneva: ILO.
2 Recent exceptions are Bulgaria, which experienced strong economic decline in 1996-7, and Romania where GDP fell by 6.7 per cent in 1997 after four years of growth.
3 These practices allow enterprises to avoid severance payments, or may offer tax advantages; they also allow workers to continue to use some of the social services provided by the enterprises.
4 Data from the Ministry of Statistics.
5 Also in the Central and South-eastern European countries differences between LFS and registered unemployment exist but they are much smaller.
6 Regional differences existed before the start of transition as well, however, they have become more apparent and the pattern has changed since the end of the 1980s.
7 On this point see for example Fazekas and Ozsvald (1998) for Hungary or UNDP (1997) for Latvia.
8 According to Scott, such forums can be essential for regional economic success in the modern world, and can be either of limited scope or more ambitious. The latter is true of regional economic councils (e.g. in Germany) that regularly bring together major local constituencies (e.g. employers, banks, workers' organisations and municipal governments) to debate questions of long-term industrial order in an effort to forge viable strategies of regional management.

References

Dijk, van J. and Oosterhaven, J. (1994) 'Past, present and future of Dutch regional policy: with special reference to regional problem indicators', in C. Verhaar and P. de Klaver (eds) *The Functioning of the Economy and Labour Market in a Peripheral Region: the Case of Friesland*, Ljouwert: Fryske Akademy, pp. 111–35.

Fazekas, K. and Ozsvald, E. (1998) 'Transition and regional policy: the case of Hungary', in M. Keune (ed.) *Regional Development and Employment Policy: Lessons from Central and Eastern Europe*, Budapest and Geneva: ILO.

Gorzelak, G. (1998) 'Regional development and planning in East-Central Europe', in M. Keune (ed.) *Regional Development and Employment Promotion: Lessons from Central and Eastern Europe*, Budapest and Geneva: ILO.

Hudson, R. (1998) *What Makes Economically Successful Regions in Europe Successful? Implications for Transferring Success from West to East*, Working Papers in Contemporary European Studies, Working Paper No. 3, Centre on European Political Economy, Brighton: Sussex European Institute.

ILO-CEET (1996) *Economic Restructuring and Social Dialogue in the Ivanovo Oblast*, Budapest: ILO-CEET.

Keune, M. (1998a) 'Economic restructuring and employment promotion in a Russian crisis region: the case of Ivanovo', in S. Clarke (ed.) *Structural Adjustment without*, MA *Unemployment? The Lessons of the Russian Experience*, Cheltenham: Edward Elgar Publishing Ltd.

Keune, M. (1998b) 'Introduction', in M. Keune (ed.) *Regional Development and Employment Promotion: Lessons from Central and Eastern Europe*, Budapest and Geneva: ILO.

Keune, M. (1998c) *Youth Unemployment in Hungary and Poland*, Employment and Training Papers 20, Geneva: ILO.

Kiss, Y. (1997) *Regional and Employment Consequences of the Defence Industry Transformation in East Central Europe*, Employment and Training Papers 32, Geneva: ILO.

Nesporova, A. (1997) 'Labour Market Institutions and Policies in Transition Countries after 1989: A Comparative Analysis', paper prepared for the National Tripartite Conference on Employment Policy in Ukraine, 14–15 October 1997, Kyiv: Government of Ukraine/ILO.

Nesporova, A. (1998) 'An active approach towards regional restructuring: the case of Ostrava, Czech Republic', in M. Keune (ed.) *Regional Development and Employment Policy: Lessons from Central and Eastern Europe*, Budapest and Geneva: ILO.

OECD (1995) *Local Responses to Industrial Restructuring in Austria,* Paris: OECD.

OECD (1996) *Transition at the Local Level: The Czech Republic, Hungary, Poland and the Slovak Republic*, Paris: OECD.

Pyke, F. (1998) *Local Development and the Management of Change in Europe*, Employment and Training Papers 31, Geneva: ILO.

Scarpetta, S. (1995) 'Spatial variations in unemployment in Central and Eastern Europe: underlying reasons and labour market policy options', in *The Regional Dimension of Unemployment in Transition Countries*, Paris: OECD.

Scott, A. (1995) 'The geographic foundations of industrial performance', *Competition and Change: The Journal of Global Business and Political Economy* 1, 1.

Sengenberger, W. and Keune, M. (1996) 'The role of proactive policies for employment creation at the industrial and regional level: international experience', in *For More and Better Jobs in the Russian Federation*, Budapest: ILO-CEET.

Swain, A. (1998) *Institutions and Regional Development: Evidence from Hungary and Ukraine*, Working Papers in Contemporary European Studies, Working Paper No. 4, Centre on European Political Economy, Brighton: Sussex European Institute.

Szczepanski, M. and Cybula, A. (1998) 'Economic restructuring and employment promotion in the Katowice Voivodship, 1989–96', in M. Keune (ed.) *Regional Development and Employment Policy: Lessons from Central and Eastern Europe*, Budapest and Geneva: ILO.

UNDP (1997) *Latvia Human Development Report 1997*, Riga: UNDP.

Vignon, J. (1996) 'A macro-economic evaluation of the potential for the creation of new jobs in Europe', in *European Commission Social Europe*, Supplement 1/96, Brussels: European Commission.

9 The significance of EU integration for transition countries

Daniel Piazolo

Introduction

The economic significance of the European Union and of the Central and Eastern European countries (CEECs) for each other in terms of trade and investment flows has increased greatly in recent years.[1] Based on various concepts of 'natural trading blocs', it can be shown that Hungary, Poland, the Czech Republic and the Slovak Republic have already become part of the economic region of Western Europe (see Piazolo 1997a). This market–induced adjustment raises the question of what additional benefit may be gained through further institutional integration between Eastern and Western Europe.

Eastern European desire for EU membership might be motivated partly by the expected transfers from the EU budget. The application of present EU transfer rules to the CEECs would create high net transfers in terms of the CEECs' GDP. However, the accession of numerous new members at a low level of economic development necessitates a reform of EU expenditures in order to avoid a collapse of the EU budget. Consequently, while the Eastern European countries can expect to receive significant net transfers, these will be substantially below the levels associated with present budget rules (see also Baldwin 1995; Baldwin *et al.* 1997).

Another possible reason for the CEECs to seek EU membership is connected with the improvement of conditions for trade with the EU through the reduction of remaining EU tariffs, the elimination of non-tariff barriers in the agricultural sector and membership of the single market. However, since tariffs on EU imports from the CEECs as well as EU non-tariff barriers are already low and will be reduced further under the Europe agreements, it is more likely to be the guaranteed access to the large EU market that motivates the CEECs to seek EU accession. Full EU membership will protect the Eastern European countries from any protectionist vogue that might raise EU trade barriers again, e.g. through anti-dumping policies.

This chapter argues that besides transfers, further reductions in trade barriers and guaranteed market access, EU membership may enhance the credibility of economic reforms in the Eastern European countries through the establishment of institutions common to the EU members. EU membership requires the transition countries to bring their legal, political and economic system into conformity with EU standards and to effectively implement the so-called *acquis communautaire*, which includes many institutional components that are crucial to the functioning of a market economy (see Bofinger 1995). Deviations from the agreed pattern of institutional reform could entail various sanctions, like formal demands by the European Commission to comply with European Union law or charges before the European Court of Justice. Greater credibility of economic reforms would enhance the speed and the effectiveness of the reforms as economic agents are more likely to believe in policy announcements and to adjust accordingly. The integration of transition countries into the EU will help to stabilise the democratic political system and promote the development of market-orientated economic institutions – not dissimilar to the experiences of Greece (as far as the political system is concerned), Portugal and Spain, when these countries entered the EC in 1981 and 1986, respectively.

In the following analysis I set out in the next section the concept of credibility, discuss how credibility problems can arise and then review the credibility problems of the Eastern European countries. In the fourth section I examine the effects of institutions on growth and provide a rough indication of the potential impact of EU integration on economic growth in the CEECs. Finally, a conclusion offers the results.

The credibility problems of policy reforms in transition countries

The transition from a socialist to a market economy involves major changes in the political, economic and social system in a short period of time. Major reforms often encounter credibility problems, since the effectiveness of far-reaching changes depends on the willingness of the economic agents to alter their behaviour. The agents will only adjust if they expect the new incentive structures established by the reforms to stay, i.e. the announced reforms have to be credible.

The credibility of an institutional arrangement or a policy can be defined as the public's subjective probabilistic belief that an arrangement or policy will in fact apply for the relevant time period (Schmieding 1993). The greater the difference between the announced government policy and the expected policy, the greater the credibility problem is. The relevant time period is that for which *ex ante* decisions have to be taken. Policy reforms, for example, trade or price liberalisation in developing countries, are initiated in order to achieve welfare gains through increased consumer surplus and through efficient allocation of resources. An efficient allocation following a reform requires the shifting of resources from one sector to another according to the new price signals. Due to sector-specific knowledge and machinery, the transfer of labour and capital between industries incurs substantial adjustment costs. The economic agents will only be prepared to shift their resources if they judge themselves able to recoup their costs i.e. if the reform is believed to be durable.

The main sources for credibility problems can be summarised into four categories (see Rodrik 1989): (a) the government's policies are inconsistent; (b) the government motives are unclear; (c) the anticipated political costs due to redistribution effects of the policies are high; (d) the macro-economic environment is unstable. A credible political and economic framework of a society needs clear, enforceable rules that are administered impartially. In particular, the failure to ensure the predictability of its actions often leads to a government suffering from credibility problems.

Three different strategies leading to increased credibility are discussed in the literature: (a) signalling commitment (Bond *et al.* 1995); (b) altering governmental incentives (Bofinger 1995); and (c) reducing the scope of governmental manoeuvring (Rodrik 1989). Various policies are feasible to follow these strategies: for example, Bond *et al.* (1995) suggest that the government might even subsidise investment in order to signal commitment and to attract foreign direct investment. However, this policy is also easily reversible and might not convince the investors to commit their long-term funds. Through joining international organisations like the World Trade Organisation, a government can also signal its commitment to liberalise its foreign trade. Ensuring convertibility for capital account transactions alters the government's incentives since the economic agents can react more quickly in the case of bad economic policies. Embarking on a reform formally agreed with the International Monetary Fund or the World Bank reduces the governmental flexibility in changing the policies arbitrarily.

By pursuing regional integration with a more advanced partner, a reform country government may use all three strategies simultaneously to increase its credibility. Regional integration requires, first, that the government signals its determination to fulfil its own goals and the commitments arising from the institutional integration. Second, the obligations through the institutional setting reduce the possibility of arbitrary changes of policies. Third, the obligations and potential sanctions change the incentive structure of the government.[2] The second strategy – making arbitrary policy shifts less likely – has been stressed recently on the grounds of political economy with particular reference to the accession of less advanced economies to the EU (Bofinger 1995). The 'hand-tying' of national governments by the various regulations of the European Union forces the member countries to follow sound economic policies (like keeping their markets completely open *vis-à-vis* other members). The influence of different national interest groups is consequently reduced, resulting in an increase in predictability of government policies.

Some important insights can be derived from the experience of institutional integration between rich and poor nations in the case of former enlargements of the then European Community and from the North American Free Trade Area (NAFTA). In the case of the European Community, trade liberalisation in preparation for accession resulted in substantial structural change in the new Member States in line with their comparative advantage. At the same time, Fratzscher (1994) emphasises that successful integration and income convergence depended critically on sound macroeconomic policies and a decisive strong government. In the case of Greece, regional integration alone could not compensate for major domestic policy deficits and unwillingness to reform. However, in Spain and Portugal, integration into the European Community acted as a catalyst for modernisation and market opening. Baldwin (1993) regards the experiences of Portugal and Spain at the time of joining the EC therefore as an example of 'investment-led' growth.

The trade accord between Mexico and the USA and Canada has been analysed by Fernandez-Arias and Spiegel (1996) with respect to its impact on the credibility of the Mexican government. They argue that the primary impact of NAFTA does not lie in the further reduction of already low tariffs between the partners, but in a fundamental change in the attractiveness of Mexico as a location for investment. Fernandez-Arias and Spiegel extend the traditional analysis of customs unions to allow for international capital movements and show how a trade accord may affect the ability of the less developed partner to attract capital. In the model, a Southern nation relies on capital from the North for production in its foreign sector and faces a standard time-inconsistency problem concerning the level of taxation on foreign investment. Hence, foreign investors fear being taxed in the future due to policy reversals ('cheating'). In a wider sense, taxation may be viewed as representing all policies that affect the profitability of FDI. Under the trade agreement, the southern nation commits itself to national treatment of foreign investment. Fernandez-Arias and Spiegel show that trade agreement can be an effective mechanism for achieving higher foreign investment if it makes the rules for the treatment of foreign investment more credible. Thus, regional integration between a poor and a rich country serves as a credibility-enhancing mechanism.

The NAFTA case also illustrates that enhanced credibility through regional integration need not be limited to trade policy reforms, but may also extend further to macro- and microeconomic reforms. It has even been stated that, during the NAFTA talks, the Mexican negotiators were more concerned with making unilateral commitments to their partners than with obtaining improved market access in the USA or Canada for themselves, in order to 'lock in domestic policy reform through this process' (Whalley 1996: 16). Despite the existence of NAFTA, there was a dramatic downturn in the Mexican domestic demand and a sharp devaluation of the Mexican peso in December 1994. However, regional integration has helped Mexico substantially to overcome the crisis, since it is questionable whether, in the absence of NAFTA, the USA would have mobilised the financial means that permitted the Mexican government to avoid default. In this respect, regional integration provided 'insurance' cover to Mexico, reducing planning uncertainties for the economic agents (Fernandez 1997).

The significance of EU membership for enhancing the credibility of reforms in transition countries

Even if one accepts that regional integration may enhance the credibility of policy reforms in the transition countries in Central and Eastern Europe, the rapid progress made especially by the candidates for EU membership in recent years raises the question of whether these countries still face any major credibility problems. It is noteworthy, however, that progress was greatest in the areas of macro-economic stabilisation and micro-economic adjustment and less pronounced in institutional reforms. Furthermore, the initial successful reforms were based on three essentially temporary factors that enhanced the ability of the governments to organise credible reforms. First, the neighbouring developed market economies could be used as examples for the design of economic policies. In that respect, the motives of the government were clear. However, policy decisions have become more and more technically complicated, and straightforward examples have become rare (e.g. in the case of financial sector reforms). Second, there was a widespread consensus among the population about the direction of the political and economic transition and only a few well-organised interest groups fought economic reforms. This reduced the expected political cost of the income redistribution associated with economic transition and thereby increased the government's credibility. More recently, various interest groups have gained strength and resist reforms that endanger their privileges and incomes. Third, the CEECs were dominated by a state-orientated understanding of society. Consequently, the governments could push through their transition policies without a long-winded process of public consensus-finding. As a result of the transition progress, democracy is now taking hold and a civil society is emerging, which will delay the decision-making process (see Wiesenthal 1995).

Because of these increasing difficulties, the commitment to further reforms has considerably weakened in all transition countries, particularly in the area of institutional reforms. Even the Czech Republic – once praised as a prime example of reform-led transition – stalled in the process of privatisation and has postponed price liberalisation in important areas. In most transition countries inappropriate legal rules and their insufficient and often arbitrary application delay economic recovery. For example, bankruptcy law is not applied consistently to state-owned firms and, as a result, obsolete industries continue to receive subsidies while the necessary restructuring of the economy is postponed. The CEECs have in common the fact that reforms in the financial sector still have a long way to go, that public procurement has to be reformed and that financial constraints will necessitate a major overhaul in the areas of health care and social security. Additionally, corruption has increased dramatically in the last years in CEE, leading to distorted price signals and undermining credibility.

In the process of economic transition, institutional reforms, structural adjustment and macro-economic stabilisation are strongly interdependent.

Widespread failure to fully implement institutional reforms therefore creates serious doubts about the governments' willingness and ability to bring economic transition to a successful conclusion. In this situation, institutional integration with the European Union provides guidance with respect to the contents of further reforms and also enhances the credibility of transition country governments. The 'Europe Agreements' between the EU and the CEECs and the prospect of EU membership have already helped to stabilise expectations about the direction of future policies and the structure of the economic and legal systems in the CEECs. EU entry will further reduce uncertainty about the long-term development of the CEECs through the EU's far-reaching coverage and institutional framework.

Institutional integration is presently based on the 'Europe Agreements' (concluded between the EU and Bulgaria, the Czech Republic, Hungary, Poland, Romania, the Slovak Republic, Slovenia and the three Baltic Republics). The Agreements grant the Eastern European countries the position of an associated country in terms of political and economic affairs. Politically, the Europe Agreements are the legal basis of the CEECs' relationship with the EU and provide a framework for dialogue and for support of the gradual integration into the Union. The institutional arrangements of the Agreements provide mechanisms to implement, control and manage all areas of economic and political interaction. Concerning economic issues, the Agreements set a timetable for the establishment of bilateral free trade in non-agricultural goods and include various provisions that have effectively led to the application of EU regulations for the domestic policies of the CEECs in some areas. For example, the Europe Agreements require the CEECs to adopt legislation within three years that mirrors the competition provisions (anti-trust and state aid) of the Treaty of Rome. Disputes concerning subsidised goods traded between the CEECs and the EU have to be dealt with on the basis of EU competition policy law. Smith *et al.* (1996) have pointed out, that the Agreements were asymmetrical in the sense that the CEECs had to complete their side of the bargain before the EU committed itself to the complete elimination of commercial defence instruments such as anti-dumping provisions. The authors continue to state that the CEECs have gained substantially from the application of the procedures of the Agreements by ensuring transparency and predictability of their economic policies. The Europe Agreements have a strong binding character for the CEECs, since the failure to fulfill the conditions might not only lead to the loss of the benefits arising from the Agreements like trade barrier reductions, but also to the denial or at least postponement of EU membership in the near future (as in the case of the Slovak Republic).

Institutional integration will be advanced through full EU membership which requires the implementation and the maintenance of the *acquis communautaire* and will effectively bind the domestic economic policies of the CEECs.[3] The 'key components' of the *acquis communautaire* which are most relevant for joining members have been outlined by the European

Commission in the 1995 'White Paper' (Commission 1995) and can be regarded as representing best practice of institutional setting in the EU. The EU demands from every candidate country to 'commit itself permanently to the economic obligations of membership' and irreversible adoption of the *acquis communautaire* 'to provide the certainty that every part of the enlarged EU market will continue to operate by common rules' (Commission 1997). The adaptation of CEECs' laws to the *acquis communautaire* can proceed either through the revision of existing laws or through new national legislation on the basis of EU law. The greatest reforms in domestic legislation will be connected to the fields in which the members of the EU carry out common policies, for example, in customs issues or agricultural sector regulations. The Commission emphasises that it is important to incorporate the *acquis communautaire* into national legislation effectively, but even more important to implement it properly via the appropriate administrative and judicial structures set up in the Member States.

Questionable practices will have to be judged by the European Commission and the European partners with reference to EU law. The Commission has a duty to ensure that all economic agents within the EU are able to operate under the same conditions. These include the obligations covering freedom of establishment, national treatment and free trade, the rules on competition, harmonisation of the rules on company law and accountancy, harmonisation of the rules on intellectual property, the opening up of public works, supply and services, tax measures, protection of personal data, implementation of proceedings and the recognition of judgements. Failure to conform to the *acquis communautaire* could entail substantial costs for the deviating government. This is especially the case due to the strong political component of the EU opening up multiple channels to sanction violations of EU regulations. Since the costs of exit are high, the maintenance of domestic policies in accordance with the EU rules is credible. Consequently, EU membership will be able to serve as a mechanism for the CEECs to commit themselves credibly to sound domestic policies.

The significance of EU integration: quantifying the effects of EU institutions

The following analysis concentrates on the impact of EU institutions for the CEECs and on transitional growth. The establishment and enforcement of EU type rules and regulations would represent a major advancement for the transition countries with their heritage of the socialist system and an as yet underdeveloped institutional setting. In this section, I try to derive an estimate of the possible impact of improved economic institutions through EU membership on economic growth in the transition countries. A production function of a standard growth model is employed to illustrate the effects of an improvement in economic institutions.[4] The representative firm maximises profit according to:

$$Max\ \pi = F(A, K, L, P) - rK - wl \tag{1}$$

with the production function:

$$Y = AP^{\beta} K^{\alpha} L^{1-\alpha} \tag{2}$$

A represents the level of technology, P the institutions, K capital and L the labour force.[5] To simplify the analysis further, the labour force is set equal to 1, yielding the production function:

$$Y = AP^{\beta} K^{\alpha} \tag{3}$$

An improvement in economic institutions (for example, in terms of lower transaction costs due to more predictability through EU membership of transition economies) entails an increase in P. The production function may be written in relative changes of the variables:

$$\hat{Y} = \beta\hat{P} + \alpha\hat{K} + \gamma(4)$$

with $\hat{A} = \gamma$ = technical progress.
The 'hat ^' denotes the relative changes of the variables. The net change in the capital stock, $\hat{K}$, can be calculated by subtracting depreciation from gross investment and by combining data for the capital coefficient, $\frac{K}{Y}$, the gross investment ratio, $\frac{I}{Y}$, and the depreciation rate, $\delta = \frac{Depr}{Y} \frac{K}{Y}$, with δ representing the depreciation rate relative to capital and 'Depr' the value of depreciation.

$$\hat{K} = \frac{I}{Y}\frac{Y}{K} - \frac{Depr}{Y}\frac{Y}{K} \tag{5}$$

Combining (4) and (5), the following regression equation can be derived:

$$\hat{Y} = \beta\hat{P} + \alpha\left[\frac{I}{Y}\frac{Y}{K} - \frac{Depr}{Y}\frac{Y}{K}\right] + \gamma + error\ term \tag{6}$$

Equation (6) will be estimated from a cross-section data set containing information about investment behaviour and economic growth in transition countries. The empirical application of the production function raises the question of how to quantify the quality of economic institutions. The ranking of institutions according to their ability to encourage and maintain economic activities has to leave behind – by its nature – 'hard' figures and has to use 'soft' indicators. While the use of such indicators might be questioned on methodical ground, their usefulness has been documented by several studies broadly similar to the present one. Fischer *et al.* (1998), for instance, work with an Economic Liberalisation Index to analyse how far away the CEECs are from Brussels in terms of adopting a market-based system. They find that

Table 9.1 Progress in institutional change in 25 transition countries, 1998

	Enterprises			*Markets and trade*			*Financial institutions*		*Legal reform*	
	Large-scale privatisation	*Small-scale privatisation*	*Governance and enterprise restructuring*	*Price liberalisation*	*Trade and foreign exchange system*	*Competition policy*	*Banking reform and interest rate liberalisation*	*Securities markets and non-bank financial institutions*	*Extensiveness and effectiveness of legal rules on investment*	*Indicator of Institutional Change*
Albania	2	4	2	3	4	2	2	2	2	23
Armenia	3	3	2	3	4	2	2	1	3	23
Azerbaijan	2	3	2	3	3	1	2	2	2	20
Belarus	1	2	1	2	1	2	1	2	2	14
Bulgaria	3	3	2	3	4	2	3	2	4	26
Croatia	3	5	3	3	4	2	3	2	3	28
Czech Republic	4	5	3	3	5	3	3	3	4	33
Estonia	4	5	3	3	4	3	3	3	3	31
FYR Macedonia	3	4	2	3	4	1	3	2	3	25
Georgia	3	4	2	3	4	2	2	1	3	24
Hungary	4	5	3	3	5	3	4	3	4	34
Kazakstan	3	4	2	3	4	2	2	2	2	24
Kyrgystan	3	4	2	3	4	2	3	2	2	25

Table 9.1 cont.

	Enterprises			*Markets and trade*			*Financial institutions*		*Legal reform*	
	Large-scale privatisation	*Small-scale privatisation*	*Governance and enterprise restructuring*	*Price liberalisation*	*Trade and foreign exchange system*	*Competition policy*	*Banking reform and interest rate liberalisation*	*Securities markets and non-bank financial institutions*	*Extensiveness and effectiveness of legal rules on investment*	*Indicator of Institutional Change*
Latvia	3	4	3	3	4	3	3	2	2	27
Lithuania	3	4	3	3	4	2	3	2	3	27
Moldova	3	3	2	3	4	2	2	2	3	24
Poland	3	5	3	3	5	3	3	3	4	32
Romania	3	3	2	3	4	2	2	2	4	25
Russian Federation	3	4	2	3	2	2	2	2	3	23
Slovak Republic	4	5	3	3	5	3	3	2	2	30
Slovenia	3	5	3	3	5	2	3	3	3	30
Tajikistan	2	2	2	3	3	1	1	1	2	17
Turkmenistan	2	2	2	2	1	1	1	1	1	13
Ukraine	2	3	2	3	3	2	2	2	2	21
Uzbekistan	3	3	2	2	2	2	2	2	2	20
Average	2.9	3.8	2.3	2.9	3.7	2.1	2.4	2.0	2.7	24.8

Source: EBRD (1998), EBRD (1996), Sachs (1996), own calculations.

Notes: Progress in institutional change is estimated for nine areas and valued on a scale from 1 (little progress) to 5 (standards and performance comparable to advanced industrial countries). The figures in the table represent the achieved level. For legal reforms in Turkmenistan na in EBRD (1998) was substituted with 1 (similar to the assessment in EBRD (1996)).

economic distance from Brussels increases with geographical distance from Brussels. Knack and Keefer (1995) use an index based on Business Environmental Risk Intelligence (BERI) data about institutional maturity measured with reference to infrastructural quality, contract enforceability, bureaucratic delays and nationalisation risks to derive the influence of the institutional setting on GDP changes. They adapt standard growth regressions by regressing GDP growth rate on initial income, investment in human capital, government consumption, the development of relative prices for investment goods and the BERI index. They find a significant positive growth elasticity of the BERI index. However, the BERI data do not exist for most transition countries.

The following analysis uses an indicator developed by the European Bank for Reconstruction and Development (EBRD) that covers institutional change in twenty-five transition countries. In the 1998 Transition Report, the progress in transition towards a market economy is assessed in nine different areas covering enterprise privatisation and restructuring, price and trade liberalisation, financial and legal reforms. The achievements are ranked on a scale ranging from 1 (i.e. no or little progress) up to 5 (i.e. standards and performance comparable to advanced industrial countries) (see Table 9.1). To obtain a general indicator of institutional change (IIC), the values for the nine areas are added. One could argue that differing weights should be given to certain sub-areas of the IIC, e.g. Sachs and Warner (1995) suggest that trade and foreign exchange reform is the most critical area for growth, whereas Fischer *et al.* (1998) argue that privatisation is decisive. Furthermore, it could be claimed that price liberalisation should be emphasised more since prices reflecting the relative scarcity of the goods are essential for the efficient allocation of resources and for long-term growth. Every weighting will be arbitrary and this article will follow Sachs (1996) in working with a simple sum of the nine indexes to test for correlation between institutional progress and macroeconomic key indicators. The IIC ranges from 13 for Turkmenistan up to 34 for Hungary, with a possible maximum of 45. This indicator of institutional change (IIC) from the EBRD can provide a proxy for P. Under the assumption that all transition countries have started with a low IIC at the beginning of their transition, the indicator $\hat{\text{IIC}}$ represents the average annual relative change in P in the equation (6).

It is assumed that the investment ratio, $\frac{I}{Y}$, in equation (6) is the distinguishing characteristic for the various transition countries, whereas the capital coefficient, $\frac{K}{Y}$, and the depreciation rate are within a limited common range. Consequently, I use the same hypothetical values for the capital coefficient and the depreciation rate in the subsequent regression analysis. This implies that old capital is depreciated once and for all when transition starts. For the investment ratio, the average of the available data for the years 1989 to 1996 from the World Bank (1998) and EBRD (1998) are used. The calculated value of for $\left[\frac{I}{Y}\frac{Y}{K}-\frac{Depr}{Y}\frac{Y}{K}\right]$ each transition country in per capita terms is called I' in the following.

For the regression with change in GDP per capita (see Table 9.2) as the dependent variable the regression estimates (with t statistics in the parentheses) are:

$$\underset{1989-1998}{\text{Average Percentage Change in GDP}} = \underset{(6.76)}{-0.13} + \underset{(4.54)}{0.37\, \hat{IIC}} + \underset{(2.54)}{0.71\, I'} \quad R^2 = 0.53$$

The coefficients attached to the indicator of institutional change and the variable representing the net change in capital stock are positive and significant. The constant is technically an estimate of the rate of technical progress ($\hat{A} = \gamma$) in equation (6), which is assumed equal for all countries. However, the negative and significant constant reflects the extent of the output collapse during the first few years of the transition. These results indicate that economic growth is positively correlated with the advancement of institutional change and with an increase in the capital stock in the transition countries. If the $\hat{IIC}$ increases by 10 per cent, *ceteris paribus*, GDP goes up by more than 3 percentage points.

These regression results can be used to analyse the effects of EU accession on the GDP growth. The EU requires from potential Member States functioning market economies in order to ensure the successful implementation of the *acquis communautaire*. Roughly speaking, a country that successfully implements the *acquis communautaire* would score a value of 4 or 5 in all nine areas of the EBRD scheme of institutional change. EU membership would consequently boost the IIC value of the transition economies close to the potential maximum of 45.

The advanced transition countries with an IIC above 30 and which are also the countries most likely to join the EU in the first round of enlargement are the Czech Republic, Estonia, Hungary, Poland and Slovenia. The IIC average of these 5 countries is 32. A country fulfilling the requirements of the *acquis communautaire* would score an IIC of almost 45, i.e. about 10 to 12 IIC points or one third higher. In terms of GDP growth this implies a possible growth bonus of more than 12 per cent.[6]

The coefficient β in equation (6), on which this estimate of the growth bonus is based indicates the 'static' effect of improved institutions with no change in the capital stock. However, in a neo-classical growth model, higher marginal productivity of capital stimulates capital formation and leads to an increase in the steady-state capital stock and, therefore, in steady-state per-capita income. This additional 'dynamic' effect is difficult to quantify, but several attempts have been made in the case of the growth effect of the completion of the European Single Market in 1992. Baldwin (1989, 1993) looks at various approaches and concludes that for the completion of the Single Market, the additional growth effect is at least of the same order of magnitude as the 'static' effect and could be up to twice its size. Therefore, the entire growth bonus of EU institutions for the CEECs could be in the range of between 24 per cent and 36 per cent of additional GDP.

These figures for expected growth changes should be seen as a 'sound

Table 9.2 Change in real GDP

	Percentage change of GDP at constant prices											*Average annual percentage change 1989–1998*	*Average annual percentage change 1989–98 per capita*
	1989	*1990*	*1991*	*1992*	*1993*	*1994*	*1995*	*1996*	*1997 Estimate*	*1998 Projection*	*1999 Forecast*		
Albania	9.8	–10.0	–27.7	–7.2	9.6	9.4	8.9	9.1	–7.0	9.0	7.0	0.4	0.5
Armenia	14.2	–7.4	–17.1	–52.6	–14.8	5.4	6.9	5.8	3.1	6.0	5.0	–5.1	–6.2
Azerbaijan	–4.4	–11.7	–0.7	–22.6	–23.1	–18.1	–11.0	1.3	5.8	6.7	6.5	–7.8	–8.7
Belarus	8.0	–3.0	–1.2	–9.6	–7.6	–12.6	–10.4	2.8	10.4	5.0	–4.0	–1.8	–2.0
Bulgaria	0.5	–9.1	–11.7	–7.3	–2.4	1.8	2.1	–10.9	–6.9	4.0	3.0	–4.0	–3.3
Croatia	–1.6	–6.9	–19.8	–11.1	–0.9	0.6	1.7	6.0	6.5	4.2	3.0	–2.1	–2.1
Czech Republic	1.4	–1.2	–11.5	–3.3	0.6	2.7	5.9	3.9	1.0	–1.0	1.0	–0.2	–0.1
Estonia	–1.1	–8.1	–7.9	–14.2	–8.5	–1.8	4.3	4.0	11.4	5.0	5.0	–1.7	–0.6
FYR Macedonia	na	–9.9	–12.1	–21.1	–8.4	–4.0	–1.4	0.8	1.5	5.0	4.0	–5.0	–5.8
Georgia	–4.8	–12.4	–13.8	–44.8	–25.4	–11.4	2.4	10.5	11.0	9.0	6.0	–8.0	–7.8
Hungary	0.7	–3.5	–11.9	–3.1	–0.6	2.9	1.5	1.3	4.4	4.6	4.4	–0.4	–0.1
Kazakstan	–0.4	–0.4	–13.0	–2.9	–10.4	–17.8	–8.9	0.5	2.0	1.0	0.5	–5.0	–4.8
Kyrgystan	4.0	3.0	–5.0	–19.0	–16.0	–20.0	1.3	7.1	6.5	4.0	4.0	–3.4	–3.9

Table 9.2 cont.

	Percentage change of GDP at constant prices											*Average annual percentage change 1989–1998*	*Average annual percentage change 1989–98 per capita*
	1989	*1990*	*1991*	*1992*	*1993*	*1994*	*1995*	*1996*	*1997 Estimate*	*1998 Projection*	*1999 Forecast*		
Latvia	6.8	2.9	–10.4	–34.9	–14.9	0.6	–0.8	3.3	6.5	4.0	2.6	–3.7	–2.5
Lithuania	1.5	–5.0	–13.4	–37.7	–24.2	1.0	3.0	4.7	5.7	3.0	3.0	–6.1	–6.1
Moldova	na	–2.4	–17.5	–29.0	–1.0	–31.2	–3.0	–8.0	1.3	–2.0	–4.0	–9.3	–9.2
Poland	0.2	–11.6	–7.0	2.6	3.8	5.2	7.0	6.1	6.9	5.2	5.0	1.8	1.5
Romania	–5.8	–5.6	–12.9	–8.7	1.5	3.9	7.1	4.1	–6.6	–5.0	1.0	–2.8	–2.4
Russia	na	na	–5.0	–14.5	–8.7	–12.6	–4.0	–3.5	0.8	–5.0	–7.0	–5.3	–5.3
Slovak Republic	1.4	–2.5	–14.6	–6.5	–3.7	4.9	6.8	6.6	6.5	5.0	3.0	0.4	0.1
Slovenia	–1.8	–4.7	–8.9	–5.5	2.8	5.3	4.1	3.1	3.8	4.0	4.5	0.2	0.3
Tajikistan	–2.9	–1.6	–7.1	–29.0	–11.0	–21.5	–12.5	–4.4	1.7	3.0	4.0	–8.5	–8.3
Turkmenistan	–6.9	2.0	–4.7	–5.3	–10.0	–19.0	–8.0	–8.0	–26.0	5.0	6.0	–8.1	–7.9
Ukraine	4.0	–3.4	–11.6	–13.7	–14.2	–23.0	–11.8	–10.0	–3.2	0.0	0.0	–8.7	–8.6
Uzbekistan	3.7	1.6	–0.5	–11.1	–2.3	–4.2	–0.9	1.6	2.4	2.0	1.5	–0.8	–2.8
Average for all 25 transition countries	1.1	–4.4	–10.7	–16.5	–7.6	–6.1	–0.4	1.5	2.0	3.3	2.6	–3.8	–3.8

Source: EBRD (1998), World Development Indicators (1998), own calculations.

institutional setting' bonus reflecting improved economic institutions. The significance of EU accession in this context lies in enhancing the credibility of reforms so that the improvements can actually be implemented. Concerning the importance of policies conducive to enhancing the functioning of the market economy, the chapter arrives at conclusions similar to the ones of Sachs and Warner (1996) and Barbone and Zalduendo (1997). However, those authors have focused on the convergence issue combining the economic fundamentals of the CEECs with econometric estimations derived from 'world-wide' cross-country analysis, while this article has established the growth enhancing effects of institutions within the specialised range of the experiences of the transition countries.

Conclusion

Even in the more advanced transition economies, economic and institutional reforms have been implemented inconsistently or have been stalled. In this chapter it has been argued that the prospect of EU membership will both require and facilitate further reforms and thereby leading to increased government credibility in the CEECs. An estimate of the potential growth effect resulting from improved economic institutions through EU membership has been derived suggesting the possibility of a 'static' growth bonus in GDP of 12 per cent (not accounting for induced capital accumulation) and an additional 'dynamic' growth bonus of up to 24 per cent. This should be regarded as a rule-of-thumb approximation of the significance of EU integration for the transition countries and as a point of departure for further, more in depth studies. Such research should analyse other indicators of credibility, like expected returns of investment or credit-ranking of various countries. These further studies might clarify in greater detail important aspects of the main conclusion of this article: adapting the CEECs' institutions according to the EU *acquis communautaire* will help to establish a functioning market-orientated framework and to lay the foundation for catching up with the EU income levels.

Notes

1 This is an amended version of a paper presented at the conference 'Integration and Transition in Europe: The Economic Geography of Interaction' organised by the Department of Planning and Regional Development of the University of Thessaly. I thank the participants at the conference, Rolf J. Langhammer and Matthias Lücke for insightful comments. Financial support from the Volkswagen-Foundation and from the Phare-ACE Program is gratefully acknowledged.

2 More generally speaking, the concept of institutional integration rests on the perceived importance of functioning institutions. That supporting institutions are essential for all economic activities has recently become part of the main body of economic thinking (see World Bank Development Report 1997). In particular, it has been shown that a *sine qua non* for economic development is a set of institutions that can enforce property rights (North 1991).

3 The *acquis communautaire* is the entirety of the EU primary legislation (the Treaties installing the three Communities with all revisions and alterations, including the Single European Act, the Treaty on the European Union and the treaties on the accession of new members), secondary legislation (Decisions of the Court of Justice, Directives and Regulations) and of all other acts that warrant the legal order of the EU.

4 More details about the employed production function is offered in Piazolo (1997b).

5 The employed production function $Y = AP^{\beta}K^{\alpha}L^{1-\alpha}$ may be regarded as a modified version of the form $Y = AK^{\alpha}L^{1-\alpha} G^{1-\alpha}$ used by Barro (1990). Barro shows that various activities of a government, described by the variable G, can be viewed as having an effect on the growth rate. The government activities considered by Barro include the provision of infrastructure services, the protection of property rights and the taxation of the economic activity. Cf. also Barro and Sala-i-Martin (1995), p. 153.

6 $\frac{IIC_t - IIC_{t-1}}{IIC_{t-1}} = \frac{43 - 32}{32} = 0.34 \approx 1/3$; Consequently, the expected growth bonus can be calculated as 0.33*0.37 equalling 0.1221 or about 12 per cent.

References

Baldwin, R.E. (1989) 'The growth effects of 1992', *Economic Policy* 4: 247–81.

Baldwin, R.E. (1993) 'On the measurement of dynamic effects of integration', *Empirica*, 20: 129–45.

Baldwin, R.E. (1995) 'The Eastern enlargement of the European Union', *European Economic Review* 39, 3/4: 474–81.

Baldwin, R., Joseph, F. F. and Portes, R. (1997) 'The costs and benefits of Eastern enlargement', *Economic Policy* 24 April: 125–76.

Barbone, L. and Zalduendo, J. (1997) *EU Accession of Central and Eastern Europe – Bridging the Income Gap*, Policy Research Working Paper No. 1721, Washington, DC: World Bank.

Barro, R. (1990) 'Government spending in a simple model of endogenous growth', *Journal of Political Economy* 98, 5: 103–25.

Barro, R. and Sala-i-Martin, X. (1995) *Economic Growth*, New York: McGraw-Hill.

Bofinger, P. (1995) *The Political Economy of the Eastern Enlargement of the EU*, CEPR Discussion Paper 1234, London: CEPR.

Bond, E., Chiu, S. and Estache, A. (1995) *Trade Reform Design as a Signal to Foreign Investors: Lessons for Economies in Transition*, Working Paper, Washington, DC: World Bank.

Commission of the European Communities (1995) *Preparation of the Associated Countries of Central and Eastern Europe for Integration into the Internal Market of the Union*, Brussels: Com(95) 163 final and 163/2 final.

Commission of the European Communities (1997) *Agenda 2000 – Commission Opinion on Poland's Application for Membership*, Brussels: Com(97) 16.

European Bank for Reconstruction and Development (1996) *Transition Report*, London: EBRD.

European Bank for Reconstruction and Development (1998) *Transition Report*, London: EBRD.

Fernandez, R. (1997) *Returns to Regionalism: An Evaluation of Non-Traditional Gains from RTAs*, Cambridge, MA: NBER Working Paper 5970.

Fernandez-Arias, E. and Spiegel, M. (1996) *North–South Customs Unions and International Capital Mobility*, Policy Research Working Paper No. 1573, Washington, DC: World Bank.

Fischer, S., Sahay, R. and Vigh, C. (1998) 'How far is Eastern Europe from Brussels?', conference volume *'Quo Vadis Europe?'*, Kiel: Kiel Institute of World Economics, pp. 97–122.

Fratzscher, O. (1994) 'European integration: lessons from the South and prospects for the East', in A. Schipke and A.M. Taylor (eds) *The Economics of Transformation*, Berlin: Springer Verlag, pp. 191–232.

Knack, S. and Keefer, P. (1995) 'Institutions and economic performance', *Economics and Politics*, 7, 3: 207–28.

North, D. (1991) 'Institutions', *Journal of Economic Perspectives*, 5: 97–112.

Piazolo, D. (1997a) 'Trade integration between Eastern and Western Europe: policies follow the market', *Journal of Economic Integration* 12 ,3: 259–97, September.

Piazolo, D. (1997b) *Gaining Credibility and Enhancing Economic Growth through Regional Integration: The Case for EU-Membership of Eastern Europe*, Kiel Working Paper No. 837, Kiel: Kiel Institute of World Economics.

Rodrik, D. (1989) 'Credibility of trade reform – a policy maker's guide', *The World Economy* 12: 1–16.

Sachs, J. (1996) 'The transition at mid decade', *American Economic Review* 86, 2/3: 128–33.

Sachs, J. and Warner, A. (1995) 'Economic reform and the process of global economic integration', *Brookings Papers on Economic Activity* 1: 1–95.

Sachs, J. and Warner, A. (1996) *Achieving Rapid Growth in the Transition Economies of Central Europe*, Working Paper No. 116, Stockholm: Institute of East European Economies.

Schmieding, H. (1993) 'From plan to market: on the nature of the transformation crisis', *Weltwirtschaftliches Archiv* 129, 1: 216–53.

Smith, A., Holmes, P., Sedelmeier, U., Smith, E., Wallace, H. and Young, A. (1996) *The European Union and Central and Eastern Europe: Pre-Accession Strategies*, Working Paper No. 15, Brighton: Sussex European Institute.

Whalley, J. (1996) *Why do Countries Seek Regional Trade Agreements?*, Cambridge, MA: NBER Working Papers, No. 5552.

Wiesenthal, H. (1995) 'Die Krise holistischer Politikansötze und das Projekt der gesteuerten Systemtransformation', *Berliner Journal für Soziologie* 4: 515–32.

World Bank (1997) *World Development Report: The Role of the State,* Oxford: Oxford University Press.

World Bank (1998) *World Development Indicators*, CD-ROM.

10 The Iron Curtain in the mind

A comparison of mental maps of business students in Vienna and Bratislava[1]

Gunther Maier and Thomas Rosenmayr

Introduction

In order to be successfull, the proposed eastern enlargement of the European Union will have to overcome substantial differences between the current Member States and the new applicants in many areas. The Iron Curtain that divided Europe for almost half a century was not only of economic and military significance. It also separated two political and social systems. On either side, children were raised, educated, and socialised according to the norms and standards of the respective part of the political ideology. The respective 'other side' was either completely neglected or misrepresented by a set of stereotypes and biased reference to selected defects that just re-emphasised the superiority of the own system.

This lack of knowledge about the respective other part of Europe was reinforced by a limited level of interaction between the two parts. While people in the West frequently travelled to other countries within their part of Europe, travel to Eastern Europe was severely constrained by administrative obstacles and political control. For most East Europeans it was practically impossible to travel to the West and even trips within the Eastern bloc were constrained in some countries.

Taking into account that this structure has persisted for more than forty years, it is easy to imagine that these biased perceptions about the respective 'other side' have become part of the common knowledge in either part of Europe. By the end of the 1980s, when the Iron Curtain was dismantled, practically all the economically and politically active population had been trained and socialised in the period of the Cold War. The graduates of our universities today started their degrees when Europe was still divided.

This chapter builds on the hypothesis that this political, social, economic, and military division has left behind its traces in the minds of people on either side of the former Iron Curtain. We are looking for these traces in the perception people have of the geography of both sides of the former divided Europe. By asking students of the Business Schools in Vienna and Bratislava a standardised set of questions and requesting them to fill in missing cities in a map of Europe, we are trying to find out about their mental maps of this part of the world and what differences there are between the two populations.

The basic hypothesis is, of course, that because of the former division of Europe each group of students will have a more accurate mental map of their own part of the continent than of the part across the former Iron Curtain. With a set of additional questions we try to control for other factors that may influence the mental maps of the respondents.

The question of the geographical perception of business students on either side of the former Iron Curtain is not only of academic interest. As argued above and in more detail below, mental maps are the result of a complex set of factors like education, experience, family relations, stereotypes, political beliefs, etc. But, these perceptions about the world surrounding us also influence our behaviour in a number of ways. As research shows (see e.g., Downs and Stea 1977; Eden 1992; Gould and White 1986), we tend to reduce the complexity of spatial behaviour by focusing on those areas we are more familiar with. Our mental maps tend to guide our behaviour. When we have to move to areas we are less familiar with, we often feel insecure, vulnerable, and disoriented. Therefore, the geographical perceptions of the business students of today will most likely influence the decision-making of the business managers of tomorrow. In economically unstable transition periods like now, the accumulated decisions of managers with biased geographical perceptions may tilt a country's economy from one development path to another.

The chapter is based on the master thesis of the second author (Rosenmayr 1996) which he conducted under the supervision of the first author. In the next section we will discuss the concept of mental maps, their generation and their impact on decision making in some more detail. Then we will present the structure of the empirical investigation and the instruments we have used and will discuss the results of the investigation. The chapter will close with a concluding section.

Mental maps

Some cognitive representation of our environment is an essential part of human life and behaviour. Day in, day out we have to make decisions that involve a spatial component. When we go to work, shop for different articles, meet friends, etc. we always have to decide about routes, places, connections, and so on.

Since optimising decisions in the context of spatial relationships easily turn out to be highly complex (see e.g. Maier 1995), we typically base such decisions on the cognitive representation of our environment. The theory of 'mental maps' deals with the structure and characteristics of those cognitive representations of space, their generation, and their influence on decision-making (see e.g. Brown 1992; Downs and Stea 1977, 1993; Gould and White 1986; Longuet-Higgins 1987; Tolman 1948; Tversky 1993).

The theory distinguishes different types of cognitive representations of space (Tversky 1993). 'Cognitive collages' are composed of patches of spatial knowledge that lack a strong relationship. This type of representation compares more to a list of independent entries than a map-like structure. In 'spatial mental models' the various points in space are put in relation to one another. In this sense they allow the orientation in space. As compared to 'mental maps' spatial mental models lack information about scale. While spatial mental models contain information about relationships in ordinal form, mental maps contain the same information in cardinal form.

The distinction between different types of spatial representations is of less importance in our context. Therefore, we will only use the term 'mental map'. Since in our empirical investigation we ask respondents to place cities in a co-ordinate system, we assume that their perception of Europe has all the characteristics of a mental map. However, we do not try to verify that this is indeed the case.

Mental maps (in the more general sense of 'cognitive representations of space') are related to spatial behaviour in two ways:

1 They are derived in part from past experience in spatial behaviour. Whenever we have to deal with a spatial problem, we implicitly or explicitly collect information about the spatial elements involved and the relationship between them. This information is used as input for a complex process of generating and updating our mental maps (Hirtle *et al.* 1989).
2 They guide and structure spatial behaviour by providing a simplified framework for making those decisions (Lee 1973). Instead of having to consider all the details in our environment, we can base spatial decisions on the filtered and structured representation of this environment in our mental maps. The use of mental maps considerably reduces the complexity of the spatial problem for the decision-maker, especially in the case of repeated, routine decisions.

The process of generating mental maps is highly complex and a research topic of psychology (e.g. Hirtle and Heidorn 1993; Longuet-Higgins 1987). In our context it is important to note that this process typically leads to certain structures of mental maps that will most likely show up in our empirical results as well, thus:

- Mental maps tend to integrate spatial representations on different scales (Freundschuh 1991). When we have structured an area by knowing certain landmarks and their relationship to one another, we tend to integrate new spatial information in reference to this existing perception of a system of points of reference. Therefore, spatial perceptions typically contain the implicit reference to other levels of aggregation. In our context this means that our respondents will locate European cities in reference to their respective countries, macro-regions of the continent, areas of influence, etc. This is an important feature because it allows us to use the placement of cities to draw conclusions about the more general perceptions of respondents.

- Because of the above mentioned relationship between spatial perceptions on different scales, mental maps tend to reflect relationships on different scales. The relative location of two cities in the mental maps of people tends to reflect the relative location of their respective states or countries. Tversky (1993), for example, reports an experiment where students from the University of San Diego were asked whether San Diego or Reno is further to the west. Since Reno is associated with Nevada which is generally to the east of California, most students erroneously thought that San Diego was further to the west.
- Another, closely related characteristic of mental maps is the tendency towards clustering. We tend to group points in space that we think are related. The relationship between these points may be of different types. We may associate them with the same country, with common history, cultural similarities, a common language, etc. By storing spatial information in our mental maps we tend to combine related information into larger units on a higher level of hierarchy.
- Commonly, distances between nearby landmarks are estimated larger than the same distance between more distant landmarks. This phenomenon is known as 'cognitive perspective' (Tversky 1993). It seems that we estimate distance based on the number of intervening landmarks. But, since the density of reference points in our mental maps tends to decline with distance, we tend to underestimate more distant stretches relative to those close by.

Research design

The main purpose of our empirical study is to compare the geographical perceptions of people on both sides of the Iron Curtain. To have a comparable and relatively homogeneous group of respondents we decided to draw our sample from business students from the Vienna University of Economics and Business Administration in Vienna, Austria, and from the Economics University in Bratislava, Slovakia. There are additional advantages in choosing this group of respondents:

- They are educated enough so that they should be able to handle the abstract problem of placing points on a map without much explanation.
- They are accessible for our analysis since the two universities are affiliated by an exchange agreement.
- They are in an age cohort that has been going to school in the time before the removal of the Iron Curtain, so that their mental maps should be influenced by the Cold War regime.

Business students are also an interesting group as far as the potential impact of different geographical perceptions is concerned. When after finishing their degree they move into management positions in their respective economy, their management decisions may be influenced by their geographical perceptions and therefore echo the divided Europe of the post-war period.

The investigation was conducted in mid-May 1995 at both universities. In each location we interviewed 120 students. The questionnaire consisted of three parts: Part A that asked general questions about the person, Part B that tried to identify the student's geographical perception, and Part C about special circumstances in an East–West context. Part B is of particular interest in our context. The results from the other parts provide additional information and are intended to be used for control and for checking the validity of the sample.

In Part A we asked typical socio-demographic questions. We asked for the respondent's age, gender, number of semesters at study, and how much money he/she has available per month. Moreover, we asked whether the respondent regularly reads a newspaper, what his/her preferred travel location is, and which east and west European languages the respondent knows. With these questions we wanted to cover some of the factors that may influence a person's geographical perception. One can hypothesise that a student who is more advanced, who regularly reads a newspaper, who knows more languages, or who prefers travelling to staying at home will have more accurate geographical perceptions.

In Part C we tried to identify people with close ties across the former Iron Curtain. We asked the Austrian students: 'How often have you visited Slovakia since 1989?', 'Do you have relatives in Eastern Europe?', and 'Do you have friends in Eastern Europe?'. The Slovak students were asked the same questions about Austria and Western Europe, respectively. Both groups of students were asked how often they had travelled to Eastern Europe and to Western Europe since 1989. In order to get a rough idea of the respondent's concept of 'Eastern' and 'Western Europe', we asked them which of a number of countries they think belong to either part of Europe.

The core of our questionnaire was Part B. In this part each respondent was asked to place six European cities on a 'map'; three from the former Eastern bloc, three from Western Europe. The 'map' was actually a blank sheet of A4-paper with minimal geographical information. We indicated only the four directions 'north', 'south', 'east', and 'west' with the corresponding letters on the sides of the paper and gave two points of reference: the location of the respective student's university town (Vienna and Bratislava) and either Rome or Warsaw. This provided enough information to fix the orientation and the scale of the map. We did not give any other information such as borders, rivers, shore lines, etc. Rome and Warsaw were chosen because they are relatively well known cities, about the same, medium distance from the area of investigation. In each city (Vienna, Bratislava) half the students were given Rome and half the students were given Warsaw as second point of reference (in addition to Vienna or Bratislava, respectively). As a basis we used a map with the relatively common scale of 1:20,000,000.

The cities the students were asked to place on the map were drawn from the pool of the following cities: Madrid, Paris, London, Oslo, Berlin, Zurich, Athens, Istanbul, Helsinki, Moscow, St Petersburg, Minsk, Kiev, Sofia, Belgrade, Krakow, Prague, and Budapest. Note that the first nine are from the former Western, the last nine from the former Eastern part of post-war Europe. Each student was asked to place three Eastern and three Western cities.

Since we planned to ask 240 students and used four base configurations (combinations of Vienna–Bratislava on the one hand, and Rome–Warsaw on the other), we generated 60 combinations of three Eastern and three Western cities each, and repeated them for the four base configurations. This gave 120 configurations for the students in Vienna and 120 configurations for the students in Bratislava. Since we always drew six cities from the pool of eighteen, each city could be found in eighty questionnaires.

There are a number of problems associated with Part B of our questionnaire. Unfortunately, most of them can hardly be avoided. Although we try to provide only the minimum of information necessary to solve the problem of placing the cities on the map, additional information may influence the results. This additional information is hard to control, thus:

- Since the students are given a sheet of paper in A4-format, they can assume that all the cities can be placed on such a piece of paper. So, when in their mental map one of the cities is further away than the sheet of paper allows, they will most likely correct their perception such that the respective city can be placed within the boundaries provided.
- Although two cities are enough to fix both scale and orientation of the map, we have added information about the orientation of the map. Because of the convention of orienting north at the top of a map, we implicitly provide additional information to the respondents as soon as we display letters for the two reference cities. In order to make this information explicit for all respondents, we added the windrose.
- The cities a respondent has already placed on the map provide additional orientation points for later cities. In this sense, the number of reference points increases during the process of answering the geographical problem. Therefore, the results may depend upon which cities a respondent has to allocate and in which sequence he/she allocates them. In order to keep this problem within reasonable bounds, we have given each respondent only six of the overall cities. Unfortunately, this reduces the number of observations for each individual city.

Empirical results

Before we turn to the results about the mental maps, let us look at some of the characteristics of the respondents. Table 10.1 summarises the socio-economic characteristics of the two samples. As we can see, the students we interviewed in Vienna are on average older and more advanced in their studies than those

Table 10.1 Basic socioeconomic characteristics

	Bratislava	*Vienna*
age	20.9	23.4
percentage female	50.4	37.3
semesters	5.5	7.6
newspaper	68%	77%

in Bratislava. The percentage of women is higher in the Slovak sample. The percentage of those who regularly read a newspaper is slightly lower in Bratislava than in Vienna.

The question about the disposable income of the students' gives remarkable differences. On average a student in Vienna has about 4,818 Austrian Schilling per month available while a student in Bratislava must live on 1,292 Slovak Crowns. This converts to about AS 430. The income distributions are shown in Figure 10.1. More than 98 per cent of the students in Slovakia must get along with less than AS 2,000 per month. In Vienna this is the case only for 25 per cent of the students.

According to the students' travel behaviour the interaction between the two cities is highly unbalanced. A student in Bratislava travelled on average more than sixteen times to Austria since 1989 while an Austrian student visited the neighbouring country on average only once. As can be seen from Table 10.2, both groups show a preference for trips to West European countries. This tendency is more pronounced in the Viennese sample.

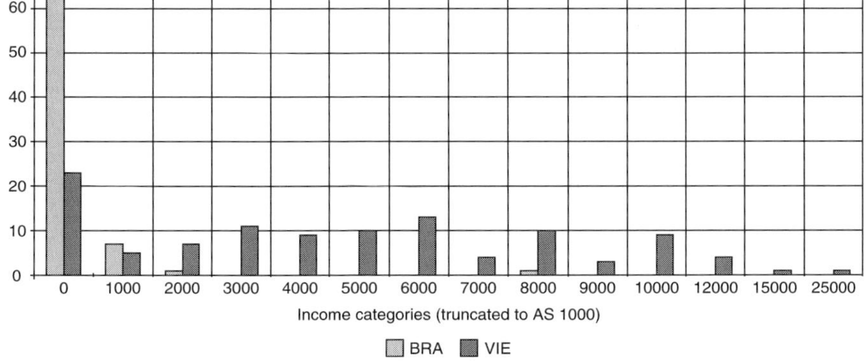

Figure 10.1 Income distribution.

Table 10.2 Average number of trips

	Bratislava	*Vienna*
to Eastern Europe	7.3	5.8
to Western Europe	13.0	14.4

Table 10.3 Knowledge of languages

	Bratislava	*Vienna*
Eastern languages	1.36	0.26
Western languages	1.84	2.12

Table 10.4 Friends and relatives across the former Iron Curtain

	Bratislava	*Vienna*
Respondents with friends	72.3%	40.7%
Respondents with relatives	28.6%	16.1%

Similarly skewed is the language knowledge of the students. Table 10.3 shows the detailed results. While a student in Vienna knows only 0.26 East European languages, the colleagues in Bratislava have command of 1.84 West European languages. Much of the knowledge of eastern languages of Viennese students can be attributed to family ties. Viennese students with relatives in Eastern Europe on average know 0.89 eastern languages while the respective figure for students without relatives is only 0.14. For the students from Bratislava the effect of family ties is only marginal. The average number of western languages rises from 1.835 (without relatives in Western Europe) to 1.853 (with relatives in Western Europe).

Overall considered it seems that students in Vienna are much less interested in Eastern Europe than the Slovak students are in Western Europe. As can be seen from Table 10.4, this shows up also in the number of friends and – surprisingly enough – the number of relatives on the other side of the former Iron Curtain that the students report. The relationship is significant for relatives and highly significant for friends.

In Part B of the questionnaire the respondents provided information about the spatial location of the above mentioned European cities according to their spatial perception. Before we analyse the results in some more detail, let us look at the average mental map of the respondents and compare it with the actual location of the cities. Figure 10.2 shows the actual location of the eighteen cities on the map of Europe and the average location they were given by the respondents. The correct location is marked by a small black arrow, the average location according to our questionnaire by a cross. Figure 10.3 gives the same information, but distinguishes between the respondents in Vienna (arrow) and Bratislava (cross).

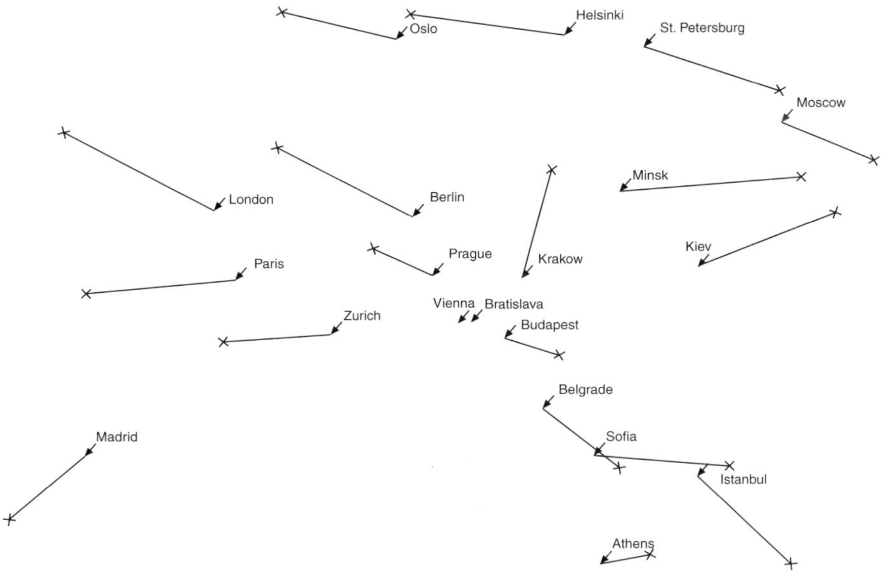

Figure 10.2 Actual and average perceived location of European cities: all respondents.

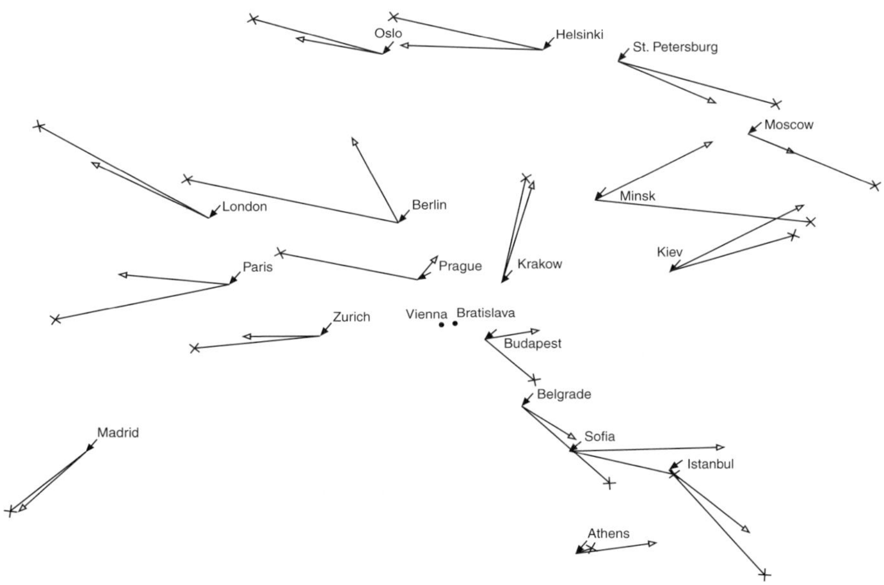

Figure 10.3 Actual and average perceived location of European cities: respondents distinguished by Vienna and Bratislava.

The two figures show some remarkable features. In general the respondents (in both samples) tend to locate the cities further away from the Vienna–Bratislava region than they actually are. London, for example, moves toward the North-West, Istanbul toward the South-East. Similarly, Madrid is moved toward the South-West. As far as the separation between Eastern and Western Europe is concerned, a line can be drawn in both maps that runs between Helsinki and St Petersburg, to Vienna–Bratislava and to Rome. Cities west of this line are in general positioned further to the West than they actually are, cities east of this line further to the east. There is only one exception to this general trend, namely the location given to Prague by the Austrian students. They place it to the east of its actual location. This is perfectly in line with the concept of mental maps when one takes into account that Austrian students associate Prague with former Eastern bloc Czechoslovakia, a country that in their perception is probably 'east' of their own. By contrast, the students in Bratislava probably associate Prague mainly with the Czech Republic, the part of their former common state that has decided to orient itself toward the west. Consequently, students in Bratislava place Prague much further to the West than it actually is.

Clustering of related observations can be found in some parts of the map. In both subsamples the former Soviet Union cities Moscow, Minsk, Kiev, and St Petersburg are located in closer proximity to one another and further away from their neighbouring cities in the sample. A similar result in weaker form holds for the two Scandinavian cities Oslo and Helsinki.

In Northern and Central Europe the above mentioned dividing line follows nicely the former Iron Curtain. In this part, former East European cities drift off to the east, former West European cities shift toward the west. In the minds of the students Helsinki and St Petersburg, which are actually only about 300 kilometers apart, on average appear to be further separated than the reference cities Vienna and Bratislava, on the one hand, and Rome and Warsaw, on the other. In Southern Europe the division is not so clear, partly because in this part of the continent the political and economic divisions do not coincide. Athens and Istanbul belong to the economically weak east Mediterranean region, but are both in NATO countries and Athens is the capital of an EU-member country.

As can be seen in Figure 10.3, the results derived from the interviews in Vienna and in Bratislava tend to be quite similar. Does this contradict our main hypothesis that there are different geographical perceptions between the students on both sides of the former Iron Curtain? We need to analyse the results in more detail in order to answer this question.

The information in Part B of our questionnaire can generate different indicators to answer this question. The vectors in Figures 10.2 (for all respondents) and 10.3 (for Vienna and Bratislava separately) show the difference between the actual location of the cities and the location given by the respondents on average. This vector can be derived as the sum of all the respective vectors of the individual respondents (standardised by the number of respondents). The co-ordinates of these vectors can be derived as the means of the respective co-ordinates of the answers given by the respondents.

These vectors generate two indicators for the deviation of the respondents' geographical perceptions from reality, namely a mean deviation in East–West direction and a mean deviation in North–South direction.[2] A larger absolute figure shows that on average the geographical perceptions are more biased. The sign of the indicator tells us whether this bias is toward the west or south (negative sign) or toward the east or north (positive sign).

The geographical perceptions of the respondents may not only be biased in different ways but may also differ in precision. A certain level of bias in the average geographical perception may result from very different individual perceptions. It may be the result of similar levels of bias in the perceptions of all respondents, or of general uncertainty about the actual location of the respective city. This difference can be captured statistically by the standard deviation of the co-ordinates given by the respondents. More homogeneous perceptions about the location of a certain city – whether biased or not – will yield a lower standard deviation. More uncertainty about its actual location will generate a larger standard deviation. Again, we get figures for East–West direction and for North–South direction. Under the assumption of the co-ordinates given by the respondents being normally distributed random variables, we can derive a statistical test for the difference in the means by use of the means and standard deviations. This test will tell us whether the observed differences between the responses in Vienna and in Bratislava are likely to be random or not.

One of the problems with the above mentioned indicators is that they generate different answers for a specific city. For one and the same city the bias in East–West direction may be larger for the respondents from Vienna, but the standard deviation in the same direction may be larger for the Slovak respondents. In the other direction, the relationship could be just reverse. Moreover, the mean value measures only the bias where the deviations of two respondents in opposite direction will cancel out. These deviations will lead to a higher standard deviation, but this indicator takes into account only the differences among the individual perceptions, but not their relationship to the actual location of the city.

An indicator that combines elements of, on the one hand, bias and precision, and, on the other hand, both directions is the average length of the vectors for each individual between actual location and perceived location. It gives a measure of the accuracy of the geographical perception of a group of respondents with respect to a certain city. It is important to keep in mind that this measure combines elements of all the previously mentioned four indications.

Table 10.5 shows the results for the average deviation in East–West direction and the respective standard deviation for the eighteen cities of our analysis separately for the respondents from Vienna and Bratislava. Since our basic hypothesis is based upon the split between Eastern and Western

Table 10.5 Deviations in East–West direction (in kilometres)

	BRATISLAVA			*VIENNA*			*comparison*		
	N	*Mean*	*StdDev.*	*N*	*Mean*	*StdDev.*	*DF*	*t–Value*	
Moscow	39	620	377	38	231	602	75	3.41	**
Kiev	32	597	519	33	653	572	63	–0.41	
St Petersburg	37	757	868	36	473	557	71	1.66	
Minsk	38	1036	496	31	569	921	67	2.69	**
Budapest	41	238	312	39	268	298	78	–0.44	
Prague	38	–650	331	39	110	386	75	–9.27	**
Sofia	39	502	564	37	744	546	74	–1.90	*
Krakow	39	123	436	32	159	325	69	–0.39	
Belgrade	38	420	801	36	265	500	72	1.00	
Oslo	39	–616	753	39	–419	638	76	–1.25	
London	37	–813	634	40	–566	452	75	–1.98	*
Paris	39	–823	431	39	–529	385	76	–3.18	**
Berlin	39	–1008	423	39	–220	446	76	–8.00	**
Madrid	38	–359	432	38	–324	308	74	–0.40	
Helsinki	40	–738	911	39	–708	792	77	–0.15	
Istanbul	39	468	869	39	394	628	76	0.43	
Zurich	38	–598	466	36	–374	298	72	–2.45	**
Athens	37	77	803	37	388	405	72	–2.10	*

Notes: * = t-statistic is significant at the 5 per cent level.
** = t-statistic is significant at the 1 per cent level.

Europe, the deviations in East–West direction are more interesting to us than those in North–South direction. The first column of Table 10.5 gives the name of the city, columns 2, 3, and 4 give the number of respondents, the mean deviation in East–West-direction and its standard deviation for the questionnaires collected in Vienna. Columns 5, 6, and 7 give the respective indicators for Bratislava. Column 8 and 9 refer to the statistical comparison between the two samples. Column 9 gives the t-statistic of the comparison of the two means, column 8 the respective degrees of freedom. One asterisk indicates that the t-statistic is significant at the 5 per cent level, two asterisks indicate significance at the 1 per cent level. In the following discussion we will call the first category 'significant' and the second one 'highly significant'.

As can be seen from Table 10.5, there is a clear distinction between the cities in Eastern and in Western Europe. While the students from Bratislava on average locate four of the nine cities in Eastern Europe better than the students from Vienna, they perform worse than their Viennese colleagues on locating eight of the nine cities from Western Europe. Only as far as Athens is concerned, do the respondents from Bratislava on average show a better result than their counterparts in Vienna. However, they are considerably more uncertain about the location of Athens. The standard deviation for the East–West position of Athens is almost twice as high in the Slovak than in the Austrian sample.

Less precision in placing the Western cities is a general result of the Slovak part of the sample. For eight of the nine Western cities the standard deviation is higher in the sample from Bratislava. For the Eastern European cities the ratio is again much more even. In four of the nine cases the students from Vienna show a higher standard deviation than their Slovak colleagues. It seems that the students from Vienna do better (both in terms of bias and in terms of precision) than those from Bratislava when allocating cities in Western Europe. This supports the first part of our hypothesis, that the students in Western Europe have a more accurate perception of the location of Western European cities. As far as the second part of our hypothesis is concerned (East European students have a more accurate perception of Eastern European cities), it is not really supported by these results.

When we take into consideration the statistical significance of the differences in the means, it even turns out that the East Europeans also perform worse with respect to the cities in the east. For six of the eighteen cities the observed differences in the means are highly significant. Three of them are from Eastern Europe (Moscow, Minsk, Prague), three from the west (Paris, Berlin, Zurich). In all these cases the students from Vienna perform better than their Slovak counterparts. So, at this level of significance we can say that the geographical perception of students in Bratislava is less accurate than that of students in Vienna, irrespective of whether the city is located in Eastern or Western Europe. Only when we reduce our level of aspiration and allow for an error probability of 5 per cent, do we find cities where the students from Bratislava perform significantly better than those from Vienna. This is the case for Sofia and for Athens. London is placed significantly more accurately by the students from Vienna at this level of significance.

The results for deviations in North–South direction are displayed in Table 10.6. Because of the basic hypothesis of our analysis, this set of results is less important than the deviations in East–West direction that we have discussed above. The results in Table 10.6 are less pronounced than those in Table 10.5 concerning the East–West direction. There are again more cities that are positioned less accurately by the Slovak students than by those from Vienna. However, we do not see a clear distinction between Eastern and Western Europe. Two of the East European and three of the West European cities are allocated less accurately by the students from Vienna. When we take into account statistical significance, the results are again mixed. For four cities the differences are highly significant, three from Eastern Europe (Minsk, Budapest, Belgrade), and one from the west (Berlin). Minsk and Berlin are positioned more accurately as far as North–South direction is concerned by the students from Bratislava. For the other two cities the Viennese students perform better. When we accept an error probability of 5 per cent, we find that for six additional cities the difference between the samples becomes significant. Only one of them is an East European city (Moscow), the other five (Oslo, London, Paris, Helsinki, Istanbul) are all from the western part of the continent. For all six cities the students from Vienna perform better than

Table 10.6 Deviations in North–South direction (in kilometres)

	BRATISLAVA			*VIENNA*			*comparison*		
	N	*Mean*	*StdDev.*	*N*	*Mean*	*StdDev*	*DF*	*t–Value*	
Moscow	39	–255	348	38	–91	352	75	–2.06	*
Kiev	32	181	434	33	328	423	63	–1.39	
St Petersburg	37	–207	539	36	–201	423	71	–0.06	
Minsk	38	–108	469	31	286	511	67	–3.34	**
Budapest	41	–195	144	39	49	149	78	–7.42	**
Prague	38	132	136	39	120	241	75	0.28	
Sofia	39	–112	333	37	20	445	74	–1.47	
Krakow	39	506	372	32	503	261	69	0.04	
Belgrade	38	–375	365	36	–163	345	72	–2.56	**
Oslo	39	177	201	39	85	195	76	2.05	*
London	37	451	413	40	279	348	75	1.98	*
Paris	39	–171	583	39	47	343	76	–2.01	*
Berlin	39	217	368	39	427	354	76	–2.57	**
Madrid	38	–283	447	38	–291	514	74	0.07	
Helsinki	40	144	260	39	9	264	77	2.29	*
Istanbul	39	–509	366	39	–304	461	76	–2.17	*
Zurich	38	–59	462	36	–3	151	72	–0.69	
Athens	37	31	306	37	58	370	72	–0.34	

Notes: *See Table 10.5.

those from Bratislava. So, at a level of significance of 5 per cent we find that for ten of the eighteen cities (four from Eastern Europe and six from Western Europe) the answers differ significantly between the two samples. In eight of these cases the students from Bratislava gave significantly less accurate responses than those from Vienna.

As we have argued above, the average distance between the actual and the perceived location of a certain city provides an indicator that combines both directions that we have discussed above and measures bias as well as precision of the perception. Table 10.7 gives the results for all the eighteen cities.

Table 10.7 provides strong support for the first part of our hypothesis. For all the Western European cities the average distance calculated for the respondents in Bratislava is higher than that calculated for the Viennese students. According to this more general indicator, the students from Vienna can allocate all the cities from their part of the former divided Europe more accurately than their colleagues from Bratislava. Parallel to the analysis of the average deviation in East–West direction above, the results in Table 10.7 provide no support for the second part of our hypothesis. Slovak respondents position only two of the nine Eastern European cities (Kiev and Sofia) more accurately than their colleagues from the west. Obviously, their geographical perception of the former communist area is no better than that of those students who were separated from this area by the Iron Curtain.

The questions in the other parts of the questionnaire were intended to

Table 10.7 Distance between actual and perceived location (in kilometers)

	BRATISLAVA		*VIENNA*	
	N	*Mean*	*N*	*Mean*
Moscow	39	785	38	609
Kiev	32	772	33	912
St. Petersburg	37	1116	36	742
Minsk	38	1136	31	1063
Budapest	41	362	39	329
Prague	38	674	39	369
Sofia	39	688	37	906
Krakow	39	646	32	618
Belgrade	38	884	36	516
Oslo	39	855	39	654
London	37	1122	40	761
Paris	39	1026	39	651
Berlin	39	1086	39	647
Madrid	38	686	38	644
Helsinki	40	981	39	876
Istanbul	39	1040	39	767
Zurich	38	774	36	421
Athens	37	704	37	603

explain some of the differences in geographical perception. Unfortunately, the number of observations we have for each individual city is too low to derive statistically significant results. Therefore, we do not report any of these results here. The overall results to these questions without reference to mental maps were reported at the beginning of this section.

Conclusion

This chapter started from the hypothesis that because of the long division of Europe people on both sides of the former Iron Curtain should have different mental maps of the continent. It was the main purpose of this chapter to identify those differences in the geographical perceptions. Since their mental maps may guide and structure people's spatial decisions, the perceptions that have formed in the minds of decision-makers during the years of the Cold War may have a long-lasting impact on the behaviour of people.

We used two samples of Business students from Vienna and Bratislava for our empirical investigation. The main results from this analysis are the following:

- There is a clear difference in the perception of Western Europe between the students in Vienna and in Bratislava. On average, students from Vienna place west European cities more accurately on the map than students from Bratislava. The reverse hypothesis, however, is not supported.

Students from Bratislava perform as badly as their Viennese colleagues when placing east European cities. It seems that geographical knowledge is generally lower in Bratislava, probably because of the tight control and restricted travel opportunities of the communist system.

- Students in Bratislava are more actively exploring the West than the Austrian students are exploring the East. They have made more trips to the West than their Austrian counterparts have made to the East. Also, they know more languages from the other part of the formerly divided continent, and have more friends and relatives on the other side. Through these contacts the students from Bratislava will probably improve their geographical knowledge and update their mental maps of Western Europe more quickly than the Austrian students will revise their perception of the East.

Although we could show deficits of the Slovak students in their mental maps of Western Europe, it seems unlikely that these deficits will have a long-term impact on their spatial behaviour. By the time they enter their professional careers they may have overcome most of these deficits because of their interest in and their intensive contacts with the West. The Austrian students, on the other hand, show little interest in the eastern part of the continent. Although the deficits in their mental maps of the East are not more severe than those of the Slovaks, they may turn out to be more persistent and more damaging in the long run.

Notes

1 Paper presented at the international conference 'Integration and Transition in Europe: The Economic Geography of Interaction', Budapest, 11–14 September 1997.

2 Alternatively we could treat the points as bivariate variable and analyse both coordinates jointly. We did not pursue this alternative.

References

Brown, S.M. (1992) 'Cognitive mapping and repertory grids for qualitative survey research: some comparative observations', *Journal of Management* 29: 287–307.

Downs, R.M. and Stea, D. (1977) *Maps in Mind: Reflections on Cognitive Mapping*, New York: Harper & Row.

Downs, R.M. and Stea, D. (eds) (1993) *Image and Environment, Cognitive Mapping and Spatial Behavior*, Chicago: Aldine Publishing Company.

Eden, C. (1992) 'On the nature of cognitive maps', *Journal of Management Studies*, 29: 261–5.

Freundschuh, S.M. (1991) 'The effect of the pattern of the environment on spatial knowledge acquisition', in D.M. Mark and A.U. Frank (eds) *Cognitive and Linguistic Aspects of Geographic Space*, NATO Advanced Science Institute Series D, Dordrecht: Kluwer Academic Publishers, 63: 167–3.

Gould, P. and White, R. (1986) *Mental Maps*, Boston: Allen & Unwin.

Hirtle, S.C. and Heidorn, B.P. (1993) 'The structure of cognitive maps: representations and processes', in T. Gärling and R.G. Golledge (eds), *Behavior and Environment: Psychological and Geographical Approaches*, Amsterdam: North Holland

Hirtle, S.C., McNamara, T.P. and Hardy, J.K. (1989) 'Subjective hierarchies in spatial memory', *Journal of Experimental Psychology, Memory, and Cognition* 15: 211–227.

Lee, T.R. (1973) 'Psychology and living space', in R.M. Downs and D. Stea (eds), *Image and Environment, Cognitive Mapping and Spatial Behavior,* Chicago: Aldine Publishing Company, pp. 87–107.

Longuet-Higgins, C.H. (1987) *Mental Processes: Studies in Cognitive Science*, Cambridge, MA: MIT Press.

Maier, G. (1995) *Spatial Search: Structure, Complexity, and Implications*, Heidelberg: Physica.

Rosenmayr, T. (1996) 'Der Eiserne Vorhang im Kopf: Unterschiede in den mentalen Karten von Wirtschaftsstudenten, in Wien und Bratislava', master thesis, Vienna: Institute for Urban and Regional Studies, Vienna University of Economics and Business Administration.

Tolman, E.C. (1948) 'Cognitive maps in rats and man', *Psychological Review* 55: 189–208.

Tversky, B. (1993) 'Cognitive maps, cognitive collages, and spatial mental models', in A.U. Frank, I. Campari and U. Formentini (eds) *Theories and Methods of Spatio-Temporal Reasoning in Geographic Space*, Pisa: Lecture Notes in Computer Science.

11 Scope and structure of Austria's foreign direct investment in Eastern Europe

Wilfried Altzinger

> Current discussion on employment effect of outward FDI from developed countries is flawed because it tends to generalise from a few visible cases of job relocation in a country to its entire FDI abroad.
>
> (Agarwal 1996)

Introduction

Since the opening of the CEECs in 1989 Austria's trade and investment relations have intensified quite rapidly. Economic co-operation has multiplied in particular with Austria's neighbouring countries Hungary, the Czech Republic, Slovenia and Slovakia. Austria has not only achieved a high surplus in its balance of trade with these countries throughout the period 1990–7, but it has also improved its overall employment through this surplus by a significant number (Altzinger 1997; Palme 1998). Moreover, Austria has shown considerable FDI activities in the CEECs. Even in other West–East European border regions such developments appeared in a very similar manner. All of these studies report huge trade surpluses and a tremendous increase in FDI by the West European countries.

Much of these developments can be explained by Austria's geographical proximity and its close historical and cultural ties to the CEECs. These features have provided Austrian companies with a substantial 'first-mover advantage' (FMA) in entering these new markets during the early 1990s. However, decreasing market share in trade and in FDI stocks indicate that FMAs have receded (Stankovsky 1996). Nevertheless, it must be noted that this development has been caused to a considerable extent by large privatisation programmes in the CEECs where Austrian companies could not participate sufficiently due to their weak financial capabilities.

To assess the impact of FDI on the domestic economy is a rather difficult task. The net result depends very much on the type of investment. As we will see, the patterns of Austria's FDI in the CEECs are rather diverse. Motives and strategies of Austrian enterprises are prompted by distinct principles for different industries. Therefore the impact on the domestic economy is rather different.

An evaluation of growth and employment effects can hardly provide accurate quantitative data (Baldwin 1994; Barrell and Pain 1997; Blomström *et al.* 1997; Cantwell 1994). The most difficult problems in calculating such effects are insufficient knowledge about the alternative scenario and the period of observation. In his survey Baldwin (1994) summarises these problems:

> Broad generalisations are difficult because of the very different employment effects one obtains from various plausible alternative assumptions about what will happen in the absence of foreign direct investment and what the magnitude of increased imports by the host country from the investing country will be.

The period of observation is important because relocation involves a sequence of events: between the closure of a local production unit and reimporting of the affiliates, there is a whole process of establishing production abroad. Moreover, in order to be able to assert with a reasonable amount of assurance that a distinctive number of jobs had been lost due to some relocation, one would have to be able to prove that these job losses would not have occurred had there been no FDI operation. On the other hand, it can also be argued that relocation can help to create jobs through the mere survival of the firm (Madeuf 1995).

There are a broad variety of factors that are important for the impact of FDI on domestic economy. Among others these are industrial mixes, investment motives, strategic and competitive considerations within FDIs are undertaken and finally it is the impact on FDI-induced trade (Agarwal 1996). To assess the impact of Austria's FDI on domestic economy we chose the following approach. First, we investigated the regional and sectoral pattern of Austria's FDI. Such an analysis provides an initial understanding of the different kinds of Austria's FDI. Furthermore, we can see which regions and industries expose the largest shares of overall FDI. Hence we will focus the subsequent analysis only on those regions and sectors.

Second, we analysed the motives of Austria's FDI. Broadly speaking we can distinguish two very different types of FDI: supply-based and market-driven FDI. The aim of the first type is to acquire some particular resources at a lower cost than at home. It is broadly assumed that for the CEECs these resources consist primarily of cheap labour.[1] This type of investment is also efficiency seeking. Such investment is mostly associated with 'relocation', reduced employment at home and increasing (re)imports from the host country. Hence domestic economy suffers (see Madeuf 1995). The second type of investment depends on the expectation of new sales opportunities. Market-based investment is often influenced by strategic considerations too. Such investment usually creates additional exports of inputs such as machinery and intermediate goods to the related foreign affiliates and of final goods which were not so far exported to the related host country but can be exported after FDI due to closer consumer relations. It is very likely that such investment will even improve the competitiveness of the parent company. As FDI motives are market-related, domestic and foreign employment can be assumed to be highly complementary.

Third, following the above considerations we would expect that supply-based FDI would show considerably larger export shares than market-driven FDI. Furthermore, we can assume that market-driven affiliates stimulate exports from the home country by the parent company while imports from the affiliates should be only of minor importance. Hence intra-firm trade should show a surplus of the parent company for market-driven FDI. On the other hand, supply-based affiliates will deliver parts and components, semi-finished or finished goods to their parent company. Although the parent company will even provide investment goods to its affiliates, intra-firm trade balances can be expected to be negative.

As we will see later, most of the empirical studies only deal with one of these two closely interrelated issues. They either investigate motives of investment or analyse trade patterns. Due to our particular data set we can analyse motives and trade patterns by different industries simultaneously. The empirical part of the chapter makes use of two data sets. The division of 'International Balance of Payments' at the Austrian National Bank provided one. This dataset presents the results of a survey that is conducted annually by roughly 4,000 Austrian enterprises that hold at least ATS 1 million of nominal capital. A second data set presents results of a questionnaire that was conducted by 1,700 Austrian enterprises in the summer of 1997.

Following the plausibility considerations above, the chapter is organised as follows: the next section provides a review of theoretical as well as empirical literature. Then we examine regional and structural patterns of Austria's FDI in the CEECs and investigate the motives of FDI. The next section proves if the postulated motives can be verified by trade patterns of the affiliates. The final section summarises and draws conclusions.

Review of the literature

Theoretical considerations

According to Dunning (1993) we can distinguish four different motives of investment: natural resources, (emerging) markets, efficiency-enhancing motives and strategic assets. The aim of the first motive is to acquire some particular resources at a lower cost than at home. These resources mainly consist of primary products. The second motive depends on the expectation of new sales opportunities from the opening of markets, to which Western companies previously had no access. The third motive, efficiency-enhancing, tries to utilise the specific comparative advantages of an economy. Hence efficiency-seeking FDI in the CEECs should mainly take place in labour- and natural resource-intensive sectors. The fourth type of investment is led by long-term strategic considerations. The final purpose of such investment is to gain an important stake in the market in the long run. Since it is not easy to separate efficiency-enhancing and strategic motives from the other two kinds of investment the empirical evidence often separates only supply-based and market-driven motives (e.g. Kurz and Wittke 1997).

Agarwal (1996) provides an explanation of what *impacts on trade* these different motives of investment have. For that purpose he distinguishes three different impacts: the substitution of former exports through FDI, growing re-imports of goods and services produced abroad by foreign affiliates of domestic firms and FDI-associated exports of goods and services. The last kind of exports can be explained by FDI which stimulates – in particular at an initial stage – exports of capital goods, spare parts, raw materials, etc. to the related affiliates. In addition, FDI may stimulate exports of other product lines neither produced by the foreign affiliate nor exported earlier by the parent firm. This is because the new unit is usually able to offer a closer market relationship to foreign customers. The overall impact of FDI on trade (and therefore on domestic employment) is the sum of negative (export substitution, re-imports) and positive effects (associated exports) and can be testified only empirically. Agarwal provides a great deal of empirical evidence and a broad array of analytical arguments. He concludes that FDI in natural resources, market-oriented manufacturing industries as well as services is likely to have a positive impact on domestic economy. Only efficiency-oriented FDI of industries and services may have negative impacts on the home economy. Because the latter generally accounts for a minor portion of total FDI the net impact on domestic economy is likely to be positive.

Empirical observations

The OECD (1994) and the EBRD (1994) carried out the very first studies on motives of investment in CEECs. Both studies challenged the 'low wage-assumption' considerably. The general conclusion of the EBRD study was straightforward:

> Most striking perhaps is the *predominance of market access* among factors of importance to investor decisions . . . Factor cost advantages are clearly rated as less important than market access in all the surveys . . . Most studies explicitly play down the role of cheap labour.
>
> (EBRD 1994: 132).

The results of the OECD study (1994, Table 4) are very similar. The key motive for FDI was to gain market access (44 per cent) and labour costs were of secondary importance only (9 per cent).

Several other studies have focused on motives of investment on a regional level (Altzinger *et al.* 1998b for the Austrian-Slovakian region; Borsos 1995 for the Finnish-Baltic region; Petrakos 1996 for the Greek-Bulgarian-Albanian region; Vincentz 1995 for the German-Polish-Czech region). All these studies report the predominance of market-driven FDI. The conclusion of the Petrakos report e.g. is as follows: 'For Greece ... capital outflows are associated in most cases with an expansion (and not dislocation) of activities to new markets that are easier to get into than the hard to compete and congested Western European ones' (Petrakos 1996: 95). Borsos' (1995) conclusion for Finland is quite similar. The main reasons for Finnish FDIs in the Eastern Baltic Rim are market-related. Factors such as low cost production, cheap resources or investment incentives fall much further down the list of priorities. By application of Dunning's theory on international production a more recent study on FDI in Poland discards the suggestion that low cost labour production is the predominant determinant of FDI (Floyd 1996). Meyer (1995) tested several hypotheses on questionnaire evidence of British and German companies. His conclusion is that labour costs differentials did not induce major investment flows. In a very recent survey on the motivations of foreign firms in CEECs, Nachum (1998) strengthens the view of the predominance of market seeking investment.

However, the above-mentioned OECD-study shows that the motives of Austria's FDI in the CEECs are a little bit different. Austrian enterprises rated market access with 35 per cent and low cost production with 6 per cent. In particular the motive 'geographical location' was rated far above the average by Austrian investors. On average this factor was rated as prime reason by 6 per cent of all conducted enterprises only. In contrast, Austrian enterprises rated this factor with 21 per cent as an important reason for investment! Gravity models also highlight the importance of geographical factors on investment (e.g. Brenton *et al.* 1998).

This geographical factor seems to be closely related to the size of the investing enterprises. Both Vincentz (1995: 112) and Kurz and Wittke (1997: 20) argue that 'low wage' options are more important for small and medium-sized enterprises (SMEs) than for large multinational enterprises (MNEs). Hence in particular these enterprises have tried to make use of the new business opportunities in the CEECs. According to Kurz and Wittke (1997) this is mainly the case if spatial proximity is of relevance. Spatial proximity reduces not only the time, risk and cost of transportation routes, but it enables Western companies to minimise the risks of managing cross-national production networks without transferring managerial or engineering staff permanently to the East. These aspects are of particular importance for companies with less experience of internationalisation. This is rather often the case for SMEs. For two adjacent EU countries to the CEECs, Finland and Germany, there is empirical evidence that SMEs are engaged in FDI activities to a considerably larger extent than before 1989 (for Finland see Borsos 1995, for Germany see Vincentz 1995). Even Meyer (1995) has tested the proximity patterns of Western FDI in Eastern Europe on survey evidence and found significant effects in favour of this factor. He also emphasises Austria's special role due to its geographic position and existing trade relations during the Cold War years.

Although Vincentz (1995) reports the dominance of market-seeking investment, he mentions that for more recent investments and in particular for prospective investments low labour-cost motives become more important. This observation is in accordance with the conjecture of a survey that was conducted by Lankes and Venables (1997) in January 1995. One of the main presumptions of this study is that the share of cost-motivated, export-oriented investments into the transition countries will increase over time, while market-oriented and natural resource investment will recede. Their argument is that for market-oriented investment the FMA was important and for natural resource investment it was in particular the opportunity to acquire strategic assets at a low cost. Hence both kinds of investment have been realised even if the country-risk perceptions among investors have been high. If the transition process proceeds and risk recedes, more investors will move in for whom cost competitiveness is a particular concern. Today there is growing evidence that at least in some industries investor motivations are no longer based exclusively on market access (e. g. Lorentzen *et al.* 1998).

Another recent study presents the results from a survey of major Western investors in Central Europe (Pye 1997). In particular, the section on export activities of the affiliates[2] provides stimulating results. On average, 41 per cent of all affiliates indicated that they were not involved in any export activity and another 22 per cent showed export activities only between 1– 10 per cent! Hence the majority of affiliates show astonishingly low export activities. Most export activities were directed at serving the markets of the CEECs and/or the FSU (Pye 1997: 52). However, we have to keep in mind that these survey data comprise *all* industries. Only 57 per cent of the enterprises belong to manufacturing, 12 per cent to wholesale and retail trade and another 10 per cent to finance and insurance. Hence this sample represents a fairly diverse section of economic fields of activities. In particular in this respect, Pye's study differs quite a lot from most other studies. Nearly all of these studies on export activities of the affiliates conclude that they provide a positive contribution to exports (see Borsos 1995; Hunya 1997; Kurz and Wittke 1997; Lemoine 1997). However, all this research is restricted to the manufacturing sector only! Due to the superior technology of foreign-owned enterprises and their inclination towards international production and distribution networks such a result can be expected.

The evidence on intra-firm trade of MNEs with FDI activities in the CEECs is rather sparse. Lemoine (1997) shows that in Hungary and Poland the overall contribution of affiliates to foreign trade balance is negative. On an aggregated level Agarwal (1996, Table 1) shows furthermore that the balance of intra-firm trade is in favour of home economies in the USA as well as Japan. For both countries increased outward FDI is accompanied by higher re-imports. But re-imports are outstripped by exports to foreign affiliates. This is the case in the earlier stages of development of the affiliates. Particularly during such a 'building-up' period the affiliates are heavily dependent on the supply of components from parent companies. However,

Dunning (1993) argues that the complementarity between FDI and exports of a parent firm diminishes with the level of FDI development. Their argument is that during an initial stage FDI is concentrated on the marketing and assembling of the parent products. As soon as the affiliates start their own production, their imports from the parent firm decline. Thus the initial intra-firm trade surplus of the parent firm declines. Similar to the results of Lankes and Venables (1997) they conclude that the stage of FDI is of considerable importance for the link between FDI and exports.

Empirical evidence for Austria

A number of empirical studies for Austria present the motives of FDI in the CEECs (Neudorfer 1997; Neudorfer and Bach 1995; Stankovsky 1995). All these studies confirm that the predominant motive of Austria's FDI in the CEECs is 'market access and to secure sales'. The dominance of 'market potential' is also the general result of a survey carried out by the Austrian National Bank (1998). In its most recent publication the predominance of market access motivation is recorded quite clearly. Weighted by capital for 80.6 per cent of all investing enterprises market access is the main motivation for their activities in Hungary, for 74.9 per cent in the Czech Republic and for 76.5 per cent in Slovenia. The percentages of enterprises which listed (low) labour costs as the main motive for their investment are 5.9 per cent for Hungary, 3.5 per cent for the Czech Republic and 16.9 per cent for Slovenia.

Concerning the trade patterns of Austria's affiliates in the CEECs there is only limited empirical evidence. The overall trade data show a staggering growth of Austria's trade surplus with the CEECs (Altzinger 1997; Neudorfer 1997). The intra-firm trade data display that Austria's parent firms have achieved a considerable surplus throughout the period 1990–6.

To summarise the empirical evidence above, we can conclude that there are numerous studies which investigate either investment motives or trade patterns. However, we cannot find many reports which deal with both of these issues simultaneously. Moreover, although it is well known that FDI–trade linkages among industries are rather diverse, we can rarely find analyses at a sectoral level. The subsequent sections provide such an analysis along the lines proposed by Agarwal (1996).

Sectoral pattern of Austria's FDI in CEECS

The GDP share of outward FDI-stock can measure the degree of countries' transnationalisation. For 1996 this indicator shows that Austria's ratio (5.8 per cent) is far below the EU average (16.8 per cent) and even far below the ratios of other small OECD countries (UN 1998: 399).[3] However, Austria's outward FDI has improved rather quickly during the period 1989–96 (see Figure 11.1). For Austria this period of 'globalisation' was characterised by two new and substantial economic developments: the pre-EU-accession period[4] and the opening of Eastern European economies. Both of them have strengthened Austria's international economic activities considerably. However, the FDI–stock–GDP ratio in 1996 was still relatively low. One of the main reasons for this low degree of internationalisation is Austria's industry structure, especially the prevalence of SMEs. Most of this specific Austrian economic feature can be explained only by history (Bellak 1997).

In Figure 11.1 we can see that Austria's FDI in OECD countries[5] has increased from ATS 30.5 billion (95.6 per cent of total FDI) in 1989 to ATS 96.9 billion (71.1 per cent of total FDI) in 1996. As mentioned above, this was mainly the result of Austria's accession to the EU and will not be further discussed. Outward FDI to the CEECs started from a ATS 1.4 billion low (4.4 per cent of total FDI) in 1989 and increased to a ATS 39.5 billion high in 1996 (28.9 per cent of total FDI). This huge increase was accompanied by gaining big shares of the overall investment in the CEECs. Although Austria's financial capabilities are not very large by international standards, its FDI stock share has attained considerable shares in CEECs (23.6 per cent in Slovenia, 21.4 per cent in Slovakia and 19.6 per cent in Hungary). Measured by this share Austria is ranked first in Slovenia and Slovakia and only second (behind Germany) in Hungary (UN/ECE 1996).

As pointed out in the literature review (see above) FDI is strongly influenced by the geographical as well as the cultural and historical proximity to countries. All four CEECs that are shown in Figure 11.1 are adjacent to Austria. Furthermore, it is not surprising that neither Austria's trade nor investment relations with Poland – although a relatively well developed CEEC – are of significance.[6]

The small decrease in the share of outward FDI to the CEECs in 1995, which continued even into 1996 (see Hunya and Stankovsky 1997), can be explained by two reasons. First, due to Austria's entry to the EU its outward FDI to this region (mainly Germany) increased quite significantly in 1995

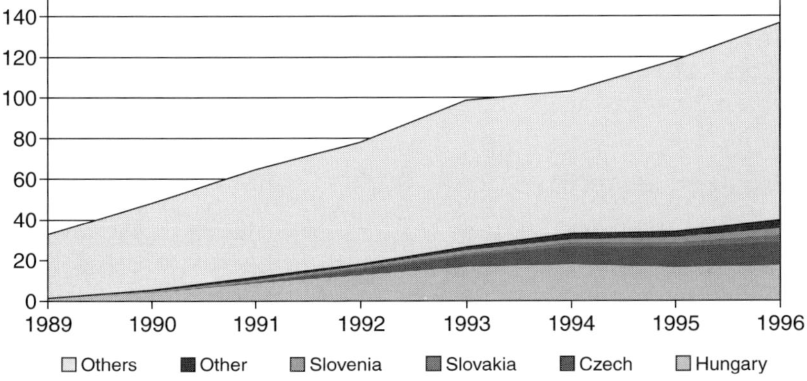

Figure 11.1 Austria's outward FDI by destination, 1989–96 (total capital).

Table 11.1 Structure and financial capabilities of Austrian affiliates in the CEECs, 1995

Firm size[a] *(number of employees)*	*Hungary*	*Czech Republic*	*Slovakia*	*Slovenia*	*other CEECs*	*Total CEECs*	*Others*	*Total*
Distribution of Austrian affiliates in the CEECs, 1995 (in %)								
1 to 19	45.7	32.1	37.1	19.0	32.7	39.2	36.9	38.0
20 to 49	6.3	5.9	4.8	4.8	7.3	6.1	7.2	6.7
50 to 99	8.7	9.6	4.8	19.0	6.4	8.8	5.4	7.0
100 to 499	22.3	27.8	25.8	28.6	31.8	25.3	22.9	24.1
500 to 999	5.2	5.9	3.2	9.5	7.3	5.7	9.9	7.9
1000+	11.9	18.7	24.2	19.0	14.5	14.9	17.8	16.4
Total	100.0	100.0	100.0	100.0	100.0	100.0	100.0	100.0
Number of affiliates[b]	462	187	62	42	110	863	933	1796
Total capital per investment, 1995 (in ATS million)								
1 to 19	33.1	63.9	24.3	58.1	39.3	39.2	83.3	61.5
20 to 49	14.2	14.2	17.6	2.0	6.2	12.7	81.7	51.2
50 to 99	20.5	18.4	20.9	9.0	22.3	19.0	33.4	24.7
100 to 499	36.1	47.8	14.9	28.1	20.3	34.3	35.3	34.8
500 to 999	29.9	45.4	127.7	76.6	13.3	38.5	134.0	100.8
1000+	61.4	77.6	62.1	174.2	34.7	69.6	172.5	127.5
Total	34.7	53.6	33.8	61.4	27.2	39.1	90.4	65.7

Source: Austrian National Bank.

Notes: [a] Firm size of the Austrian parent company.
[b] If the parent company has two (or more) affiliates they are accounted twice (or more often).

and 1996. Second, the boost in Austria's outward FDI to the CEECs seems to be slowing down after a few tough initial years of business which were characterised by specific FMAs. Partly, this can be explained by the fact that most of the privatisation in the period 1994–6 (i.e. large state-owned enterprises and former public industries such as telecommunications, energy, etc.) required huge amounts of capital. Due to their small size such financial support has been only sparsely available for most Austrian enterprises. For example, in 1995 in Hungary only US $ 1 billion of the total FDI of US $ 3.5 billion was non-privatisation-related FDI. The remaining part of FDI was the result of large utility and telecommunication sell-offs. Likewise, some 60 per cent of the Czech Republic's inflow of 1995 was related to the privatisation of the telecommunications company, SPT Telecom, and a major oil refinery (UN/ECE 1996). Furthermore, Neudorfer (1997) argues that more and more multinational firms, which have performed considerable FDI via their Austrian affiliates before 1994, have started to invest directly in CEECs through their parent firms. Hence the bridgehead function of such (foreign-owned) affiliates has diminished.

Table 11.1 shows the specific FDI feature of 'low capital requirement' in the CEECs. First, Table 11.1 presents the structure of Austria's FDI in the CEECs by the size of the Austrian parent company. In 1995 only 28.6 per cent of total capital was invested in the CEECs although almost 50 per cent of the affiliates (863 entities out of 1,796) were established there. Second, total capital per investment in CEECs was only ATS 39.1 million and thus considerably lower than those of affiliates established in OECD countries (ATS 90.4 million per investment).

Furthermore there are large differences between Hungary, the Czech Republic, Slovakia and Slovenia. In Hungary the huge majority of FDI (45.7 per cent) was accomplished by Austrian enterprises with less than twenty employees. We should bear in mind, however, that this category also includes holding companies. Thus it makes sense to focus on the second part of Table 11.1 where total capital per investment is calculated. There it appears that in Hungary total capital per investment is the lowest of all CEECs, followed by Slovakia, the Czech Republic and Slovenia. The last two countries show total capital per investment which is much higher than in Hungary and Slovakia although far below the amounts of the affiliates established in OECD countries. This confirms the presumption that the opening of Central and Eastern Europe gave SMEs with weak financial capacities greater opportunity for internationalisation. To many of them it was the first time that they had expanded their economic activities across the Austrian border. As mentioned above this specific feature is very similar to the eastward economic activities of German and Finnish SMEs.

Table 11.2 shows the structure of Austria's FDI in the CEECs by industries for 1996, registered by the industries of the host countries. Although there are differences between the four CEECs listed in Table 11.2 we can mainly see six industries in which Austria's FDI is concentrated: finance and insurance

Table 11.2 Austrian total capital by host countries and foreign economic sectors at end of 1996 (%)

	Hungary	*Czech Republic*	*Slovak Republic*	*Slovenia*	*Other CEECs*	*CEECs total*	*Other countries*	*Total*
mining and quarrying	2.4	0.4	2.2	0.0	0.4	1.4	2.6	2.2
food, beverages, tobacco	11.6	3.2	4.5	1.4	1.3	6.6	0.7	2.4
textiles, clothing, leather	1.0	0.3	0.0	0.0	1.3	0.7	0.5	0.5
wood processing	1.5	1.4	0.9	0.0	0.3	1.2	0.1	0.4
paper, printing and publishing	6.1	1.1	0.0	8.0	1.0	3.8	1.6	2.2
chemical products and refined petroleum	4.4	7.5	4.9	16.9	15.8	7.7	4.9	5.7
non-metallic products	6.2	16.4	2.0	2.9	6.1	8.6	2.0	3.9
metal products	3.7	1.0	3.2	2.7	2.2	2.6	5.7	4.8
mechanical products	1.0	1.6	0.3	1.1	3.0	1.3	2.3	2.0
electric and electronic equipment	7.0	2.3	22.3	0.2	1.4	5.6	2.5	3.4
motor vehicles	1.0	–0.2	0.0	0.0	0.0	0.4	0.4	0.4
other manufacturing	1.5	0.3	0.0	0.0	0.0	0.7	0.3	0.4
engineering sector[a]	14.2	5.0	25.8	4.0	6.6	10.7	11.3	11.1
industrial sector	45.0	35.1	38.1	33.2	32.4	39.2	21.0	26.2
construction	9.3	4.5	2.9	0.0	4.3	6.0	2.6	3.6
wholesale and retail trade	16.9	18.2	20.7	27.9	12.2	18.1	10.7	12.8
tourism	2.8	12.8	0.3	0.1	0.3	5.0	0.1	1.5
transport and communication	1.0	0.7	0.0	0.0	1.3	0.8	0.2	0.4
credit and finance	12.6	19.9	33.7	21.6	43.7	20.5	19.5	19.8
real estate (incl. holdings)	8.7	6.6	1.6	17.0	4.9	7.9	42.7	32.7
miscellaneous	1.3	1.7	0.5	0.3	0.3	1.2	0.7	0.8
non-industrial sector	52.6	64.5	59.7	66.8	67.1	59.5	76.4	71.5
Total ATS million	17,002	11,590	3,173	3,647	4,071	39,478	96,900	136,378

Source: Austrian National Bank.

Note: [a] metal products, mechanical products, electric and electronic equipment, motor vehicles, other manufacturing.

(20.5 per cent), wholesale and retail trade (18.1 per cent), non-metallic products (8.6 per cent), chemicals and petroleum (7.7 per cent), food and beverages (6.6 per cent) and construction (6.0 per cent). Additionally, we have assembled an 'engineering sector' which consists of metal products, mechanical products, electric and electronic equipment, motor vehicles and other manufacturing products. This sector accounts for 10.7 per cent of total FDI. Together these seven sub-categories account for 78.1 per cent of Austria's FDI in the CEECs.

On average nearly 60 per cent of Austria's FDI in CEECs is located in the service sector while the share of manufacturing is only close to 40 per cent. Interestingly, the manufacturing share of German FDI in Hungary was 54.8 per cent and in the Czech Republic 65.6 per cent respectively at the end of 1993 (Lemoine 1997). The dominance of service-related FDI is a specific Austrian feature.

Within the service sector the trading sector is of extraordinary significance. Austria's activities in trade have mainly been a result of buying up merchandise trading chains and in addition building up its own sales units. This pattern is rather similar for the financial and insurance sector. Investments within these service sectors are mainly aimed at taking advantage of the new distribution markets. Even the construction sector shows a strong standing. These activities are mainly a result of the strong build-up requirements of the transformation countries that on the whole could not be satisfied by their own construction industries. As several case studies indicate, most of this investment was a complementary investment in the Austrian home-based construction industry (Altzinger *et al.* 1998a).

FDI within the manufacturing sector is also concentrated in a few sectors only. The strong investment activities of the petroleum industry is a typical resource-motivated FDI which was brought about through joint ventures between refineries of Austria, Slovenia, Slovakia and partially Hungary. Further investments have been carried out in food and beverages as well as non-metallic products. The patterns of these investments are not so simple and will be discussed in more detail in the next two sections. One sector, which is of particular interest, is the 'engineering sector'. FDI within this sector is very often associated with the relocation of specific units of production (e.g. Madeuf 1995). However, this sector comprises only 10.6 per cent of Austria's total FDI in CEECs.

In absolute numbers by far the largest share of Austria's FDI in the CEECs has been invested in Hungary. In 1996 the four adjacent countries to Austria (Hungary, the Czech Republic, Slovenia and Slovakia) accounted for 90 per cent of Austria's overall FDI in the CEECs. This regional pattern emphasises the importance of geographical proximity and confirms the theoretical considerations above.

This brief outline of the sectoral and regional patterns of Austria's FDI in the CEECs shows three important issues: the importance of geographical proximity, the significance of investments in the non-manufacturing sectors, and a

Table 11.3 Motives for FDI in CEECs, ranked by their importance[a,b]

		Market-driven motives				*Supply-based motives*			
Sectors		*Market potential*	*proximity to customers*	*to create an export base*	*low wage costs*	*human capital*	*intermediate inputs*	*procurement*	*know-how of the affiliated firm*
Food & Beverages	mean	3.78	3.00	3.75	3.14	2.29	2.50	2.00	1.57
	N	9	7	8	7	7	6	6	7
Petroleum, chemicals	mean	3.63	3.33	3.38	2.86	2.29	1.71	2.00	1.50
	N	8	9	8	7	7	7	7	6
Non-metallic products	mean	3.50	3.11	3.00	3.00	2.14	2.50	2.38	2.22
	N	8	9	8	8	7	8	8	9
Engineering	mean	3.21	3.13	3.16	3.46	2.37	1.91	2.00	1.67
	N	24	24	25	26	19	22	22	21

Table 11.3 cont.

Sectors		*Market-driven motives*				*Supply-based motives*			
		Market potential	*proximity to customers*	*to create an export base*	*low wage costs*	*human capital*	*intermediate inputs*	*procurement*	*know-how of the affiliated firm*
Construction	mean	3.75	2.00	3.14	2.75	2.75	2.57	2.75	2.00
	N	8	6	7	8	8	7	8	6
Trade	mean	3.75	3.47	3.46	2.91	2.40	2.21	1.95	1.47
	N	28	30	26	23	20	19	20	17
Finance & Insurance	mean	4.00	4.00	2.86	1.50	2.00	1.00	1.00	1.83
	N	7	7	7	6	6	6	6	6
Others	mean	3.61	3.37	3.15	2.65	2.67	2.33	2.18	2.13
	N	33	27	26	26	24	18	17	16
Total mean	3.60	3.27	3.25	2.91	2.43	2.12	2.05	1.78	
	N	125	119	115	111	98	93	94	88

Notes: [a] Several respondents did not rate all the various motives
[b] Source: Questionnaire conducted in 1997.

significant activity of SMEs. Consequently, the subsequent analysis on motives and trade patterns will focus on those seven sectors which show the strongest FDI activities (trade, construction, finance and insurance, petroleum and chemicals, food and beverages, non-metallic products and engineering).

Motives for Austria's FDI in the CEECs

To discuss the motives of the FDI of Austrian enterprises we can rely on the results of a questionnaire which was conducted in 1997 by 1843 Austrian firms.[7] A total of 283 firms (15.4 per cent) returned completed questionnaires. 150 of these firms (52.0 per cent) had invested in the CEECs. Only the answers of these firms will be analysed in this chapter.

Concerning the motives, the following question was asked: 'Which factors were the most important ones for your initial investment decision?' The question was of a close-ended variety where the degrees of importance were based upon a four-point scale, using (1) very unimportant; (2) unimportant; (3) important and (4) very important. The responses to this question are shown in Table 11.3. Only those industries are presented which are the most important ones for Austria's FDI in the CEECs.

Due to our specific interest we have grouped the responses into two different groups. The first one can be summarised as 'market-driven' factors and consists of the following factors: 'market potential', 'customer proximity', 'to create an export base'. The second group we call 'supply-based' motives. This category consists of the following factors: 'low wage costs', 'to gain access to intermediate products', 'to gain access to procurement', 'human capital' and 'access to local technology'.

In Table 11.3 the motives of FDI have been ordered by importance. This ranking leads automatically to an interesting sub-division of the motives of FDI. The three factors which are rated highest are all market-driven factors while the remaining five factors are supply-based factors. Table 11.3 shows the number of respondents. As indicated above, only 150 firms of the total sample have invested in the CEECs. Due to the fact that several respondents only replied to certain statements the number of answers is always below 150.

The factor 'market potential' yields by far the highest mean of 3.60 followed in second place by 'customer proximity' with a mean of 3.27. In third place is the factor 'export base' with a mean of 3.25. Hence all three factors with the highest ranking are 'market-driven' factors although the last one indicates some very specific strategy. Because domestic markets do not drive this FDI, the labelling 'market-driven' for this factor is to some extent ambiguous. Therefore we will make the following distinction: if this FDI is being used as an export base for markets further East, it is indeed market-driven FDI. In contrast, if it is used as an export base for markets within the EU, it seems to be more of the supply-based type. We will discuss this issue in more detail.

The most important supply-based factor is 'low wage costs' with a mean of 2.91. However, for some industries this factor is of importance (engineering sector, food and beverages, non-metallic products). Even other supply-based factors such as 'human capital' (2.43), 'to gain access to intermediate products' (2.12) and 'to gain access to procurement' (2.05) are all rated rather low. The lowest rating was given to the factor 'know-how of the associated company' (1.78). These results confirm clearly the dominance of market-driven factors. However, remarkable differences remain between industries. Therefore, a breakdown by industries seems to be of considerable importance.

Table 11.3 shows (at least) two industries where market-driven factors are of particular importance: finance and insurance, trade and petroleum and chemicals. For finance and insurance, domestic market-driven factors are far above the mean and all supply-based factors (with the exception of the 'know-how of the associated company') are rated low. Noticeably, labour costs are of least importance. As expected, the export base factor is not of any significance. Even for trade all market-driven factors are far above the mean and supply-based factors (with the exception of 'intermediate inputs') are rated low. Hence, for these two industries in particular the objectives of investment are clearly market-driven.

Even food and beverages show the prime importance of market-driven factors. However, for food and beverages not only the domestic market is of importance but even 'to create an export base' scored high (3.75). In addition, this sector also shows considerable importance of intermediate inputs. The factor 'low labour costs' scored second in all industries. There are two other industries where non-labour supply-based factors are of considerable importance: both the construction sector and the non-metallic sector are very much dependent on procurement and intermediate inputs.

Of particular interest is the engineering sector. This sector considers low wage costs as very important (3.46). It is the only sector where low wage costs are evaluated as the most important factor. Market-driven factors are rated favourably but well behind the wage costs. Other supply-based factors are rather insignificant.

To summarise these features we should emphasise the overall importance of market-driven factors. In particular 'market potential' is of top priority. This is especially the case for finance and insurance, food and beverages, construction and trade. Only one industry, the engineering sector, rated low wage costs rather high. Due to the remarkable importance of supply-based motives within this sector we should keep an eye on it. There are two sectors where other supply-based motives play a role, construction and non-metallic products. Both of them are dependent on intermediate products and procurements above the average. Generally speaking, although market-driven factors dominate the overall objectives of Austria's FDI in the CEECs, the patterns are very different among industries.

Sales and trade patterns of Austrian affiliates

Finally we want to look at the sales and trade patterns of Austrian affiliates. In particular it is of interest to discover which markets affiliates are providing their goods and services. For that purpose it is useful to distinguish once again between 'supply-based' and 'market-driven' motives. Supply-based motives would presumably indicate that the dominant factor of investment is to gain access to a cheap industrial workforce. As long as the national purchasing power of the host country remains low – which is a necessary requirement of this approach – large parts of the production will be exported to developed countries with strong demand. As discussed above, such a scenario would presumably substitute exports from the home country and encourage re-imports to the home country. Such patterns are usually associated with 'relocation'. In contrast, market-driven FDI should be accompanied by considerable demand in the 'new emerging' markets. Therefore the production of the affiliates should be sold to a large extent to local markets. Such a scenario is likely to stimulate 'associated exports' from the home country and hence would have a positive impact on domestic economy. Due to the predominance of market-driven FDI we would expect high local market shares throughout the sample with the exception of the engineering sector.

Table 11.4 shows the regional sales structure of the affiliates. Again, these are the results of a survey. On average 65.5 per cent of the total production of the affiliates was sold to local markets. One third of total production was sold to foreign markets; 23.2 per cent was exported to the EU, thereof 10.6 per cent to Austria; another 8.5 per cent were destined for other CEECs. A comparison by industries reveals that indeed six out of seven industries which account for the bulk of Austria's FDI in these countries display rather high shares of local markets.[8] Construction shows a local market share of 89.2 per cent, followed by food and beverages (83.0 per cent), petroleum and chemicals (81.6 per cent), non-metallic products (78.7 per cent) and trade (75.1 per cent). This evidence confirms in a convincing manner the predominance of market-driven motives. However, there is one industry which yields important exports to the EU. The engineering sector sells 51.3 per cent to EU markets. The share of local markets is just 39.5 per cent. This distinctive feature is of substantial importance because it indicates rather clearly that within this engineering sector some highly specialised division of labour has already taken place. And it is not only Austria where these products are shipped to. Even other EU countries are involved in this new emerging European division of labour to a large extent. Close to 35 per cent of the overall output is sold to EU markets other than Austria.

In addition to this evidence it is worth taking a look at intra-firm trade data. Such intra-firm trade between the Austrian parent firm and its affiliates in CEECs has reached considerable proportions relative to countries' trade. During the period 1989–95 intra-firm exports of Austrian companies which

Table 11.4 Regional sales structure of the affiliates, 1995[a]

Sectors		*local market*	*EU (incl. Austria), 1995*	*thereof: Austria*	*other CEECs*	*Others*
Food & Beverages	mean	83.0	8.6	4.1	8.3	0.1
	N	9	9	9	9	9
Petroleum, Chemicals	mean	81.6	17.2	17.2	1.2	0
	N	5	5	5	5	5
Non-metallic products	mean	78.7	9.1	6.3	6.1	6.1
	N	9	9	9	9	9
Engineering	mean	39.5	51.3	17.4	6.1	3.1
	N	23	23	23	23	23
Trade	mean	75.1	13.0	6.7	7.0	4.8
	N	31	31	31	31	31
Others	mean	56.9	27.3	12.9	14.4	1.4
	N	33	33	33	33	33
Total	mean	65.5	23.2	10.6	8.5	2.7
	N	119	119	119	119	199

Note: [a] Source: Questionnaire conducted in 1997.

have affiliates in Hungary, the Czech Republic and Slovakia have grown from 1.8 per cent in 1989 to 9.7 per cent in 1995. On the import side these changes were less dramatic. The share of intra-firm imports from these three countries increased only from 0.1 per cent in 1989 to 5.1 per cent in 1995 (Neudorfer 1997).

The outcome of the intra-firm relations of Austria's MNEs with CEECs is a large trade surplus. To assess this development in greater detail it is interesting to compare intra-firm trade by industries (see Table 11.5). In 1996 intra-firm exports to the CEECs amounted to ATS 9.1 billion while the imports accounted only for ATS 3.6 billion. Hence the intra-firm trade surplus was ATS 5.4 billion. If we look at the structure of these exports we can see that only two sectors account for two-thirds of all intra-firm exports: trade and electric and electronic equipment. The large share of intra-firm exports in trade is in line with the strong investment activities of this sector. Within the trading sector FDI and intra-firm exports in particular show a complementary relationship. One specific feature of trade is that these exports consist entirely of final goods. Hence it is not a result of an improved international division of labour. However, the trade surplus of this sector is remarkable and accounts for two-thirds of the overall trade surplus. On the import side we can see that nearly all intra-firm imports have been carried out by the manufacturing sector. Chemicals and petroleum and electric and

Table 11.5 Intra-firm trade of goods, 1996 (in ATS million)

	Exports	*Imports*	*Balance*
mining and quarrying	0	0	0
food, beverages, tobacco	97	194	–97
textiles, clothing, leather	84	169	–85
wood processing	57	328	–271
paper, printing and publishing	351	40	311
chemical products and refined petroleum	786	722	64
non–metalic products	440	129	311
metal products	69	286	–217
mechanical products	408	315	93
electric and electronic equipment	2363	840	1523
motor vehicles	348	445	–97
other manufacturing	24	18	6
engineering sector[a]	3212	1904	1308
manufacturing sector	5027	3486	1541
construction	119	34	85
wholesale and retail trade	3915	95	3820
Tourism	0	0	0
transport and communication	13	0	13
credit and finance	0	0	0
real estate (incl. holdings)	1	2	–1
Miscellaneous	3	1	2
Non–manufacturing sector	4051	132	3919
Total ATS million	9078	3617	5461

Source: Austrian National Bank.

Note: [a] metal products, mechanical products, electric and electronic equipment, motor vehicles, other manufacturing.

electronic equipment are responsible for the largest part of these imports. Furthermore there are several manufacturing sectors which show (small) intra-firm trade deficits: food and beverages, textiles and clothing, wood processing and metal products. Nearly all of them are labour-intensive industries. Within the engineering sector only metal products display a negative intra-firm trade balance. These pattern seem to indicate that although this sector is largely dependent on exports to the EU, it also stimulates intra-firm exports from the Austrian parent firm and therefore helps to compensate for export substitution to some extent.

Conclusion

Geographically Austria's FDI to the CEECs is strongly concentrated in its adjacent countries (Hungary, Czech Republic, Slovakia and Slovenia). Spatial proximity and cultural and historical affinity have enabled Austrian companies to enter these new emerging markets immediately. Therefore these companies have reaped an essential FMA. Moreover, these factors enabled Austrian companies to minimise risks and therefore even SMEs took new opportunities for their internationalisation. Investment was undertaken to a large extent by SMEs. For many of them it was the first time that they had performed an outward FDI.

A breakdown by industry reveals that the non-manufacturing sector (trade, finance and insurance, construction) has invested most strongly in CEECs. Within the manufacturing sector three industries comprise the bulk of FDI: chemicals and petroleum, food and beverages and non-metallic products. As has been shown by the results of a survey the principal motive of these investments is 'market access'. With the exception of food and beverages all sectors show a strong reliance of their FDI on market-driven motives. There is only one sector, the engineering sector (metal products, mechanical products, electrical and electronic equipment and motor vehicles), which rated low wage costs rather high. In particular within this sector some new European division of labour seems to be developing. The importance of supply-based FDI within this sector indicates that production activities are being relocated in order to gain overall competitive strength.

Sales and trade patterns of Austrian affiliates in the CEECs indicate that two-thirds of the overall output is sold on local markets. All industries with large amounts of FDI yield high local market shares. Hence for these industries the dominance of market-driven factors is strongly confirmed by these sales patterns. Only the engineering sector indicates a strong dependence on EU markets. Within this sector the share of local markets is only 39.5 per cent. More than 50 per cent of the output is shipped to the EU while this share is only 23.2 per cent on average. Hence for this sector a new European division of labour seems to be established.

Additionally, overall intra-firm trade data display that much of this trade is not performed in a way that is associated with established MNEs operating in global industries. First of all it is the trading sector which has improved its performance by trading final goods to its affiliates. Within the manufacturing sector only labour-intensive sectors show (small) intra-firm trade deficits.

To sum up the empirical evidence, we are tempted to conclude that Austria's FDI in the CEECs presents a considerable push of the internationalisation of Austria's industry. However, the internationalisation process differs from the typical pattern stated by established theory: Austria's FDI in the CEECs can be mainly explained by geographical proximity and close historical and cultural ties which gave Austrian firms a considerable FMA. Most of this FDI has been undertaken by SMEs with little experience of internationalisation. For all industries which display strong FDI activities in CEECs, market-driven motives were of overwhelming importance. The predominance of market-driven factors is strongly confirmed by sales patterns of the affiliates, which demonstrate rather clearly the dominance of local markets. However, one exception remains: the engineering sector rates production cost advantages far above the average. Additionally, this sector shows a rather different sales pattern with high exports to the EU. It is this sector in particular where some detrimental impacts on domestic economy may have occurred. Nevertheless, until now this part of FDI has only been of minor importance. At the end of 1996 only 10.7 per cent of total FDI stock had been allocated to this sector. The bulk of Austria's FDI in the CEECs is predominantly market-driven, produced to a very large extent for local markets, thereby encouraging additional 'associated' exports, and displaying intra-firm trade surpluses by the Austrian parent firms. Hence it is very likely that these investments have had positive net effects on Austria's economic performance.

Acknowledgements

I am grateful to Christian Bellak and Klaus Meyer for helpful comments, to the Division of 'International Balance of Payments' at the Austrian National Bank for assistance with the data, and to the 'Jubiläumsfonds' at the Austrian National Bank for financial support under grant 6,370. The author takes sole responsibility for the use and interpretation of the data and for any errors therein.

Notes

1 For a rather different view see Lemoine (1997).
2 Export activities are by definition the share of total sales which is destined for exports.
3 In 1996 only Greece and Portugal showed lower outward FDI–stock–GDP ratios than Austria.
4 Austria became a member of the EU on 1 January 1995.
5 Weighted by their nominal capital the share of OECD countries within the group 'Others' is 98 per cent. Hence for simplicity this group will be labelled as OECD group.
6 Hence Poland is not displayed separately in any figure or table.
7 This questionnaire was conducted by a research group at the University of Economics and Business Administration, Vienna. The project team included Elisabeth Beer, Christian Bellak, Markus König, Renate Tolunay, Richard Winklhofer and myself. I would like to thank all of them for their help and cooperation throughout the research project.
8 We did not get enough responses from finance and insurance. However, this sector is certainly dependent on the local market to a very large extent.

References

Agarwal, J. (1996) *Does Foreign Direct Investment Contribute to Unemployment in Home Countries? – An Empirical Survey*, Kiel Working Paper 765, Kiel: Institut für Weltwirtschaft.

Altzinger, W. (1997) 'Gewinner und Verlierer – Die Auswirkungen des Osthandels auf den österreichischen Arbeitsmarkt', in *Wege zu einem anderen Europa: Beirat für gesellschafts-, wirtschafts- und umweltpolitische Alternativen*, Cologne: Papyrossa Verlag, pp. 168–97.

Altzinger, W., Beer, E., Bellak, C. (1998a) 'Exportieren Österreichische Unternehmen Arbeitsplätze nach Osteuropa?', *Wirtschaft und Gesellschaft* 24, 4: 475–503.

Altzinger, W., Maier, G. and Fidrmuc, J. (1998b) 'Crossborder development in the Vienna-Bratislawa-region: a review', in U. Graute (ed.) *Sustainable Development for Central and Eastern Europe: Spatial Development in the European Context*, Vienna, Berlin and New York: Springer-Verlag, pp. 89–114.

Austrian National Bank (1998) 'Österreichische Investitionen im Ausland und ausländische Direktinvestitionen in Österreich', Stand per Ende 1996, *Statistische Monatshefte der Nationalbank*, vol. 6/1998, Vienna: ÖNB.

Baldwin, R. (1994) 'The effects of trade and foreign direct investment on employment and relative wages', *OECD Economic Studies* 23: 7–54, Winter.

Barrel, R. and Pain, N. (1997) 'Foreign direct investment, technological change, and economic growth within Europe', *The Economic Journal* 107, 445: 1770–86, November.

Bellak, C. (1997) 'Austrian manufacturing MNEs: long-term perspectives', *Business History* 39, 1: 47–71.

Blomström, M., Fors, G. and Lipsey R.E. (1997) 'Foreign direct investment and employment: home country experience in the United States and Sweden', *The Economic Journal*, 107, 445: 1787–97, November.

Borsos, J. (1995) 'Domestic employment effects of Finnish FDIs in Eastern Europe', *ETLA* B.111, Helsinki: The Research Institute of the Finnish Economy (ETLA).

Brenton, P., Mauro, F.D. and Lücke, M. (1998) 'Economic integration and FDI: an empirical analysis of foreign investment in the EU and in Central and Eastern Europe', *Kieler Arbeitspapier*, No. 890, November.

Cantwell, J. (1994) 'The relationship between international trade and international production', in D. Greenaway and L. Alan Winters (eds) *Surveys in International Trade*, Oxford: Blackwell. pp. 303–28.

Dunning, J.H. (1993) *Multinational Enterprises and the Global Economy*, Harlow: Addison-Wesley.

EBRD (1994) *Economic Transition in Eastern Europe and the Former Soviet Union*, Transition Report, 1994, London: EBRD.

European Commission (1997) *Agenda 2000: For a Stronger and Wider Europe*, Brussels: EC.

Floyd, D. (1996) 'Foreign direct investment in Poland: Is low cost labour really the sole determinant?', *Economic Issues*, 2: 29–39, September.

Hunya, G. (1997) *Foreign Direct Investment in Central and Eastern Europe*, Vienna: Bank Austria.

Hunya, G. and Stankovsky, J. (1997) *Foreign Direct Investment in Central and Eastern European Countries and the Former Soviet Union*, Vienna: Österreichisches Institut für Wirtschaftsforschung and Wiener Institut für internationale Wirtschaftsvergleiche.

Kurz, C. and Wittke, V. (1997) 'From "Supply Base Driven" to "Market Driven" integration: patterns of integrating Central-East European economies by using their industrial capacities', background paper, presented at the Berkeley Roundtable on the International Economy, Vienna, 5–6 June.

Lankes, H.-P. and Venables, A.J. (1997) 'FDI in economic transition: the changing pattern of investment', *Economics of Transition* 4, 2: 331–47.

Lemoine, F. (1997) 'Integrating Central and Eastern Europe in the European trade and production network', Background Paper, presented at the Berkeley Roundtable on the International Economy, Vienna, 5–6 June.

Lorentzen, J., Møllgaard, P. and Rojec, M. (eds) (1998) 'Corporate networks, EU enlargement, and the global economy', *Journal of International Relations and Development* 1, 1–2: 85–105.

Madeuf, B. (1995) *Foreign Direct Investment, Trade and Employment – Delocalisation*, Paris: OECD, pp. 41–66.

Meyer, K.E. (1995) 'Direct foreign investment in Eastern Europe: the role of labour costs', *Comparative Economic Studies* 37, 4: 69–88.

Nachum, L. (1998) 'Motivations of TNCs for investment in Eastern and Central Europe: some policy implications', Discussion Papers in International Investment and Business Studies, vol. XI (1998/99), no. 260.

Neudorfer, P. (1997) 'The opening of Central and Eastern Europe: the case of Austrian foreign direct investment', *Focus on Transition* 2: 52–68, Österreichische Nationalbank.

Neudorfer, P. and Bach, W. (1995) '5 Jahre Ostöffnung' in *Österreichische Unternehmensbeteiligungen in Osteuropa, Informationen über multinationale Konzerne*, special edition. '5 Jahre Ostöffnung', 14–21.

OECD (1994) *Assessing Investment Opportunities in Economics in Transition*, Paris: OECD.

OECD (1995) *Foreign Direct Investment, Trade and Employment*, Paris: OECD.

Palme, G. (1998) 'Auswirkungen der EU-Osterweiterung auf die Österreichische Sachgüterproduktion', *WIFO-Monatsberichte*, 11/1998, pp. 761–9.

Petrakos, G. (1996) *The New Geography of the Balkans: Cross-Border Cooperation between Albania, Bulgaria and Greece*, Volos: University of Thessaly.

Pye, R.K. (1997) *Foreign Direct Investment in Central Europe – Results from a Survey of Major Investors*, Finance Working Paper A.97/1, London: City University.

Stankovsky, J. (1995) 'Österreichische Direktinvestitionen in Osteuropa', in Bundeskanzleramt der Republik Österreich, Europa 1996 – Auswirkungen einer EU-Osterweiterung, *Schriftenreihe Europa*, pp. 157–92.

Stankovsky, J. (1996) 'Direktinvestitionen in Osteuropa: Österreich auf dem Rückzug?', *WIFO-Monatsberichte* 5: 349–53.

UN (1998) *World Investment Report 1998*, Geneva: United Nations Publications, (various yearbooks).

UN/ECE (1996) 'Statistical survey of recent trends in foreign investment in Eastern European countries', *Economic and Social Council/Economic Commission for Europe/Committee on the Development of Trade*, 23 November, Geneva: United Nations, Economic Commission for Europe.

Vincentz, V. (1995) *Auswirkungen der wachsenden Arbeitsteilung zwischen Deutschland und seinen östlichen Nachbarn auf Arbeitsmarkt, Investitionen und Güterströme*, Munich: Osteuopa-Institut München, working paper no. 188.

12 Export competition between Central and Eastern European countries in the EU market

Dimitris Kyrkilis and Evangelos Nikolaidis

Introduction

In the standard Hecksher–Ohlin theoretical framework international trade flows are determined by differences in national comparative advantages, and their volume increases as countries limit production in sectors where they enjoy competitive advantages, i.e. inter-industry trade. In that context protectionism curtails international trade, since tariffs distort international differences of factor prices, which constitute the basis of national comparative advantages. Therefore, trade liberalisation will encourage production and international trade patterns compatible with national comparative advantages differences and it will eventually increase the volume of international trade. As the existence of trade barriers encourages domestic production of a greater variety of products within sectors than competitive advantages dictate, it results in domestic producers operating at suboptimal plant levels and at relatively high production costs. Again trade liberalisation leads to production rationalisation within domestic industries, taking the form of reducing the number and varieties of products, and thus to increased intra-industry specialisation according to economies of specialisation at the product and plant levels.

To the extent that the countries liberalising their bilateral trade are at different stages of development, differences in relative factor prices and demand patterns are likely to be greater. Besides, developing economies have lower per capita incomes, less availability of human and financial capital compared to developed countries and so it is anticipated that the former cannot specialise in differentiated products. Therefore, the possibility of observing to a larger extent inter-industry than intra-industry production and trade specialisation is greater in that case than it is in the case of countries being at similar levels of development.[1]

Trade liberalisation between the EU and CEE is expected to increase the volume of bilateral inter-industry trade, due to the fact that the two areas differ substantially in their levels of development. If it is accepted that development proceeds in stages,[2] CEE countries are currently in the second stage of development. That means that their advantages are directed towards low cost in sectors of standardised technology. Production takes advantage of cheap but adequately trained labour in industries characterised either by labour intensity or by medium capital intensity, e.g. chemicals, iron and steel, shipbuilding, synthetic fibres, electrical appliances, etc.

The exporting effort of CEE countries is therefore expected to concentrate on rather traditional sectors.[3] There is some evidence that price but not income elasticities are significant determinants of trade between CEE and the EU,[4] an indication that exports from the former to the latter consist of non- or low differentiated products.

Another implication of the above analysis is that CEE countries have to some extent overlapping production structures on the basis of rather common comparative advantages. That in turn leads to similar export structures. If this is valid, then competition between these countries in export markets and consequently in the EU market is anticipated to be significant.

Nevertheless, CEE countries differ among themselves in levels of production and organisation abilities, education and training of the labour force, success in the transformation effort from central plan to free market, proximity to the main EU markets, etc. There is no doubt that these differences give rise to differences in production specialisation among them and affect export patterns, influencing in that way the degree of competition between CEE countries in the EU market.

In addition, according to the recently announced Agenda 2000, five CEE countries, namely Poland, Hungary, the Czech Republic, Slovenia and Estonia, which happen to be, with the exception of Estonia, the most successful in the transformation towards the market economy[5] will proceed to become full members of the EU. Full membership status is expected to give them a relative advantage *vis-à-vis* the other CEE countries in their export penetration of the EU market.

The aim of this chapter is to test the validity of the above stated hypothesis, that CEE countries have to some extent similar export structures, centred around rather traditional industries, that affect their export success in the EU market. The analysis will be based on the comparison of export patterns per pair of the following countries: Poland, Hungary, the Czech Republic, Slovenia, Romania and Latvia. These countries have been chosen due to the availability of data on exports to the EU. The methodology adopted is the estimation of the Finger–Kreinin index. The presentation and discussion of the results are organised after grouping industries in three main categories: primary products, manufactured products, and raw materials and fuels.

Methodology and data

Finger and Kreinin (1979) have proposed a measure of the export pattern similarity between two countries or groups of countries, to a third country or group of countries. This measure is given by the following formulae:

$$XS_{\alpha\beta} = \Sigma\ minimum\ (Xi_{ac}, Xi_{bc})\ 100$$

where:

XS_{ab} is the export similarity between two countries or group of countries *a* and *b*.

Xi_{ac} and Xi_{bc} is the share of commodity *i* in the exports of country *a* to a third market *c* and in the exports of country *b* to the same third country *c* respectively. Commodity shares are expressed in percentages of either total exports, or exports of a specific commodity group, e.g. primary products if patterns of total exports, or of specific commodity groups are investigated respectively.

Σ stands for summation across commodities *i*.

The measure takes the value of 100 if the patterns of exports of countries *a* and *b* to the market *c* are identical, and the value 0 if the export patterns are completely different. It is obvious that as the value of the index approaches 100 the export similarity between countries *a* and *b* increases.

In fact, the Finger–Kreinin index is the equivalent of country's *a* exports to country *c* in terms of country's *b* exports to country *c*. For example, if the index takes the value of 40, it can be interpreted that the *b*'s exports to *c* correspond to the 40 per cent of *a*'s exports to *c*. In that respect the Finger–Kreinin index resembles the well-known Grubel–Lloyd intra-industry index, which assesses the similarity of export and import structures of country *a* with respect another country *b*.[6] Since the Finger–Kreinin index is a summation across commodity sectors, in a similar manner to the Grubel–Lloyd measure, it is open to the same criticism about the influence of the aggregation level. The higher the data aggregation level, i.e. the closer it comes to the one digit sectoral level of the Standard International Trade Classification (SITC), the higher the value of the index is expected to be, since the likelihood of commom export structures of any two countries *a* and *b* increases as the classification of commodities becomes broader and hence the elasticity of substitution between the commodities of each product group tends to decrease.[7]

Sectoral data on exports from CEE to the EU are available for the following countries: Poland, Hungary, the Czech Republic, Slovenia, Romania and Latvia. Data are retrieved from the United Nations Statistical Papers, Commodity Trade Statistics – Series D and they are available up to the two-digit level of the SITC for all the above countries. With the exception of Hungary, data are also available at the three-digit level of the SITC. For the purpose of unifying the analysis, calculations are made at the two-digit sectoral level. However, as a next step, and after excluding Hungary, estimations of export similarity indices are also made at the three digit level of SITC. Data refer to the year 1994, the last year for which trade data exist for the aforementioned countries.

Commodities are grouped in the following categories: Primary raw and processed products, i.e. SITC classes 0 = food and live animals; 1 = beverages and tobacco; and 4 = animal and vegetable oils and fats. Raw materials and fuels, i.e. SITC classes 2 = raw materials except fuels; and 3 = mineral fuels, lubricants and related materials. Manufactured products, i.e. SITC classes 5 = chemicals and related products; 6 = manufactured products classified chiefly by raw materials; 7 = machinery and transport equipment; 8 = miscellaneous manufactured articles. Comparisons are made per pair of countries for both each product category and between commodity groups. The intention is to establish the main country competitors in EU markets per product group, to draw some conclusions on the export competition intensity for each commodity group, and finally to point out any policy implications.

Empirical results

Results for each commodity group are presented in Table 12.1. It is evident that all countries under investigation have considerable export similarity in all product categories, although in the case of raw materials and fuels it seems reduced.

Primary raw and processed products

The index takes values of 50 and above in all cases with the exception of the export structures of Hungary and Latvia. The higher export similarity is demonstrated in the cases of Hungary–Romania, Slovenia–Romania, the Czech Republic–Latvia, and Slovenia–Poland, while the lower indices are observed for the pairs of Latvia–Slovenia, Latvia–Poland, Hungary–the Czech Republic, Latvia–Romania, and Latvia–Hungary.

From the countries not facing immediate entry, Latvia seems to meet relatively lower competition in EU export markets of primary products, while Romania is in a more difficult position, especially because two of its main competitors, namely Hungary and Poland, show some considerable export intensity of agricultural products, concentrating 14.8 and 9.3 per cent respectively of their EU exports in the primary sector (see Table 12.2), an indication that they are relatively successful in overcoming the protection measures of the Common Agricultural Policy. In that respect their entry is expected to facilitate, and thus to increase further their agricultural exports through the elimination of trade barriers, an event not applicable in the case of Romania. The latter demonstrates an agricultural export share equal to 3.9 per cent (see Table 12.2).

On the other hand, Hungary, Poland and the Czech Republic appear to be competing against each other, not only because they demonstrate relatively high export similarity values, but also because they show the highest primary products export intensity among all countries (see Table 12.2). Slovenia, although it shows high export similarity values with all other countries, is a less important competitor since the share of agricultural products in its total exports to the EU is only 2.2 per cent.

Table 12.1 The Finger–Kreinin export similarity index values for CEE country exports to the EU, 1994

Countries	*Hungary*	*Poland*	*Slovenia*	*Romania*	*Latvia*
	Primary Products (0,1,4)				
The Czech Republic	52 (–)	61 (52)	60 (51)	59 (53)	73 (59)
Hungary	-	58 (–)	65 (–)	76 (–)	44 (–)
Poland	–	–	71 (48)	68 (58)	52 (46)
Slovenia	–	–	–	73 (49)	55 (42)
Romania	–	–	–	–	50 (44)
	Materials and Fuels (2,3)				
The Czech Republic	46 (–)	65 (57)	61 (47)	31 (24)	41 (38)
Hungary	–	36 (–)	45 (–)	57 (–)	24 (–)
Poland	–	–	38 (32)	27 (22)	28 (26)
Slovenia	–	–	–	33 (21)	54 (37)
Romania	–	–	–	–	14 (13)
	Manufactured products (5–8)				
The Czech Republic	60 (–)	65 (59)	66 (59)	49 (40)	50 (36)
Hungary	–	69 (–)	70 (–)	60 (–)	50 (–)
Poland	–	–	72 (59)	66 (56)	59 (41)
Slovenia	–	–	–	53 (46)	54 (37)
Romania	–	–	–	–	56 (42)

Source: UN Statistical Papers. Commodity Trade Statistics. Series D (Own calculations).

Notes: Figures in brackets are the index values calculated on the basis of the three-digit sectoral level of SITC:

0	Food and live animals	5	Chemicals and related products
1	Beverages and tobacco	6	Manufactured goods classified chiefly by raw material
2	Crude materials inedible, except fuels	7	Machinery and transport equipment
3	Mineral fuels, lubricants, etc.	8	Miscellaneous manufactured articles
4	Animal and vegetable oils and fats	9	Commodities and transactions not classified by category

Table 12.2 Distribution of CEE country exports to the EU at the one-digit level of SITC, 1994, (%)

	The Czech Rep.	*Hungary*	*Poland*	*Slovenia*	*Romania*	*Latvia*
		Primary products				
0	4.4	14.0	8.9	1.9	3.4	2.9
1	0.6	0.6	0.3	0.2	0.4	0.3
4	0.2	0.2	0.1	0.0	0.1	0.0
(0+1+4)	(5.3)	(14.8)	(9.3)	(2.2)	(3.9)	(3.2)
		Raw materials and fuels				
2	10.6	6.4	5.2	2.1	2.2	40.4
3	5.1	3.9	9.0	0.3	5.7	1.8
(2+3)	(15.7)	(10.3)	(14.2)	(2.4)	(7.9)	(42.2)
		Manufactured products				
5	8.6	8.4	5.0	4.0	5.8	3.0
6	32.4	18.3	28.4	28.2	18.8	28.0
7	21.8	25.3	18.1	35.1	9.8	5.0
8	16.1	22.9	25.0	28.1	53.7	15.0
(5+6+7+8)	(79.0)	(74.9)	(76.5)	(95.4)	(88.1)	(50.9)
9	0.1	0.1	0.1	0.0	0.0	3.6
TOTAL	(100.0)	(100.0)	(100.0)	(100.0)	(100.0)	(100.0)
	100.0	100.0	100.0	100.0	100.0	100.0

Source: UN Statistical Papers. Commodity Trade Statistics. Series D (Own calculations).

Note: For the SITC code numbers see Table 12.1.

At the three-digit level of analysis (see figures in brackets in Table 12.1) lower values of the export similarity indices are observed for all countries. In some cases, as between Poland and Slovenia, Romania and Slovenia, Latvia and the Czech Republic the decrease in the index is significant. In general, though, with the exception of Slovenia, which becomes an even less important competitor in all cases, the relative positions of countries do not seem to be affected.

Raw materials and fuels

Export similarity seems to be significantly lower in that commodity group compared with the one of primary commodities. Relatively high index values are demonstrated by the following country pairs: Poland and the Czech Republic, Slovenia and the Czech Republic, Hungary and Romania, Latvia and Slovenia (values between 65 and 54), while Latvia and Poland, Poland and Romania, Latvia and Hungary, Latvia and Romania show relatively low export similarity (values are in the range between 28 and 14).

In general, both Latvia and Romania appear to have the least similar export patterns to the rest of the countries and in that respect are in an advantageous position after the entry of the latter. However, this is a limited advantage since both countries show a considerable raw material export concentration in sectors where some serious competition exists. Latvia concentrates 90.3 per cent of its raw material exports to the EU in the cork and wood sector, and it faces considerable competition from both Slovenia and the Czech Republic, which concentrate in the same sector 48.7 and 30.9 per cent respectively of their EU raw material exports. Romania with a 72.0 per cent concentration ratio in the petroleum and petroleum product sector is in direct competition with Hungary, with a sectoral export intensity at the level of 34.1 per cent (see Table 12.3).

The Czech Republic demonstrates greater export similarity to almost all other countries, with the exception perhaps of Romania. Its export similarity is higher to Poland and Slovenia than Hungary, Latvia and Romania. Again, the sectoral source of the Czech Republic's high similarity indices is narrow with only three sectors being responsible for common export structures. More specifically, cork and wood in all cases, and in addition coal-coke and briquettes in the case of Poland, and metalliferous ore and scrap in the case of Hungary.

Manufactured products

Index values are significant in all cases with Latvia demonstrating the lowest export similarity in general. Pairs with relatively high export similarity are: Hungary and Poland, Hungary and Slovenia, Poland and Slovenia, the Czech Republic and Slovenia, the Czech Republic and Poland, Poland and Romania, whereas the Czech Republic and Romania show the lowest index value, i.e. $XS = 49$. Relatively less similar export patterns are demostrated between Latvia and Hungary, Latvia and the Czech Republic, Latvia and Slovenia, Slovenia and Romania.

Overall, all countries appear to be in direct competition, with Slovenia demonstrating the highest degree of competition, especially with the Czech Republic, Poland and Hungary. Besides, Slovenia has an impressive EU manufacturing export intensity. Manufacturing accounts for 95.4 per cent of its total exports to the EU, while Latvia has both the lowest manufacturing export intensity, i.e. 50.82 per cent (see Table 12.2) and the lowest similarity of manufacturing export patterns. Latvia seems to be in stronger competition with Poland. Romanian exports of manufactures appear to be more similar with their Slovenian and Polish counterparts. This may cause some further difficulties in Romanian exports after Slovenia and Poland have entered the EU and the consequent intensification of their export orientation towards its market. However, EU markets will be a field of strong competition between all countries eligible for immediate entry, given both their strong export similarity and export intensity in manufacturing industries.

The basis of this high export similarity seems to be rather diversified due to equally diversified manufacturing export structures of the countries involved. Only Romania concentrates almost 51 per cent of its manufacturing exports to the EU in three sectors, namely clothing and accessories, furniture and cushions etc., and non-ferrous metals. These sectors account for 37 per cent of the total Polish manufacturing exports to the EU. In general, manufacturing

Table 12.3 Distribution of CEE country exports to the EU at the two-digit level of SITC, 1994, (%)

	The Czech Rep.	*Hungary*	*Poland*	*Slovenia*	*Romania*	*Latvia*
			Primary products			
00	10.78	11.63	15.61	1.46	20.35	6.34
01	5.38	43.56	13.24	24.75	24.46	8.21
02	26.09	1.33	9.27	8.17	1.68	16.00
03	4.22	0.72	7.88	3.86	1.04	17.27
04	3.72	5.64	0.30	1.35	5.04	14.06
05	20.81	26.23	42.40	34.78	31.36	16.53
06	1.83	1.68	3.11	5.61	1.38	0.00
07	1.38	3.28	0.43	2.73	0.34	1.53
08	7.75	0.00	2.78	4.89	0.76	7.88
09	1.80	1.39	1.10	0.34	0.62	0.00
11	11.37	3.45	0.66	8.56	10.42	11.24
12	0.92	0.64	2.22	1.41	0.00	0.00
41	0.75	0.00	0.07	1.73	0.00	0.94
42	1.16	0.46	0.00	0.12	1.42	0.00
43	2.04	0.00	0.91	0.25	1.12	0.00
TOTAL	100.00	100.00	100.00	100.00	100.00	100.00
			Raw materials and fuels			
21	2.24	1.75	0.77	10.15	3.34	1.16
22	1.04	12.16	0.09	0.00	1.35	0.25
23	4.10	0.02	1.62	0.13	0.08	0.00
24	30.95	16.87	18.55	48.69	7.74	90.29
25	5.20	0.00	1.16	13.13	0.05	0.00
26	5.30	2.51	2.58	1.68	4.91	1.84
27	4.01	0.76	4.61	1.27	1.90	0.32
28	13.62	14.64	3.32	9.83	5.00	1.37
29	0.96	14.82	3.63	3.24	3.22	0.45
32	22.56	1.39	53.27	0.00	0.38	3.67
33	7.15	34.10	6.38	10.76	72.02	0.66
34	0.41	0.99	0.14	0.24	0.00	0.00
35	2.47	0.00	3.87	0.88	0.00	0.00
TOTAL	100.00	100.00	100.00	100.00	100.00	100.00

Table 12.3 cont.

	The Czech Rep.	Hungary	Poland	Slovenia	Romania	Latvia
			Manufactured products			
51	3.49	3.46	1.85	0.81	2.81	0.31
52	0.95	0.84	1.49	0.77	0.49	0.39
53	1.21	0.13	0.26	0.78	0.04	0.00
54	0.59	0.82	0.36	0.24	0.87	0.44
55	0.11	0.06	0.12	0.26	0.04	0.00
56	0.88	0.18	1.17	0.00	0.71	0.33
57	2.85	4.22	0.71	0.56	1.32	1.81
58	0.41	0.93	0.11	0.40	0.01	0.00
59	0.46	0.94	0.40	0.36	0.33	2.56
61	0.55	0.78	0.85	1.19	0.44	3.06
62	1.53	1.60	1.10	2.22	0.71	0.12
63	2.70	1.48	4.21	4.07	1.05	17.44
64	2.01	1.13	1.53	3.64	0.45	0.52
65	5.90	3.71	2.78	4.50	2.52	12.51
66	9.60	2.76	4.31	2.33	3.13	1.44
67	9.47	4.65	5.62	3.23	7.51	16.29
68	1.45	4.49	9.69	3.97	3.53	0.57
69	7.80	4.61	7.04	4.39	2.10	3.05
71	1.99	1.46	1.10	3.13	1.14	0.45
72	3.87	3.06	1.71	1.80	0.53	1.77
73	1.70	0.48	0.29	0.66	0.56	0.00
74	3.49	3.74	1.90	3.66	2.26	1.55
75	0.67	0.37	0.14	0.21	0.07	0.30
76	0.43	6.26	0.67	0.80	0.17	0.81
77	4.53	12.88	5.51	10.40	3.29	3.34
78	9.73	3.23	7.93	15.35	1.07	1.25
79	1.21	3.38	4.47	0.78	1.66	0.08
81	2.31	1.28	0.62	1.86	0.81	0.49
82	3.75	0.00	8.44	6.01	12.17	9.54
83	0.39	0.00	0.22	0.18	0.37	0.07
84	4.37	17.72	18.91	13.44	35.42	15.34
85	1.70	4.93	1.50	2.23	10.72	2.07
87	0.60	0.95	0.66	2.22	0.19	0.11
88	0.30	0.35	0.02	0.81	0.05	0.00
89	6.99	3.10	2.30	2.73	1.43	2.01
TOTAL	100.00	100.00	100.00	100.00	100.00	100.00

Source: UN Statistical Papers. Commodity Trade Statistics. Series D (Own calculations).

Note: For the SITC code numbers see the Appendix.

industries such as electrical machinery, road vehicles, furniture etc., and clothing account for some significant export activity of CEE countries. If sectors with noticeable shares, such as non-metallic minerals, iron and steel, and metal are added, then the prediction that CEE specialises in products of standardised medium-scale technology is verified. This fact intensifies competition for export market shares, provided that for most of these products markets in advanced countries are saturated and competition is a matter of prices and thus of lower labour costs. To the extent that CEE countries will accelerate their development process and incomes will rise, this type of advantage will erode. This prospect is more potent for the relatively advanced CEE countries, such as the Czech Republic, Hungary, Poland and Slovenia. Consequently, the need for both faster increases in productivity and production diversification is expected to arise soon.

In general, it can be argued that, given the high manufacturing export similarity of the CEE countries and their coming need for production diversification and productivity advances, the dependence of their exporting effort on the conditions of EU markets in terms of incomes, demand patterns and competition from other sources will increase. Needless to say, CEE domestic restructuring strategies will play a critical role, through their success in mobilising, directing and creating local tangible and intangible resources.[8]

Conclusion

This chapter is investigating the similarity of export patterns of the CEE countries by applying the Finger–Kreinin formulae in three groups of commodities: primary products, raw materials and fuels, and manufactured products. With the exception of the second category of commodities, export similarity among the CEE countries seems to be significant and that is expected to stiffen competition for export shares in the EU market, provided that all countries except Latvia show high export intensity in manufacturing goods. In the case of agricultural products competition is stronger among Poland, Hungary and the Czech Republic, which show some export intensity for these products.

Latvia is going to be the country relatively less affected by the entry of Poland, Hungary, the Czech Republic and Slovenia given both its relatively low index values in all commodity groups and its smaller dependence on manufacturing exports. However, the country's raw material exports concentrate on the cork and wood sector at a level of 90.3 per cent where competition exists from almost all the other CEE countries. Romania demonstrates a significant export similarity to all countries eligible for entry in both the primary and manufacturing commodities, and to Hungary in the raw materials and fuels category, mainly in petroleum products. That implies rather stiffer competition for EU market shares, especially after the five CEE countries enter the Union. The commodity base for export similarity is rather narrow in agriculture and raw materials due to considerable export concentration, and more extensive in manufacturing industries.

It should be noted that as the level of disaggregation increases, the degree of export similarity lowers for all countries and product groups. The implication is that export structures differentiate as the level of analysis comes closer to individual commodity base and that decreases the competition intensity between countries for export market shares. A more complete picture of competition structures can be drawn if export similarity calculations are made for specific export markets and not for the total EU market, given that countries have closer commercial links with some individual countries than others, due to tradition, proximity, demand pattern similarity, etc.

However, the Finger–Kreinin formulae gives some insight into competition structures both at country and product level. As the level of aggregation decreases, the information becomes more precise and policy recommendations can be achieved as to what direction diversification of both products and markets should take in order to avoid direct competition with other countries, and thus to increase success in export markets.

Appendix

The SITC third version two-digit level code numbers

Primary products
00 Live animals
01 Meat, meat preparations
02 Dairy products, bird's eggs
03 Fish, crustaceans, molluscs
04 Cereals, cereal preprtns
05 Vegetables and fruit
06 Sugar,sugar preprtns honey
07 Coffee, tea, cocoa, spices
08 Animal feed stuff
09 Misc. edible products etc.
11 Beverages
12 Tobacco, tobacco manufactures
41 Animal oils and fats
42 Fixed veg. fats and oils
43 Animal, veg. fats, oils, nes

Materials and fuels
21 Hides, skins, furskins, raw
22 Oil-seed, oleaginous fruit
23 Crude rubber
24 Cork and wood
25 Pulp and waste paper
26 Textile fibres
27 Crude fertilizer, mineral
28 Metalliferous ore, scrap
29 Crude animal, veg. material
32 Coal, coke, briquettes
33 Petroleum, petrol. product
34 Gas, natural, manufactured
35 Electric current

Manufactured products
51 Organic chemicals
52 Inorganic chemicals
53 Dyes, colouring materials
54 Medicinal, pharm. products
55 Essential oils, perfume, etc.
56 Fertilizer, except grp 272
57 Plastics in primary form
58 Plastic, non-primary form
59 Chemical materials nes
61 Leather, leather goods
62 Rubber manufactures, nes
63 Cork, wood manufactures
64 Paper, paperboard, etc.
65 Textile yarn, fabric, etc.
66 Non-metal. mineral manufactures
67 Iron and steel
68 Non-ferrous metals
69 Metals manufactures, nes
71 Power generating machines
72 Special. indust. machinery
73 Metalworking machinery
74 General indust. machinery
75 Office machines, adp
76 Telecomm. sound equip etc.
77 Elec. mch. apparatus parts, nes
78 Road vehicles
79 Other transport equipment
81 Prefab building, fitting etc
82 Furniture, cushions, etc
83 Trunk, suit-cases, bags, etc
84 Clothing and accessories
85 Footwear
87 Scientific equipment nes
88 Photo. apparat. nes; clocks
89 Misc. manufactured goods nes

Notes

1 For a brief analysis of that issue see Kyrkilis and Nikolaidis (1998).
2 For a presentation of this argument see Rostow (1959), Porter (1990) and Ozawa (1992).
3 For a discussion on the EU–CEE countries bilateral trade see Kyrkilis and Pantelidis (1996a).
4 See Kyrkilis and Pantelidis (1996b).
5 According to the estimations of the European Commisssion, as they are revealed in the Agenda 2000 proposal, the per capita income of Poland, the Czech Republic, Hungary, Slovenia and Estonia as percentage of the EU average is equal to the 31, 55, 37, 59 and 23 per cent respectively, while that for Bulgaria, Lithuania, Latvia, Romania and Slovakia equals the 24, 24, 18, 24, and 41 per cent of the EU average respectively (Slovakia has not become eligible for immediate entry on political and not economic grounds). It is also expected that countries with the higher per capita income, such as Poland, the Czech Republic, Slovenia, or Hungary and under the assumption of an annual growth rate between 4.3 and 4.8 per cent will reach the average EU per capita income in the year 2010.
6 See Grubel and Lloyd (1975).
7 For criticism on the Grubel–Lloyd index see Vona (1991) and Shelburne (1993), and for the Finger–Kreinin index see Pomfret (1981).
8 For some further comments on that issue see Pantelidis and Kyrkilis (1995) and Kyrkilis and Pantelidis (1996a).

References

Finger, J.M. and Kreinin, M.E. (1979) 'A measure of export similarity and its possible uses', *The Economic Journal* 89: 905–12, December.

Grubel, H.G. and Lloyd, P. J. (1975) *Intra-industry Trade*, London: Macmillan.

Kyrkilis, D. and Nikolaidis, E. (1998) 'Trade flows between Greece and Central and Eastern Europe: inter-industry vs. intra-industry trade', *International Review of Economics and Business*, XLV, 1: 139–50.

Kyrkilis, D. and Pantelidis, P. (1996a) 'European Union and Central and Eastern European countries integration, foreign direct investment and international trade', paper presented at the Conference on Problems, Policies and Strategies of CEE Countries towards European Integration, Kracow Academy of Economics, Kracow, 8–10 November.

Kyrkilis, D. and Pantelidis, P. (1996b) 'A model on European Union – Central and Eastern Europe bilateral trade', in Innovation and International Business, Proceedings of the 22nd EIBA Annual Conference, Institute of International Business, Stockholm, 15–17 December.

Ozawa, T. (1992) 'Foreign direct investment and economic development', *Transnational Corporations* 1, 1: 27–54.

Pantelidis, P. and Kyrkilis, D. (1995) 'Foreign direct investment and trade patterns of Eastern European Economies', *Economia Internazionale* XVLIII, 3, August.

Pomfret, R. (1981) 'The impact of EEC enlargement on non-member Mediterranean countries' exports to the EEC', *The Economic Journal* 91: 729–62, September.

Porter, M. (1990) *The Competitive Advantage of Nations*, New York: Free Press.

Rostow, W. (1959) *The Stages of Economic Growth*, London: MacMillan.

Shelburne C.R. (1993) 'Changing trade patterns and the intra-industry trade index: a note', *Weltwirtschaftliches Archiv*, 129: 829–33.

Vona, S. (1991) 'On the measurement of intra-industry trade: some further thoughts', *Weltwirtschaftliches Archiv*, 127: 678–700.

13 Greece and the Balkans

The challenge of integration

George Petrakos and Nikos Christodoulakis

Introduction

It is now beyond any doubt that in the cosmogony of changes that is shaping the new Europe by the interacting forces of integration and transition, the worst performing area in all accounts is the Balkan region. For a number of reasons discussed in the literature (Dobrinsky 1997; Jackson and Petrakos 1999; Petrakos and Christodoulakis 1998; Petrakos and Pitelis 2000; Petrakos and Totev 2000) on the northern Greek borders one meets those paradigms of integration and transition in Europe that face the greatest difficulties and have the weakest performance to this point. On the one side of the borders is Greece, which, despite its recent progress, is one of the weakest EU states and the only country that failed to meet the Maastricht criteria for participation in the first round of the EMU. On the other side of the borders are a heterogeneous group of formerly planned Balkan economies that have experienced an unstable transition path characterised by repeated crises, open conflict and a real divergence from the EU with respect to welfare and development levels. In this context, the Greek economic relations in the Balkans and the future developments in this region present a special analytical and policy-making interest as they concern (a) relations between EU and Central and East European (CEE) countries with an East–West character; that is, important systemic and institutional differences; (b) relations between countries with relatively lower level of development compared to the other EU or CEE countries, respectively; (c) relations between countries that are to varying degrees perimetric with respect to the geographical and economic gravity centre of Europe; and (d) relations between countries that have adjusted in a relatively poor way to the pressures of EU economic integration (Greece) and transition (the other Balkan countries) respectively.

It is clear that the Balkan region is entering the third millennium severely damaged by the Yugoslav conflicts, with many unsolved problems and difficult choices ahead. It is also clear that the countries in the region are now searching for a new less fragile place and a more productive role in the new European space, seeking to cover some of the ground lost in the 1990s. In this context, this chapter intends to explore the options available for both Greece and the other Balkan countries (BCs). In the next section we examine the initial conditions that existed in the BCs in the pre-1989 period and the new conditions in the post-1989 period with respect to structural adjustments and aggregate economic performance, trade relations and regional structures. In the last section we draw our conclusions concerning the policies that are needed in the Balkans in order to successfully overcome the constraints imposed by the new internal and external environment.

The pre-1989 conditions in Greece and the other Balkan countries

Greece was confronted in the post-World War II period with a uniquely unfavourable situation not found anywhere else in Europe. This situation results from the interaction of (a) a peripheral location in South-eastern Europe, away from major markets and the European development centre and (b) distorted economic relations, as the northern borders of the country were, due to the post-war realities, meant to be real barriers to communication and trade with neighbouring countries. This type of 'border condition' where practically the entire continental border-line of the country operated as a barrier to economic and social relations, is a rare situation in the history of international relations.

These two conditions generated an overall unfavourable index of geographic location within the post-war European economic space, with serious long-term implications for the economic structure and performance of the country. The isolation and distance from the European core and the other EU members implied in general limited accessibility of domestic products to large foreign markets that (by definition of the EU) were supposed to be accessible, explaining the low export-to-GDP ratios (Petrakos and Pitelis 2000). In addition, the 'missing factor' in the trade relations with its neighbours generated serious disadvantages. Theoretical and empirical research has shown the importance of geographical factors such as adjacency and proximity in trade relations (Krugman 1994). As a result, it is only natural that the 'missing factor' in the trade relations of Greece has caused a significant reduction in the trade potential of the country, limiting market accessibility for exporting industries and limiting the prospects for export-led growth.

Because of these conditions the trade relations of Greece took on an inter-industry character with the more advanced and distant countries of Western Europe, with a serious impact on the industrial structure of the country. Trade theory indicates (Grimwade 1989) that trade with neighbouring countries is more intensive and usually takes on an intra-industry character, implying greater room for more industries to develop, as international specializations are not mutually exclusive and the division of labour takes place *within* and not *between* sectors.

Therefore, the lack of trade relations with the other Balkan countries pushed Greece further towards an inter-industry type of specialisation with the technologically more advanced Western European countries[1] that was rather unfavourable for the industrial development of the country. In that respect, the post-war 'border conditions' of the country have generated a 'missing factor' in trade relations that in its turn has imposed additional constraints on the already weak structure of the economy. In addition, due to the small size of the country and the lack of accessible markets of a critical size, industrial firms could not benefit from economies of scale. As a result the industrial base of the country became the most fragmented in Europe, with very small firms by international standards (Petrakos and Zikos 1996; Petrakos 1997a) that exacerbated the structural problems of the economy and reduced overall economic efficiency.

Taking into consideration the fact that, due to the ongoing conflict in the Middle East and the Greek-Turkish dispute, Greece lost in this region significant markets in the early 1970s, the operation of these two factors (limited accessibility to European markets and no economic relations with neighbouring countries) may explain some aspects of the Greek economic performance during the last decades. Distance and the 'missing factor' in trade relations may explain, for example, why the dynamism of the economy in the 1950s and the 1960s was exhausted so quickly afterwards, or why the public sector in the 1970s and the 1980s became so popular and so large. As export-led growth was not possible due to limited accessible markets and the predominantly inter-industry structure of trade, the industrial sector unavoidably took on an inward-looking character, became more fragmented, less efficient and of course smaller in size, leaving to the public sector the principal responsibility of absorbing the expanding, due to strong urban migration flows, labour force.

Overall, it is claimed here that the post-World War II and pre-1989 period performance of the Greek economy was affected by the restrictions imposed on the structure and level of the external economic relations of the country by the limitations of geography and the artificial division of Europe into two camps. Although there is no direct empirical evidence to support it, we are confident that a simple spatial trade model would predict for Greece a different level and structure of trade (in terms of its composition by product and origin-destination by country) than the existing one, if barriers to trade with the neighbouring countries had not been imposed.

The post-World War II conditions in the other Balkan countries are in some respects similar to the other CEE countries. Besides the central planning mechanism, a significant distortion in international economic relations took place with an eastward trade orientation within the CMEA block that caused significant trade diversion[2] from traditional partners, including neighbouring countries. In addition, in the pre-1989 period the Balkan socialist countries were politically and ideologically divided, showing an unusually low degree of interaction. Bulgaria was a close ally and trade partner of the Soviet Union, Yugoslavia and Romania were less oriented towards the Soviet bloc and relatively more open to the West, while Albania followed for the most period an autarky strategy that led to economic isolation from the rest of the world. The peculiarity of the Balkan region is that, even within the socialist bloc, economic relations and interaction were very limited in the pre-1989 period (Petrakos and Totev 2000).

Another characteristic of the post-war period in the central planning countries including the Balkans, was a strong reliance on economies of scale and a strong ideological preference for huge industrial plants and mass production. Although this reliance on large-scale enterprises was a reasonable outcome of the international division of labour within the Soviet bloc, it is perhaps a historical accident that it took momentum at a time where the model of mass production and the Fordist-Taylorist types of industrial organisation and growth strategies were in serious crisis and being openly questioned in the West (Piore and Sabel 1984).

While in the 1980s post-Fordist strategies of industrial restructuring and development emphasising flexibility were being discussed or even being implemented in the West, in the East, mass production and vertical division of labour were the dominant trends contributing to the bottlenecks, the inefficiency, the failure and the eventual collapse of the system. In the Balkans this divide was even more evident. On the one hand, Greece has practically never followed the Fordist mode of large-scale mass production, maintaining the smaller average industrial firm size in Europe,[3] while on the other, the BCs in transition experienced an industrial structure based on extremely large firm sizes, even by Western European standards.[4] In addition to that, the command economies in the Balkans followed an industrialisation strategy that laid strong emphasis on the development of heavy industry and led to a total neglect of the light, consumer-oriented industry and the tertiary sector, failing to develop specialisations and branches critical for the development of a modern economy (Petrakos 1997a).

The post-1989 conditions in the Balkans

The recent changes in CEE countries and the Balkans in particular have affected in a fundamental way their economic structure and the geography of trade and economic relations in the region, as well as the prospects for regional co-operation and development. In this section we present and discuss the elements of change that are related to economic performance at the macro level, to structural adjustment at the sectoral level, as well as trade relations, factor mobility and the existing spatial structure of the region. In the next section we discuss the policy implications of the new conditions in the Balkans.

GDP structure and change

Examining the GDP index in Table 13.1 we observe that all transition countries in the Balkans have experienced a deep recession in the post-1989 period.

Table 13.1 GDP and GDP per capita in the Balkan countries and the EU, 1997

Country	*GDP (1989=100)*	*Sectoral GDP Structure Primary*	*Secondary*	*Tertiary*	*GDP per capita (USD)*
Albania	79.13	55.0	22.0	23.0	711
Bosnia					1114
Bulgaria	62.26	10.0	33.0	57.0	1239
Croatia	73.98	12.0	25.0	63.0	3851
FYR of Macedonia	55.33	11.0	25.0	64.0	1494
Greece	110.98	12.0	26.0	62.0	10828
FR of Yugoslavia		27.0	36.1	36.9	1429
Romania	82.44	21.0	40.0	39.0	1521
Slovenia	98.47	5.0	38.0	57.0	8995
EU	110.05	2.4	32.5	65.1	21640

Source: World Bank, World Development Report (1992), (1998).

In 1997 real GDP was equal to 79 per cent of the 1989 level in Albania, 62 per cent in Bulgaria, 73 per cent in Croatia, 55 per cent in FYROM, 82 per cent in Romania, and 98 per cent in Slovenia. The time-path of the recession has not been the same for all countries. Albania, despite its early recovery in 1993, has again sunk into a deep recession after the 1997 economic and political crisis. Bulgaria experienced a second recession in the 1996–7 period, with some signs of stabilisation and growth in 1998 and 1999. Romania, on the other hand, was not able to maintain the 1997 level of output and has experienced a recession in 1998 and 1999. Slovenia and Croatia seem to follow a steady path of recovery after 1993, although the war in Kosovo is very likely to have affected the performance and the short-term prospects of the latter. Finally, FYROM is going through a continuous recession in the entire post-1989 period, which has become deeper because of the Kosovo crisis. Besides FR of Yugoslavia, which has been devastated by the war, it is estimated that the Kosovo crisis has negatively affected growth prospects in all neighbouring countries. As shown in the tables, Greece is the only country in the region that has experienced a positive and significant growth rate of GDP in the 1989–97 period.

In Table 13.1 we present information about the structure of GDP in the EU and the Balkan countries by sector, respectively. A comparison of the figures reveals some important characteristics that need to be evaluated. First, we see that compared to the average EU figures, Greece appears to be a unique case of EU country structurally lagging behind with a share of primary sector equal to 12 per cent of GDP, which is more than four times the EU average. This high dependence on the primary sector is unavoidably followed by one of the lowest shares of secondary and tertiary sectors in GDP in the EU.

Second, this high dependence on the primary sector is a common feature of the Balkan economies that, with the exception of Slovenia, have primary sector shares in GDP that are similar or greater than that of Greece. In addition, comparisons with earlier analysis (Petrakos 1997a; Petrakos and Totev 1999) indicate that a number of countries such as Albania, Romania, FR of Yugoslavia and FYROM, have seen their GDP shares of agriculture increase at various rates in the 1990–7 period.

In general, it can be stated that the direction of change of the primary sector share in GDP is affected by the severity of the industrial restructuring process and the level of development. The greater the decline of the industrial share in GDP, the higher the possibility for the share of primary sector to increase, as the return to land is the last resort for displaced labour to avoid open unemployment. On the other hand, Slovenia has experienced a much lower dependence on agriculture and in that sense has a productive structure similar to that of the advanced CE countries and the EU (Petrakos 1997a). A corollary of this statement is that the more advanced transition economies (with stronger industrial bases) have experienced low and stable or declining shares of primary sector in GDP, while the less advanced transition economies have experienced higher and often increasing shares.

Excluding Slovenia, which has a GDP structure approaching that of the EU,[5] the other Balkan transition countries are approaching the structure of Greece, having a significantly greater dependence on agriculture. This indicates perhaps a north–south divide in CEE countries, with the Balkan countries having a less advanced economic structure than the Central European ones (Petrakos 1997a).

Third, some Balkan transition economies have a GDP share of industry greater than the EU average, indicating that the process of industrial restructuring has not been completed yet. Taking the superiority of Western European industry (especially in R&D and capital-intensive or knowledge-intensive sectors) for granted (Landesmann 1995), one would expect that adjustment to new international standards, restructuring and import penetration, at least in the foreseeable future, will further reduce the industrial share in the Balkan transition economies to below the EU share.

Finally, the relatively lower than the EU average shares of the tertiary sector in the transition economies also reveal that a certain amount of resources is still employed in industry by virtue of the various protection schemes and devices that serve as a buffer to unemployment until a sustainable strategy of development is formulated and implemented. Although the increase of the tertiary sector's share in GDP in transition economies is very impressive, its composition is by no means similar to that of the average EU country. Instead of a strong presence of banking, financial and business services highly interacting with industry, as well as activities related to culture, amenity, civilisation and leisure or personal services, one would more commonly meet in transition economies a tertiary sector dominated by non-tradable activities such as retail trade and an overmanned public sector. Although there are certain important differences, this structure retains some aspects of the internationalisation–tertiarisation process in Southern Europe and especially in Greece.

In Table 13.1 we present GDP per capita figures for 1997. We observe that even before the recent crisis in Kosovo, the level of welfare and development in the region was significantly lower and diverging from that of the EU. GDP per capita in USD in Albania is less than 4 per cent of the GDP per capita of the EU, while the same figure for Bulgaria, Bosnia, FR Yugoslavia, FYROM and Romania is in the range of 5–7 per cent of the EU. Croatia and especially Slovenia differentiate from the other transition countries with figures close to 18 per cent and 42 per cent of the EU, respectively. Overall, the Balkan transition countries had in 1997 a GDP per capita level (1825 US dollars) that was less than 9 per cent of the GDP per capita of the EU. This figure, which is expected to be lower in 1999, due to the war in Kosovo, is less than half the average GDP per capita of the Central European countries in transition (3,383 US dollars). If one excludes Greece and Slovenia, in the 1990s the other countries in the region have experienced continuous or repeated economic and political crises. This process seems to resemble a vicious cycle that seems more and more difficult to break without external intervention and assistance.

Trade relations of Greece in the Balkans

The geographical composition of Greek trade in the Balkans[6] has changed significantly in the 1989–97 period. The Balkan share of Greek exports has increased from 3.16 per cent in 1989 to 11.43 per cent in 1997, while the Balkan share of the volume of trade (exports and imports) has increased from 2.72 per cent in 1989 to 5.58 per cent in 1997. Clearly, the 1997 figures would have been much higher than the ones presented in the absence of the wars in former Yugoslavia and the embargoes imposed in the area. As a result of the transition process and the severe structural difficulties in the Balkan countries, their share in total Greek imports has increased less than the export figures in the same period.

Although in 1989 Yugoslavia was the most significant trading partner of Greece in the Balkans, because of the embargoes and the war, this picture has now changed considerably. Bulgaria[7] appears to be in 1997 the most important trading partner of Greece in the Balkans followed by FYROM,[8] Albania[9] and Romania[10] while trade with the other new states in the territory of former Yugoslavia was until 1997 virtually non-existent. Examining the export and import shares of Greece with Albania, Bulgaria and Romania (the three countries with trade relations uninterrupted by the war) we can see the impact of factors such as country (and market) size, distance and non-economic preference factors on trade relations. Clearly the adjacency and proximity factors explain the higher shares of Bulgaria and Albania, compared to that of Romania, in total Greek trade, while the size and the capacity of the market explain the higher share of Bulgaria compared to that of Albania. Other factors, such as religious or historical ties, the existence of minorities and various types of implemented policies of external

Table 13.2 The geographical composition of Greek trade in the Balkans, 1989–97

	Exports		*Imports*		*VOT*	
	1989	*1997*	*1989*	*1997*	*1989*	*1997*
Balkans	3.16	11.43	2.50	3.17	2.72	5.58
EU	65.20	49.81	64.72	62.58	64.88	58.85
World	100.00	100.00	100.00	100.00	100.00	100.00

Source: Petrakos (1997b) and National Hellenic Exporters Association database.

Table 13.3 The evolution of Greek trade with the Balkans, the EU and the world, 1989–97

	Exports		*Imports*		*Volume of trade*	*Balance of trade*	*Exports/imports*
year	*index*	*share*	*index*	*share*	*index*	*value*	
Trade of Greece with the Balkans, 1989–97							
1989	100.00	3.16	100.00	2.50	100.00	–144627	0.62
1990	129.67	3.88	121.09	2.41	124.39	–154623	0.67
1991	144.16	3.98	119.03	2.21	128.68	–112043	0.75
1992	163.31	3.96	83.30	1.41	114.02	70872	1.22
1993	289.60	8.21	85.85	1.60	164.07	363090	2.10
1994	314.11	8.00	121.42	2.23	195.40	285189	1.61
1995	420.63	9.18	186.73	2.76	276.52	289275	1.40
1996	519.83	10.48	184.67	2.47	313.34	534417	1.75
1997	529.98	11.43	222.02	3.17	340.25	415338	1.49
Trade of Greece with the EU, 1989–97							
1989	100.00	65.20	100.00	64.72	100.00	–4998360	0.50
1990	103.12	63.73	127.04	65.55	119.10	–7532522	0.40
1991	111.41	63.51	129.47	62.36	123.47	–7363539	0.43
1992	130.49	65.39	147.36	64.56	141.76	–8199406	0.44
1993	95.48	55.95	132.52	63.96	120.22	–8454041	0.36
1994	102.59	54.03	138.92	66.19	126.86	–8739338	0.37
1995	127.67	57.56	173.77	66.61	158.46	–10964025	0.37
1996	123.69	51.51	177.88	61.63	159.88	–11568868	0.35
1997	111.78	49.81	169.25	62.58	150.17	–11299493	0.33
Total trade of Greece, 1989–97							
1989	100.00	100.00	100.00	100.00	100.00	–7780578	0.49
1990	105.51	100.00	125.43	100.00	118.84	–11268527	0.42
1991	114.38	100.00	134.35	100.00	127.75	–11967531	0.42
1992	130.12	100.00	147.73	100.00	141.91	–12828412	0.43
1993	111.28	100.00	134.08	100.00	126.55	–12161013	0.41
1994	123.82	100.00	135.83	100.00	131.86	–11478478	0.45
1995	144.62	100.00	168.82	100.00	160.83	–14969591	0.42
1996	156.57	100.00	186.79	100.00	176.81	–16824536	0.41
1997	146.34	100.00	175.03	100.00	165.55	–15792430	0.41

Source: Petrakos (1997b) and National Hellenic Exporters Association.

Note: Share means %.

relations have certainly affected in various ways the level and the growth rate of trade between Greece and the other Balkan countries (Petrakos 1997b).

As we can see in Table 13.2, in the period 1989–97 the share of Greek exports that go to the rest of the EU countries has declined significantly from 65.22 per cent to 49.8 per cent. In the same period the share of Greek imports that come from the rest of the EU countries has remained relatively stable. As a result, in the 1989–97 period we have two opposite trends with respect to the geographical distribution of Greek trade relations. On the one hand we observe the declining performance of Greek products in the EU markets, as indicated by falling exports and relatively stable imports shares and on the other, the improving performance of Greek products in the Balkan markets, indicated by increasing export and relatively stable import shares. These differences in performance are certainly very important and will be examined in more detail in the next sections.

The evolution of Greek trade in the Balkans

The evolution of Greek trade with the BCs is given in Table 13.3. From the examination of the data we observe that the value of Greek exports to the BCs in US dollars has increased in the period 1989–97 by 429 per cent, accounting in 1997 for 11,43 per cent of total Greek exports. This indicates a major development in the structure of Greek exports in a short period of time when compared to the 1989 figure. This impressive increase comes in at a period when Greek exports to the EU have been almost constant in dollar value but declining as a share to total exports. This development indicates the declining competitiveness of Greek products in the EU markets, which is partly attributed to the structural difficulties of Greek industry (Petrakos and Zikos 1996) and partly to the strength of the drachma. The latter is the outcome of anti-inflationary policies applied in accordance with the convergence criteria of Maastricht. As far as total Greek exports are concerned a positive change (+46 per cent) is recorded in the 1989–97 period.

Interestingly, the Greek imports from the BCs as a whole have increased by 122 per cent in the 1989–97 period, an impressive figure if one considers the conflict in former Yugoslavia and the embargoes imposed in the region. As a result the share of Greek imports from the BCs has increased from 2.5 per cent in 1989 to 3.17 per cent in 1997.

The volume and balance of trade and the export/import ratios

As a result of the expansion of exports and imports of Greece with the BCs, the volume of trade (VOT) increased by 240 per cent in the 1989–97 period. The magnitude of this increase can be better appreciated if compared to the 50 per cent and 65 per cent increase in the Greek VOT with the EU and the rest of the world, respectively. This explosive expansion of trade indicates that the economic, geographical, historical, cultural or other factors in operation favour cross-border interaction and trade in the area. As expected due to the difficulties of the transition process, but also due to the conflict in the territory of former Yugoslavia, Greece has increased its exports faster than its imports. As a result, its balance of trade (BOT) in the period 1989–97 has turned from negative to positive in the case of trade with the BCs.

The export/import ratio measures the degree of relative penetration of a foreign market by Greek products. Looking at the export/import ratio in Table 13.3, we see first, the Greek export/import ratio with the BCs has turned from smaller than one to greater than one. Second, the Greek export/import ratio with the EU has dropped from 0.50 in 1989 to 0.33 in 1997, indicating that for each dollar of imports from the EU, Greece manages to export to the EU countries products worth only $0.33. Similarly, and to a certain extent, affected by the relative weight of the Greek–EU trade, the export/import ratio of Greece with the rest of the world has declined from 0.49 in 1989 to 0.41 in 1997.

The observations made above indicate that in the post-1989 period two processes different in direction take place, with respect to Greek performance in international markets. On the one hand, there is the deteriorating position of Greek exports in the EU and world markets and on the other hand, there is a successful in all terms, export performance in the neighbouring Balkan countries. Interpreting these facts, it becomes obvious that the competitiveness of the Greek economy in the EU and world markets is quite low and declining, while its competitiveness in the Balkan countries is at high levels and increasing. Although higher competitiveness in the Balkans is certainly affected by the difficulties of transition in these countries, the fact remains that Greece has managed to improve its overall export performance in the region while other Southern European countries have not.

It is also interesting to observe that despite the existence of the single European market and the fact that Greek products do not face any barriers, their ability to penetrate the EU market is lower, compared to Balkan and world markets, where certain barriers to trade exist. This may be an indication of the difficulties of integration among basically unequal partners and the fact that the qualitative standards of the EU market are higher and more difficult to meet than that of the world (and certainly the Balkan) markets. It may also be an indication that geography is, after all, an important factor that affects the trade performance of a country.

Sectoral trends in the trade of Greece with the BCs

Besides the examination of the evolution of exports, imports, export/import ratios and the VOT, a question that frequently arises is related to the sectoral structure and composition of trade between two countries. The issues usually examined are those of inter-industry or intra-industry specialisation, that is whether two countries tend to specialise and trade products that belong to different industries or tend to trade products within the same industry more intensively. The first is known as inter-industry or Heckscher–Ohlin (H–O) type of trade, while the second as intra-industry type of trade (IIT).

The standard international trade theory has shown that in the case of H–O type of trade, where countries specialise in different products and then exchange them, there are well-defined welfare gains for them, known as gains from specialisation and gains from exchange (Caves and Johnes 1981). H–O types of relations, however, have also been criticised as suitable only for countries with comparable levels of development. This is because in the case of trade between a developed and a developing country, the second will necessarily specialise in labour-intensive or resource-intensive products, missing the opportunity to industrialise and therefore missing the opportunity to develop. Also the H–O type of trade relations are considered to cause, in several cases, severe adjustments to the productive base of a country as some sectors shrink and some others expand, a process that is not always free from social friction.

On the other hand, trade within the same industry is usually associated with welfare gains (Greenway and Milner 1986; Grimwade 1989) to the extent that consumer preference functions have an additive form, that is, consumers derive more satisfaction when offered a greater selection of similar products. IIT is not associated with major structural adjustment (as adjustment takes place within the industry or even within the firm) and it usually characterises neighbouring countries with similar levels of development and similar tastes.

IIT is also often used as a measure of economic integration (Grimwade 1989). That is, the higher the level of IIT between two countries, the greater the similarities in their productive bases, the more homogeneous their consumer preferences and therefore the greater the degree of economic integration. On the other hand, the higher the level of H–O type of trade between two countries, the higher the possibility of having dissimilar productive bases and development levels.

In Table 13.4 we present sectoral data for the trade of Greece with the BCs and EU, as well as total trade by one-digit International Standard Trade Classification (ISTC) categories. The first observation in Table 13.4 is that the Greek exports to the BCs are more evenly distributed to sectors than exports to the rest of the EU countries. In the case of BCs, seven sectors have significant shares close to or greater than 10 per cent of total exports to the region. In the case of EU, however, three sectors concentrate more than 70 per cent of Greek exports. Turning to Greek imports, we see that differences in sectoral structures among the BCs and the EU are less important.

Measures of Revealed Comparative Advantage (RCA)

In an attempt to further analyse the 1-digit SITC data of Greek trade with the BCs, we have estimated in Table 13.5 the sectoral coefficients of Revealed Comparative Advantage (RCA) for the Greek exports to the BCs and the EU. The RCA coefficients are measured as a share of a sector's *i* exports to a country *j*, divided by the share of sector's *i* total exports {RCA = $(Xij/Xj)/(Xi/X)$}.

Table 13.4 Greek trade with the Balkans, the EU and the world by one-digit SITC sector, 1989–97

Greek exports		*Balkans* *1989–97*	*1989–97*	*EU* *1989–97*	*1989–97*	*World* *1989–97*	*1989–97*
SITC	*Sectors*	*value in '000 US $*	*(% structure)*	*value in '000 US $*	*(% structure)*	*value in '000 US $*	*(% structure)*
0	Food and live animals	1215548	19.5	11350802	22.8	16654640	19.4
1	Beverages and tobacco	537972	8.6	2038757	4.1	4994466	5.8
2	Crude materials inedible	557740	8.9	2676984	5.4	5259930	6.1
3	Mineral fuels, etc.	1007885	16.1	1252699	2.5	6564059	7.6
4	Animal, vegetable oils, fats	46713	0.7	3485501	7.0	3851016	4.5
5	Chemicals, etc.	400170	6.4	1489025	3.0	3930089	4.6
6	Manuf. goods, classified by mat.	1051903	16.8	10533399	21.2	18513357	21.6
7	Machinery and transp. equip.	664678	10.6	2380038	4.8	5367990	6.3
8	Misc.manufactured articl.	729251	11.7	13521071	27.2	18985845	22.1
9	Commod. not elsewhere clas.	32554	0.5	989033	2.0	1719271	2.0
0–9	Total	6244414	100.0	49717310	100.0	85840664	100.0
Greek imports							
0	Food and live animals	564207	11.8	20344567	15.7	24975264	12.2
1	Beverages and tobacco	15048	0.3	3460733	2.7	3966207	1.9
2	Crude materials inedible	418017	8.8	2223623	1.7	7720805	3.8
3	Mineral fuels, etc.	397398	8.3	1118820	0.9	18252995	8.9
4	Animal, vegetab. oils, fats	11148	0.2	638545	0.5	837784	0.4
5	Chemicals, etc.	645181	13.5	18418893	14.3	24109371	11.8
6	Manuf. goods, class. by mat.	1859075	39.0	26332541	20.4	39344860	19.2
7	Machinery and transp. equip.	492006	10.3	40648400	31.5	62980116	30.7
8	Misc. manufactured articl.	368795	7.7	15820967	12.2	22290692	10.9
9	Commod. not elsewhere clas.	99	0.0	225548	0.2	502513	0.2
0–9	Total	4770975	100.0	129232638	100.0	204980608	100.0

Source: Petrakos (1997b) and own estimates from the Hellenic Exporters Association database.

Table 13.5 The coefficient of Revealed Comparative Advantage (RCA) for Greek trade with the Balkans and the EU

RCA sectors	*Balkans 1989–97*	*EU 1989–97*
0	1.00	**1.18**
1	**1.48**	0.70
2	**1.46**	0.88
3	**2.11**	0.33
4	0.17	**1.56**
5	**1.40**	0.65
6	0.78	0.98
7	**1.70**	0.77
8	0.53	**1.23**
9	0.26	0.99
TOTAL	1.00	1.00

Source: Petrakos (1997b) and own estimates from the Hellenic Exporters Association database.

A value of RCA coefficient greater than one (RCA > 1) in a sector, indicates a better exporting performance than average and therefore a specialisation and a possible comparative advantage (CA).

From the examination of Table 13.5 we can see first, that Greek exports to the Balkan countries appear to have a CA in sectors 1 (beverages and tobacco), 2 (crude materials), 3 (fuels), 5 (chemicals) and 7 (machinery and transportation equipment). Second, these specialisations appear to be complementary to that developed with the EU where Greece appears to have a CA in sectors 0 (food), 4 (oils and fats) and 8 (miscellaneous manufacturing articles). Therefore, on the basis of one-digit ISTC data, Greece appears to have a potential CA in more sectors when trading with the BCs than when trading with EU countries. This observation is also verified from the analysis of two-digit ISTC data (Petrakos 1999).

This analysis reveals two points with significant long-term implications for the trade relations of Greece. First, it indicates that Greece has developed its trade in the Balkans in such a way that more sectors can take the opportunity and expand their activities because of trade, finding a CA in a new market that was not available before. Second, Greece appears to have CA in more sectors when trading with its Balkan neighbours, than when trading with the other EU members.

Measures of Intra-Industry Trade (IIT)

As discussed earlier, measures of IIT are usually estimated in an attempt to find the share of the total trade of a country with another country or a group of countries that takes place within sectors (rather than between sectors). On the basis of these estimates, conclusions can be drawn about the existing type of trade relations, with all the implications about the structure and the required adjustments in the production base, as well as the type and

Table 13.6 The Intra-Industry Trade (IIT) coefficient for Greek trade with the Balkans, the EU and world (one-digit SITC sectors)

Sectors	*Balkans 1989–97*	*EU 1989–97*	*World 1989–97*
0	63	72	80
1	5	74	89
2	86	91	81
3	57	94	53
4	39	31	36
5	77	15	28
6	72	57	64
7	85	11	16
8	67	92	92
9	1	37	45
TOTAL	68	51	55

Source: Petrakos (1997b) and own estimates from the Hellenic Exporters Association database.

the strength of the ongoing process of economic integration. Table 13.6 presents IIT coefficients for Greek trade by one-digit SITC sectors with the BCs, EU and total trade, estimated from the standard Grubel–Lloyd (1975) equation.

From the examination of the data we see that for the entire 1989–97 period, 68 per cent of the Greek–Balkan, 51 per cent of the Greek-EU and 55 per cent of the total Greek trade was of an intra-industry character, that is trade within (1-digit SITC) sectors. The trade of Greece with the BCs is characterised by a higher IIT coefficient. About two-thirds of the Greek–BCs trade takes place within industries in the 1989–97 period, while only a little more than half of the Greek–EU trade takes place within sectors.

Similar findings based on two-digit ISTC data are reported by Petrakos (1999). Although the IIT coefficients based on two-digit data are (as expected) lower, the general picture is maintained. In the 1990–7 period, Greece had 42 per cent of its trade with the BCs and 32 per cent of its trade with the EU taking place within two-digit sectors. Paradoxically, the IIT figure for the Greek–EU trade is consistently lower than that for Greece–Balkan countries and total Greek trade. To the extent that the IIT coefficient is an indication of economic integration, this means that seventeen years of membership in the EU (EC), have not brought the Greek economy closer to the EU than the World economy, since Greek–EU trade relations basically retain an inter-industry character. This type of integration is probably explained by the large distance (and the lack of adjacency) separating Greece from the other EU members (Petrakos and Zikos 1996) as well as the significant Greek deviations from the production structure of the average EU country (Petrakos and Pitelis 1999).

These figures also indicate that the Greek trade relations in the Balkans have a greater intra-industry component than the Greek–EU or the total Greek trade relations. Proximity, similar consumer preferences and tastes, or the technology level and the requirements of the two markets probably explain this fact. Although it is rather early to draw any firm conclusions and further examination of this issue is certainly necessary, it seems that this development in Greek–Balkan trade relations has two significant implications.

First, it allows for the expansion of economic relations in a sectorally more diversified manner, without exerting pressure for a strict H–O type of specialisation that would perhaps require severe structural adjustments in the Balkan region. This leaves some room to restructuring policies in order to reorganise productive resources *within* sectors, maintaining existing specialisations and avoiding major sectoral shifts of resources that could generate structural unemployment and reduce the diversity of the production base. Second, it offers Greece the missing component in its trade relations, that is cross-border trade of a strong intra-industry character that would balance and ameliorate the implications of the existing inter-industry type of specialisation and trade with the distant EU markets.

Factor mobility between Greece and the other Balkan countries

Cross-border labour mobility in the Balkan region

Besides trade relations that imply cross-border flows of goods and services, another important characteristic of the level of interaction between different countries is the level and the direction of production factor flows. It can be stated that factor mobility in the Greek–Albanian and Greek–Bulgarian borders has followed, in general terms, the predictions of a simple neo-classical model applied for transition economies. Under the pressure imposed on labour markets and labour relations by the transition and restructuring process, intensive labour emigration has been recorded, mainly in Albania but also in Bulgaria, while capital has followed the opposite route, flowing into these countries from various directions, to various destinations and rates.

Cross-border labour migration from Albania to Greece has been much more massive, persistent and mostly illegal, (although in most of the period with the tolerance of the Greek state). Estimations of the level of migration range, depending on the source, from 300,000 to 400,000 people. This number increases during the summer months, when border crossing is easier and decreases during the winter. A small portion of this number enters Greece with a tourist visa (usually for a month) which is violated, since most of the visa holders stay either for a longer period of time or permanently. The rest of them cross the borders illegally in remote mountainous sites.

On the other hand, labour migration from Bulgaria to Greece has been much less and it is estimated at about 50,000 people mostly concentrated in Northern Greece. The Bulgarian migrants are in fact long-term commuters that stay for a few months in Greece with a tourist visa and ‘bend’ the rules probably with the ‘understanding’ or the tolerance of the state. Most of them work in the fields having rather stable contacts with employers in Northern Greece. A very small number of them obtain a work permit.

Overall, there are estimated to be more than 500,000 migrants in Greece from the former Socialist countries. Besides Albanians (that are by far the majority) and Bulgarians, migrants from Romania, Poland, former Soviet Union and former Yugoslavia are found in significant numbers in Greece. In general, it can be claimed that the relatively homogeneous and mono-cultural Greek society has reacted to the shock of the new post-1989 conditions of population inflows from other Balkan countries in a relatively modest way. Anti-migration, racist or ultra-nationalist movements are marginal and have very limited influence on public opinion which seems to consider migration flows as an unavoidable by-product of an overall positive development (the transition process) in the region.

Despite fears of labour displacement in a period where unemployment is rising in Greece, there are no official reports or documentation providing any evidence in support of that allegation. On the contrary, sporadic reports in the press indicate that the migrants have been absorbed in the informal sector of the economy (irregular or sporadic work, repairs, painting, housekeeping, gardening, hauling, construction, etc.) or in the fields where in several cases, their assistance has been gratefully acknowledged by the farmers.

While a significant number of migrants (legal and illegal) consider their stay in Greece as permanent, another (perhaps larger) group of them consists in fact of long-distance commuters in a continuous, but irregular, in-and-out of the country motion. Incomes and remittances from Albanian migrants in Greece are estimated to be a significant supplement to the disposable income of Albania. Over time, labour mobility is expected to have beneficial effects for the entire region. Migration reduces the pressure on limited production resources in Albania and Bulgaria, while in Greece, given the dual structure of the economy, labour immigration has resulted in cost related advantages and has rather improved the competitiveness of several sectors of the economy.

Greek–Balkan capital mobility

Following the predictions of a simple West–East neo-classical model of capital flows, inward FDI in transition economies has increased significantly, but in a geographically unbalanced way. Recent data compiled by the Economist Intelligent Unit for the period 1990–7 indicates that the Balkan countries in transition have managed to attract only 13.5 per cent of cumulative FDI going to Central and East European Countries. On the other hand, the Visegrad countries have managed to attract 86.5 per cent of the FDI directed in the CEE region (Petrakos and Christodoulakis 1998). Most FDI flows originate from EU countries, with Germany (by far the largest), The Netherlands, France and Italy being the most significant investors. This geographical pattern is expected to continue in the future, driven by cultural and geographical proximity, access to large markets, economic recovery and political stability (Colis *et al.* 1997; UNCTAD 1996). Should this be the case, the Balkan transition countries will only marginally benefit from the west–east flows of capital in the post-transition period.

One positive and significant factor that offsets some of the consequences of the weak prospects of the Balkan transition countries with respect to FDI, is the rapidly increasing presence of Greek outward investment in the region. Although Greece until recently was more a host to FDI than an investing country, it is estimated that in the post-transition period Greek firms have invested more than 1 billion US dollars in the region (Petrochilos 1997). Despite the dominance of hundreds of small Greek firms investing in the area (that, however, increase economic and social mobility in Greece), a significant number of large projects have also been present in virtually all sectors of economic activity. As a result, Greece appears to be a serious investor in the Balkan region, ranking in the top-four position in Albania, Bulgaria and FYROM in terms of its share in the total invested foreign capital.

Again here, the role of geography (adjacency and proximity) seems to be a decisive factor affecting the allocation of Greek investment in the region. Greek investors select more often as a host country Albania, Bulgaria (and with an increasing frequency FYROM) than the more distant Romania. Within each country, however, spatial investment patterns differ. In Albania the majority of Greek investment is located close to the Greek borders and in an area with a significant presence of the Greek minority. This geographical pattern is explained by the convenience of a Greek-speaking population, the incentives provided by the Greek investment law and the re-exporting character of many activities (Petrakos 1996b). In Bulgaria the spatial pattern is different, as the majority of Greek investment is located in the metropolitan area of Sofia, taking advantage of the largest and more developed domestic market. Nevertheless, a significant (and perhaps increasing) share of investment is taking place near the Greek borders. To the extent that market dynamics and local or national policies result in an increasing presence of cross-border type of investment, this may improve the development prospects of the border regions. This may have a significant long-term impact on the regional patterns of development, as due to the post-war realities and the multiple divisions in the Balkans, border regions have been the least developed in all countries (Petrakos 1996b, 1997c).

According to official sources, Petrakos (1996b) and Rizopoulos (1997), the level of Greek FDI in Albania in 1997 amounted to 52 million US dollars. This figure represents 40 per cent of the total capital invested in Albania, putting Greece second in the list of foreign investors after Italy and before Austria, Germany and the USA.

Until now, more than 600 foreign firms have been located in Albania, of which 200 are of Greek interests. Several of these enterprises have received financial assistance (grants) from the Greek State (Ministry of National Economy) under the provisions of the (amended) Greek Investment Law.

The average size of these investments is small to modest and in the great majority (93 per cent) represent new enterprises with an Albanian partner. Only 5–7 per cent of Greek investment concerns existing enterprises that have been privatised.

Information on the sectoral composition of Greek investment activity in Albania indicates first that the bulk of the Greek investment in Albania is concentrated in the secondary sector (food, textiles, clothing and tobacco industries), which make up 91.7 per cent of the total capital invested by Greek firms. Another 7 per cent of investment goes to the primary sector (agriculture and aquaculture), while the tertiary sector attracts very limited investment activity (1.3 per cent of total) The overwhelming majority of Greek investment projects are concentrated in labour-intensive industrial activities, indicating the importance of the labour cost factor in the decision to invest in Albania and revealing a re-exporting nature of these activities.

The total stock of foreign direct investment in Bulgaria in 1997 is estimated to be equal to 1,200 million US dollars. In terms of the country of origin of investment, first is Germany, followed by Switzerland, Greece, Belgium, the Netherlands and the USA. Greece, although third in terms of invested capital, takes first place in terms of the number of enterprises with about 1,000 or 20 per cent of the total number. The level of invested Greek capital in Bulgaria at the end of 1997 was 120 million US dollars. The largest share of Greek enterprises (47 per cent) are joint ventures with a domestic firm, which in almost all cases is a private one, a small share (5–7 per cent) represents privatised state firms and the rest is entirely Greek-owned (and usually very small) enterprises.

Detailed sectoral data for foreign investment activity in Bulgaria are unfortunately not available from official sources. From unofficial sources, a sample of 283 Greek enterprises operating in Bulgaria and a survey of the Greek economic press, we have estimated that the majority of Greek firms in Bulgaria are active in the fields of trade and commerce. There is also a significant share of Greek enterprises active in Business Services (business advisors, tax and legal consulting, market research, etc.), while some activity is also found in transportation and travel. The industrial firms, that are the largest in terms of capital invested, are mainly concentrated in the food and drink industries. The investments by Delta (dairy products and ice cream), 3E and Athens Brewery (beers and bottling) are among the largest made by foreign firms in Bulgaria. Noticeable (and very crucial for the other Greek activities) is the presence of Greek banks in Bulgaria. Xiosbank was the first foreign bank permitted in Bulgaria, followed soon by Egnatia Bank, Ionian Bank, Macedonia & Thrace Bank, National Bank of Greece and Agricultural Bank. Other Greek banks such as the Industrial Bank and the Commercial Bank are expected to get an operation permit in the near future.

Finally, in Romania about 1,500 Greek enterprises were established in 1997, with activities in commerce, industry (food, clothes and footwear, wood, furniture, and chemicals), construction, transportation and tourism.

The total stock of Greek foreign direct investment in Romania is equal to 70 million US dollars, putting Greece in the 11th place in the list of foreign investors in the country.

Overall, in terms of capital flows, Greece appears to be a serious investor in the Balkan region, ranking second in Albania, third in Bulgaria and 11th in Romania in terms of its share in the total invested foreign capital. Recent developments seem to further strengthen its position, as Greece has undertaken in the 1998–9 period large-scale investment projects in public utilities in the Balkans. Examples of this investment activity are the acquisition of the Telecommunication Organisations in Serbia and Bulgaria and the largest oil refinery in FYROM. As the situation in the territory of former Yugoslavia stabilises, it is estimated that a strong attraction force will be exerted on Greek firms to invest in the region. All other factors in the region remaining constant, Greek capital inflows to the Balkan region will continue in larger scale and scope, while labour outflows will gradually diminish and cease. The larger and faster the inflows of capital, the more likely it is that labour outmigration will stop.

The regional geography of development in the Balkans

The analysis of the economic characteristics of neighbouring countries requires in most cases a geographical perspective and the examination of their spatial economic structure, in order to detect differences or similarities in the existing development patterns. This is particularly important in our case, considering that the existing geographical distribution of activities in the Balkan countries, their location, concentration or dispersion have probably been affected by the fact that borders acted as real barriers to economic and social relations for decades. Given that development and economic cooperation are a geographically determined process (Krugman 1994; Petrakos 1996b), influenced by factors such as distance, proximity, agglomeration economies, critical market size, etc., it can be asserted that the post-World War II artificial division of the Balkan economic space has negatively affected all countries in the region.

A recent study (Petrakos 1996b) examines the spatial dynamics of Albania, Bulgaria and Greece on the basis of demographic and economic indicators, land resources and level of infrastructure at NUTS II level and depicts, in broad lines, the existing spatial pattern of development in each country. It concludes that in the three countries the most dynamic part of economic activity is concentrated in limited geographical development areas that include (and start from) the metropolitan area and take the form of a development axis.

In the case of Albania, the development axis includes (mainly) Tirana and extends along the Adriatic Sea coastal region, down to the Greek–Albanian borders. The Bulgarian development axis extends in a parallel mode to the River Danube and the Greek–Bulgarian borders from Sofia to the Black Sea coast, including important cities like Plovdiv, Varna and Burgas. Finally the Greek development axis starts from Athens and extends to Thessaloniki, including the major cities in the intermediate zone, with weak extensions to Patras (southwest) and Kavala (northeast) (see Map 13.1).

Another study of the regional structure of Romania (Anton *et al.* 1996) indicates that the southeastern region is the more densely populated part of the country with important industrial cities such as Bucharest, Costantza and Craiova, although large centres such as Timisoara (in the west), Brasov (centre) and Iasi (in the northeast) are scattered throughout the country. Although it seems that Romania has a relatively balanced territorial structure, it is possible to identify a formation of development centres starting from the southeastern part of the country and extending to the western, leaving out many less developed regions in the central and northern part.

Finally, in the territory of former Yugoslavia, a north–south pattern of development was present for most of the post-war period (Kukar 1996), with

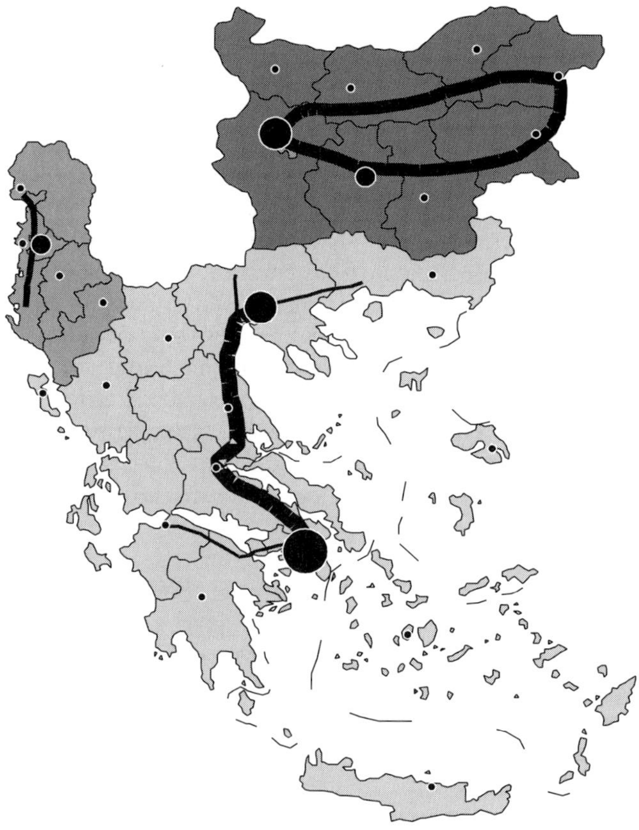

Map 13.1 Development axes of Albania, Bulgaria and Greece.
Source: Petrakos (1997c).

the northern part of the country having a twice as high level of development compared to the country as a whole. Here a development axis with a rather northwest orientation, connecting Belgrade with Zagreb and Ljubliana is clearly identified, with weak extensions to Skopje and Serajevo.

Overall, available evidence (Anton *et al.* 1996; Minassian and Totev 1996; Petrakos 1996b; Petrakos 1997c) indicates that capital regions have a higher share of employment in the tertiary sector and a better mix of activities. On the other hand, regions outside the development axes and regions at the borders either depend on the primary sector as in the case of Albania and Greece, or are excessively dependent on a secondary sector burdened with serious restructuring problems. These spatial differences in sectoral specialisations are expected to intensify regional disparities with the process of transition. In addition, the spatial dynamics in the Balkan countries with respect to the development process, has left in several cases (including the Greek–Albanian and the Greek–Bulgarian frontiers) a wide stripe of border land with lower levels of economic activity and development.

Analysing the Balkan peninsula as a European macro-region (Petrakos 1997c), a strange but also interesting observation can be made that national development axes do not meet or cross anywhere. The Greek axis is vertical with an eastward orientation ('looking' at the Aegean Sea) since it covers the eastern part of the country, the Albanian axis is also vertical, but with a westward orientation ('looking' at the Adriatic Sea) since it is in the western part of the country, the Bulgarian axis is horizontal, with an orientation towards the Black Sea countries, while the Yugoslavian axis has been (even before fragmentation) relatively distant. Neither common orientation nor a point of interaction exists among existing axes of development in the Balkans. It looks as if for each one of them the others simply do not exist, which is an indication that existing axes have grown independently from each other for a long period of time. In a geographic region with no major territorial barriers, this fact, which can only be explained by the interruption of social and economic relations imposed on these countries by the post-World War II realities, is seriously affecting the prospects for regional cooperation and development.

Policy implications and conclusion

After some forty years of separation by military blocks a large regional market of 70 million people in South-eastern Europe has taken shape, including Greece (a EU member), Albania, Bulgaria, Romania and the territory of ex-Yugoslavia, where significant opportunities for co-operation, specialisation and trade exist. To the extent that geography plays a role in shaping preferences in economic interaction (something clearly evident by the bulk and type of relations between countries in Northwestern Europe), a regional market will gradually emerge in the Balkans, driven by distance (of the countries in the region from the European core), size and proximity (to each other). The main characteristic of this new market is the existence of intensive economic relations, especially between bordering countries.

To the extent that the ethnic-territorial arrangements in Yugoslavia have a permanent character, and taking into consideration that most Balkan transition countries are found to be in relatively early stages of accumulation, a long period of recovery may start now if domestic and international conditions become more favourable. With a population of 68 million people (18 per cent of the EU population), the Balkan region represents a substantial regional market with increasing demand for all types of goods and services and significant opportunities for intra-regional economic co-operation.

Available statistics indicate that the basic characteristic of the Greek–Balkan trade relations is the fast expansion of the volume of trade, a relatively high diversification in sectoral specializations and a relatively high share of IIT compared to the figures of Greek trade with the EU and the world. This implies that from the efficiency point of view, Greece could seek an integration process parallel in nature and complementary to that with the EU, based on the advantages generated by geographic and other non-economic preference factors, as well as the needs of the Balkan neighbours that have accrued from the transition process.

Factor mobility is also expected have long-term beneficial effects for the entire region. Migration reduces the pressure on limited production resources in Albania and Bulgaria, while capital inflows generate working positions, incomes and entrepreneurial capacity and know-how. For Greece, labour immigration has resulted in cost-related advantages and has rather improved the efficiency of several sectors, while capital outflows are associated in most cases with an expansion (and not dislocation) of activities to new markets that are easier to get in than the hard to compete and congested Western European ones. The well-known operation of the export-multiplier also guarantees that incomes generated by Greek investment in the Balkans will have a positive impact on incomes and work positions in Greece, to the extent that the positive business climate encourages the promotion of Greek exports. In other words, a virtuous cycle may be in operation, where Greek investments in the Balkans generate incomes that are used for consumption and result in an increase of Greek exports. These generate in their turn incomes in Greece, that can induce new investments to, or imports from the region, etc. Overall, the higher the level of interaction, the greater the long-term benefits for all the countries in the region.

Finally, existing evidence reveals that the regional structure of the Balkan countries is, to varying degrees, characterised by significant concentration of activities and the formation of development axes that, however, due to the interruption of relations between the three countries imposed by the post-World War II realities, do not meet or cross anywhere, limiting the prospects, the intensity and the benefits of co-operation.

From this analysis two points emerge and deserve consideration from the policy-making point of view, the first one concerning Greece and the second, all the countries in the region. Perhaps for the first time since its membership in the EU, a real opportunity has been given to Greece to effectively deal with the difficulties and the pressures imposed by the process of European integration on its economic structure. This opportunity is related to the prospect of gradually re-composing the economic space in its vicinity with the creation of a regional Balkan market, in which it will have a central and highly influential role. For the first time also, in the post-war period, a real opportunity has been given to the Balkan countries to interact and cooperate without systemic or military barriers, leaving the level and type of their relations to be an affair of markets, preferences and geography.

From the strategic point of view, the long-term interests of Greece and the other countries in the region require stable relations, successful implementation of the policies of transition and a policy mix promoting the unification and coherence of the European economic space, the development of the European Southeastern region and the facilitation of cross-border cooperation. Since Greece, of all the other Balkan countries, has the highest 'degree of freedom' in influencing policies for the region, it also has the greater responsibility for promoting them.

The appropriate policy mix should include the steady and energetic support of the efforts of all Balkan countries to join the EU in the foreseeable future, according to the progress they make in meeting the requirements and the criteria set. This policy is a cornerstone for the future of the Balkan region and it is the only one that allows in the long run the unification of the Balkan and European space and the better accessibility and connection of Southern with Northern and Western Europe. Second, it should include the promotion of an EU strategic development plan for the Balkan region at various spatial, operational and sectoral levels with the active participation of Greece and a special emphasis on the issues of intra-regional co-operation and integration. This development plan should include effective transportation and telecommunication networks that will allow the integration of the existing development axes, or areas in the Balkans and reveal the special weight of Southeastern Europe as an emerging regional market with significant size, strong intra-regional relations, efficient infrastructure and a strategic advantage for the expansion of the EU economic relations in the Black Sea region, Eastern Mediterranean and the Middle East.

Notes

1 This may explain why from all the EU countries, Greece has the lowest share of intra-industry trade.
2 Trade distortions were especially strong in Bulgaria that was the most dependent of all CEE countries on trade with the Former Soviet Union (Totev 1997b).
3 Over 93 per cent of the industrial firms in Greece employ less than 10 employees while the average industrial firm size in Greece has been close to 5 employees per firm for the last 20 years (Petrakos and Zikos 1996).
4 The average industrial firm size in Bulgaria was in 1990 close to 500 employees per

firm while 47 per cent of the industrial firms employed more than 100 employees in 1993. In Romania the situation is similar, while in a sample of 150 firms the average employment was found to be more than 2,000 employees per firm (Jackson 1996). Even in Albania that is a small country, the average firm size in its border regions with Greece ranged in 1992 from 20 to 80 employees per firm (Petrakos 1996b). For comparison, in the EU only 2.1 per cent of the industrial firms employ more than 100 employees, while the average employment is 18 employees per firm (Petrakos 1997a).

5 Of the other CEE countries, the Czech Republic, Poland, and the Slovak Republic also approach the GDP structure of the EU (Petrakos 1997a)

6 Although Turkey certainly belongs to the Balkans, it is not included in the analysis, as the emphasis is on the Greek economic relations with the transition economies in the Balkans, where significant changes have occurred in the last years.

7 Bulgaria accounted in 1997 for 2.85 per cent of total Greek exports and 1.47 per cent of total Greek imports.

8 FYROM accounted in 1997 for 2.45 per cent of total Greek exports and 0.22 per cent of total Greek imports.

9 Albania accounted in 1997 for 2.24 per cent of total Greek exports and 0.13 per cent of total Greek imports.

10 Romania accounted in 1997 for 1.57 per cent of total Greek imports and 0.74 per cent of total Greek imports.

References

Anton, I., Danciu, D. and Mitu, C. (1996) 'The role of SMEs in the regional development of Romania', in M. Jackson and G. Petrakos (eds), 'Regional Problems and SME development in transition countries', *Eastern European Economics* 34, 2: 65–95, Special Edition.

Caves, R., and Johnes, R. (1981) *World Trade and Payments*, 3rd edition, Boston: Little Brown.

Colis, C., Berkeley, N. and Noon, D. (1997) 'Attracting foreign direct investment to east European economies: can lessons be learned from the UK experience?' paper presented at the Regional Studies Association, Regional Frontiers conference, Frankfurt (Oder), September 1997.

Dobrinsky, R. (1997) 'Multi-speed transition and multi-speed integration in Europe: recent economic developments in the Balkans and their implications', paper presented at the conference for Economic Cooperation in the Balkans: A Regional Approach to European Integration, PHARE-ACE Program, Volos: University of Thessaly, Department of Planning and Regional Development, 16–19 January 1997.

Greenway, D. and Milner, C. (1986) *The Economics of Intra-Industry Trade*, Oxford: Blackwell.

Grimwade, N. (1989) *International Trade: New Patterns of Trade, Production and Investment*, London: Routledge.

Grubel, H. and Lloyd, P. (1975) *Intra-Industry Trade: The Theory and Measurement of International Trade in Differentiated Products*, London: Macmillan.

Jackson, M. (1996) *Restructuring large enterprises in Central and Eastern Europe*, COST/PHARE Program, Interim Report, Leuven Institute for Central and East European Studies, Katholieke Universiteit Leuven.

Jackson, M. and Petrakos, G. (1999) 'Regional differences in the impact of EU integration on the industrial structure and competitiveness of CEFTA countries', paper prepared for the Phare ACE P96-6071–R project: Competitiveness of CEFTA countries: measurement and trends in the period of preparation to join the EU.

Krugman, P. (1994) *Geography and Trade*, Cambridge, MA: MIT Press.

Kukar, S. (1996) 'Regional policy in Slovenia: results, problems and alternatives', *Eastern European Economics* 34, 3, Special Edition.

Landesmann, M. (1995) *The Pattern of East–West European Integration: Catching up or Falling Behind?*, Vienna: The Vienna Institute for Comparative Economic Studies, No 212.

Minassian, G. and Totev, S. (1996) 'The Bulgarian economy in transition: the regional after-effects', *Eastern European Economics*, 34, 3: 49–92, Special Edition.

Ministry of National Economy (MNE) (1996) *Greek Enterprise Activity in the Balkans*, General Secretariat MNE, Athens: Ministry of National Economy.

Petrakos, G. (1996a) 'The regional dimension of transition in Eastern and Central European countries: an assessment', *Eastern European Economics*, 34, 5: 5–38.

Petrakos, G. (1996b) *The New Geography of the Balkans: Cross-border Cooperation between Albania, Bulgaria and Greece*, Series on Transition in the Balkans, Volos: 1, University of Thessaly, Department of Planning and Regional Development.

Petrakos, G. (1997a) 'Industrial structure and change in the European Union: comparative analysis and implications for transition economies', *Eastern European Economics*, 35, 2: 41–63.

Petrakos, G. (1997b) 'A European macro-region in the making? The Balkan trade relations of Greece', *European Planning Studies*, 5, 4: 515–33.

Petrakos, G. (1997c) 'The regional structure of Albania, Bulgaria and Greece: implications for cooperation and development', *European Urban and Regional Studies*, 4, 3: 193–208.

Petrakos, G. (1999) 'Greece and the Balkans: geography lost and found', *Revue d'Etudes Comparatives Est-Ouest*, 30, 4: 1–23

Petrakos, G. and Christodoulakis, N. (1998) 'Transition in the Balkans: patterns of change and policies to overcome marginalisation and disintegration', paper prepared for the Phare-ACE Program *Structural Changes and Spillovers in the East European Reform Process*, Final Report, Imperial College Management School, University of London.

Petrakos, G. and Pitelis, C. (2000) 'Peripherality and integration: the experience of Greece as a member of the EU and its impications for the Balkan economies in transition', in G. Petrakos and S. Totev (eds) *The Development of the Balkan Region*, Aldershot: Ashgate, forthcoming.

Petrakos, G. and Totev, S. (2000) 'Economic structure and change in the Balkan region: implications for integration, transition and economic cooperation', *International Journal of Urban and Regional Research*, 24,1: 95–113.

Petrakos, G. and Zikos, S. (1996) 'European integration and industrial structure in Greece, prospects and possibilities for convergence', in C. Paraskevopoulos, R. Grinspun and Georgakopoulos, T. (eds) *Economic Integration and Public Policy*, London: Edward Elgar, pp. 247–59.

Petrochilos, G. (1997) 'Explaining Greek outward foreign direct investment: a case of regional economic integration', paper presented at the Regional Studies Association, Regional Frontiers conference, Frankfurt (Oder), September 1997.

Piore, M. and Sabel, C. (1984) *The Second Industrial Divide: Possibilities for Prosperity*, New York: Basic Books.

Rizopoulos, G. (1997) 'Foreign direct investment and western firms' internationalization strategies in the Balkans', paper presented at the conference Economic Cooperation in the Balkans: A Regional Approach to European Integration, PHARE-ACE Program, Volos: University of Thessaly, Dept. of Planning and Regional Development, 16–19 January 1997.

Totev, S. (1997a) *Economic Co-operation in the Balkans: A Regional Approach to European Integration*, Final Report, PHARE-ACE Program, Institute of Economics, Bulgarian Academy of Sciences.

Totev, S. (1997b) 'The Bulgarian economy in transition: possibilities for Balkan regional integration', paper presented at the conference, Economic Cooperation in the Balkans: A Regional Approach to European Integration. PHARE-ACE Program, Volos: University of Thessaly, Dept of Planning and Regional Development, 16–19 January 1997.

UNCTAD (1996) *World Investment Report: Investment, Trade and International Arrangements*, Geneva: United Nations.

Index